VANCOUVER

CAROLYN B. HELLER

CONTENTS

MAPS

1	the Seawall in Yaletown
2	Granville Island Public Market
3	Tofino sunset
4	Olympic rings in Whistler
5	totem poles in Stanley Park
6	signs for biking, walking, and craft beer

DISCOVER
VANCOUVER

Vancouver cuts a dramatic urban figure. Set on Pacific coastal inlets with forested mountains beyond, it's frequently named one of the world's most livable cities. When you stroll along the waterfront, or through rainforest parks where evergreens reach the sky, it's easy to see why. Steel-and-glass towers grow like cedars on the downtown peninsula, but in green Vancouver, you're never far from a beach, mountain, or public park.

When the sun shines (and even when it doesn't), Vancouverites are outdoors, running or cycling on the seaside paths, kayaking or paddleboarding local waters, or sipping a pour-over coffee or local craft beer in a sidewalk café. And unlike many North American cities, where the city center empties out when the office workers go home, many Vancouver residents live and work downtown, keeping the streets active from early morning into the night.

Home to 2.5 million people, Vancouver looks to the Pacific Rim. More than 40 percent of the metro area's population is of Asian descent, influencing everything from art and urban design to food. Vancouver boasts some of the best Chinese cuisine outside China.

The indigenous people who've lived on this continent for thousands of years have also made their mark on the city. Vancouver has several museums, galleries, and other attractions where you can explore First Nations culture. An extensive collection of indigenous art at the airport welcomes visitors to the region.

Vancouver is a convenient starting point for trips along the British Columbia coast, north to the mountain resort of Whistler or across the Strait of Georgia to BC's capital city, Victoria. There's much to explore in this part of the world, and it all starts here.

10 TOP
EXPERIENCES

1 **Hike and Bike Stanley Park:** The rainforest meets the city in this parkland crisscrossed with trails (page 46).

2 **Wander Dr. Sun Yat-Sen Classical Chinese Garden:** This Chinatown oasis was the first authentic Ming Dynasty garden built outside China (page 73).

3 **Graze Away at Granville Island Public Market:** Nibble on charcuterie, cheeses, pastries, fudge, and other treats at this food lover's heaven (page 114).

4 **Visit the Museum of Anthropology:** This striking modern museum illuminates the culture of British Columbia's indigenous peoples and traditional cultures from around the world (page 146).

5 **Feast on Chinese Food:** More than half the population is of Asian descent in Richmond, where you can dig into some of the best Chinese food in North America (page 195).

6 **Sample Craft Brews:** Numerous craft breweries in the city welcome visitors for sampling and sipping (page 177).

7 **Summit Grouse Mountain:** Ride the tram up this North Shore peak for mountaintop hiking trails, a wildlife refuge, and spectacular views (page 204).

8 **Find Outdoor Adventures:** You don't have to venture far from the city center to experience the rainforest, the mountains, or the sea, whether on a hiking trail, ski run, or paddling route (page 26).

9 **Appreciate Indigenous Culture:** Stay in Canada's first indigenous arts hotel, sample traditional foods at a First Nations bistro, and find works by contemporary indigenous artists (page 21).

10 **Take a Day Trip to Victoria:** Ferry across the Strait of Georgia for a day trip to visit world-class Butchart Gardens, take afternoon tea at the grand Fairmont Empress Hotel, or go whale-watching (page 234).

EXPLORE
VANCOUVER

THE BEST OF VANCOUVER

In just a few days, you can experience the best of Vancouver, combining outdoor activities, cultural explorations, and time for strolling, snacking, and sipping. Vancouver's public transit system makes it easy to get around without a car; this itinerary includes tips for the most convenient transit options.

>DAY 1:
DOWNTOWN AND
GRANVILLE ISLAND

Get your first glance of the city and orient yourself with the 360-degree view from the observation platform at the **Vancouver Lookout** downtown. Save your ticket to return later for the nighttime views.

Catch bus 50 on Granville Street to **Granville Island.** Browse the stalls and stop for a morning snack in the **Granville Island Public Market** before checking out the galleries and shops in the **Net Loft,** on **Railspur Alley,** and throughout the island. Don't miss the museum-quality indigenous art at the **Eagle Spirit Gallery.**

view of Vancouver

BEST VIEWS

Vancouver is a city of amazing views, so keep your camera handy.

CANADA PLACE
The white sails of Canada Place are one of Vancouver's most recognizable landmarks. Follow the walkway for up-close views, with the water and mountains beyond (page 43).

VANCOUVER LOOKOUT
From this downtown tower, you have 360-degree vistas across the city, overlooking Stanley Park, Gastown, and other districts. It's a good place to get oriented (page 44).

STANLEY PARK
Follow the Seawall around Stanley Park for views across Burrard Inlet to the city skyline and North Shore mountains. At one point, you'll pass under the Lions Gate Bridge, which makes a dramatic photo backdrop (page 46).

OLYMPIC VILLAGE
Stop along False Creek near the Olympic Village to snap photos of city landmarks, including Science World and BC Place stadium. You'll have good views of the downtown skyline (page 95).

GROUSE MOUNTAIN
On a clear day, the vistas from the top of Grouse Mountain stretch north toward Howe Sound, over Burrard Inlet, and across metropolitan Vancouver (page 204).

LIGHTHOUSE PARK
Located on the North Shore, this West Vancouver park offers beautiful views across the water toward downtown (page 212).

For lunch, return to the Public Market or sit down for a more leisurely meal, highlighting Canadian products, at **Edible Canada Bistro.**

To start your afternoon on an active note, rent a kayak or a stand-up paddleboard at **Ecomarine Paddlesports Centre** and spend an hour paddling around the island. Back on land, refresh yourself with a sake sampling at the **Artisan Sake Maker** or a craft cocktail made from the small-batch spirits at **Liberty Distillery** before catching the bus back downtown.

Liberty Distillery sign

Your next stop is the **Bill Reid Gallery of Northwest Coast Art,** which shows works by the noted First Nations artist. Nearby, you can wander the exhibits at the **Vancouver Art Gallery,** making sure to see paintings by BC's renowned Emily Carr.

In the late afternoon, rent a bike and take a leisurely ride along the **Seawall** in **Stanley Park,** stopping to see the **totem poles at Brockton Point,** then pedal past landmark **Siwash Rock.** Pause to rest at **English Bay Beach,** which is also one of Vancouver's best spots to watch the sun set over the ocean. Across the street from the beach, smile at *A-maze-ing Laughter,* a public art piece comprising 14 grinning bronze figures.

Have dinner downtown,

perhaps the imaginative contemporary fare at **Royal Dinette** or a creative pizza at **Nightingale,** then return to the **Vancouver Lookout** to gaze over the city's twinkling lights.

>DAY 2:
UBC, GASTOWN, AND CHINATOWN

Enjoy breakfast at **Forage** or **Medina Café** before exploring more of the city's cultural highlights.

From Granville Street, catch bus 4 or 14 west to the **University of British Columbia** and the **Museum of Anthropology.** This first-rate museum has a particularly strong collection of First Nations art, including an awe-inspiring gallery of totem poles. After exploring the museum, take a walk through the serene **Nitobe Japanese Garden** nearby.

When you're finished on campus, take bus 4 back toward Kitsilano for lunch on West 4th Avenue: Thai food at **Maenam** or French bistro fare at **Au Comptoir.** Check out the 4th Avenue shops before stopping for dessert at **Beaucoup Bakery & Café.**

Bus 4 or 7 will take you from Kits to Gastown. Walk along Water Street, watch the **Gastown Steam Clock** toot its steam whistle, and stop into several of the First Nations art galleries, like **Coastal Peoples Fine Arts Gallery.**

Continue into **Chinatown** for a late-afternoon tour of the **Dr. Sun Yat-Sen Classical Chinese Garden,** the only authentic Ming Dynasty garden outside China.

Stay in Chinatown for dinner. Try the unusual combination of Italian and Japanese elements at speakeasy-style **Kissa Tanto** or share modern Canadian plates at **Juniper Kitchen & Bar.** After your meal, have a drink at **The Keefer Bar,** or take a cab back downtown for a nightcap at **Uva Wine & Cocktail Bar** or elegant **Prohibition Lounge.**

>DAY 3:
THE NORTH SHORE

Today, you're exploring the mountains and rainforests on Vancouver's North Shore. Catch the free shuttle from **Canada Place** to **Grouse Mountain.** If you're up for a challenge, walk up the **Grouse Grind,** a trail nicknamed "Mother Nature's Stairmaster." But there's no shame in taking the **Skyride;** it's North America's largest tram system. At the top, laugh at the lumberjack show, explore the wildlife refuge, and go for a short hike. The views are spectacular on a clear day.

Come down the mountain, and at the Grouse entrance, catch bus 236 to the **Capilano Suspension Bridge.** This 450-foot (137-m) span swings over a canyon high above the Capilano River. If you're feeling brave, follow the **Cliffwalk,** a series of boardwalks cantilevered over the rushing river. Do you dare stand on the glass platform and look down (way down)?

Get back on bus 236 to **Lonsdale Quay.** Stop for a drink, with views of the city skyline, at **Pier 7 Restaurant & Bar,** or at any of other the spots in the Shipyards District, a short walk from the quay. Then take the **SeaBus** across

Burrard Inlet to Waterfront Station downtown.

Have dinner in Gastown, where **L'Abbatoir** serves French-accented west coast fare on the site of Vancouver's first jail or stylish **Chambar** combines flavors of North Africa and Belgium with local ingredients.

With More Time

DAY 4: RICHMOND

Ride the Canada Line to spend a day in Vancouver's "new Chinatown" in the city of Richmond. First up: dim sum in the Golden Village along No. 3 Road. At Chef Tony Seafood Restaurant, choose from a mix of traditional and modern Hong Kong-style plates, or at Su Hang Restaurant, try Shanghai-style dim sum.

After you've eaten, catch bus 403 southbound along No. 3 Road to the International Buddhist Temple, one of the largest Chinese Buddhist temples in North America. Visitors are welcome to tour the gardens and the peaceful temple complex.

From the temple, head to the village of Steveston, an active fishing port where the Asian communities have historic roots. Visiting the Gulf of Georgia Cannery National Historic Site or the Britannia Shipyards National Historic Site will introduce you to the area's multicultural history. Walk along the wharf, where fishing boats sell their fresh catch. Pajo's on the pier makes first-rate fish-and-chips.

Bus 401, 402, 406, or 407 will take you back to the Golden Village, where you can browse the Asian shops at Aberdeen Centre.

If you're in town on Friday-Sunday mid-May-mid-October, take the Canada Line to Bridgeport Station for the Richmond Night Market. Graze your way through this Asian-style festival of street foods. Return downtown on the Canada Line.

DAY 5: CAMBIE CORRIDOR AND EAST VANCOUVER

From downtown, take bus 17 to VanDusen Botanical Garden and spend your morning strolling among the blossoms. When you're ready to eat, hop on a northbound bus 17 for lunch at Salmon n' Bannock, a modern indigenous bistro.

Continue east on Broadway through the Cambie Corridor to browse the neighborhood's boutiques. There's a cluster of shops near Main and Broadway, and more clothing and accessories purveyors on Main between 20th and 30th Avenues (if you don't want to walk, bus 3 can take you along Main Street).

When you're done shopping, it's time for a beer crawl to try the city's craft breweries. Both 33 Acres Brewing and Brassneck Brewery are a short walk from the intersection of Broadway and Main.

For a more serious exploration of Vancouver's microbrewery scene, head for the Commercial Drive and East Village neighborhoods. Parallel 49 Brewing Company has a large tasting room that's a popular neighborhood gathering spot. To sample some spirits, visit Odd Society Spirits, a small-batch distillery in a former motorcycle garage. To get to this district from Broadway and Main, take bus 99 eastbound on Broadway to Commercial Drive, then change to bus 20 going north and get off on Hastings Street.

When you've tasted your fill, bus 4 or 7 (on Powell St.) or bus 14 or 16 (on Hastings St.) will bring you back downtown for dinner at lively Guu Garden (a Japanese *izakaya*) or at Boulevard Kitchen & Oyster Bar for local seafood in a stylish setting.

VANCOUVER'S BEST SIGHTS

EXPLORE

BILL REID GALLERY OF NORTHWEST COAST ART

The **Bill Reid Gallery of Northwest Coast Art** is dedicated to the life and work of the notable eponymous indigenous artist (page 44).

DR. SUN YAT-SEN CLASSICAL CHINESE GARDEN

Tour **Dr. Sun Yat-Sen Classical Chinese Garden,** the first authentic Ming Dynasty garden outside China (page 73).

SCIENCE WORLD

Take the youngsters to **Science World,** inside a geodesic dome on the banks of False Creek (page 94).

GRANVILLE ISLAND PUBLIC MARKET

Find an artistically arranged food-lover's heaven at **Granville Island Public Market** (page 114).

RAILSPUR ALLEY

Seek out narrow **Railspur Alley,** a hidden gem where you can chat with artists at work in their studios (page 115).

MUSEUM OF VANCOUVER

The **Museum of Vancouver** takes you on a hands-on journey through the city's past (page 130).

Dr. Sun Yat-Sen Classical Chinese Garden

MUSEUM OF ANTHROPOLOGY

The **Museum of Anthropology** houses one of the world's top collections of First Peoples' art, including massive cedar canoes, elaborate carvings, and towering totem poles (page 146).

NITOBE JAPANESE GARDEN

Stroll among the flowers, waterfalls, and koi ponds in the serene **Nitobe Japanese Garden** (page 147).

VANDUSEN BOTANICAL GARDEN

Among the 250,000 plants at the peaceful **VanDusen Botanical Garden,** the city seems far away (page 160).

PARALLEL 49 BREWING COMPANY

Parallel 49 Brewing Company is both a craft beer tasting hall and a spirited neighborhood gathering place (page 176).

ODD SOCIETY SPIRITS

Odd Society Spirits makes small-batch vodka, gin, and a "moonshine" whiskey that you can sip in a fun and funky lounge (page 176).

RICHMOND NIGHT MARKET

The large and lively **Richmond Night Market** is an amazing Asian food adventure and sells everything from kebabs to bubble tea (page 190).

GROUSE MOUNTAIN

For zip-lining, paragliding, skiing, and snowboarding, head for **Grouse Mountain** (page 204).

CAPILANO SUSPENSION BRIDGE

The **Capilano Suspension Bridge** sways high above the Capilano River in a rainforest park (page 206).

EXPLORE

Capilano Suspension Bridge

VANCOUVER WITH KIDS

With so many outdoor attractions, cool ways to get around the city, and kid-friendly restaurants, Vancouver is a fantastic destination for families. Whether you're exploring a rainforest park, riding a ferry, or following the Dumpling Trail, Vancouver serves up plenty of family-focused fun. Tip: Always ask about special family rates or discounts when you're buying tickets to any sights or attractions.

Kids Market on Granville Island

kids enjoy watching the dumpling makers at work at **Dinesty Dumpling House,** or you can dig into Japanese-style hot dogs at **Japadog.**

Granville Island Public Market

>DAY 1: STANLEY PARK

Pack a picnic lunch and spend the day in **Stanley Park,** Vancouver's rainforest green space at the end of the downtown peninsula. Visit the **Vancouver Aquarium Marine Science Centre** first (it's less crowded in the mornings), then enjoy your picnic near Lost Lagoon.

After lunch, **rent bikes** to explore more of the park; there are several rental shops just outside the park's West Georgia Street entrance. Follow the **Seawall** to see the majestic **totem poles at Brockton Point,** stop to cool off in the splash park near Lumberman's Arch, and let the kids play in the sand or go for a swim at **Second Beach,** where there's a large pool, restrooms, and a snack bar.

For dinner, try one of the Asian restaurants downtown. Most

>DAY 2: GRANVILLE ISLAND AND FALSE CREEK

Buy a day pass for the Aquabus ferry, so you can hop on and off these cute little boats as you travel around Granville Island and False Creek. Take the Aquabus to **Science World** and spend the morning exploring the hands-on exhibits. When it's time for lunch, cruise over to **Granville Island,** where there are plenty of family-friendly food options in the **Granville Island Public Market.**

Don't miss the **Kids Market,** with its kid-approved shops and indoor playground. Check out **Sea**

INDIGENOUS CULTURE

Indigenous people have lived in western Canada for more than 10,000 years. For many visitors, the opportunity to explore this traditional culture and its present-day manifestations is a highlight.

Here are just a few of the numerous places where traditional culture remains strong. Another valuable resource for visitors interested in First Nations culture is the Indigenous Tourism Association of British Columbia (604/921-1070 or 877/266-2822, www.indigenousbc.com).

traditional indigenous pit house at the Squamish Lil'wat Cultural Centre

BILL REID GALLERY OF NORTHWEST COAST ART

Dedicated to the work of Haida First Nations artist Bill Reid, this gallery showcases Reid's sculptures, carvings, and jewelry (page 44).

TALKING TREES WALK

Several First Nations made their traditional home in Vancouver's Stanley Park. Tour Stanley Park with an indigenous guide to learn more about the park's First Nations' heritage (page 46).

MUSEUM OF ANTHROPOLOGY

This excellent museum illuminates the culture of British Columbia's indigenous peoples and traditional cultures from around the world (page 146).

SALMON N' BANNOCK

This contemporary indigenous bistro uses traditional ingredients in its elk burgers, game sausages, and bison tenderloin. They serve plenty of salmon and bannock (a type of bread) too (page 162).

SKWACHÀYS LODGE

Stay at Canada's first indigenous arts and culture hotel, where works by First Nations artists adorn the one-of-a-kind guest rooms (page 225).

SQUAMISH LIL'WAT CULTURAL CENTRE

In Whistler, learn about the history and present-day culture of the region's First Nations communities at this modern gallery (page 304).

Village to let the kids imagine what it would be like to live on a houseboat. When you're done exploring the island, rent kayaks for an excursion along False Creek.

Have an early dinner at Go Fish (it's a short stroll along the waterfront from Granville Island),

then catch the Aquabus back downtown.

›DAY 3: CANADA PLACE AND THE NORTH SHORE

Start your day at Canada Place with a virtual flight across the country at **FlyOver Canada.** You even feel the spray as you soar (virtually) over Niagara Falls.

bird of prey at Grouse Mountain

In front of Canada Place, catch the free shuttle to **Grouse Mountain.** Ride the **Skyride** tram to the top, where you can visit the grizzly bears at the **Grouse Mountain Refuge for Endangered Wildlife,** watch the falcons soar at the **Birds in Motion** demonstration, and get some chuckles at the **Lumberjack Show.** Go for a hike, and have lunch overlooking the city and water below.

Your next stop is the **Capilano Suspension Bridge** (from the Grouse Mountain entrance, take bus 236 down Capilano Road). Give the kids a thrill as they look from the bridge to the canyon way below. Explore the **Treetops Adventure,** where you follow a network of gently swaying wooden bridges to eight treehouse platforms in the forest. When you're ready to go back downtown, catch the free shuttle.

For supper, let the kids play with the jukeboxes at retro diner

BEST PEOPLE-WATCHING

Many of the city's top people-watching locales are beaches and walkways. For more urban people-spotting, head for Gastown, Yaletown, or Granville Island.

THE SEAWALL

Stroll the Seawall in Yaletown, the West End, or near the Olympic Village, particularly on a weekend afternoon or summer evening. You'll have plenty of company (page 43).

ENGLISH BAY BEACH

On the downtown peninsula near Stanley Park, this curve of sand attracts local seniors, gay couples, hordes of visitors, and pretty much anyone who wants to enjoy the views across the water. It's especially busy at sunset (page 57).

YALETOWN

Bars and restaurants with outdoor seating line Hamilton and Mainland Streets. Try WildTale Coastal Grill, where you can spot well-dressed millennials out for an evening and yoga mat-toting residents on their way home from the studio (page 97).

GRANVILLE ISLAND

Sit outside along the water behind the Granville Island Public Market to survey an endless parade of tourists hopping on and off the tiny False Creek ferries, locals taking a break from shopping, and kayakers out for some exercise (page 114).

KITSILANO BEACH

Serious beach volleyball enthusiasts, families with kids, groups of UBC students, and sunbathers congregate at busy Kits Beach (page 136).

The Templeton or slurp up a bowl of ramen at **Hokkaido Ramen Santouka.**

>DAY 4:
UBC AND POINT GREY

Today, you'll tour the museums on the **University of British Columbia** campus, check out another rainforest park, and then have time to relax at **Jericho Beach.**

From downtown, catch any UBC-bound bus to the campus bus loop. Walk over to the **Museum of Anthropology,** where there's a fantastic collection of First Nations totem poles and other artifacts. Another short walk takes you to the **Beaty Biodiversity Museum,** which has more than two million specimens of bugs, fish, plants, and fossils that the kids can explore, as well as a massive blue whale skeleton. One more campus attraction, located at the **UBC Botanical Garden,** is the **Greenheart TreeWalk,** a network of aerial bridges that takes you high into the rainforest canopy.

Catch bus 99 to Point Grey Village (get off along W. 10th Ave. at Sasamat St.), where you can have a sandwich and a sweet at **Mix the Bakery.** After you've refueled, walk south to West 16th Avenue, where you can go for a stroll in the rainforest at **Pacific Spirit Regional Park,** which has more than 40 miles (70 km) of hiking trails. The trails are fairly well marked, but the park is large, so you'll need to pay attention to your route.

If the kids aren't too tired, you can walk down to the **Jericho Sailing Centre,** 1.25 miles (2 km) straight down Trimble Street; if you'd rather go by bus, it's fastest to take bus 25 or 33 on 16th Avenue back to the UBC Bus Loop, then change to bus 84, which will drop you on West 4th Avenue just above the beach. Have dinner overlooking the sand at **The Galley Patio and Grill,** go for a **sunset kayak paddle,** or simply sit on the beach and watch the sunset. When you're ready to go back downtown, take bus 4 from West 4th Avenue.

>DAY 5:
RICHMOND

Plan a **whale-watching cruise** today. Several operators run trips from **Steveston Village** in the suburb of **Richmond,** and most will include transportation from downtown. Spend the morning on the water looking for orcas, sea lions, and other aquatic life. Back on land, check out the fishing boats and vendors along the wharf, and stop for a fish-and-chips lunch at **Pajo's.**

Richmond is the center of Vancouver's Asian community, so instead of heading straight back downtown, catch bus 401, 402, 406, or 407 from Steveston to Richmond's **Golden Village,** where you can choose from countless Chinese restaurants for dinner. The kids might enjoy mapping out their route along Richmond's **Dumpling Trail** (get a map at www.visitrichmondbc.com) or choosing from the long list of bubble teas at **Pearl Castle Café.** If you're in town on a weekend mid-May-mid-October, wrap up your day at the **Richmond Night Market,** where there's plenty of Asian food to sample, before catching the Canada Line back downtown.

A DAY OUTDOORS

Spring-fall, head for the North Shore to enjoy a day outdoors. Although it's possible to do this excursion by public transport, it's easier if you have a car.

➤MORNING: DEEP COVE

Start your day of adventure by assembling a picnic for lunch outdoors. Make a quick shopping stop at the **Granville Island Public Market.** Then go east from downtown, and cross the Second Narrows Bridge to the North Shore.

kayaks on the shore at Deep Cove

Begin your visit to the scenic waterfront village of **Deep Cove** with a freshly made treat from local institution **Honey Donuts.** When you've sated your sweet tooth, rent a **kayak** for a leisurely paddle between the forests and mountains of **Indian Arm fjord.** If you'd rather go with a guide, **Deep Cove Kayaks** offers kayak tours, including a three-hour **Deep Cove Explorer** route that's suitable for novice and more advanced paddlers alike.

BEST FOR ROMANCE

Visiting Vancouver with a special someone? Start by cycling around Stanley Park on a bicycle built for two or paddling around Granville Island in a tandem kayak. Then check out these other romantic spots.

SIP

Have a drink at **Reflections: The Garden Terrace** (page 55), hidden on the 4th floor of the Rosewood Hotel Georgia, or sink into the leather chairs at posh **Bacchus Lounge** (page 55) to enjoy your cocktails with live piano music.

EAT

For dinner, **Hawksworth Restaurant** (page 48) always wows for its setting and service. Book a table at sunset overlooking False Creek at **Ancora Waterfront Dining and Patio** (page 97), and enjoy both the views and the distinctive Peruvian-Japanese dishes. If you consider oysters to be an aphrodisiac, or if you simply crave fresh seafood, reserve your spot for two at **Boulevard Kitchen & Oyster Bar** (page 49).

TREAT

Share two scoops of excellent gelato at downtown's **Bella Gelateria** (page 53). Detour to Gastown to indulge in a lemon chèvre brownie or other decadent sweet at **Purebread** (page 81).

SLEEP

When you're ready to call it a day, Yaletown's boutique **Opus Hotel Vancouver** (page 226) will appeal to contemporary couples, while the **Wedgewood Hotel & Spa** (page 222) is a good choice for more traditional romantics. The deluxe **Fairmont Pacific Rim** (page 219) will pamper any pairs, particularly if you book a couple's treatment in the posh Willow Spring Spa.

>AFTERNOON: LYNN CANYON AND GROUSE MOUNTAIN

Back on shore, it's a short drive to **Lynn Canyon Park,** which has a **suspension bridge** that was built in 1912—and it's free. Find a shady spot to enjoy your picnic lunch. When you're done eating, follow a forested hiking trail to one of the popular swimming areas and go for a dip.

enjoying the view from Grouse Mountain

Late in the afternoon, you'll still have time for a visit to **Grouse Mountain.** Take the **Skyride** up the mountain, or if you have energy to spare, hike up the famous **Grouse Grind** trail. Nicknamed "Mother Nature's Stairmaster," it's essentially a mountain staircase with an elevation gain of 2,800 feet (850 m). However you get to the top, there's plenty to do when you arrive: Go **zip-lining,** watch one of the wildlife shows, or try out a **paragliding** adventure. When you're ready to relax, have a drink in the lounge overlooking the city.

>EVENING: SUNSET ON THE BEACH

Return to Vancouver in time to watch the sunset from **English Bay Beach.** Ready for dinner? Stroll along Denman Street for tapas at **España Restaurant,** walk up Robson Street for farm-to-table fare at **Forage,** or go for high-end sushi overlooking Canada Place at **Miku.**

Wrap up your day downtown with drinks at all-Canadian gastropub **Timber,** where Caesars (Canada's version of a Bloody Mary) are a signature, or head over to Granville Island for an always-entertaining improv show at **Vancouver Theatre Sports League.** Then get a good night's sleep; with this active day, you've earned it.

brunch at Forage

OUTDOOR ADVENTURES

If you love the outdoors, Vancouver is your city—in any season. With its stellar natural setting, you don't have to venture far from the city center to experience the rainforest, the mountains, or the sea, whether on a hiking trail, a ski run, or a paddling route. Even on damp winter days, you'll find locals playing soccer, going for a run, or strolling along the beach, and when the sun shines, it seems like the entire city is outdoors.

kayakers on False Creek

PARKS

Just steps from the downtown skyscrapers, there's Stanley Park (page 46), the city's 1,000-acre (400-ha) green space to explore on foot, by bike, or in a kayak. The Seawall (page 43), a walking and cycling path, circles the park's perimeter and continues around downtown's waterfronts, along both Burrard Inlet and False Creek; with a couple of detours, you can follow this waterside path all the way out to the University of British Columbia campus. There, on the city's west side, is another rainforest park to explore: Pacific Spirit Regional Park (page 153).

BEACHES

You can go to the beach in Stanley Park at Second Beach or Third Beach (page 46), or right downtown at English Bay Beach (page 57). Kitsilano Beach (page 136) is one of the city's most popular. Families gravitate to the Point Grey sands at Jericho Beach (page 151), Locarno Beach (page 151), and Spanish Banks Beach (page 152).

WATER SPORTS

Want to get out on the water? Rent a kayak at Jericho Beach's Ecomarine Paddlesports Centre (page 152) or take a stand-up paddleboard or kayak out on False Creek via Creekside Kayaks (page 103). Or head to the North Shore to paddle the scenic Indian Arm fjord with a kayak or paddleboard from Deep Cove Kayaks (page 211).

THE NORTH SHORE

For more outdoor adventures, the North Shore is your day-trip destination. Go hiking, skiing, or snowshoeing at Grouse Mountain (page 204) or Cypress Mountain (page 213), explore the walking trails in West Vancouver's waterfront Lighthouse Park (page 212), or take a wildlife cruise from Horseshoe Bay (page 208).

VANCOUVER'S ASIAN CULTURE

> **MORNING:**
> **CHINATOWN**

Get a sweet start to your day in Gastown with coffee and a treat from **Purebread,** or pair your caffeine with an avocado toast at **Nelson the Seagull.** Walk from Gastown to **Chinatown,** then spend the rest of your morning at the peaceful **Dr. Sun Yat-Sen Classical Chinese Garden.** Take a guided tour to learn more about the garden's construction and rest up on a bench overlooking the koi pond.

> **AFTERNOON:**
> **RICHMOND AND**
> **STEVESTON**

Catch bus 23, Beach, outside the Chinese Garden at the corner of Keefer and Columbia Streets, and change to the Canada Line (Richmond branch) at Yaletown-Roundhouse Station. You're heading for the suburb of **Richmond** for a dim sum lunch in the **Golden Village,** which is full of Asian restaurants and shopping malls. Good dim sum options include **Chef Tony Seafood Restaurant,** walking distance from the Canada Line's Aberdeen Station, and **Golden Paramount Seafood Restaurant,** a short walk from Richmond-Brighouse Station.

After you've eaten, continue south to the fishing port of **Steveston.** Bus 401, 402, 406, or 407 can bring you to Steveston Village from Number 3 Road. Take a walk on the wharf, check out the fish vendors, then learn about the Asian, European, and First Nations workers who once staffed the **Gulf of Georgia Cannery** or the **Britannia Shipyards,** which are both now national historic sites. If you have time when you've finished your Steveston visit, detour to the peaceful **International Buddhist Temple,** one of the largest traditional temples in North America.

> **EVENING:**
> **DINNER IN RICHMOND**

Return to the Golden Village on and around Number 3 Road to sit down for dinner at one of Richmond's hundreds of Chinese eateries. If you love lamb, try the many western Chinese-style preparations at **Hao's Lamb Restaurant** or sample the spicy Sichuan-influenced seafood at **The Fish Man.** For milder fare, **Bamboo Grove** is an excellent upscale Cantonese option. Alternatively, graze your way through the Asian food stalls at the **Richmond Night Market,** near the Bridgeport Canada Line station.

Take the Canada Line back to downtown Vancouver for a nightcap at a Japanese *izakaya* like **Guu Garden,** or at **The Keefer Bar,** an Asian-inspired lounge in Chinatown. Or if you're ready for a late-night snack, stop for a unique-to-Vancouver Japanese-style hot dog at **Japadog.**

VANCOUVER'S BEST FOOD

Vancouver is known for seafood, particularly salmon, halibut, oysters, and spot prawns, caught in regional waters. The city's restaurants have embraced the "eat local" movement, so look for seasonal produce and locally raised meats. With a large Asian population, Vancouver has some of the best Chinese food in North America, as well as good Japanese, Korean, and Vietnamese fare. Many non-Asian restaurants incorporate Pacific Rim influences in their dishes.

Some of Vancouver's most innovative restaurants are in Gastown, Chinatown, and along Main Street. In the West End, you'll find a concentration of noodle shops, *izakayas,* and other Asian eateries. For the region's top Chinese food, head to the suburb of Richmond, which has hundreds of Asian dining spots, both large and small.

British Columbia wines, from the Okanagan Valley or Vancouver Island, are good accompaniments to most Vancouver meals, as are regionally brewed craft beers. Plenty of bartenders have adopted an "eat local" philosophy, incorporating locally grown herbs, house-made bitters, and other fresh ingredients into creative cocktails and alcohol-free drinks.

NIGHTINGALE

Nightingale serves gourmet pizzas in a buzzing dining room (page 49).

GUU GARDEN

Guu Garden is a spirited spot for Japanese tapas, even before the sake comes out (page 50).

CHAMBAR

From waffles in the morning to *moules frites* at night, **Chambar** takes you from Belgium to North Africa (page 78).

L'ABBATOIR

L'Abbatoir serves creative cocktails and a changing menu of west coast plates—on the site of Vancouver's first prison (page 78).

KISSA TANTO

At **Kissa Tanto,** the chef draws on Japanese and Italian flavors to craft inventive dishes (page 79).

ANCORA WATERFRONT DINING AND PATIO

Ancora Waterfront Dining and Patio serves delicious seafood in one of the city's most scenic restaurants (page 97).

BURDOCK & CO

Relaxed neighborhood bistro **Burdock & Co** delivers a creative menu sourced from local ingredients (page 161).

ANH & CHI

Sit on the breezy outdoor patio at **Anh & Chi** and dig into fresh, updated Vietnamese dishes (page 163).

THE PIE SHOPPE

The Pie Shoppe bakes up delicious sweet things in a crust (page 180).

BAMBOO GROVE

High-end **Bamboo Grove** has an elaborate Cantonese menu emphasizing fresh seafood (page 193).

SU HANG RESTAURANT

Slurp soup dumplings at **Su Hang Restaurant,** which specializes in *xiao long bao* and other Shanghai-style fare (page 193).

HAO'S LAMB RESTAURANT

Hao's Lamb Restaurant uses every part of the sheep (page 194).

CHEF TONY SEAFOOD RESTAURANT

Chef Tony Seafood Restaurant prepares traditional and innovative dim sum (page 196).

LIFT BREAKFAST BAKERY

Before or after a hike or other adventure on the North Shore, dig into a hearty meal at **Lift Breakfast Bakery** (page 210).

waffles at Chambar

PLANNING YOUR TRIP

WHEN TO GO

High season in Vancouver and Victoria runs May-October, when the weather is generally warm and relatively dry. **July-August** are the region's peak travel months, with sunny, temperate conditions balancing the big crowds and high prices. In summer, comfortable daytime temperatures rarely rise above 75°F (24°C), and the sun doesn't set until after 9pm.

Prices may be somewhat more moderate in spring (April-June) and fall (September-October), although you can expect more rain than in midsummer.

During the winter months of November-February, prices are lowest; except during the Christmas and New Year's holidays, accommodations can drop to half of their summer rates. The cultural calendar is full with theater, music, and other arts events, and you can ski on the local mountains or just two hours away at Whistler-Blackcomb. Daytime temperatures in the city average 43-46°F (6-8°C) during winter. The trade-off is that winter is the rainy season, with rain—sometimes quite heavy—and clouds most days. Snow typically falls only at higher elevations,

fall colors in Vancouver

Vancouver SkyTrain

although it occasionally snows in the city.

ENTRY REQUIREMENTS

Visitors to Canada must have a valid **passport**. U.S. citizens entering Canada by land can use a **NEXUS** card or **U.S. Passport Card** instead, but note that these documents aren't valid for air travel.

Depending on your country of origin, you may also need either a **visitor visa** or an **Electronic Travel Authorization (eTA)**. See more information in the "Essentials" chapter of this guide, and check with Citizenship and Immigration Canada (www.cic.gc.ca) to confirm what documents you require.

TRANSPORTATION

Vancouver International Airport is south of downtown in the suburb of Richmond. The **Canada Line** subway stops at

the airport and can take you downtown in just 25 minutes.

Visitors arriving by train or bus come into **Pacific Central Station** on the edge of Chinatown. Cabs typically wait outside the station. To get downtown, you can also catch the **SkyTrain** from Main Street Station, one block from the train and bus depot.

Vancouver has a very good public transit system, with subway lines, buses, and ferries that can take you almost everywhere around the city. You don't need a car to explore most city attractions. A car is useful, though not essential, for excursions around the North Shore mountains or up the Sea-to-Sky Highway to Whistler. You can get to Victoria from Vancouver without a car by air, or on the **BC Ferries Connector,** a combination bus-ferry-bus route.

RESERVATIONS

If you're traveling in the summer, particularly in July-August, book your **hotel reservations** in advance. Car reservations are recommended on **BC Ferries** trips between Vancouver and Victoria in the summer as well.

Many Vancouver restaurants fill up with advance reservations, particularly on Friday-Saturday nights. Book a weekend table at least a few days ahead; most local eateries take reservations online. Don't despair if you can't get a reservation, since many spots save room for walk-ins.

PASSES AND DISCOUNTS

Many Vancouver attractions offer discounted admission for seniors (age 65 and up), students, and families, typically including two adults and up to two children.

If you're going to visit several attractions on the University of British Columbia campus, the **UBC Gardens and MOA Pass** (adults $27, seniors, students, and children $23) can save you money. It includes admission to the Museum of Anthropology, Nitobe Japanese Garden, and UBC Botanical Garden, as well as a 10 percent discount on the Greenheart TreeWalk. Purchase the pass at any of the participating attractions.

Tickets Tonight (604/684-2787, www.ticketstonight.ca) sells same-day, half-price theater tickets online only. Check the current day's availability on the website; same-day tickets go on sale at 9am, and sales continue until 4pm or until tickets are sold out. Tickets Tonight also sells full-price

DAILY REMINDERS

- **Monday:** Mid-May-early September, most Vancouver attractions stay open every day, but some museums close Monday, particularly during the winter months. Monday can be a good day to visit Granville Island or tour Stanley Park, which can be extremely crowded on weekends.

- **Tuesday:** On Tuesday evening, admission to the Vancouver Art Gallery is by donation.

- **Thursday:** In Kitsilano, the Museum of Vancouver and the Vancouver Maritime Museum both stay open late on Thursday, closing at 8pm. The Museum of Anthropology is open until 9pm, and evening tickets are discounted.

- **Friday:** The Richmond Night Market operates Friday-Sunday evenings mid-May-mid-October.

- **Saturday:** The West End Farmers Market is open Saturday late May-late October. The UBC Farm Market is also open Saturday June-November.

- **Sunday:** The Vancouver Art Gallery runs free drop-in art activities for kids on Sunday afternoon. The Kitsilano Farmers Market sells fresh produce and baked goods on Sunday early May-late October.

advance tickets to many local productions, online or by phone (8am-4pm Mon.-Fri.).

GUIDED TOURS

Several companies offer Vancouver city tours or explorations of particular neighborhoods, including **Tours by Locals** (www.toursbylocals.com) and **Context Travel** (www.contexttravel.com). For a guided tour by bike, contact **Cycle City Tours** (http://

samples from Japadog on a Vancouver Foodie Tour

cyclevancouver.com) or **Vancouver Bike Tours** (http://biketourvancouver.com).

Vancouver Foodie Tours (http://foodietours.ca) runs several excellent and entertaining food tours, including an eating tour of Granville Island and restaurant adventures downtown and in Gastown.

Want to forage in the rainforest for wild edibles or learn to catch your own crab? Contact **Swallow Tail Culinary Adventures** (www.swallowtail.ca), which also organizes pop-up dinners and other food events. **Vancouver Brewery Tours** (http://vancouverbrewerytours.com) runs regular tasting tours of the city's craft breweries.

The nonprofit **Vancouver Heritage Foundation** (www.vancouverheritagefoundation.org) offers periodic walking tours of different Vancouver neighborhoods, focusing on the architecture and history of each community. Other options for architecture buffs are the Architectural Walking Tours that the **Architectural Institute of BC** (http://aibc.ca) runs throughout July-August.

CALENDAR OF EVENTS

JANUARY-MARCH

Dozens of restaurants offer special menus, and you can join in food events, from chef dinners and wine-tastings to food tours, during **Dine Out Vancouver** (www.dineoutvancouver.com, Jan.), the city's annual celebration of dining that has grown into one of Canada's largest food and drink festivals.

With its large Asian population, Vancouver hosts plenty of festivities to mark the **Lunar New Year** (Jan.-Feb.), including parades, lion dances, music, fireworks, and other special events held in China-town and throughout Richmond.

APRIL-JUNE

A good introduction to the region's growing micro-brewery scene, the annual **Vancouver Craft Beer Week** (http://vancouvercraftbeerweek.com, May-June) includes tasting events and other activities that showcase small brewers and their products.

With nearly two weeks of concerts around the city, from big-name big-ticket shows to free music in the park, the **TD Vancouver International Jazz Festival** (www.coastaljazz.ca, June-July) has tunes for any jazz, Latin, funk, and world music lover.

Vancouver Folk Festival at Jericho Beach

JULY-AUGUST

Vancouver celebrates Canada's birthday, **Canada Day** (www.canadaplace.ca, July 1), with a parade, outdoor concerts, and celebratory fireworks over Burrard Inlet. Canada Place is the center of the festivities.

It's not just folk music at the long-established **Vancouver Folk**

WHAT'S NEW?

- **Short-term rental restrictions:** The city of Vancouver has implemented regulations to manage the proliferation of short-term rentals from services such as Airbnb and VRBO. Owners must be licensed, and many rentals are limited to 30 days or more, which has reduced the availability of short-term accommodations. Book early, particularly in the busy summer months.

- **Ride sharing:** After extended deliberations, the city of Vancouver has given approval to ride-sharing companies. Both Uber and Lyft have announced plans to begin local service by 2020.

- **More places to pedal:** Vancouver continues to add bike lanes throughout the city and expand its bike-sharing program, making it easier to get around on two wheels.

- **Fun at the Shipyards:** On the waterfront, a short walk from Lonsdale Quay in North Vancouver's Lower Lonsdale neighborhood, the redeveloping Shipyards District now has a cool contemporary art museum, the Polygon Gallery; several pubs and eateries; and a popular summer night market with live music and numerous food trucks.

Festival (http://thefestival.bc.ca, July). This musical extravaganza draws world beat, roots, blues, and yes, folk musicians from across Canada and around the world to Jericho Beach for three days of always-eclectic music on multiple outdoor stages. It's great fun for all ages.

Fireworks displays over English Bay bring thousands of Vancouverites and visitors out for the **Celebration of Light** (http://hondacelebrationoflight.com,

July-Aug.) that takes place over several summer evenings. The best viewing spots are at English Bay Beach, but you can see them from Kitsilano Beach and other points around False Creek.

The **Vancouver Pride Festival** (http://vancouverpride.ca, July-Aug.) features more than 20 events celebrating the city's large gay, lesbian, bisexual, transgender, and queer community, culminating in a festive parade through the downtown streets.

SEPTEMBER-DECEMBER

For two weeks, the **Vancouver Fringe Festival** (www. vancouverfringe.com, Sept.) takes over Granville Island and other stages around town with innovative, quirky, and often surprising theater, comedy, puppetry, and storytelling performances.

The VanDusen Botanical Garden marks the holiday season with its annual **Festival of Lights** (http://vandusengarden.org, Dec.), illuminating its garden paths with thousands of sparkling lights.

Festival of Lights at VanDusen Botanical Garden

Downtown and West End Map 1

Downtown is a vibrant mix of residential and commercial development, dotted with pocket parks and green spaces. Visitors and locals walk and bike the Seawall and play at the beach.

Apartment buildings, historic houses, and a growing number of modern towers line the **leafy streets** of the West End, bounded by English Bay, Stanley Park, Burrard Inlet, and downtown. Most of the city's **hotels** are located downtown or in the West End, as are plenty of **dining** and **drinking spots.** Robson is a major shopping street, Granville Street is the center of Vancouver's nightclub district, and the city's LGBTQ community congregates in the bars and cafés along Davie Street.

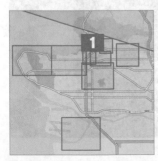

TOP SIGHTS

- Most Renowned Indigenous Art: **Bill Reid Gallery of Northwest Coast Art** (page 44)

TOP RESTAURANTS

- Most Glam Pizza Spot: **Nightingale** (page 49)
- Liveliest Japanese Restaurant: **Guu Garden** (page 50)

TOP NIGHTLIFE

- Most Scenic Views: **LIFT Bar & Grill** (page 54)
- Best Themed Night Out: **Prohibition Lounge** (page 55)
- Best Secret Drinking Hideaway: **Reflections: The Garden Terrace** (page 55)

TOP RECREATION

- Best Place to Get Sandy Downtown: **English Bay Beach** (page 57)

TOP FESTIVALS AND EVENTS

- Best Reason to Wear a Rainbow: **Vancouver Pride Festival** (page 61)

TOP SHOPS

- Most Historic Shopping Destination: **Hudson's Bay** (page 62)

GETTING THERE AND AROUND

- SkyTrain lines: Canada Line, Expo Line
- SkyTrain stops: Waterfront (Canada, Expo Lines); Vancouver City Centre (Canada Line); Burrard, Granville (Expo Line)
- Bus lines: 2, 5, 6, 19, 23

1 Lost Lagoon
To ❶ Just Singin' Round
2
3

Devonian Harbour Park

SIGHTS

7	B5	Olympic Cauldron	36	D5	Vancouver Art Gallery
10	C1	A-maze-ing Laughter	47	D6	Vancouver Lookout
23	C6	The Seawall	68	E5	Vancouver Central Library
24	C6	Canada Place			
34	D5	Bill Reid Gallery of Northwest Coast Art			

Marina Square Park

Spokes Bicycle Rentals

Freedom Bikes

Stanley Park

CHILCO ST

GILFORD ST

DENMAN ST

HARO ST

ALBERNI ST

BARCLAY ST

WEST END

W GEORGIA ST

BEACH AVE

The Seawall

COMOX ST

BIDWELL ST

NELSON ST

CARDERO ST

NICOLA ST

ROBSON ST

A-maze-ing Laughter

PENDRELL ST

DAVIE ST

Barclay Heritage Square Park

BROUGHTON ST

English Bay Beach Park

English Bay Bike Rentals

JERVIS ST

BUTE ST

Nelson Park

RESTAURANTS

4	B2	Dinesty Dumpling House	32	D4	Caffé Artigiano
5	B3	Marutama Ramen	33	D5	Royal Dinette
6	B3	Hokkaido Ramen Santouka	39	D5	Hawksworth Restaurant
9	C1	España Restaurant	46	D5	Peaceful Restaurant
14	C3	Forage	48	E3	West End Farmers Market
15	C3	Timber	53	E4	Le Crocodile
19	C5	Meat and Bread	56	E4	Guu Garden
20	C5	Nightingale	62	E5	Japadog
21	C5	Tractor Foods	63	E5	Medina Café
22	C5	Bella Gelateria	74	F3	Musette Caffè
26	C6	Miku	77	F4	The Templeton
30	D4	Boulevard Kitchen & Oyster Bar			

NIGHTLIFE

2	A3	LIFT Bar & Grill	57	E4	The Roxy
29	D4	Gerard Lounge	61	E5	The Commodore Ballroom
40	D5	Prohibition Lounge	64	E5	Uva Wine & Cocktail Bar
41	D5	Reflections: The Garden Terrace	65	E5	Red Card Sports Bar
50	E3	Fountainhead Pub	75	F4	Johnnie Fox's Irish Snug
51	E3	Celebrities Nightclub			
54	E4	Bacchus Lounge			

DAVIE VILLAGE

BURNABY ST

PACIFIC ST

DAVIE

DRAKE ST

PACIFIC BLVD

Sunset Beach Park

| 0 | | 200 yds |
| 0 | | 200 m |

DISTANCE ACROSS MAP
Approximate: 1.7 mi or 2.7 km

4   **5**   **6**

RECREATION

11 C1 English Bay Beach	**58 E5** Robson Square Ice Rink	
38 D5 Cycle City Vancouver	**73 F2** Sunset Beach	

ARTS AND CULTURE

1 A2 Just Singin' Round	**71 E6** Ballet BC
37 D5 Pendulum Gallery	**72 E6** DanceHouse
70 E6 CBC Musical Nooners	

SHOPS

3 B2 Ayoub's Dried Fruits and Nuts	**45 D5** Hudson's Bay
27 D4 RYU	**59 E5** Nordstrom
28 D4 Indigo	**60 E5** Winners
31 D4 Lululemon Athletica	**66 E5** Viti Wine & Lager
44 D5 Holt Renfrew	**69 E6** Bookmark
	78 F5 Designhouse

HOTELS

8 C1 Sylvia Hotel	**42 D5** Rosewood Hotel Georgia
12 C3 Barclay House B&B	**43 D5** EXchange Hotel Vancouver
13 C3 West End Guest House	**49 E3** Sunset Inn and Suites
16 C3 Listel Hotel	**52 E3** Burrard Hotel
17 C4 Loden Hotel	**55 E4** Wedgewood Hotel & Spa
18 C5 Fairmont Pacific Rim	**67 E5** Moda Hotel
25 C6 Pan Pacific Hotel Vancouver	**76 F4** Hotel Belmont
35 D5 Fairmont Hotel Vancouver	

© MOON.COM

Canada Place

DOWNTOWN AND WEST END WALK

TOTAL DISTANCE: 2.5 miles (4 km)
TOTAL WALKING TIME: 1 hour

This walking tour takes you from Canada Place on the Burrard Inlet side of downtown, through the city to English Bay, passing numerous landmarks, artworks, and places to eat. You can do this walk anytime, but if you start in the early afternoon, you can wrap up your stroll at west-facing English Bay Beach as the sun is shining over the sea.

1 Begin your walk at **Canada Place,** the waterfront landmark with its billowing white sails. Follow the Seawall path one block toward the Vancouver Convention Centre's west building, and note the building's living roof. Keeping the water on your right, continue along the Seawall behind the convention center, passing *The Drop,* a 65-foot (20-m) bright blue raindrop sculpture that a Berlin-based art collective created in 2009.

2 At the back of the convention center, after watching the floatplanes taking off and landing on the harbor, turn left up the stairs to Jack Poole Plaza. Look for *Digital Orca* (2009), by Vancouver artist Douglas Coupland, a sculpture of a whale that appears to be breaching toward the sky. Also on the plaza is the **Olympic Cauldron,** which was lit when Vancouver hosted the 2010 Winter Olympic Games.

3 Turn left (east) onto Canada Place, then in one block, turn right (south) onto Burrard Street. Walk one more block to the corner of Burrard and Cordova, and look up. Wrapping around the exterior of the **Fairmont Pacific Rim** are the words "Lying on top of a building the clouds looked no nearer than when I was lying on the street." It's an art installation by New York artist Liam Gillick.

4 Ready for refreshments? In front of the Fairmont, stop for gelato or sorbetto at **Bella Gelateria.**

5 When you've finished your treats, continue walking south on busy Burrard Street, away from the water. After three blocks, turn left (east) onto Dunsmuir Street and take your first right (south) onto Hornby Street. In the middle of the block is the **Bill Reid Gallery of Northwest Coast Art,** one of the best places downtown to explore indigenous art. Allow about an hour to walk through the gallery.

6 Exit the gallery and turn right (south) on Hornby. In one block, at the corner of Hornby and Georgia Streets, cross the street and go into the HSBC Building (885 W. Georgia St.). Why stop at a bank office? In the lobby is a massive, swinging stainless steel pendulum, an art piece

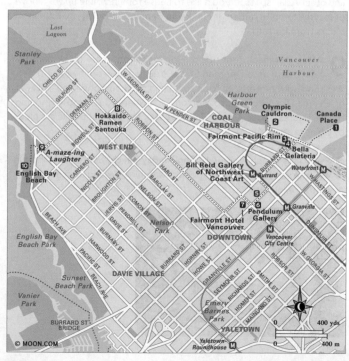

© MOON.COM

called *Broken Column* (1987) by Alan Storey. The building's air circulation system powers its movement. Also in the lobby, the free **Pendulum Gallery** mounts small changing art exhibitions.

7 Diagonally across Hornby and Georgia Streets is the landmark **Fairmont Hotel Vancouver,** built in 1939. Duck into the lobby for a quick look, and then exit the building, turning left (south) onto Burrard Street.

Fairmont Hotel Vancouver

8 In one block, cross Burrard and turn right (west) onto Robson Street. Robson is one of downtown's main shopping streets, and while many of the stores are international chains, it's still a lively district. This retail route gradually gives way to restaurants—primarily noodle shops, Korean eateries, and other Asian spots. If you'd like to pause for lunch, line up for a bowl of *tokusen toroniku* ramen at **Hokkaido Ramen Santouka,** on Robson six blocks from Burrard.

9 After your meal, continue on Robson for one more block, and turn left (south) onto Denman Street. You're now in the heart of the West End, with more small food spots and neighborhood shops. Stay on Denman for six blocks to Morton Park, where you'll spot 14 grinning bronze figures. That's *A-maze-ing Laughter,* the popular public art piece by Chinese artist Yue Minjun.

10 Cross Beach Avenue to **English Bay Beach,** where you can sit in the sand and do some people-watching, resting up from your downtown explorations.

English Bay Beach

Sights

Canada Place

Among Vancouver's most famous downtown landmarks is Canada Place, its billowing white sails recalling a ship ready to set off to sea. Canada Place does have a seafaring function; the building, with its five 90-foot (27-m) white sails made of Teflon-coated fiberglass, houses the city's cruise ship terminal. Also inside are the east wing of the Vancouver Convention Centre, the Pan Pacific Hotel Vancouver, and several tourist attractions.

The coolest reason to visit Canada Place is FlyOver Canada (604/620-8455, www.flyovercanada.com; 9:30am-10pm daily, adults $33, seniors, students, and ages 13-18 $27, under age 13 $23), a multimedia simulated flight ride that has you swoop and soar across the country, flying over Arctic peaks, past Toronto's CN Tower, and across the Canadian Rockies. You even feel the spray as you hover above Niagara Falls, and at one point the northern lights spread out around you. The FlyOver Canada experience lasts about 30 minutes; the flight itself is eight minutes long. Tickets are discounted if you buy them online in advance.

While you're at Canada Place, follow the Canadian Trail, a walkway along the building's west promenade. Check out interpretive panels about Canada's 10 provinces and 3 territories while enjoying the views of Stanley Park, Burrard Inlet, and the North Shore mountains. You'll frequently see massive cruise ships at the docks spring-fall.

MAP 1: 999 Canada Pl., 604/665-9000, www.canadaplace.ca

Olympic Cauldron

When Vancouver hosted the 2010 Winter Olympic Games, the candelabra-like Olympic Cauldron burned brightly. The 33-foot-tall (10-m) landmark, comprising four diagonal columns leaning together, stands next to the Vancouver Convention Centre's west building, near the Coal Harbour waterfront downtown—although it's now lit only for special events.

MAP 1: Jack Poole Plaza, foot of Thurlow St.

the Seawall along Vancouver's waterfront

The Seawall

Snaking along the waterfront on both sides of the downtown peninsula, extending around Stanley Park, through the West End and Yaletown, and along False Creek to Granville Island, Kitsilano Beach, and beyond, the Seawall is Vancouver's most popular walking, running, and cycling path. The first sections of the Seawall were built in Stanley Park, beginning in 1917. Now, this 17.5-mile (28-km) pathway, officially called the Seaside Greenway, may be the world's longest uninterrupted waterfront path.

The majority of the Seawall is paved, although in a few areas it's made of packed gravel. In most places the Seawall is divided, with pedestrians routed to one side and cyclists, skaters, and anything with wheels on the other; watch for the signs to stay on the proper side, particularly when the pathway is busy.

MAP 1: On the waterfront from Canada Place to Stanley Park, English Bay, Yaletown, and along False Creek to Granville Island, Kitsilano, and the city's west side

Vancouver Lookout

Ride the glass elevator to the top of this observation tower for views across the city, Stanley Park, the waterfront, and the North Shore mountains. Although many downtown buildings now dwarf this 30-story tower, which opened in 1977, it's a good place to get oriented. Admission includes a 20-minute tour highlighting local sights as you circle the observation platform, which offers a 360-degree view. Even if you don't follow a tour, you can ask the guides to point out particular locations and landmarks.

Lookout tickets are good all day, so you can check out the daytime views, then return to see the sunset or watch the evening lights twinkle.

MAP 1: 555 W. Hastings St., 604/689-0421, www.vancouverlookout. com, 8:30am-10:30pm daily May-Sept., 9am-9pm daily Oct.-Apr., adults $18.25, seniors $15.25, students and ages 13-18 $13.25, ages 6-12 $9.50

view from the Vancouver Lookout

✪ Bill Reid Gallery of Northwest Coast Art

The Bill Reid Gallery of Northwest Coast Art, which you enter through a courtyard in the Cathedral Place complex off Hornby Street, is dedicated to British Columbia artist Bill Reid's life and work. Born to a Haida First Nations mother and a European father, Reid created more than 1,500 sculptures, carvings, and pieces of jewelry, most of which explore Haida traditions. Among the highlights on display are Reid's *Mythic Messengers,* a 28-foot (8.5-m) bronze frieze; more than 40 pieces of his gold and silver jewelry; and several of Reid's works that the Canadian government features on Canada's $20 bill.

With exhibits both in its main high-ceilinged exhibition space and on an art deco-style mezzanine, the downtown gallery also showcases other First Nations art, including a full-size totem pole carved by James Hart of Haida Gwaii, and hosts changing exhibits of indigenous art of the Northwest Coast region. Stop into the gift shop for First Nations prints, jewelry, and other artwork.

MAP 1: 639 Hornby St., 604/682-3455, www.billreidgallery.ca, 10am-5pm daily mid-May-early Oct., 11am-5pm Wed.-Sun. early Oct.-mid-May, adults $13, seniors $10, students $8, ages 13-17 $6

Vancouver Art Gallery

The permanent collection at the Vancouver Art Gallery includes more than 10,000 artworks, emphasizing artists from western Canada, including indigenous artists, photographers, and artists with connections to the Pacific Rim region. The gallery has a strong collection of works by British Columbia-born Emily Carr, one of Canada's most important early-20th-century painters. Carr is known for her paintings of BC's landscapes and its indigenous people.

Hosting changing exhibitions throughout the year, the gallery is housed in the former 1906 court building designed by architect Francis M. Rattenbury (who also designed Victoria's Parliament Building). Noted BC modern architect Arthur Erickson incorporated the stone courthouse into the expanded gallery that was completed in 1983. Built around a grand rotunda, the art gallery has exhibit spaces on four levels.

The gallery offers guided tours (hours vary Thurs. and Sat.-Sun., free with museum admission). The gallery also runs programs for kids and families on Sunday afternoons that range from child-focused exhibit tours to hands-on art workshops.

The Vancouver Art Gallery has announced plans to relocate to a new building to be constructed at West Georgia and check the website MAP 1: 750 Hornby St., 6 www.vanartgallery.bc.ca, 10a Wed.-Mon., 10am-9pm Tues., adu $24, seniors $20, students $18, ages 6 $6.50 (by donation 5pm-9pm Tues.)

Vancouver Central Library

The Vancouver Central Library is both an architectural landmark and a hub of information, art, and events. Designed by Israeli Canadian architect Moshe Safdie and opened in 1995, the building has a distinctive curved shape, modeled after Rome's Colosseum. Before you even get to the books, you can have coffee or a snack in one of several cafés in the library's light and airy interior atrium. On the 9th floor, you can take a break on the rooftop terrace as you take in the city views.

The library regularly hosts lectures, author talks, movie screenings, and other events, mostly free. In front of the library, near the corner of Homer and Robson Streets, is a public art piece, *The Words Don't Fit the Picture*, a neon sign by Vancouver artist Ron Terada.
MAP 1: 350 W. Georgia St., 604/331-3603, www.vpl.ca, 10am-9pm Mon.-Thurs., 10am-6pm Fri.-Sat., 11am-6pm Sun., free

A-maze-ing Laughter

One of Vancouver's most popular public art pieces, *A-maze-ing Laughter*, by Beijing-based contemporary artist Yue Minjun, is composed of 14 larger-than-life bronze figures, with oversize grins dominating their equally oversize faces. Though the 8.5-foot-tall (2.6-m) statues appear to be chortling

...Y PARK

...on the downtown peninsula, Stanley Park incorpo-
...d waterfront trails, First Nations culture and heritage,
...n, and spectacular views

...5-mile (9-km) walking and cycling path, circles the pe-
...y Park and passes many of the park's attractions. You
...he park's outer edge by car along Stanley Park Drive.
It's wor... ...ring the park's interior trails, too, many of which pass
through old-growth rainforest.

Among Stanley Park's highlights are the totem poles at Brockton
Point and Siwash Rock, an offshore rock formation that figures in First
Nations legends. A family-friendly stop is the Vancouver Aquarium Marine Science Centre (845 Avison Way, 604/659-3474, www.vanaqua.org,
9:30am-6pm daily July-early Sept., 10am-5pm daily early Sept.-June,
adults $38, seniors and students $30, ages 4-12 $21), one of Canada's
largest aquariums.

On a finger of land jutting into the harbor on Stanley Park's east side,
the red and white Brockton Point Lighthouse was built in 1914.

From Prospect Point, the highest spot in Stanley Park, you have
great views of Burrard Inlet, the North Shore mountains, and the Lions
Gate Bridge, one of the world's longest suspension bridges.

A giant western red cedar, roughly 800 years old, is another park
landmark. The massive Hollow Tree stopped growing in the 1800s and
was essentially a 42-foot-tall (13-m) tree stump. After a 2006 windstorm
caused it to lean precipitously, locals campaigned to save it, and the historic tree was stabilized with a steel core and underground steel "roots."
Find it along Stanley Park Drive, north of Third Beach.

TOURS

Several First Nations, including the Burrard, Musqueam, and Squamish
people, made their home for centuries in what is now Stanley Park. Learn
about these indigenous connections on the 1.5-hour Talking Trees Walk
with First Nations' owned Talaysay Tours (604/628-8555 or 800/605-4643,
www.talaysay.com, daily Feb-Oct., adults $45, ages 3-18 $36).

West Coast Sightseeing (604/451-1600 or 877/451-1777, http://
westcoastsightseeing.com) runs a year-round hop-on hop-off tour (48-
hour pass adults $59, ages 3-12 $30) that takes visitors to six stops within
the park and to 24 other locations throughout the city.

BEACHES

Along the Seawall, you can swim or watch the sunset at sandy Second Beach, which has a seasonal snack bar and children's playground
nearby. Quieter Third Beach has views toward the North Shore.

WATER SPORTS

To explore Stanley Park from the water, rent a kayak from Vancouver Water Adventures (1700 Beach Ave., 604/736-5155, www.
vancouverwateradventures.com, 11am-7pm daily late May-early Sept.)
on English Bay Beach, and paddle toward Siwash Rock.

HIKING

The City of Vancouver publishes an online park trail map (http://

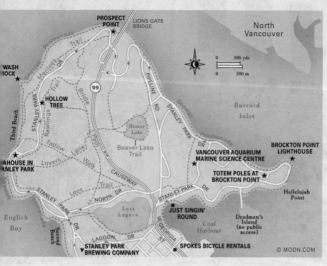

vancouver.ca). Don't hike alone on these interior trails, as they can be surprisingly secluded. Trails include **Tatlow Walk**, between Third Beach and Lost Lagoon; **Rawlings Trail**, open to cyclists and pedestrians, which parallels Park Drive and takes you past the Hollow Tree; and **Beaver Lake Trail**, which circles this small lake near the park center.

CYCLING

Vancouver's most popular cycling route runs along the **Seawall**.

The **Mobi bike share program** (778/655-1800, www.mobibikes.ca) has locations near Stanley Park. Or you can rent bikes from several West End shops just outside the park's boundaries, including **Spokes Bicycle Rentals** (1798 W. Georgia St., 604/688-5141, www.spokesbicyclerentals. com, 8am-9pm daily, from $8.50 per hour), **Freedom Bikes** (730 Denman St., 604/623-2837, www.freedombikes.ca, 8am-9:30pm daily, from $7 per hour), and **English Bay Bike Rentals** (1754 Davie St., 604/568-8490, www.englishbaybikerentals.com, 9am-9pm daily, from $8.50 per hour, electric bikes $18 per hour). Another rental shop with good-quality bikes, **Cycle City Vancouver** (page 57) is centrally located downtown, along the Hornby Street bike lane that leads to the Seawall. All the cycle shops reduce their hours October-May.

PRACTICALITIES

Enter Stanley Park from West Georgia Street, near Coal Harbour, or from English Bay, near the intersection of Denman and Davie Streets. Stanley Park's parking lots are fee-based ($3.50 per hour Apr.-Sept., $2.50 per hour Oct.-Mar.). Daily passes ($13 Apr.-Sept., $7 Oct.-Mar.) are good at any park lot.

Stop for a beer and a sandwich, salad, or pizza in the heritage sports pavilion that's now **Stanley Park Brewing Company** (8901 Stanley Park Dr., 604/681-0460, www.stanleyparkbrewing.com, 11am-11pm Mon.-Fri., 10am-11pm Sat.-Sun., $16-26). Above Third Beach, the **Teahouse in Stanley Park** (Ferguson Point, 604/669-3281, www.vancouverdine.com, 11:30am-10pm Mon.-Fri., 10:30am-10pm Sat.-Sun., $22-32) has a crowd-pleasing west coast menu and lovely patio.

the rooftop terrace at the Vancouver Central Library

hysterically, the artist has said that these smiling faces actually mask the misery of life in China's post-Tiananmen Square era. The artwork faces English Bay in the West End.

MAP 1: Morton Park, Denman St. at Davie St.

Restaurants

PRICE KEY

$ Entrées less than CAD$15
$$ Entrées CAD$15-25
$$$ Entrées more than CAD$25

MODERN CANADIAN

Hawksworth Restaurant $$$

In a chandelier-bedecked space at the Rosewood Hotel Georgia downtown, sophisticated Hawksworth Restaurant attracts expense-account diners, couples celebrating occasions, and gourmets savoring a fine meal with solicitous service. With foie gras, aged beef sirloin, and papardelle with wild mushrooms and truffle, it's all about the luxe ingredients in regionally influenced contemporary fare. If the dinner prices are too rich, splurge on a leisurely lunch or light bites at the bar.

MAP 1: 801 W. Georgia St., 604/673-7000, www. hawksworthrestaurant.com, 7am-10:30am, 11:30am-2pm, and 5pm-10:30pm Mon.-Thurs., 7am-10:30am, 11:30am-2pm, and 5pm-11pm Fri., 7am-2pm and 5pm-11pm Sat., 7am-2pm and 5pm-10:30pm Sun.

✪ Nightingale $$

Owned by chef David Hawksworth of the high-end Hawksworth Restaurant, Nightingale sings a slightly less formal song, though you still get the chef's trademark glamour in the buzzing two-level dining room downtown. The lengthy menu pairs sharing plates and pizzas, with dishes like grilled kanpachi collar with grated radish, roasted cauliflower with charred lemon dressing, and fried chicken with sumac and pickles, with straightforward and wilder (braised beef, pickled mushrooms, and *fior di latte*) pies. To drink are inventive cocktails or beer from a local craft brewery.

MAP 1: 1017 W. Hastings St., 604/695-9500, http://hawknightingale.com, 11am-midnight daily

pizza at Nightingale

Forage $$

The kitchen team at Forage, the contemporary dining room at the West End's Listel Hotel, sources ingredients from local farmers, fisherfolk, and, yes, foragers, and crafts them into locavore plates to share. Snack on bison carpaccio as you sip a BC craft beer or wine on tap. Then graze on summer carrots with Vietnamese herbs, fir-smoked duck sauced with haskap berry jus, or pan-seared halibut with geoduck bottarga. Around a large U-shaped bar and furnished with lots of natural wood, the restaurant is a good choice for breakfast or brunch too.

MAP 1: 1300 Robson St., 604/661-1400, www.foragevancouver.com, 6:30am-10am and 5pm-late Mon.-Fri., 7am-2pm and 5pm-late Sat.-Sun.

Royal Dinette $$

Styled like a Parisian brasserie, Royal Dinette is a lively spot for inventive farm-to-table dining downtown. Start with a craft beer or fun cocktail, like the Kumbaya (cedar-smoked rye, amaro, cherry cedar bitters, and burnt cinnamon marshmallow). The kitchen makes its pasta fresh daily for dishes like tagliatelle with rabbit, leeks, and wild mushrooms or gnocchi with asparagus, spinach, and sweet garlic. If you can't choose between duck breast with gooseberries or ash-rubbed bison steak, order a family-style feast ($65 pp) and let the chef send out a parade of dishes.

MAP 1: 905 Dunsmuir St., 604/974-8077, http://royaldinette.ca, 11:30am-2pm and 5pm-10pm Mon.-Fri., 5pm-10pm Sat.

SEAFOOD
Boulevard Kitchen & Oyster Bar $$$

Sink into a cream-colored banquette at elegant Boulevard Kitchen & Oyster Bar, where the service is polished and dishes like *kanpachi* paired with a ramen-style quail egg, soy- and sake-glazed sablefish with local bull kelp, or lingcod with wild rice crunch highlight local seafood in refined Asian-accented

49

preparations. Stop in for a glass of bubbly and fresh oysters at the long marble bar. Boulevard shares its space with the Sutton Place Hotel downtown.

MAP 1: 845 Burrard St., 604/642-2900, www.boulevardvancouver.ca, 6:30am-10pm daily

CHINESE
Dinesty Dumpling House $$

Watch the dumpling makers at work at Dinesty Dumpling House; that's what you should order: Shanghai-style soup dumplings, pan-fried pork buns, and steamed vegetable and egg dumplings. Handmade noodles, fresh greens with garlic, and the unusual omelet with pickles are also tasty choices in this bustling West End eatery, where the tables are packed in tightly. They also have several locations in Richmond.

MAP 1: 1719 Robson St., 604/669-7769, www.dinesty.ca, 11am-3pm and 5pm-10pm Mon.-Fri., 11am-10pm Sat.-Sun.

Peaceful Restaurant $$

Visit this simple and friendly place for northern Chinese dishes, including hand-pulled noodles, lamb, and dumplings. Try the mustard-seed salad (carrots, celery, and vermicelli in a mustardy dressing), the Xinjiang cumin lamb, or the "cat ear" stir-fried noodles, shaped like orecchiette and tossed with vegetables and pork. Peaceful Restaurant has several other locations across town.

MAP 1: 602 Seymour St., 604/313-1333, www.peacefulrestaurant.com, 11am-9:30pm Sun.-Thurs., 11am-10pm Fri.-Sat.

JAPANESE
✪ Guu Garden $$

Part of a local mini chain of *izakayas,* lively Guu Garden serves Japanese tapas designed to share, like grilled black cod cheeks, crispy cauliflower *karaage,* and sashimi-style tuna *tataki,* to pair with sake, *shochu,* or Japanese beer. Guu is on the top floor of a downtown complex with a similarly named eatery on the main level, so be sure to go upstairs. Nab a seat on the terrace if you can.

MAP 1: 888 Nelson St., 604/899-0855, www.guu-izakaya.com/garden, 11:30am-2:30pm and 5:30pm-midnight Mon.-Thurs., 11:30am-2:30pm and 5:30pm-12:30am Fri., noon-3pm and 5:30pm-12:30am Sat., noon-3pm and 5:30pm-midnight Sun.

sushi at Guu Garden

Hokkaido Ramen Santouka $

In the West End, there are ramen shops on seemingly every corner. At Hokkaido Ramen Santouka, the local outpost of a Japan-based noodle shop chain, the signature dish is *tokusen toroniku* ramen, a rich, almost creamy soup made from pork cheek meat. This ramen revelation is worth the inevitable queue, but lingering in this cramped space is discouraged, so diners slurp and move on. There's another location on Broadway near Cambie Street.

MAP 1: 1690 Robson St., 604/681-8121, www.santouka.co.jp, 11am-11pm daily

Marutama Ramen $

Japanese import Marutama Ramen makes its noodle soup with a velvety chicken broth. The *tamago* ramen comes with roast pork and an egg, while the *tanmen* is full of fresh vegetables. In addition to this compact West End branch, you'll find a second location near the Vancouver Central Library downtown.

MAP 1: 780 Bidwell St., 604/688-8837, www.marutama.ca, 11:30am-10pm Mon.-Thurs., 11:30am-10:30pm Fri., 11am-10:30pm Sat., 11am-10pm Sun.

Miku

Miku $$$

For sushi with a water view, visit Miku, an upscale Japanese dining room opposite Canada Place downtown. They're known for *aburi*

sushi, fresh fish seared with a blowtorch, but any of their raw fish options should please *nigiri* and maki lovers. The waterside location and the solicitous service make a meal here feel like a classy night out.

MAP 1: 200 Granville St., 604/568-3900, www.mikurestaurant. com, 11:30am-10:30pm Sun.-Wed., 11:30am-11pm Thurs.-Sat.

Japadog $

A unique-to-Vancouver mash-up of hot dogs and Japanese flavors, fast-casual Japadog concocts their signature sausages, like the *kurobuta* pork *terimayo*, sauced with teriyaki, mayonnaise, and seaweed, at a diminutive downtown counter-service restaurant (also open for breakfast) and at several downtown food stands.

MAP 1: 530 Robson St., 604/569-1158, www.japadog.com, 7am-11pm Mon.-Fri., 8am-midnight Sat., 8am-10pm Sun.

FRENCH
Le Crocodile $$$

Classic French cuisine never goes out of style at Le Crocodile, a long-standing downtown favorite where standards from *la belle France* are updated with west coast ingredients. Grilled salmon sauced with a saffron velouté, locally raised duck breast served with foie gras in an apple cider reduction, and rack of lamb with a mustard sabayon are some of the menu offerings. Expect white tablecloths and polished service, appropriate for a business lunch or a special night out.

VANCOUVER'S FOOD TRUCKS

Vancouver's fleet of food trucks park downtown, purveying a global gamut of meals to go. A cluster of trucks sets up shop around the Vancouver Art Gallery along Howe and Hornby Streets, while others locate closer to the waterfront along Burrard or Thurlow Streets. Most operate 11am or 11:30am to 2:30pm or 3pm. The best way to find what trucks are where is with the Vancouver Street Food app (http://streetfoodapp.com/vancouver). Some favorites include:

- **Mom's Grilled Cheese** (Howe St. at Robson St.) for, as you'd expect, grilled cheese sandwiches
- **Chickpea** (W. Cordova St., near Burrard St., www.ilovechickpea.ca) for Mediterranean-inspired vegetarian fare
- **Via Tevere Neapolitan Express** (Burrard St. at W. Pender St., http://viateverepizzeria.com) for the "Neapolitan Saltimbocca," a pizza-style sandwich cooked in a wood-fired oven
- **Aussie Pie Guy** (www.aussiepieguy.com) for handheld Australian-style meat or vegetable pies

MAP 1: 909 Burrard St., Suite 100, 604/669-4298, http://lecrocodilerestaurant.com, 11:30am-2:30pm and 5:30pm-10pm Mon.-Thurs., 11:30am-2:30pm and 5:30pm-10:30pm Fri., 5:30pm-10:30pm Sat.

SPANISH

España Restaurant $$

At España Restaurant, a narrow storefront tapas bar in the West End, you could almost be in Spain, though here, some of the Spanish classics, like sautéed *padrón* peppers, fried anchovies, or paella, might be made with Pacific Northwest ingredients. To drink, try a sherry flight or choose from the list of Spanish wines by the glass. The restaurant is tiny, and they don't take reservations, so don't be in a rush.

MAP 1: 1118 Denman St., 604/558-4040, www.espanarestaurant.ca, 5pm-11pm Sun.-Thurs., 5pm-1am Fri.-Sat.

BREAKFAST AND BRUNCH

Medina Café $

Expect a queue at cheerful window-lined Medina Café, known for its sugar-studded Liège waffles (check out the waffle case on the dark wood counter) and for its North African-influenced brunch fare downtown. Try the tagine, a flavorful vegetable stew topped with poached eggs, merguez sausage, and preserved lemon.

MAP 1: 780 Richards St., 604/879-3114, www.medinacafe.com, 8am-3pm Mon.-Fri., 9am-3pm Sat.-Sun.

GASTROPUBS

Timber $$

From the deep-fried cheese curds, ketchup chips, bison burgers, and mushroom poutine to the beaver tail-like fried dough or the gooey butter tart, Timber, an all-Canadian West End gastropub, serves fun updates on classic Canuck comfort food. The beer list trends toward local craft labels, or choose from several types of Caesar, Canada's version of a Bloody Mary, made with

Clamato juice. The TVs are tuned to hockey, of course.

MAP 1: 300 Robson St., 604/661-2166, http://timbervancouver.com, noon-midnight Mon.-Thurs., noon-1am Fri., 11am-1am Sat., 11am-midnight Sun.

DINERS
The Templeton $

Retro diner The Templeton, complete with tabletop jukeboxes and soda-fountain stools, has morphed into a cool purveyor of comfort foods among the downtown bars on the Granville strip. Dig into hearty plates of pancakes, creative omelets, or burgers, which you can pair with coffee or "big people drinks" (craft beer, local wines, and cocktails). Save room for an ice cream sundae or old-fashioned banana split.

MAP 1: 1087 Granville St., 604/685-4612, http://thetempleton. ca, 8:30am-3pm Mon., 8:30am-10pm Tues.-Thurs. and Sun., 8:30am-11pm Fri.-Sat.

QUICK BITES
Meat and Bread $

Pull up a stool at the communal table in this downtown sandwich shop catering to the weekday lunch crowd. The signature sandwich at Meat and Bread is the hearty porchetta topped with salsa verde and crackling, but the simple menu typically includes several other varieties, perhaps roast chicken with pickled daikon and lemongrass-ginger sauce or a vegetarian eggplant, mozzarella, and gremolata. A soup and a salad, which change daily, are the only accompaniments. There's another downtown location on Robson Street and a branch in Gastown.

MAP 1: 1033 W. Pender St., http:// meatandbread.ca, 11am-4pm Mon.-Fri.

Tractor Foods $

For fresh salads, soups, rice bowls, and sandwiches near Canada Place downtown, plow a path to cafeteria-style Tractor Foods. Build your own rice bowl or choose half or whole sandwiches, with options like grilled chicken, arugula, and pear, or hummus with roasted beets and avocado. Breakfast selections run from wraps to parfaits. Other locations are on Robson Street downtown, at the Olympic Village, in Kitsilano, and in the Broadway-Cambie neighborhood.

MAP 1: 335 Burrard St., 604/979-0500, www.tractorfoods.com, 7am-9:30pm Mon.-Fri., 8am-9:30pm daily

DESSERT
Bella Gelateria $

When gelato makers are obsessive about fresh ingredients and traditional Italian techniques, naturally they make some of Vancouver's best gelato. Find it downtown at tiny Bella Gelateria, near the Fairmont Pacific Rim hotel. Expect a line, particularly on warm summer nights.

MAP 1: 1001 W. Cordova St., 604/569-1010, http://bellagelateria.com, 11am-10pm Mon.-Thurs., 11am-11pm Fri., 10:30am-11pm Sat., 10:30am-10pm Sun.

FARMERS MARKETS
West End Farmers Market $

The West End Farmers Market purveys produce, baked goods, and prepared foods on Saturday late May-late October. There's always a line for the sweets at whatever bakeshop is at the market, and local cheesemaker Little Qualicum Cheeseworks frequently offers samples. Eli's Serious Sausage, Chouchou Crepes, and The Aussie Pie Guy are among the food trucks regularly parked here, and a musician or two usually performs during market hours. Local distillers, like Odd Society Spirits or craft breweries, offer tastings and sell their brews.

MAP 1: Comox St. at Thurlow St., www.eatlocal.org, 9am-2pm Sat. late May-late Oct.

COFFEE AND TEA
Caffé Artigiano $

Local Italian-style coffee chain Caffé Artigiano has several downtown branches, including this convenient location just off Robson Street, opposite the Vancouver Art Gallery. Come for the carefully prepared coffee, which they source from small producers around the world. The baristas here frequently win local competitions for their latte art. To pair with your drinks are a small selection of pastries and sandwiches. There are three other center-city locations, as well as a branch in Yaletown and one on Main Street.

MAP 1: 763 Hornby St., 604/694-7737, www.caffeartigiano.com, 5:30am-7pm Mon.-Fri., 6am-7pm Sat.- Sun.

Musette Caffè $

Cyclists congregate at bike-friendly Musette Caffè, a spacious downtown coffeehouse with double-height windows and a sunny patio. You don't have to bring your bicycle to enjoy an espresso, a beer, or a breakfast plate. To encourage patrons to be social, the café has a no-laptops-on-weekends policy.

MAP 1: 1325 Burrard St., 778/379-4150, www.musettecaffe.com, 7am-5pm Sat.-Tues., 7am-8pm Wed.-Fri.

Nightlife

PUBS
✪ LIFT Bar & Grill

Enjoy one of the best views of Vancouver while you raise your glass at LIFT Bar & Grill, an upscale waterfront pub and Pacific Northwest eatery on Coal Harbour that draws a mix of visitors, local businesspeople, and after-work meet-ups. Look across to Stanley Park as you take your craft beer, BC wine, or favorite cocktail on the terrace, where, if you were any closer to the water, you'd be swimming.

MAP 1: 333 Menchions Mews, 604/689-5438, http://liftbarandgrill.com, 11:30am-late Mon.-Fri., 11am-late Sat.-Sun.

Johnnie Fox's Irish Snug

Amid the nightclubs along Granville Street downtown, Johnnie Fox's Irish Snug is a classic Irish pub, where a diverse crowd settles in at the bar or wooden booths for a whiskey or a pint. Irish breakfast (served all day), Yorkshire pudding, and steak and Guinness pie add a Gaelic twist to the otherwise standard pub menu.

MAP 1: 1033 Granville St., 604/685-4946, www.johnniefox.ca, 11:30am-1am Sun.-Thurs., 11:30am-2am Fri.-Sat.

LIVE MUSIC

The Commodore Ballroom

First opened in 1930, The Commodore Ballroom downtown hosts live concerts in its art deco ballroom, featuring performers as diverse as the Tragically Hip, Lady Gaga, and Katy Perry and drawing crowds of over 900. Its original "sprung" dance floor, which cushioned dancers' feet with a layer of horsehair, was one of the first in North America.

MAP 1: 868 Granville St., 604/739-4550, www.commodoreballroom.com, tickets $35-100

The Roxy

Head to The Roxy, a dark neon-lit club downtown on the Granville strip, when you want to dance. Their rockin' house bands play several nights a week, drawing a young partying crowd; the club accommodates 200-plus people. Sunday is country-and-western night.

MAP 1: 932 Granville St., 604/331-7999, www.roxyvan.com, 8pm-3am daily, cover $7-14

COCKTAIL BARS AND LOUNGES

✪ Prohibition Lounge

Elegant Prohibition Lounge at the Rosewood Hotel Georgia has a Roaring Twenties theme, with music or DJs on weekend nights. Wear something stylish when you stop in to try an absinthe tasting, or go

for a classic cocktail, like the Hotel Georgia Circa 1951 (gin, lemon, orgeat, orange blossom water, and egg white) or Mandarin Mist (potato vodka, mandarin and lemon juices, yuzu syrup, and coconut foam).

MAP 1: 801 W. Georgia St., 604/673-7089, www.rosewoodhotels. com, 8pm-3am Fri.-Sat.

✪ Reflections: The Garden Terrace

Secreted away on the 4th floor of the Rosewood Hotel Georgia, the posh outdoor Reflections lounge, where you can sip your wine or classic cocktail on teak couches around a fire pit, brings Los Angeles glamour to downtown Vancouver. Because the lounge is exposed to the elements, it's typically only open April-October.

MAP 1: 801 W. Georgia St., 604/673-7043, www.rosewoodhotels. com, 11:30am-11pm daily Apr.-Oct.

Bacchus Lounge

Polished Bacchus Lounge at the Wedgewood Hotel is appropriate for cocktails and quiet conversation with a colleague or a consort. Don a cocktail dress or suit, then sink into the leather chairs or velvet banquettes and listen to the live piano music every evening.

MAP 1: 845 Hornby St., 604/608-5319, www.wedgewoodhotel.com, 2:30pm-midnight Sun.-Wed., 2:30pm-1am Thurs.-Sat.

Gerard Lounge

Styled like an English club room, with dark wood paneling, leather chairs, and oriental rugs, Gerard Lounge at the Sutton Place Hotel has a popular happy hour (3pm-6pm daily), where the after-work crowd loosens their ties over craft beer flights and discounted highballs. With french fries that are hand-cut and crispy chicken wings spiced with sambal chili, the bar snacks go beyond the ordinary.

MAP 1: 845 Burrard St., 604/642-2900, www.suttonplace.com, noon-late daily

Uva Wine & Cocktail Bar

Snug Uva Wine & Cocktail Bar serves creative cocktails, craft beer, and a long list of wines by the glass to a hip crowd. In the evening, arancini, charcuterie plates, or tapas-sized pastas make a snack or a light meal.

MAP 1: 900 Seymour St., 604/632-9560, www.uvavancouver.com, 2pm-2am daily

LGBTQ

Celebrities Nightclub

Davie Street, in the West End, is the center of Vancouver's LGBTQ community, where nightspots include Celebrities Nightclub, a frequently packed party-hard dance club that's open to all, known for its light shows and booming sound system. Stereotype Fridays (10pm-3am) are electronic music nights; Playhouse Saturdays (10pm-3am) get dancers moving with a mix of club hits and house anthems.

MAP 1: 1022 Davie St., 604/681-6180, www.celebritiesnightclub.com, cover varies

Fountainhead Pub

A West End local hangout since 2000, the easygoing Fountainhead Pub is a classic neighborhood bar with a heated patio (especially busy at brunch), a pool table, and room to talk. It has long been a popular spot for the area's gay community, although all are welcome. Cocktails get a little racy with drinks like the Porn Star (blue curacao, Sour Puss raspberry, and cranberry juice) or a Slippery Nipple shooter of Sambuca and Bailey's.

MAP 1: 1025 Davie St., 604/687-2222, www.fthdpub.com, 11am-midnight Sun.-Thurs., 11am-2am Fri.-Sat.

Uva Wine & Cocktail Bar

SPORTS BARS

Red Card Sports Bar

Want to watch the hockey game? Red Card Sports Bar downtown has 16 TVs and two massive projection screens, so you won't miss any of the action. It's not all hockey either, although Vancouver Canucks games get priority over football, baseball, and other sports. Beers come from around the world, and to ward off mid-match munchies, choose from Italian classics (pizzas, pastas), burgers, sandwiches, and other comfort food.

MAP 1: 560 Smithe St., 604/602-9570, www.redcardsportsbar.ca, 11:30am-1am Sun.-Thurs., 11:30am-2am Fri.-Sat.

Recreation

BEACHES

❂ English Bay Beach

You don't have to leave downtown Vancouver to go to the beach. English Bay Beach, in the West End, is the busiest of the city-center beaches, fun for people-watching, swimming, or enjoying the sunset. A landmark on English Bay is the Inukshuk, made of granite boulders. This type of traditional Inuit sculpture was used as a trail marker or symbol of welcome. Carver Alvin Kanak, of Rankin Inlet, Nunavut, crafted the 20-foot (6-m) English Bay Inukshuk, which weighs nearly 70,000 pounds (31,500 kg).

You can follow the Seawall path from English Bay into Stanley Park or around to Yaletown. In summer, you can rent kayaks and stand-up paddleboards on the beach from Vancouver Water Adventures (1700 Beach Ave., 604/736-5155, www.vancouverwateradventures. com, May-Sept.).

MAP 1: Beach Ave. at Denman St., http://vancouver.ca, 6am-10pm daily, free

Sunset Beach

As you'd expect from the name, Sunset Beach, along the Seawall near English Bay, is a west-facing beach with sunset views. Near the beach, built into the hillside at the foot of Broughton Street, is the AIDS Memorial, a public art piece installed in 2004. The names of nearly 800 people from BC who died of AIDS are engraved on its rust-oxidized steel panels.

MAP 1: Beach Ave. at Thurlow St., http://vancouver.ca, 6am-10pm daily, free

CYCLING

Cycle City Vancouver

In a spacious shop, centrally located downtown along the Hornby Street bike lane that leads to the Seawall, Cycle City Vancouver rents good-quality bikes, including electric bikes, and offers several cycling tours.

MAP 1: 646 Hornby St., 604/618-8626, http://cyclevancouver.com, 8am-9pm daily May-Sept., hours vary Oct.-Apr., rentals from $9.50 per hour, electric bikes $32 for 2 hours

ICE-SKATING

Robson Square Ice Rink

December-February, you can ice-skate downtown at the Robson Square Ice Rink, under a dome outdoors beneath Robson Square, near the Vancouver Art Gallery. The rink is particularly busy on weekend afternoons, when families take to the ice, and on Friday-Saturday evenings. You can rent skates ($5) if you don't have your own.

MAP 1: 800 Robson St., 604/209-8316, www.robsonsquare.com, 9am-9pm Sun.-Thurs., 9am-11pm Fri.-Sat. Dec.-Feb., free

Arts and Culture

GALLERIES
Pendulum Gallery
In the lobby of the HSBC Building, this small gallery space mounts different exhibits throughout the year. Recent shows have varied from "The Art of Dr. Seuss" to paintings by several Canadian landscape artists in "Land, Sea & Sky," to "Canstruction," featuring sculptures made entirely from cans of food; the dismantled creations were donated to the local food bank at the end of the exhibition. Also on view in the atrium-style lobby is a massive swinging stainless steel pendulum, an art piece called *Broken Column* by Alan Storey, which HSBC Bank commissioned. The building's ventilation system provides the power that keeps the pendulum moving.
MAP 1: 885 W. Georgia St., 604/250-9682, www.pendulumgallery. bc.ca, 9am-6pm Mon.-Wed., 9am-9pm Thurs.-Fri., 9am-5pm Sat., free

MUSIC
CBC Musical Nooners
Looking for lunchtime entertainment? CBC Musical Nooners is a free summertime concert series that brings pop, blues, folk, and world music performers to the plaza in front of the CBC building downtown for an hour of weekday live music. Bring your lunch.
MAP 1: CBC Plaza, 700 Hamilton St., www.cbc.ca, noon Mon.-Fri. early July-mid-Aug., free

Just Singin' Round
The Vancouver-based Synergy Collective Society hosts Just Singin' Round, a monthly dinner and music night featuring local performers, at the Vancouver Rowing Club overlooking the water on the edge of Stanley Park. Each event, typically held on the first Tuesday of the month October-June, benefits a different area charitable organization. Doors open at 6pm, dinner starts at 6:30pm, and musicians take the stage 7:30pm-10pm, with a break for dessert and coffee. Call for reservations, which are required.
MAP 1: Vancouver Rowing Club, 450 Stanley Park Dr., 604/726-5277, www. synergycollective.ca, adults $25, seniors and students $15

Vancouver Opera
Canada's second largest opera company, the Vancouver Opera stages its productions downtown in the 2,765-seat **Queen Elizabeth Theatre** (630 Hamilton St.) or at the adjacent **Vancouver Playhouse** (600 Hamilton St.). Recent shows have included Verdi's *La Traviata*, the contemporary opera *Dead Man Walking*, and *Stickboy*, a work about bullying, with a libretto by Canadian spoken word artist Shane Koyczan. Attend a preview talk, free to all ticketholders, an hour before each performance, for an introduction to the show.
MAP 1: 604/683-0222, www. vancouveropera.ca, $40-182

CYCLING IN THE CITY

Vancouver is becoming one of North America's top bicycling cities. Throughout the metropolitan area, you can pedal along a growing number of urban cycling routes, from downtown bike lanes to the popular Seawall route, which circles Stanley Park and follows False Creek through Yaletown, past the Olympic Village, and on to Granville Island, continuing west to the beaches in Kitsilano and Point Grey. The city-managed Arbutus Greenway follows a former rail line from Kitsilano south to the Fraser River, while another city cycling path, the Central Valley Greenway, takes you through Vancouver's eastern suburbs. Check the City of Vancouver website (http://vancouver.ca) for a map of bike routes around town.

cycling in Stanley Park

TIPS FOR CYCLING THE SEAWALL

One of the most pleasant ways to explore Vancouver is by bike on the paved, mostly flat Seawall that follows the water around the edge of Stanley Park and along False Creek. To help ensure a safe cycling excursion, keep these tips in mind:

Stay on the cyclist side of the path. In most places, there's a parallel walking path for pedestrians, but at some points, which are clearly marked, the path is shared.

Watch for pedestrians. Many people unwittingly wander onto the cycling path to snap a photo or enjoy the view. Stay alert whenever pedestrians are nearby.

To avoid collisions, don't stop suddenly and make sure no one is directly behind you when you slow down, particularly on the Seawall's narrower stretches. And when you do stop, pull off the path to let other cyclists pass.

Wear a helmet. Vancouver law requires all cyclists to wear a bike helmet.

Note that within Stanley Park, while pedestrians can follow the Seawall in either direction, it's one-way for cyclists. Whether you enter the park near English Bay or Coal Harbour, you must ride only in a counterclockwise direction, keeping the water on your right side.

BIKE SHARING IN VANCOUVER

The city of Vancouver has a bike-sharing program that enables you to rent a bike at one location and return it at another. For visitors, the easiest way to use the Mobi bike share system (778/655-1800, www.mobibikes.ca) is to sign up online for a day pass. For $12 per day, you can take an unlimited number of 30-minute rides within a 24-hour period.

After you register online, you'll receive a user code that will unlock your bike. Bikes are stationed throughout the downtown area and in parts of the Kitsilano, South Granville, Cambie, and East Side neighborhoods; search the Mobi website for the bikes nearest to you. Helmets, which local laws require cyclists to wear, are available at each rental station.

If you keep the bike for more than half an hour during any ride, you'll pay an extra $6 for each additional 30 minutes, so it's more cost-effective to dock your bike when you stop to sightsee, shop, or eat. You can check out another bike after your stop.

Vancouver Symphony Orchestra

Established in 1919, the Vancouver Symphony Orchestra performs 150 concerts every year. Their main venue is the historic Orpheum Theatre (601 Smithe St.) downtown. They also play at the Chan Centre for the Performing Arts (6265 Crescent Rd.) on the UBC Campus and at several other spaces. In addition to traditional classical performances, the orchestra presents pops concerts, a new music festival, events for children, and even movie nights, where the musicians accompany a film. If you're under age 35 or a full-time student, sign up online for the All-Access Pass, which lets you buy up to two $15 tickets to many performances.

MAP 1: 604/876-3434, www. vancouversymphony.ca, $20-95

the historic Orpheum Theatre

DANCE
Ballet BC

Vancouver's professional contemporary ballet company, Ballet BC presents several productions a year at the Queen Elizabeth Theatre downtown. The company frequently stages new pieces by BC-based choreographers, including Crystal Pite, Wen Wei Wang, and Emily Molnar. They have also collaborated with international choreographers, including Barcelona's Cayetano Soto and Ohad Naharin of Israel's Batsheva Dance Company.

MAP 1: 630 Hamilton St., 855/985-2787, www.balletbc.com, $35-95

DanceHouse

Fans of contemporary and modern dance should check out the offerings from DanceHouse, which brings Canadian and international dance companies to downtown's Vancouver Playhouse stage. It produces several shows each year, which have included Momix, Finland's Tero Saarinen Company, and Hofesh Shechter from Britain. DanceHouse also presented *Betroffenheit,* a unique dance-theater collaboration between two Vancouver-based organizations, Kidd Pivot Dance and the Electric Company Theatre.

MAP 1: 600 Hamilton St., 604/801-6225, www.dancehouse.ca, $40-80

Festivals and Events

Vancouver International Wine Festival

Wine-tastings, seminars, and dinners show off more than 700 wines from around the world at the Vancouver International Wine Festival, a weeklong event usually in late February. Many events are held downtown at the Vancouver Convention Centre's West Building, but restaurants and other venues host festivities as well.

Various locations: http://vanwinefest.ca, Feb.

Vancouver Sun Run

Close to 50,000 runners and walkers take to the streets for the Vancouver Sun Run, a fun-for-all 10K that starts and ends downtown, usually the 3rd Sunday in April.

Downtown and West End: www.vancouversun.com/sunrun, Apr.

Canada Day

Vancouver celebrates Canada's birthday, Canada Day, with a parade, outdoor concerts, and celebratory fireworks over Burrard Inlet. Canada Place is the center of the festivities. The fireworks, which start at 10:30pm, draw big crowds. You'll need tickets to watch from the outdoor Fireworks Viewing Zone (adults $15) at Canada Place, but you can see them anywhere along Burrard Inlet, including Harbour Green Park on the Coal Harbour Seawall and in Stanley Park near the Nine O'Clock Gun, east of the Brockton Point totem poles.

Downtown and West End: Canada Place, www.canadaplace.ca, July 1

Celebration of Light

Fireworks displays over English Bay bring thousands of Vancouverites and visitors out for the Celebration of Light that takes place on three summer evenings. The best viewing spots are at English Bay Beach, but you can see them from Kitsilano Beach and other points around False Creek. Held the last week of July and the first week of August on Wednesday and Saturday evenings, the fireworks start at 10pm. Try to arrive no later than 9pm to find a place to sit; many people come early and bring picnic suppers to enjoy before the displays begin.

Downtown and West End: http://hondacelebrationoflight.com, July-Aug.

✪ Vancouver Pride Festival

The Vancouver Pride Festival features more than 20 events celebrating the city's large gay, lesbian, bisexual, transgender, and queer community. Several days of parties, cruises, picnics, and other celebrations culminate in a festive parade through the downtown streets on the Sunday before BC Day, the 1st Monday in August.

Downtown and West End: http://vancouverpride.ca, July-Aug.

CITYWIDE FESTIVALS AND EVENTS

DINE OUT VANCOUVER

More than 250 restaurants offer special menus, and you can join in food events, from chef dinners and wine-tastings to food tours, during Dine Out Vancouver (www.dineoutvancouver.com, Jan.-Feb.), the city's annual celebration of dining that has grown into one of Canada's largest food and drink festivals. The festival runs for two and a half weeks late January-early February. Organizers publish the event schedule and a list of participating restaurants on the website the 2nd week of January. Make reservations right away, since many restaurants and events sell out.

PUSH INTERNATIONAL PERFORMING ARTS FESTIVAL

An eclectic selection of theater, music, dance, and multimedia events brighten up the winter nights at the PuSh International Performing Arts Festival (http://pushfestival.ca, Jan.-Feb.), featuring local and international performers. At theaters and performance spaces across Vancouver, the festival begins in mid-January and runs for three weeks.

VANCOUVER CRAFT BEER WEEK

A good introduction to the region's growing microbrewery scene, the annual Vancouver Craft Beer Week (http://vancouvercraftbeerweek.com; May-June), normally the last week of May into the first week of June, includes tasting events and other activities that showcase small brewers and their products around town.

EAT! VANCOUVER FOOD + COOKING FESTIVAL

Dinners featuring chefs from across Canada, cooking workshops, and other delicious events draw foodies to the week-long EAT! Vancouver Food + Cooking Festival (www.eat-vancouver.com, Nov.).

Shops

SHOPPING DISTRICTS

Granville Street

Department stores, outdoor gear shops, and mid-priced boutiques line Granville Street downtown, in between the nightclubs and tattoo parlors. The Hudson's Bay flagship store is located on Granville.

MAP 1: Granville St. between Davie St. and Cordova St.

Robson Street

Vancouver's main downtown shopping district is along Robson Street, between Jervis and Granville Streets. Mid-priced Canadian and international chains predominate; a few small shops sell trinkets and souvenirs. One block north of Robson, on Alberni Street between Burrard and Bute Streets, look for luxury brands like Tiffany and Burberry.

MAP 1: Robson St. between Jervis St. and Granville St.

DEPARTMENT STORES

✪ Hudson's Bay

The Vancouver flagship location of Hudson's Bay, Canada's original department store, is in a six-story 1914 downtown building, selling clothing and accessories for women, men, and kids, as well as housewares, luggage, and small appliances. One

Hudson's Bay flagship store

department carries striped Hudson's Bay blankets and other Canadiana. The Hudson's Bay Company opened their first Vancouver store in Gastown in 1887. They subsequently added a branch on Granville Street and then built this store, which has remained its Vancouver base for more than 100 years.

MAP 1: 674 Granville St., 604/681-6211, www.thebay.com, 9:30am-9pm Mon.-Sat., 11am-7pm Sun.

Holt Renfrew

For high-fashion designer clothing, with prices to match, visit Holt Renfrew downtown, built around a gleaming white atrium at the Pacific Centre Mall. You can book an appointment with their personal shoppers to help you navigate the chic designs.

MAP 1: 737 Dunsmuir St., 604/681-3121, www.holtrenfrew.com, 10am-7pm Mon.-Tues., 10am-9pm Wed.-Sat., 11am-7pm Sun.

Nordstrom

Seattle-based Nordstrom has a sizable store at Vancouver's Pacific Centre Mall downtown, in a multistory glass-clad space at the corner of Robson and Granville Streets. This high-end department store

chain got its start as a shoe retailer and still has a large selection of footwear. The store has three food outlets: Bistro Verde, a contemporary restaurant; Ebar for coffee and smoothies; and Habitant, a wine and cocktail bar.

MAP 1: 799 Robson St., 604/699-2100, www.nordstrom.com, 10am-9pm Mon.-Sat., 11am-7pm Sun.

Winners

You can often find deals on designer apparel, other clothing, shoes, and accessories at Winners, a discount department store that carries both men's and women's garments. In addition to their large downtown location, there's a branch near Broadway and Cambie.

MAP 1: 798 Granville St., 604/683-1058, http://winners.ca, 9am-9pm Mon.-Sat., 10am-8pm Sun.

CLOTHING AND ACCESSORIES
Lululemon Athletica

The now-ubiquitous yoga- and workout-wear maker Lululemon Athletica got its start in Vancouver and still has its flagship store downtown, where you'll find yoga pants, running gear, and clothing for other athletic pursuits or for just lounging around looking cool. There are other locations in the Pacific Centre Mall downtown and in Kitsilano.

MAP 1: 970 Robson St., 604/681-3118, www.lululemon.com, 10am-9pm Mon.-Sat., 10am-8pm Sun.

RYU

Another Vancouver-based athletic wear company, RYU ("Respect Your Universe"), sells stylish running, yoga, and other active wear

yoga-wear store Lululemon Athletica

for men and women. In addition to this downtown location off Robson Street, you'll find another RYU branch in Kitsilano.

MAP 1: 805 Thurlow St., 778/379-4232, http://ryu.com, 10am-9pm Mon.-Sat., 11am-7pm Sun.

BOOKS AND STATIONERY

Bookmark

Run by the Friends of the Vancouver Public Library, Bookmark, the gift shop in the library's central branch downtown, carries a small selection of gently used books, along with cards, stationery, T-shirts, and gift items with literary themes. Sales benefit the library and its programs.

MAP 1: 350 W. Georgia St., 604/331-4040, www.friendsofthevpl.ca, 10am-5:30pm Tues.-Fri., noon-5pm Sat.

Indigo

Canada's largest bookstore chain has a two-level location on downtown's Robson Street. Find all types of books, including fiction, travel, food, and titles for kids and teens, by both Canadian and international authors; there's plenty of room for browsing. It carries gift items, stationery, and magazines as well. There's another large location in the South Granville district.

MAP 1: 1033 Robson St., 778/783-3978, www.chapters.indigo.ca, 9am-10pm daily

DESIGN AND GIFTS

Designhouse

Cool furniture, housewares, and other fun design-y stuff, including watches, bags and backpacks, and gift items, fill Designhouse downtown. This sleek Scandinavian-style store carries packs from Vancouver-based Herschel Supply Company, stainless steel water bottles from S'well, and the "Anna G." corkscrew from Alessi that resembles a smiling woman. The shop shares its space with **Marimekko Vancouver** (604/609-2881, http://

marimekkovancouver.com), which stocks brightly patterned clothing, accessories, household items, and fabrics from the Finnish design company.

MAP 1: 851 Homer St., 604/681-2800, http://designhouse.ca, 10:30am-6pm Mon.-Sat., noon-5pm Sun.

SPECIALTY FOOD AND DRINK

Ayoub's Dried Fruits and Nuts

The aroma of freshly roasted nuts may draw you into Ayoub's Dried Fruits and Nuts, which sells in-house roasted almonds, pistachios, cashews, walnuts, and more, attractively displayed in ornate silver tureens. They also carry dried fruits, vegetable chips, Mediterranean spices, and Persian-style pastries and candies. Try their unique lime-and-saffron seasoned nuts. In addition to this West End shop, you'll find this nut vendor in Kitsilano and North Vancouver.

MAP 1: 986 Denman St., 604/732-6887, www.ayoubs.ca, 10am-9pm Mon.-Thurs., 10am-10pm Fri.-Sat., 10am-8pm Sun.

Viti Wine & Lager

Viti Wine & Lager, a compact shop at the Moda Hotel downtown, stocks an extensive selection of BC wines, particularly labels from the Okanagan region. They also carry more than 300 types of beer and a large collection of whiskeys. In the coolers lining the walls, they always keep a selection of chilled wine and beer, ready to drink.

MAP 1: 900 Seymour St., 604/683-3806, www.vitiwinelagers.com, 10am-11pm Mon.-Sat., 11am-11pm Sun.

Gastown and Chinatown   Map 2

Gastown, centered on Water and Cordova Streets between Richards and Main Streets, is one of the city's oldest neighborhoods, with brick and stone buildings dating to the early 1900s. Beyond its historic facades, Gastown is known for its **stylish boutiques** and **indigenous art galleries.**

The ornate **Millennium Gate** on Pender Street marks the entrance to Vancouver's fast-changing Chinatown. Though a few traditional herbalists, tea shops, and produce markets remain, more and more **hip eateries** are moving in. Some of Vancouver's most **innovative restaurants** have opened here.

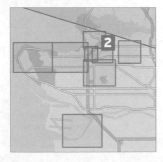

TOP SIGHTS

- Most Zen Urban Escape: **Dr. Sun Yat-Sen Classical Chinese Garden** (page 73)

TOP RESTAURANTS

- Best Global Journey: **Chambar** (page 78)
- Best Reason to Go to Jail: **L'Abbatoir** (page 78)
- Most Imaginative Cuisine Coupling: **Kissa Tanto** (page 79)

TOP NIGHTLIFE

- Freshest Cocktails: **The Pourhouse** (page 82)

TOP ARTS AND CULTURE

- How to Get Acquainted with Indigenous Art: **Coastal Peoples Fine Arts Gallery** (page 83)

TOP SHOPS

- Where to Find Yoga Wear No One Else Has: **Lululemon Lab** (page 85)
- Most Unusual Shoe Store: **John Fluevog** (page 86)

GETTING THERE AND AROUND

- SkyTrain lines: Canada Line, Expo Line
- SkyTrain stops: Waterfront (Canada, Expo Lines), Stadium-Chinatown (Expo Line), Main Street-Science World (Expo Line)
- Bus lines: 4, 7, 14, 16, 19, 20, 22, 23

1 **2** **3**

Vancouver Harbour

W WATERFRONT RD

M Waterfront

HOWE ST

GRANVILLE ST

W CORDOVA ST

SEYMOUR ST

RICHARDS ST

HOMER ST

1

2

Gastown Steam Clock

3

5

4

6 7 WATER ST

GASTOWN

10 Gassy Jack Statue

11

13 14

9 BLOOD ALLEY

15 16

8

CAMBIE ST

HAMILTON ST

SEE MAP 1

Cathedral Square

21

20

Victory Square Park

22

Woodward's Building

23

W CORDOVA ST

W HASTINGS ST

25

26

CARRALL ST

DUNSMUIR ST

D

W PENDER ST

ABBOTT ST

27 28 Millennium Gate

29

24

BEATTY ST

36

35

International Village

TAYLOR ST

Dr. Sun Yat-Sen Classical Chinese Garden 37

KEEFER PL

M Stadium-Chinatown

W GEORGIA ST

CITADEL PARADE

DUNSMUIR VIADUCT

Andy Livingstone Park

E

EXPO BLVD

Rogers Arena

EXPO BLVD

BC Place

GEORGIA VIADUCT

PACIFIC BLVD

PACIFIC BLVD

SEE MAP 3

© MOON.COM

F

4   5   6

Crab Park

E WATERFRONT RD

RAILWAY ST

ALEXANDER ST

POWELL ST

GORE AVE

E CORDOVA ST

COLUMBIA ST

Vancouver Police Museum

E HASTINGS ST

MAIN ST

E PENDER ST

Rennie Museum

CHINATOWN

KEEFER ST

SEE MAP 7

E GEORGIA ST

DUNSMUIR VIADUCT

UNION ST

PRIOR ST

0   100 yds
0   100 m

DISTANCE ACROSS MAP
Approximate: 1.1 mi or 1.7 km

SIGHTS
3	C2	Gastown Steam Clock	
14	C3	Gassy Jack Statue	
23	D2	Woodward's Building	
29	D3	Millennium Gate	
30	D4	Rennie Museum	
32	D5	Vancouver Police Museum	
37	E3	Dr. Sun Yat-Sen Classical Chinese Garden	

RESTAURANTS
8	C2	Revolver
15	C3	L'Abbatoir
19	C6	Ask for Luigi
22	D2	Purebread
24	D2	Tsuki Sushi Bar
25	D3	Nelson the Seagull
26	D3	Pidgin
34	D5	Kissa Tanto
35	E2	Chambar
36	E2	Jam Café
39	E4	Bao Bei Chinese Brasserie
40	E4	Juniper Kitchen & Bar
41	E4	Juke
42	F5	Crackle Crème

NIGHTLIFE
7	C2	The Pourhouse
12	C3	Salt Tasting Room
13	C3	Six Acres
16	C3	The Diamond
18	C4	The Alibi Room
38	E4	The Keefer Bar

ARTS AND CULTURE
5	C2	Coastal Peoples Fine Arts Gallery
6	C2	Inuit Gallery of Vancouver
27	D3	Urban Aboriginal Fair Trade Gallery
31	D5	Movies in the Morgue
33	D5	Firehall Arts Centre

SHOPS
1	B2	Oak + Fort
2	C2	One of a Few
4	C2	Kit and Ace
9	C3	Tees.ca
10	C3	John Fluevog
11	C3	Örling & Wu
17	C3	Lululemon Lab
21	D1	The Paper Hound Bookshop

HOTELS
20	D1	Victorian Hotel
28	D3	Skwachàys Lodge

GASTOWN AND CHINATOWN WALK

TOTAL DISTANCE: 1.8 miles (3 km)
TOTAL WALKING TIME: 45 minutes

This walk takes you through two of Vancouver's oldest neighborhoods. Begin with lunch, and stop to explore indigenous art galleries, the city's serene Chinese garden, and the unusual Police Museum, and then wrap up your afternoon with cocktails in Gastown.

1 Fuel up for your walk with lunch at **Chambar,** adjacent to the Stadium-Chinatown SkyTrain station. In a heritage brick building on Beatty Street, this restaurant creatively mixes flavors of Belgium and North Africa with local ingredients.

2 After lunch, turn right out of the restaurant, following Beatty Street one block to Pender Street. Turn right onto Pender and go east two blocks. On the left side of Pender, stop at the **Urban Aboriginal Fair Trade Gallery,** inside Skwachàys Lodge, Canada's first indigenous

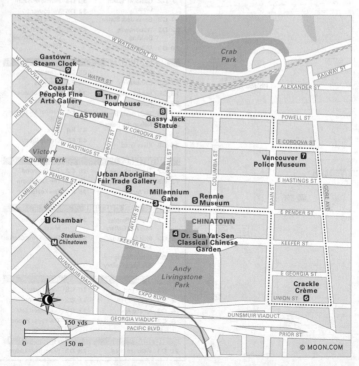

arts hotel, for a look at the works by First Nations artists. As you leave, notice the large sculpture atop the hotel building.

3 Turn left out of the gallery, cross under the ornate **Millennium Gate,** which marks the entrance to Chinatown, and walk one more block east on Pender.

4 At Carrall Street, turn right, walk half a block, and turn left at the garden wall to find the entrance to the **Dr. Sun Yat-Sen Classical Chinese Garden.** It's worth stopping to tour this peaceful retreat, the first authentic Ming Dynasty garden outside China.

5 From the garden, retrace your steps back north toward Pender Street and turn east (right) to find the **Rennie Museum,** a private art museum. The brick building that houses the museum, constructed in 1889, is the oldest structure in Chinatown.

6 Continue one block east on Pender to Main Street and turn right. As you walk south on Main, notice Chinatown's mix of new condos and old-time shops. Stay on Main three blocks, then turn left onto Union Street. Midway down the block is **Crackle Crème,** a café that specializes in crème brûlée.

7 After your break, turn left out of the café, and in half a block, turn north (left) onto Gore Avenue. Follow Gore five blocks north. At Cordova Street, turn left to find the entrance to the **Vancouver Police**

Gastown Steam Clock

Museum on your left. The exhibits at this museum, in the former city morgue, detail Vancouver's seamier side.

8 When you leave the museum, turn left onto Cordova, take the first right onto Main, and in one block, turn left onto Powell Street, which takes you toward Gastown. Follow Powell Street two blocks west to Maple Leaf Square, where Water, Alexander, Powell, and Carrall Streets meet. Stop for a photo at the **statue of Gassy Jack,** the British sailor for whom Gastown is named.

9 Continue west on Water Street, the main street in Gastown, to the corner of Cambie Street, where you'll see the **Gastown Steam Clock,** which toots its whistle every quarter hour.

10 One block past the clock on Water Street is one of several Gastown galleries that specialize in works by indigenous artists. **Coastal Peoples Fine Arts Gallery** shows masks, carvings, jewelry, and other works by First Nations and Inuit artists.

11 Ready for a drink? Retrace your steps one block east on Water Street, where you can wrap up your walk with a cocktail at **The Pourhouse.**

Sights

TOP EXPERIENCE

✪ Dr. Sun Yat-Sen Classical Chinese Garden

From the building tiles to the pathway pebbles, all the components of the Dr. Sun Yat-Sen Classical Chinese Garden came from China, as did the 52 master craftspeople who arrived from Suzhou in 1985 to construct the first authentic Ming Dynasty garden outside China. Named for the Chinese revolutionary leader and politician who is considered a father of modern China, the garden was built for the Expo '86 world's fair to promote understanding between Chinese and North American cultures.

The garden is compact, encompassing just one-third of an acre (1,200 square m). As traditional Chinese garden design dictates, it's built with a balance of four elements: rocks, water, plants, and architecture. The garden contains several pavilions, with elaborately scalloped roofs, lattice screens, and red columns; one of these structures, the Jade Water Pavilion, appears to float atop a pond. Wheelchair-accessible walkways meander between fish ponds and fountains, and around limestone outcroppings, bamboo groves, and native pine trees. The garden's covered paths provide shelter on rainy days.

Take one of the informative

Dr. Sun Yat-Sen Classical Chinese Garden

45-minute **garden tours** (included with admission) to learn more about the peaceful garden's design and construction. Mid-June-August, tours start on the hour 10am-4pm daily, with an additional tour at 5:30pm (tour times vary the rest of the year). After your tour, you're free to wander the garden or simply linger in the serene setting.

Adjacent to the garden is the free city-run **Dr. Sun Yat-Sen Park,** which local architects Joe Wai and Donald Vaughan designed at the same time that the garden was constructed. While lacking the classical garden's Chinese pedigree, this smaller park is still a pretty spot to sit. Head for the shaded pagoda and watch the fish swim past.

MAP 2: 578 Carrall St., 604/662-3207, www.vancouverchinesegarden.com, 10am-6pm daily May-mid-June and Sept., 9:30am-7pm daily mid-June-Aug., 10am-4:30pm daily Oct., 10am-4:30pm Tues.-Sun. Nov.-Apr., adults $14, seniors $11, students and ages 6-17 $10

NEARBY:

- Make an advance reservation to tour the large private art collection of the **Rennie Museum** (page 74).

- Linger over modern Canadian bites and a cocktail at **Juniper Kitchen & Bar** (page 79).
- Stop into **Juke** for crispy, juicy fried chicken (page 80).

Rennie Museum

Vancouver real estate marketer Bob Rennie has assembled one of Canada's largest private collections of contemporary art. At the Rennie Museum, a private gallery in Chinatown's oldest structure, the 1889 Wing Sang Building, you can see changing exhibitions by both established and emerging international artists.

To visit, you must reserve a spot on a free 50-minute guided tour, typically offered Saturday. Book in advance on the museum website, which indicates available tour times; the gallery doesn't allow walk-in visitors.

The docents lead tour groups through the multilevel gallery's current exhibit, introducing you to the artists and providing background both about the Rennie Museum's holdings, which include works by about 200 artists, and about the building itself. Originally a two-story brick Victorian, the Wing Sang Building belonged to Chinese Canadian businessman Yip Sang. Sang expanded the building, adding a 3rd floor in 1901, and in 1912 he constructed a six-story brick building across the alley, with an elevated passageway connecting the two structures. His family—three wives and 23 children—lived in this adjacent building.

Tours end in the rooftop sculpture garden, which has views across Chinatown. Installed on the building's facade above the garden is British artist Martin Creed's 2008 neon sculpture, *Work No. 851: EVERYTHING IS GOING TO BE ALRIGHT*. This string of text is illuminated at night, making it visible throughout the neighborhood. Rennie selected this work as a symbol of optimism for the future of Vancouver's Chinatown.

MAP 2: 51 E. Pender St., 604/682-2088, www.renniemuseum.org, by guided tour only, free

Millennium Gate

Topped with three staggered gold roofs, the three-story Millennium Gate welcomes visitors to Vancouver's Chinatown. Erected in 2002, this ornamental gateway spans Pender Street near the International Village mall, a half block east of Abbott Street. The Chinese characters on the gate's east side exhort visitors to "remember the past and look forward to the future."

MAP 2: E. Pender St. at Taylor Way

Vancouver Police Museum

If you're curious about some of shiny Vancouver's darker moments, plan a visit to the Vancouver Police Museum, where the exhibits about policing, criminology, and various misdeeds are housed in the 1932 former city morgue and autopsy facility.

The museum's holdings include more than 20,000 artifacts, photos, and documents about crime and police work in the city, from the region's early days to the present. In the Sins gallery, you can check out the collection of counterfeit money, illegal drugs, and weapons confiscated from criminals. The True

Rennie Museum

Crime gallery exhibits photos and evidence from notorious crimes, many of which remain unsolved. You can also visit the autopsy suite, last used in 1980 but still looking ready for its next casualty, which has a collection of preserved human organs. Some people may find the graphic exhibits rather creepy; the museum may not be appropriate for younger children.

The museum runs several 1.5-hour Sins of the City Walking Tours (www.sinsofthecity.ca, late Apr.-Oct., adults $18, seniors and students $14), where you can explore the underbelly of Gastown and Chinatown. The Red Light Rendezvous Tour (4pm Sat.) tells you about the neighborhoods' brothels and the women who ran them, while on the Vice, Dice, and Opium Pipes Tour (6pm Fri., 2pm Sat.), you walk the beat of a 1920s cop, on the lookout for gambling dens, bootlegging joints, and other nefarious activity. The Soul Food and Shotguns Tour (11am Sat.) highlights the cultural history of Vancouver's African Canadian and Italian communities, focusing on the city's multicultural heritage and social change movements. While kids are allowed in the police museum at their parents' discretion, the minimum age for the walking tours is 16.

The Vancouver Police Museum is east of Gastown, on the edge of Chinatown. Buses 4 and 7 from downtown stop nearby.
MAP 2: 240 E. Cordova St., 604/665-3346, www. vancouverpolicemuseum.ca, 9am-5pm Tues.-Sat., adults $12, seniors and students $10, ages 6-18 $8

Gassy Jack Statue

At Maple Tree Square is a statue of Gassy Jack, a fast-talking British sailor and riverboat pilot turned saloonkeeper, from whom Vancouver's historic Gastown district got its name. In 1867, Captain John Deighton, nicknamed "Gassy Jack" for his habit of telling tall tales, promised local millworkers that he'd serve them drinks if they'd build him a saloon on the shores of Burrard Inlet. The motivated millworkers constructed the bar in just one day, and the fledgling Gastown neighborhood took its title from Deighton's "Gassy" nickname. Artist Vern Simpson crafted the copper statue of the hat-wearing Deighton, who is standing atop a barrel. A gift to the city, the statue was installed in 1970.
MAP 2: Maple Tree Square, intersection of Alexander, Carrall, Water, and Powell Sts.

Gastown Steam Clock

Sure, it's touristy, but you'll still find yourself in front of this local icon, waiting for it to toot its steam whistle every 15 minutes. The historic-looking Gastown Steam Clock actually dates only to 1977, when area businesses commissioned clockmaker Ray Saunders to create the clock as part of the neighborhood's revitalization. Saunders based his clock on an 1875 design; it draws power from the city's underground steam heating system and three electric motors. Weighing over two tons, with steam whistles above its dial, the clock stands 16 feet (5 m) tall.
MAP 2: Water St. at Cambie St.

THE EVOLUTION OF CHINATOWN

In 1858, gold was discovered along British Columbia's Fraser River. Among the miners and adventurers who flocked to the province for this emerging gold rush were a number of Chinese settlers. Many came north from California, while some arrived directly from China, primarily from Guangdong Province and other southern regions.

Throughout the late 1800s, Chinese immigrants continued to arrive in BC, including thousands who found work building the Canadian Pacific Railway. Others worked in the canneries in Steveston, or in logging and mining. By the 1890s, more than 1,000 Chinese people had settled in Vancouver's Chinatown, clustered on what is now Pender Street, between Carrall and Columbia Streets. By 1911, Vancouver's Chinatown was the largest in Canada.

In 1923, Chinese immigration came to an abrupt halt when the Canadian government passed the Chinese Immigration Act—often called the Chinese Exclusion Act—which effectively stopped any additional Chinese immigrants from settling in Canada. This lack of new residents, combined with the Great Depression of the 1930s, sent the neighborhood into decline.

The population of Vancouver's Chinatown ebbed and flowed during the second half of the 1900s. Beginning in the 1980s, many new Chinese residents arrived in the Vancouver area, first from Hong Kong and more recently from Taiwan and mainland China. Most of these newcomers, many of whom were more well-to-do than earlier immigrants, avoided settling in the aging Chinatown, preferring to locate throughout the city or in Richmond, the suburb to the south that has become something of a "new Chinatown."

Some of Chinatown's signature produce markets, herbalists, tea shops, bakeries, and Chinese restaurants still remain, with bins piled high with ginseng, winter melons, and *yu choy* (greens), or display cases filled with tea leaves, coconut buns, and various herbal remedies. In recent years, however, many apartment and condominium buildings have sprouted up, and chic restaurants, cafés, and bars have opened, making it a newly vibrant destination for eating and drinking. While many applaud these businesses and the increased life that they're bringing to Chinatown streets, some residents are expressing concern at the pace and extent of the neighborhood's changes.

With its mix of historic and modern, Vancouver's Chinatown remains an exciting district to explore, but the neighborhood will undoubtedly continue to evolve.

Woodward's Building

Charles Woodward started his career as a grocer in Ontario before opening a shop in Vancouver in the late 1800s. In 1903, he moved his Woodward's Department Store to Gastown. Woodward's sold clothing for men, women, and children, along with housewares and food. Growing to occupy most of a city block, the store developed into a prime Vancouver shopping destination. On its roof was a tower crowned with a red neon "W" that became a city landmark and is visible to this day.

In 1992, Woodward's declared bankruptcy. It wasn't until 2006 that the former store was converted into a mixed-use complex, combining residential, commercial, and arts spaces.

MAP 2: Hastings St. and Abbott St.

77

Restaurants

PRICE KEY

$ Entrées less than CAD$15
$$ Entrées CAD$15-25
$$$ Entrées more than CAD$25

MODERN CANADIAN

✪ Chambar $$$

Combining tastes of North Africa and Belgium with local ingredients, Chambar pleases patrons in a window-lined rehabbed warehouse with a spacious outdoor terrace. Kick off your morning with a waffle studded with pearl sugar or breakfast paella topped with spicy sausage and a fried egg. Later, sup on roasted ling cod with sea asparagus or braised lamb shanks with almond couscous and figs. *Moules frites* (mussels with french fries) are a specialty.

MAP 2: 568 Beatty St., 604/879-7119, www.chambar.com, 8am-midnight daily

✪ L'Abbatoir $$$

On the site of Vancouver's first jail, transformed into a multilevel space with exposed brick and polished wood, Gastown's L'Abbatoir detains diners with creative cocktails (how about an avocado gimlet with herb-infused gin, avocado, and lime?) and a changing menu of west coast plates. Bite into pan-fried sweetbreads, baked oysters, or slow-cooked halibut with mussels and summer squash. At brunch, order

a breakfast salad at Chambar

the oversize scone mounded with house-made jam and clotted cream.
MAP 2: 217 Carrall St., 604/568-1701, www.labattoir.ca, 5:30pm-10pm Mon.-Thurs., 5:30pm-10:30pm Fri., 10am-2pm and 5:30pm-10:30pm Sat., 10am-2pm and 5:30pm-10pm Sun.

Juniper Kitchen & Bar $$

From the sleek backlit gray bar to the distillery-inspired copper light fixtures, this high-ceilinged Chinatown room emphasizes cocktails along with modern Canadian fare. As the "juniper" name suggests, there's a long list of gin and tonics, although local breweries and cideries are also well represented. Share one of the charcuterie boards—they offer a changing selection of house-made meat or vegan options—or sample gnocchi with basil and sunflower seed *pistou*, mussels steamed in Vancouver Island gin, or duck with spaetzle and red cabbage.
MAP 2: 185 Keefer St., 604/681-1695, www.junipervancouver.com, 4:30pm-midnight Sun.-Thurs., 4:30pm-1am Fri.-Sat.

ASIAN
Bao Bei Chinese Brasserie $$

At Bao Bei Chinese Brasserie, many of the menu items, from *mantou* (steamed buns) to fried rice, would be at home in a traditional Chinatown kitchen, but this modern lounge and eatery isn't your grandmother's Chinese restaurant. The buns are stuffed with Hunan-spiced beef and Chinese leeks, the fried rice is amped up with turmeric-marinated rock fish and fried peanuts, and other dishes, like octopus carpaccio with kale and *kabocha*

salad, start in Asia but wander the world. Clever cocktails include the Midnight Lucky, which blends sake, Aperol, hibiscus tea, pink peppercorn, and *shiso*.
MAP 2: 163 Keefer St., 604/688-0876, www.bao-bei.ca, 5:30pm-midnight Mon.-Sat., 5:30pm-11pm Sun.

Pidgin $$

Shishito peppers with miso dressing and puffed rice, Korean rice cakes with *gochujang* Bolognese, or a foie gras rice bowl with chestnuts and daikon are a few of the Asian-inspired dishes that might grace your light wood table at this Gastown dining and drinking spot. Order a few plates to share and pair with drinks like the Game.Set. Matcha, a blend of Japanese whiskey, matcha tea, lemon, and ginger.
MAP 2: 350 Carrall St., 604/620-9400, www.pidginvancouver.com, 5pm-midnight daily

JAPANESE
Tsuki Sushi Bar $

Opposite the International Village mall, casual Tsuki Sushi Bar does one thing and does it well: preparing fresh sushi and sashimi. See what's on special, or try the *chirashi* bowl, an assortment of raw fish on rice.
MAP 2: 509 Abbott St., 604/558-3805, http://tsukisushibar.ca, 11:30am-2:30pm and 4pm-9:30pm Mon.-Fri., noon-9:30pm Sat., noon-9pm Sun.

JAPANESE-ITALIAN
✪ Kissa Tanto $$

This intriguing mash-up of Japanese and Italian flavors, run by the same team that operates nearby Bao Bei Chinese Brasserie, is in a classy 2nd-floor Chinatown space that draws its

fried chicken at Juke in Chinatown

design style from 1960s Tokyo jazz cafés. The fun, adventurous menu might include pasta with lamb *ragù*, braised greens, and toasted nori or fish *crudo* with *shiso* vinaigrette, olives, and pickled almonds. They serve plenty of eclectic cocktails too.

MAP 2: 263 E. Pender St., 778/379-8078, www.kissatanto.com, 5:30pm-midnight Tues.-Sat.

ITALIAN
Ask for Luigi $$

Why should you Ask for Luigi? Because this highly regarded trattoria serves first-rate handmade pastas along with modern Italian small plates that might include fried cauliflower with chickpeas or *bocconcini fritti* (fried mozzarella balls), plus a good selection of wines by the glass. This small spot doesn't take reservations, so expect a line. To find the restaurant, follow Alexander Street

east from Gastown; Luigi is at the corner of Gore Avenue, one block east of Main.

MAP 2: 305 Alexander St., 604/428-2544, www.askforluigi.com, 11:30am-2:30pm and 5:30pm-10:30pm Tues.-Thurs., 11:30am-2:30pm and 5:30pm-11pm Fri., 9:30am-2:30pm and 5:30pm-11pm Sat., 9:30am-2:30pm and 5:30pm-9:30pm Sun.

FRIED CHICKEN
Juke $

This smart-casual Chinatown eatery has a single specialty: crisp and juicy fried chicken that will have you licking your fingers. The kitchen starts with locally raised birds, coats the pieces in gluten-free batter, and fries them till the skin crackles and the meat is meltingly tender. Add a side or two, like fried brussels sprouts or nutty pork and peanut slaw. The joint is laid-back enough to bring the kids (during the day, you order at the counter), but with local microbrews and a full bar, it's cool enough for the grown-ups.

MAP 2: 182 Keefer St., 604/336-5853, www.jukefriedchicken.com, 11am-10:30pm Sun.-Thurs., 11am-midnight Fri.-Sat.

BREAKFAST AND BRUNCH
Jam Café $

Lines are common at Jam Café, a relaxed no-reservations import from Victoria, as hungry diners wait for overflowing plates of hearty breakfast and brunch fare. The red velvet pancakes are as big as a cake, while savory options include the Charlie Bowl (hash browns, crumbled biscuit, ham, and cheddar cheese topped with gravy and sunny-side eggs) and the Gravy Coupe (a biscuit piled with fried chicken and eggs slathered with sausage gravy).

MAP 2: 556 Beatty St., 778/379-1992, http://jamcafes.com, 8am-3pm daily

the Gravy Coupe at Jam Café

BAKERIES AND CAFÉS
Nelson the Seagull $

A popular destination for Gastown's coffee drinkers, Nelson the Seagull, with classic schoolhouse-style wooden chairs on a historic tile floor, serves light breakfasts (poached eggs, avocado toasts), sandwiches, and salads to pair with your caffeine. They're known for the bread as much as for coffee.

MAP 2: 315 Carrall St., 604/681-5776, www.nelsontheseagull.com, 8am-4pm Mon.-Fri., 9am-4pm Sat.-Sun.

sweets at Purebread bakery

Purebread $

Vancouverites used to have to drive to Whistler for the decadent pastries and wholesome breads at Purebread. But now Gastown has a Purebread of its own, with drool-inducing treats like freshly baked scones, lemon chèvre brownies, and giant meringues. Enjoy your snack with coffee inside this friendly café, or take your goodies to go.

MAP 2: 159 W. Hastings St., 604/563-8060, www.purebread.ca, 8:30am-6pm daily

DESSERT
Crackle Crème $

A café that specializes in crème brûlée? Why, yes, please. Chinatown's Crackle Crème concocts custards in flavors from salted caramel to matcha. They serve Belgian-style Liège waffles, macarons, and ice cream too.

MAP 2: 245 Union St., 778/847-8533, www.cracklecreme.com, 10am-noon and 2pm-10pm Mon.-Fri., 11am-10pm Sat., 11am-9pm Sun.

COFFEE AND TEA
Revolver $
Gastown is Vancouver's coffee central, where hip coffee shops abound.

Sip your java among the designers, techies, and laptop-toting cool kids at Revolver, which offers a changing menu of beans from roasters across North America.

MAP 2: 325 Cambie St., 604/558-4444, www.revolvercoffee.ca, 7:30am-6pm Mon.-Fri., 9am-6pm Sat.

Nightlife

CRAFT BEER
The Alibi Room
Beer lovers need no excuse to visit The Alibi Room, a low-key Gastown pub with 50 taps of local and imported craft beers. Housed in a century-old building with big curved windows, brick walls, and long communal tables, this laidback bar draws a diverse crowd, united by their love of microbrews. In summer, you can sit on the narrow street-side patio.

MAP 2: 157 Alexander St., 604/623-3383, www.alibi. ca, 5pm-11:30pm Mon.-Thurs., 5pm-12:30am Fri., 10am-12:30am Sat., 10am-11:30pm Sun.

Six Acres
In Vancouver's oldest brick building, near the Gassy Jack statue, this cozy pub has a rotating selection of local beers (with more options in bottles) and a menu of creatively comforting small plates. It's a good place to meet up for drinks and conversation.

MAP 2: 203 Carrall St., 604/488-0110, www.sixacres.ca, 11am-midnight Mon.-Thurs., 11am-1am Fri., 10:30am-1am Sat., 10:30am-11pm Sun.

COCKTAIL BARS AND LOUNGES
✪ The Pourhouse
With a name like The Pourhouse, you'd expect a joint that serves great cocktails—and you'd be right. The resident mixologists at this upscale Gastown saloon, set in a 1910 building lit with vintage lamps, concoct drinks like L'Amour Rouge (bourbon, amontillado, lemon, and sparkling wine) and the Bitter Southside, a blend of Quebec's Ungava gin, Fernet Branca, lime, and peppermint. Enjoy yours at the 38-foot (11.5-m) bar, crafted from reclaimed Douglas fir planks.

MAP 2: 162 Water St., 604/568-7022, www.pourhousevancouver.com, 5pm-midnight Mon.-Thurs., 5pm-1am Fri., 11am-2:30pm and 5pm-1am Sat., 11am-2:30pm and 5pm-midnight Sun.

The Diamond

A lively speakeasy-style cocktail bar with exposed brick walls and tall windows overlooking Gastown's Maple Leaf Square, The Diamond groups its cocktails by adjective, from "Refreshing" to "Overlooked." There's a short eclectic menu—currywurst, flatbreads, tartares—to snack on too.

MAP 2: 6 Powell St., 604/568-8272, http://di6mond.com, 5:30pm-1am Sun.-Thurs., 5:30pm-2am Fri.-Sat.

The Keefer Bar

The Keefer Bar, a swank Chinatown hideout, concocts aromatic cocktails using house-made bitters, teas, and syrups. Join the well-dressed crowd in this dark den, and pair the Opium Sour (bourbon, grapefruit, tamarind, lemon, and poppy seeds) or the Dragon Fly (dragon fruit-infused gin, sake, ginger, lemon, and magnolia bark tincture) with the Asian-inspired small plates.

MAP 2: 135 Keefer St., 604/688-1961, www.thekeeferbar.com, 4pm-1am Sun.-Thurs., 4pm-2am Fri.-Sat.

WINE BARS
Salt Tasting Room

A wine bar hidden in a Gastown alley, tiny Salt Tasting Room offers a long list of wines by the glass that's strong on BC labels, along with craft beers, ciders, sherries, and meads. In this warm inviting room, with solid wooden tables and brick walls, you can pair your drinks with a cheese and charcuterie board, then nibble and sip the night away.

MAP 2: 45 Blood Alley, 604/633-1912, www.salttastingroom.com, 3:30pm-late daily

Arts and Culture

GALLERIES
✪ Coastal Peoples Fine Arts Gallery

Coastal Peoples Fine Arts Gallery specializes in Northwest Coast and Inuit artwork in a spacious modern gallery in a brick Gastown building. On view are masks, carvings, and jewelry, with works ranging in price from hundreds to thousands of dollars.

MAP 2: 332 Water St., 604/684-9222, www.coastalpeoples.com, 10am-7pm daily May-Sept., 10am-6pm daily Oct.-Apr., free

Inuit Gallery of Vancouver

A specialist in Canadian indigenous art, the Inuit Gallery of Vancouver, operating since 1979, exhibits works by First Nations and Inuit people in a light and open 2nd-floor Gastown space. The gallery showcases an extensive collection of sculpture in stone, alabaster, and bone. They also show drawings, prints, wall hangings, carvings, and jewelry.

MAP 2: 206 Cambie St., 604/688-7323, www.inuit.com, 10am-6pm Mon.-Sat., 11am-5pm Sun., free

Urban Aboriginal Fair Trade Gallery

On the main floor of Skwachàys Lodge, a boutique indigenous art hotel, the small Urban Aboriginal Fair Trade Gallery showcases works by Canadian aboriginal artists, including many from British Columbia. The nonprofit Vancouver Native Housing Society owns the gallery, and proceeds from the prints, carvings, and jewelry sold here help support the society's mission to provide affordable urban housing for indigenous people.

MAP 2: 29 W. Pender St., 604/558-3589, www.skwachays.com, 10am-5pm Mon.-Fri., noon-5pm Sat.-Sun., free

THEATER

Firehall Arts Centre

A venue for diverse theatrical, dance, and musical productions, the 136-seat Firehall Arts Centre is housed in a 1906 former city fire station on the edge of Chinatown. From the exterior, with its brightly painted garage doors, the building still resembles the fire station that it was until the 1970s. The theater produces contemporary works that highlight Canada's multicultural communities, with productions throughout the year by an assortment of companies and performers.

MAP 2: 280 E. Cordova St., 604/689-0926, http://firehallartscentre. ca, tickets $23-33

CINEMA

Movies in the Morgue

The Vancouver Police Museum, located in the former city morgue, presents a monthly film series, Movies in the Morgue, on the 2nd Tuesday of the month September-April. Though the setting may be spooky, they're not all horror films. They do sell out, so book tickets at least a few days in advance on the website.

MAP 2: 240 E. Cordova St., 604/665-3346, www. vancouverpolicemuseum.ca, 2nd Tues. of the month Sept.-Apr., tickets $10

Festivals and Events

Lunar New Year

With its large Asian population, Vancouver hosts plenty of festivities to mark the Lunar New Year, including parades, lion dances, music, fireworks, and other special events in Chinatown and throughout Richmond. Chinatown's Spring Festival Parade draws crowds of nearly 100,000 spectators every year, and nearby, the Dr. Sun Yat-Sen Classical Chinese Garden organizes more New Year's festivities.

Chinatown and Richmond: www.cbavancouver.ca, http:// vancouverchinesegarden.com, and www.visitrichmondbc.com, Jan.-Feb.

Indian Summer Festival

A unique celebration of South Asian, Canadian, and international culture, the Indian Summer Festival serves up two weeks of films, lectures, food events, theater, and other thought-provoking programming in mid-July. SFU's Goldcorp Centre for the Arts (Woodward's Bldg., 149 W. Hastings St.) in Gastown hosts many events, as do other venues downtown and elsewhere in the city.

Various locations: http://indiansummerfest.ca, July

Shops

SHOPPING DISTRICTS

Gastown

Visit Gastown for smaller fashion boutiques and clothing by local designers.

MAP 2: Water St. and Cordova St., between Richards St. and Carrall St.

CLOTHING AND ACCESSORIES

✪ Lululemon Lab

Operated by the Vancouver-based yoga-wear maker in a warehouse-style Gastown space, Lululemon Lab is a concept store that offers prototypes and other limited-edition clothing not carried at the company's regular retail outlets. Watch the designers at work while you browse for unique active and casual wear. The city is also home to several regular Lululemon locations.

MAP 2: 50 Powell St., 604/689-8013, www.lululemonlab.com, 11am-7pm Mon.-Sat., noon-6pm Sun.

Kit and Ace

Ready to upgrade your yoga look? Shannon Wilson, who's married to Lululemon founder Chip Wilson, and J. J. Wilson, Chip's son, founded Kit and Ace, which designs and sells hip men's and women's work-to-weekend clothing made from "technical cashmere" and other luxury fabrics, designed to dress up while still being comfortable. The soft, comfy garments may be too pricey for the gym, but are lovely for the office or a casual evening out. They have a second location in Kitsilano.

MAP 2: 165 Water St., 604/559-8363, www.kitandace.com, 10am-7pm Mon.-Wed., 10am-8pm Thurs.-Sat., 11am-6pm Sun.

Oak + Fort

Launched in Vancouver, Oak + Fort has a spacious Gastown store purveying stylishly relaxed, moderately priced clothing for men and women, along with jewelry and accessories. Both the monochromatic designs and the airy, high-ceilinged shop have a minimalist, almost Japanese aesthetic, and the well-spaced racks are comfortable for browsing.

MAP 2: 355 Water St., 604/566-9199, www.oakandfort.ca, 11am-7pm Mon.-Wed., 11am-8pm Thurs.-Fri., 10am-7pm Sat., 11am-6pm Sun.

One of a Few

This small but chic boutique in Gastown sells women's clothing by emerging and established designers from around the world. Catering to the young, style-conscious, and well-heeled, One of a Few carries distinctive fashions that you might

BEST SOUVENIRS

What should you bring home to remember your Vancouver visit? Besides a camera full of photos of this scenic waterfront city, look for the following souvenirs:

INDIGENOUS ARTS AND CRAFTS

Pick up artwork, jewelry, and other crafts by indigenous artists at the Coastal Peoples Fine Arts Gallery (page 83), Urban Aboriginal Fair Trade Gallery (page 84), or Hill's Native Art (page 168).

LOCAL SALMON

Several seafood vendors in the Granville Island Public Market (page 114) sell locally caught, cured

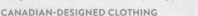

smoked salmon

salmon, packed for travel. Try "salmon candy," a sweetened, cured, and surprisingly addictive fish snack.

CANADIAN-DESIGNED CLOTHING

Browse boutiques like One of a Few (page 85) or Two of Hearts (page 139) to find clothing and accessories from Canadian designers.

BC WINE OR CRAFT BEER

Look for wines from the Okanagan or Vancouver Island, and craft beers brewed in Vancouver or elsewhere around the province at Viti Wine & Lager (page 65), Legacy Liquor Store (page 109), and Liberty Wine Merchants (page 125). Or visit any of the microbreweries across the city.

---

wear to work or for a night out at an of-the-moment bistro.

MAP 2: 354 Water St., 604/605-0685, www.oneofafew.com, 11am-6pm Mon.-Thurs. and Sat., 11am-7pm Fri., noon-5pm Sun.

Tees.ca

Pop into Tees.ca for funky T-shirts designed by local artists and other creatives. In this tiny storefront, piled high with tees, many have Vancouver motifs and would make fun souvenirs.

MAP 2: 227 Abbott St., www.tees.ca, 11am-6pm Mon.-Sat., noon-5pm Sun.

SHOES

✪ John Fluevog

Canadian shoemaker John Fluevog started his funky footwear line in Vancouver, offering high-end, unconventional designs for both men and women, many of which feature bright colors and distinctive heel shapes. His two-level Gastown shop, with massive windows and a greenhouse-like ceiling, looks more like an art studio than a shoe store. There's a second Fluevog branch among the Granville Street nightclubs downtown.

MAP 2: 65 Water St., 604/688-6228, www.fluevog.com, 10am-7pm Mon.-Wed. and Sat., 10am-8pm Thurs.-Fri., noon-6pm Sun.

BOOKS

The Paper Hound Bookshop

The floor-to-ceiling shelves at The Paper Hound Bookshop are crammed with a diverse array of used (and some new) titles, sorted into sometimes quirky categories that range from literature and Eastern enlightenment to "books with folding maps." In this chockablock Gastown shop, kids books get the same tongue-in-cheek treatment, organized into sections from "indomitable orphans" to "the rodent as hero." If you can't find what you need, ask the helpful bibliophile staffers.

MAP 2: 344 W. Pender St., 604/428-1344, http://paperhound. ca, 10am-7pm Sun.-Thurs., 10am-8pm Fri.-Sat.

HOUSEWARES

Örling & Wu

The carefully curated collection of hip housewares draws you into this window-lined storefront in a rehabbed Gastown building, where it's fun to browse for things you didn't know you needed. Örling & Wu carries cards and paper goods, coffee- and tea-making supplies, tableware, soaps and bath products, and even stylish dog collars. You'll find a second location in Kitsilano.

MAP 2: 28 Water St., 604/568-6718, www.orlingandwu.com, 10am-6pm Mon.-Thurs., 10am-7pm Fri.-Sat., 11am-6pm Sun.

The Paper Hound Bookshop

Yaletown and False Creek Map 3

Yaletown's renovated brick warehouses, once part of an industrial district, today house a chic mix of restaurants, boutiques, and **drinking spots.** Browse the **fashionable shops,** meet for cocktails on street-side patios, and dine on local seafood in the **upscale restaurants.** The city's sports arenas, including the home ice of the **Vancouver Canucks,** are also nearby.

False Creek is home to **Science World,** the family-friendly science museum in a geodesic dome. Also here is the **Olympic Village,** where athletes stayed during the 2010 Winter Games, now a complex of pubs, cafés, and condos. South of False Creek, on and

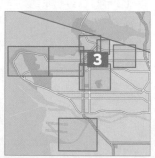

off Main Street, is a district of **craft breweries** and **beer-centric pubs,** perfect for strolling and sipping.

TOP SIGHTS

- Best Museum for Kids: **Science World** (page 94)

TOP RESTAURANTS

- Best Seafood with a View: **Ancora Waterfront Dining and Patio** (page 97)

TOP NIGHTLIFE

- Where to Pair Waffles with Craft Beer: **33 Acres Brewing** (page 100)
- Where to Hang Out on a Blue-Sky Day: **Tap & Barrel** (page 102)
- Coolest Cocktail Lounge: **Opus Bar** (page 102)

TOP RECREATION

- Local Team with the Most Devoted Fans: **Vancouver Canucks** (page 104)

TOP SHOPS

- Best Discoveries: **Fine Finds Boutique** (page 108)

GETTING THERE AND AROUND

- SkyTrain lines: Canada Line, Expo Line
- SkyTrain stops: Yaletown-Roundhouse, Olympic Village (Canada Line); Stadium-Chinatown, Main Street-Science World (Expo Line)
- Bus lines: 3, 6, 19, 23, 50, 84
- Ferries: Aquabus, False Creek

SIGHTS

13 **B1** Long Table Distillery	38 **C5** Olympic Village
27 **B3** Engine 374 Pavilion	39 **C6** Science World
28 **B4** BC Place and the BC Sports Hall of Fame	

RESTAURANTS

2 **A1** Giardino	17 **B2** La Pentola
6 **A3** Homer Street Café and Bar	20 **B3** Small Victory Bakery
8 **A4** Fanny Bay Oyster Bar	21 **B3** Blue Water Café
14 **B1** Ancora Waterfront Dining and Patio	22 **B3** WildTale Coastal Grill
15 **B2** House Special	36 **C5** Terra Breads Bakery Café
16 **B2** Rodney's Oyster House	

NIGHTLIFE

7 **A4** Red Racer Taphouse	34 **C5** Tap & Barrel
11 **A4** Frankie's Jazz Club	44 **E5** 33 Acres Brewing
18 **B2** Opus Bar	45 **E6** Brassneck Brewery
23 **B3** Yaletown Brewing Company	

RECREATION

1 **A1** Bicycle Sports Pacific	32 **C2** David Lam Park
12 **A5** Vancouver Canucks	33 **C3** Reckless Bike Stores
29 **B4** BC Lions	35 **C5** Creekside Kayaks
30 **B4** Vancouver Whitecaps	

ARTS AND CULTURE

3 **A2** Scotiabank Dance Centre	42 **D6** Equinox Gallery
5 **A3** Contemporary Art Gallery	43 **D6** Monte Clark Galler
40 **D5** Goldcorp Stage at the BMO Theatre Centre	

SHOPS

4 **A2** My Sister's Closet	26 **B3** Global Atomic Designs
24 **B3** Fine Finds Boutique	37 **C5** Legacy Liquor Stor
25 **B3** Woo To See You	41 **D6** MEC

HOTELS

9 **A4** YWCA Hotel Vancouver	19 **B2** Opus Hotel Vancouver
10 **A4** Hotel BLU	31 **B4** Parq Vancouver

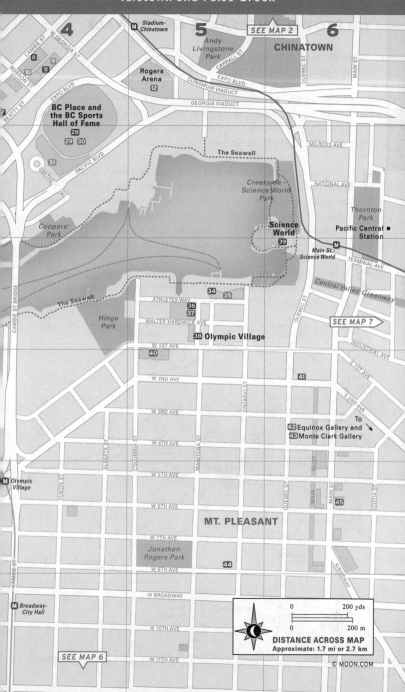

YALETOWN AND FALSE CREEK WALK

TOTAL DISTANCE: 2.6 miles (4.2 km)
TOTAL WALKING TIME: 1.5 hours

On this excursion, which includes a combination of walking and ferry-hopping, you'll start and end in Yaletown. In between, you'll explore the Olympic Village, the False Creek waterfront, and the craft beer district around Main Street.

1 Start your stroll with coffee and pastries at Yaletown's **Small Victory Bakery.** When you're ready to wander, exit the bakery, turning left on Homer Street, and take an immediate left onto Helmcken Street. Follow Helmcken two blocks down the hill, and turn right onto Mainland Street, checking out the neighborhood's restored warehouse buildings. In one block, at Davie Street, turn left to walk south toward the waterfront.

2 In two blocks, at the corner of Davie and Pacific Boulevard, stop for a quick look at the **Engine 374 Pavilion** to see the locomotive that pulled the first transcontinental passenger train into Vancouver in

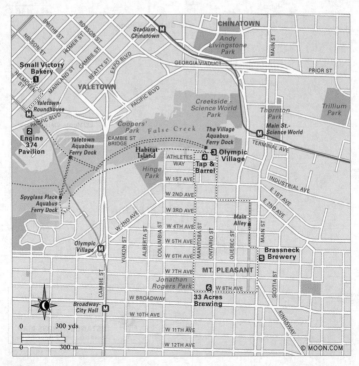

1887. Continue south on Davie Street one more block to False Creek and the Aquabus ferry dock, where colorful ferries shuttle across False Creek, which British naval officer and explorer George Henry Richards is credited with naming. In 1859, Richards traveled up what he thought was a creek in search of coal deposits but discovered that this "false creek" was actually an inlet of the Pacific Ocean. Board the ferry headed east to The Village.

3 When you get off the ferry, explore the cluster of contemporary buildings in front of you: the **Olympic Village,** also known as the Village at False Creek. The neighborhood's buildings, which housed athletes during the 2010 Olympic Games, have been converted into condominiums, and the district has several brewpubs, cafés, public art pieces, and a community center.

4 If you're ready for a break, nab a patio seat at **Tap & Barrel,** where they've got a long list of BC beer and wines on tap and great views of the city skyline.

5 From the Olympic Village, you'll detour away from the water to check out other craft breweries and explore some street art en route. Walk south through the plaza on Salt Street, past the massive sculptures *The Birds,* and continue three blocks to West 2nd Avenue. Turn left onto 2nd, and go one and a half blocks east to **Main Alley,** just east of Quebec Street. Turn right and wander up the alley, checking out the murals on the back sides of the warehouse and office buildings. When you reach 5th Avenue, turn left to Main Street, to find your next stop, **Brassneck Brewery,** where you can do a tasting of their small-batch beer.

6 Turn left out of the brewery onto Main and walk two blocks south. At 8th Avenue, turn right, walk two more blocks, and you'll see **33 Acres Brewing** on your right. Stop for another beer tasting and a snack. To get back to the False Creek waterfront, turn right onto 8th Avenue and take the first right onto Manitoba Street. Follow Manitoba 10 blocks north, back to the Olympic Village. Pause to take photos of the city skyline and Science World's dome. For more waterfront views, follow the Seawall west along the water. You'll pass tiny **Habitat Island,** created when the Olympic Village was constructed, and under the Cambie Bridge. You can board the Aquabus here at the Spyglass Place dock to return to Yaletown.

Sights

✪ Science World

What's that dome thing? Kids may want to check out the distinctive geodesic dome, constructed for the Expo '86 world's fair, that houses Vancouver's cool science museum, even before they venture inside. Clad in aluminum and illuminated at night with 400 lights, the 155-foot-tall dome looks like a colossal shiny golf ball, shimmering on the edge of False Creek.

Officially called Science World at Telus World of Science, the museum is full of hands-on exhibits about the natural world, light and sound, and puzzles and illusions. The BodyWorks exhibit helps kids explore what's inside of them and where they came from. The littlest visitors have their own Kidspace, designed for children under age six, stocked with giant building blocks, water features, and games for exploring light and color. Live science shows and demonstrations take place throughout the day, entertaining (and educating) with fire, electricity, balloons, and other science themes—even grossology ("the impolite science of the human body"). A rotating selection of films plays on the five-story-tall screen in the immersive OMNIMAX Theatre ($6.50).

Outside in Ken Spencer Science Park, you can explore more interactive exhibits about the local

Science World

environment and issues of sustainability. The park even has its own chicken coop.

MAP 3: 1455 Quebec St., 604/443-7440, www.scienceworld.ca, subway: Main Street-Science World, 10am-6pm Fri.-Wed., 10am-9pm Tues. late June-early Sept., 10am-5pm Mon.-Fri., 10am-6pm Sat.-Sun. Apr.-late June and early Sept.-Mar., extended hours Dec. winter break and Mar. spring break, adults $27, seniors and students $22, ages 3-12 $18

Olympic Village

A new neighborhood developed on the south side of False Creek thanks to the 2010 Winter Olympic Games. The residential buildings where athletes lived during the games have been transformed into the Olympic Village, also known as the Village at False Creek, comprising stylish condominiums, brewpubs, cafés, a community center, and several public art pieces. Look for *The Birds* in the Southeast False Creek Plaza, two 18-foot-tall (5.5-m) sparrows crafted by Vancouver artist Myfanwy MacLeod. The Olympic Village provides a great vantage point for skyline photos.

MAP 3: Bounded by Ontario St., Athletes Way, Columbia St., and W. 2nd Ave., subway: Olympic Village or Main Street-Science World

BC Place and the BC Sports Hall of Fame

The odd-looking structure along False Creek that resembles a giant spaceship is BC Place, a sports and concert arena. Major League Soccer's Vancouver Whitecaps (www.whitecapsfc.com) play here, as do the Canadian Football League's BC Lions (www.bclions.com). Built in 1983, the arena hosted the Expo '86 opening ceremonies, the opening and closing ceremonies of the 2010 Winter Olympics, the FIFA Women's World Cup Canada 2015, as well as concerts by Michael Jackson, the Rolling Stones, Madonna, Paul McCartney, Taylor Swift, and many others.

Inside BC Place, the BC Sports Hall of Fame (Beatty St. at Robson St., Gate A, 604/687-5520, http://bcsportshall.com, 10am-5pm daily, adults $18, seniors $14, students and ages 6-17 $12) highlights regional sports history and offers interactive games where kids (and accompanying adults) can test their athletic prowess. Exhibits feature topics like Vancouver's 2010 Winter Olympics, women and indigenous sports figures, and a Hall of Champions showcasing BC athletes.

You can also book the All Access Experience ($24), which includes a BC Place tour along with access to the Hall of Fame. Tours visit the field, media room, premium boxes, and (when available) the locker rooms. The All Access Experience tours are offered on specific dates, so check ahead.

Outside the arena, near the intersection of Robson and Beatty Streets, is the Terry Fox Memorial, a series of four progressively larger sculptures by Vancouver artist Douglas Coupland. The memorial honors Fox, the BC man who embarked on a cross-Canada run in 1980 to raise money for cancer research after losing his own leg to the disease.

THE ISLAND THE OLYMPICS BUILT

Before hosting the 2010 Winter Olympic Games, Vancouver embarked on numerous building projects: the Canada Line subway connecting downtown and the airport, the Olympic Cauldron on the Coal Harbour waterfront, and the former Athletes Village on the shores of False Creek, which housed competitors during the games and is now the fashionable Olympic Village district.

Yet one of the Olympics' most unusual legacies may be an artificial island. To build the Athletes Village, developers excavated a vast amount of rocks, sand, and gravel. More than 2 million cubic feet (60,000 cubic m) of this excavated material was used to construct tiny Habitat Island, along Southeast False Creek. Now city-owned parkland, Habitat Island has more than 200 native trees, shrubs, flowers, and grasses, and, as befits its name, it provides a habitat for birds, crabs, starfish, and other land and sea creatures.

Habitat Island is on the False Creek waterfront, near the foot of Columbia Street, east of the Cambie Bridge. A rock pathway leads onto the island from the Seawall path. You can wander over to the little island for a stroll or a picnic, or simply explore the island that the Olympics built.

MAP 3: 777 Pacific Blvd., 604/669-2300, www.bcplace.com, subway: Stadium-Chinatown

Engine 374 Pavilion

The Canadian Pacific Railway completed its cross-Canada train route in 1885, when rail workers drove the last spike of the transcontinental railroad into the ground at Craigellachie, near the town of Revelstoke, in eastern British Columbia. A year and a half later, in 1887, the first transcontinental passenger train rolled into Vancouver, pulled by Engine 374.

This historic locomotive is now on view at the Engine 374 Pavilion, next to Yaletown's Roundhouse Community Centre. Posing next to the engine makes a fun photo op for rail enthusiasts of all ages. The Engine 374 Pavilion is typically open every day, but hours can vary, as the staff are volunteers; call ahead.

MAP 3: 181 Roundhouse Mews, 604/713-1800, http://roundhouse. ca, subway: Yaletown-Roundhouse, 10am-4pm daily July-Aug, 11am-3pm daily Sept.-June, free

Long Table Distillery

Vancouver's first micro-distillery produces several varieties of gin and vodka in their 80-gallon (300-liter) copper-pot still. Long Table Distillery also makes small batches of seasonal spirits, like Akvavit or Amaro, so stop by their Yaletown tasting room to see what's brewing. In the 28-seat space, with a polished wood bar and a wall of windows into the distilling room, you can choose a flight of three spirits ($6); the staff can explain what you're drinking and how it's made. They also host popular Gin & Tonic Fridays (4pm-9pm) and Cocktail Saturdays (3pm-9pm), when they offer custom cocktails, and you can purchase snacks from food trucks parked out front.

MAP 3: 1451 Hornby St., 604/266-0177, http://longtabledistillery.com, 1pm-6pm Wed.-Thurs., 1pm-9pm Fri.-Sat.

Restaurants

PRICE KEY

$ Entrées less than CAD$15
$$ Entrées CAD$15-25
$$$ Entrées more than CAD$25

MODERN CANADIAN

Homer Street Café and Bar $$$

Savory rotisserie chicken and other upscale comfort foods draw hearty appetites to Yaletown's Homer Street Café and Bar. Choose from starters like grilled tuna with sweet pepper salsa or bison terrine with pickled cherries. Then, go for the chicken (available in quarter, half, or whole birds), or peruse the daily "fresh sheet" for other seafood, pasta, and meat options. Save room for the peanut butter cookies with Nutella cream, and note the unique architecture; the dining room encompasses space in both a heritage building and a contemporary tower, with ornate tile work, lots of marble, and a shady sidewalk patio.

MAP 3: 898 Homer St., 604/428-4299, http://homerstreetcafebar.com, 11:30am-10pm Mon.-Thurs., 11:30am-11pm Fri., 10:30am-2:30pm and 5pm-11pm Sat., 10:30am-2:30pm and 5pm-10pm Sun.

SEAFOOD

✪ Ancora Waterfront Dining and Patio $$$

Does chic Ancora Waterfront Dining and Patio have the loveliest outdoor dining space in the city? Its sunny terrace overlooking False Creek in Yaletown is certainly among Vancouver's most scenic waterside dining destinations. Come at sunset or on a sunny day for the best views. Expect an innovative hybrid of Japanese and Peruvian flavors crafted from west coast ingredients. Ceviche and sashimi are highlights. Another location is on the North Shore.

MAP 3: 1600 Howe St., 604/681-1164, www.ancoradining.com, noon-2:30pm and 5pm-10pm Mon.-Fri., 5pm-10pm Sat., 11am-2:30pm and 5pm-10pm Sun.

Blue Water Café $$$

Busy with business diners and couples celebrating occasions, this long-standing high-end seafood spot in a rehabbed Yaletown warehouse does an excellent job with fresh fish. The chef often spotlights underutilized species—the restaurant hosts an annual "Unsung Heroes" festival—so look for seafood that you might not find elsewhere alongside more familiar varieties. A lengthy wine list and well-trained staff make your evening more special.

MAP 3: 1095 Hamilton St., 604/688-8078, www.bluewatercafe.net, 5pm-11pm daily

WildTale Coastal Grill $$$

Fresh seafood, simply prepared, is the lure at WildTale Coastal Grill. Start with oysters or ceviche from the raw bar, then order the day's fresh catch, with most of the fish options from Pacific waters. Inside, where the furnishings are sturdy wood and leather, the well-spaced tables encourage comfortable conversation. On a sunny day, nab a patio seat to watch all of Yaletown go by. A second location is in the Olympic Village.

MAP 3: 1079 Mainland St., 604/428-9211, www.wildtale.ca, 11am-midnight Mon.-Sat., 11am-11pm Sun.

Fanny Bay Oyster Bar $$

West coast shellfish producer Taylor Shellfish Farms runs Fanny Bay Oyster Bar, which bills itself as the city's first "tide to table" oyster bar. Sit at the long marble counter and watch the shuckers at work while you dig into platters of whatever bivalves are freshest that day; the servers can help you choose from the regularly changing list. Besides oysters, the menu at this smart-casual spot with industrial-style lighting, exposed pipes, and a polished wood floor includes crab cakes, ceviche, fish-and-chips, and other seafood preparations. Near BC Place in Yaletown, it's handy for pre- or post-game drinks and snacks.

MAP 3: 762 Cambie St., 778/379-9510, www.fannybayoysters.com, 11am-late Mon.-Fri., 10:30am-late Sat.-Sun.

Rodney's Oyster House $$

Bring the gang, raise a glass, and start slurping—oysters, that is—at lively Rodney's Oyster House. This nautical-themed pub-style fish house in Yaletown, outfitted with buoys, model ships, and a pile of fresh oysters on ice at the bar, specializes in simple seafood dishes, from chowders and steamers to the namesake bivalve. To drink, choose from several beers on tap or wines from BC and farther afield. There's a second Rodney's in Gastown.

an oyster platter at Fanny Bay Oyster Bar

MAP 3: 1228 Hamilton St.,
604/609-0080, http://rohvan.com,
11:30am-11pm daily

VIETNAMESE
House Special $$

A modern Vietnamese eatery in a refurbished Yaletown warehouse, House Special is named for the house special pho. From the menu of innovative sharing plates that pair well with cocktails and craft beers, try the spicy-sweet chicken wings, the soft-boiled "son-in-law egg" in a crispy panko crust, or the sautéed green beans with mushroom-based "XO" sauce. Many dishes can be adapted for vegetarians and vegans.
MAP 3: 1269 Hamilton St.,
778/379-2939, www.housespecial.
ca, 11:30am-10pm Sun.-Thurs.,
11:30am-10:30pm Fri.-Sat.

noodles and spring rolls at House Special

ITALIAN
Giardino $$$

Longtime Vancouver restaurateur Umberto Menghi operates the elegant Tuscan-inspired Giardino near Yaletown, pairing Old World service with updated plates like fettuccine with prosciutto and peas, horseradish-crusted sablefish, or seared venison sauced with a chianti reduction. Don't miss the sweets, like chocolate *fonduta*, a baked chocolate soufflé with chestnut crème anglaise, or almond cannoli served with blood orange sorbet. The dining room could be a refined restaurant in Florence, with its vaulted wood-beamed ceilings, Italian tile work, and European paintings; in summer, sit on the garden patio, hidden behind the restaurant.
MAP 3: 1328 Hornby St., 604/669-2422,
www.umberto.com, 5:30pm-10pm
Mon.-Sat.

La Pentola $$$

The best way to dine at La Pentola, the fashionable dining room at Yaletown's Opus Hotel, is family-style ($60-70 pp), when the kitchen sends out a procession of contemporary Italian dishes. For a less opulent feast, choose from antipasti like grilled squid with green onion puree, house-made tagliatelle bolognese or taglierini with clams, and mains like BC ling cod with braised octopus or flank steak with grilled polenta. The signature dessert is a sweet-tart lemon cream. With street-level windows bringing in light from two sides and tables well laid out for conversation, La Pentola is a pleasant spot for lunch or a business meeting.
MAP 3: 350 Davie St., 604/642-0557,
www.lapentola.ca, 7am-2pm and
5pm-10pm Sun.-Thurs., 7am-2pm and
5pm-11pm Fri.-Sat.

BAKERIES AND CAFÉS
Small Victory Bakery $

At times, it can seem like a small victory to get a seat at this Yaletown café that's filled with blond wood tables and lots of enticing aromas.

At Small Victory Bakery, the coffee is excellent, and the short menu includes pastries, breads, and a few sandwiches. The almond croissants are a special treat. The bakery has another branch on South Granville Street.

MAP 3: 1088 Homer St., 604/899-8892, http://smallvictory.ca, 7:30am-6pm Mon.-Fri., 8am-6pm Sat.-Sun.

Terra Breads Bakery Café $

With floor-to-ceiling windows and seats inside and out, cheery Terra Breads Bakery Café in the Olympic Village makes a handy rest stop for coffee and muffins while you're strolling the False Creek Seawall, or as a treat for the kids after visiting Science World. Sandwiches, salads, soups, and a range of sweet and savory pastries are available, along with hot and cold drinks, beer, wine, and cider. Terra Breads has other sit-down locations in Kitsilano and off Main Street.

MAP 3: 1605 Manitoba St., 604/877-1183, www.terrabreads.com, 7am-7pm daily

Nightlife

CRAFT BEER

✪ 33 Acres Brewing

You can sample a flight or raise a glass at 33 Acres Brewing, which draws a casual hipster crowd to its 60-seat tasting room between Cambie and Main Streets, a sleek white-walled space with shared tables and stools along the counter. Their well-regarded brews include 33 Acres of Sunshine (a blond summer ale) and 33 Acres of Darkness (a malty dark beer). Flights of four six-ounce samplers are $9. They serve snacks all day and cook wood-fired pizzas at lunch and dinner. The weekend waffle brunch has legions of fans. Next door, at 33 Brewing Experiment (25 W. 8th Ave., 604/620-4589, http://33brewingexp. com; noon-11pm Mon.-Fri., 11am-11pm Sat.-Sun.), the tasting room in their "experimental brewery," you can sample test brews or new beers before they're officially released.

MAP 3: 15 W. 8th Ave., 604/620-4589, www.33acresbrewing.com, 9am-9pm Mon.-Tues., 9am-11pm Wed.-Fri., 10am-11pm Sat., 10am-9pm Sun.

waffles at 33 Acres Brewing

Brassneck Brewery

The communal tables in the compact Main Street tasting room at

Yaletown Brewing Company

hip Brassneck Brewery fill up fast, particularly on weekend evenings, with fans of their frequently changing small-batch brews. Brassneck is the craft brewery that other local brewers often recommend. Choose from 8-10 brews that might include the signature Brassneck Ale, a straightforward pale ale; the dry-hopped Passive Aggressive pale ale; or Joe's Ukelele, a saison. Six-ounce samples are $2.50, a flight of four is $8. There's no kitchen, but food trucks sometimes park outside.

MAP 3: 2148 Main St., 604/259-7686, www.brassneck.ca, 2pm-11pm Mon.-Fri., noon-11pm Sat.-Sun.

Red Racer Taphouse

Known for its Red Racer label, especially the popular IPA, Central City Brewing has been making beer at their brewery in the Vancouver suburb of Surrey since 2003. Red Racer Taphouse, their Yaletown brewpub, is a roomy warehouse-style space with a long bar, exposed brick walls, and communal wooden tables, showcasing Central City's brews and other local varieties from 40 taps. Close to the sports arenas, it attracts hockey and soccer fans; if you're not headed for the game, you can sip your beer here and watch the match on TV.

MAP 3: 871 Beatty St., 778/379-2489, ww.redracertaphouse.com, 11am-11pm Sun.-Thurs., 11am-1am Fri.-Sat.

Yaletown Brewing Company

The always-busy Yaletown Brewing Company, with a rotating selection of taps, is a lively spot to meet up for a drink or bring the gang for appetizers and beer. It can get loud inside, so ask for a table on the wraparound patio, where the added benefit is a front-row seat for the Yaletown neighborhood scene. Look over the lengthy menu of sandwiches, salads, pizzas, and other pub fare if you need sustenance with your brews.

MAP 3: 1111 Mainland St., 604/681-2739, www.mjg.ca/yaletown, 11:30am-midnight Sun.-Wed., 11:30am-1am Thurs., 11:30am-3am Fri.-Sat.

PUBS
✪ Tap & Barrel

With a sunny patio facing False Creek lined with their signature umbrellas, the Olympic Village branch of local pub chain Tap & Barrel is perpetually packed on summer days. Yet, even in winter, you can take in the city views through the oversize windows. They serve a long list of BC beer on tap, from producers like 33 Acres, Four Winds, and Whistler Brewing. Order a flight of five ($12.50) to sample a few different options. They've got taps for BC wines as well. The comfort food menu amps up basic pub fare with dishes like a PBJ burger (slathered with chipotle peanut butter and bacon jam) and craft beer macaroni and cheese. For an interesting brunch twist, try the pork belly and soft egg pizza. You'll find other Tap & Barrel locations at the Convention Centre downtown and in North Vancouver. The company also runs smaller Tap Shack pubs (http://tapshack.ca).

MAP 3: 1 Athletes Way, 604/685-2223, www.tapandbarrel.com, 11am-midnight Sun.-Thurs., 11am-1am Fri.-Sat.

LIVE MUSIC
Frankie's Jazz Club

A venue for serious jazz fans, Frankie's Jazz Club hosts performances by local and international musicians several nights a week. Sax player Cory Weeds, a longtime fixture on Vancouver's jazz scene, is a frequent performer. Other musicians who've entertained here include Canadian acoustic string ensemble Van Django; Canadian jazz vocalist Maya Rae; and Philadelphia-based organist Lucas Brown, performing with his quartet.

MAP 3: 755 Beatty St., 604/688-6368, www.frankiesjazzclub.ca, hours vary, cover $10-25

LOUNGES
✪ Opus Bar

In the lobby of Yaletown's hip Opus Hotel Vancouver, the Opus Bar is styled like a trendy living room, where well-dressed young people gather in curvaceous lounge chairs in front of the fireplace to chat over drinks like the Little Chile (pisco, campari, egg white, and orange blossom water) or Room 207 (tequila, Cointreau, Galliano, and citrus). Come at happy hour (3pm-6pm) for discounted drinks and snacks. Earlier in the day, you can linger over coffee.

MAP 3: 322 Davie St., 866/642-6787, http://vancouver.opushotel.com, 7am-late Mon.-Fri., 8am-late Sat.-Sun.

Recreation

PARKS

David Lam Park

Between Yaletown's condo towers and the waterfront, you can sit by the water in the grassy expanse of David Lam Park, named for the Hong Kong-born philanthropist, real estate mogul, and politician who became Canada's first Asian Canadian lieutenant governor. The 10.7-acre (4.34-ha) park along the Seawall has a playground, tennis and basketball courts, and plenty of space for picnics. The park hosts free outdoor concerts during the annual Vancouver Jazz Festival in late June. MAP 3: 1300 Pacific Blvd. at Drake St., http://vancouver.ca, 6am-10pm daily, free

KAYAKING AND STAND-UP PADDLEBOARDING

Creekside Kayaks

False Creek is an especially beautiful spot for a late-in-the-day paddle, with views of the city skyline. At the Olympic Village on False Creek, Creekside Kayaks rents kayaks and stand-up paddleboards spring-fall. MAP 3: 1495 Ontario St., 604/616-7453, www.creeksidekayaks.ca, 11am-dusk Mon.-Fri., 9am-5pm Sat.-Sun. late-Apr.-early-Oct., single kayak $20 per hour, double kayak $35, paddleboard $20

kayaking in Yaletown

CYCLING
BIKE RENTALS
Bicycle Sports Pacific

Opposite the Burrard Bridge, where Yaletown meets the West End, Bicycle Sports Pacific rents seven-speed cruiser or hybrid bikes. You can reserve a rental in advance or simply drop in when you're ready to ride.

MAP 3: 999 Pacific St., 604/682-4537, http://bspbikes.com, 10am-6pm Mon.-Sat., noon-5pm Sun., 2 hours $20, all-day $40

Reckless Bike Stores

Reckless Bike Stores rents city bikes and cruisers along the Seawall in Yaletown. The shop gets busy on summer weekends, so don't be in a rush when picking up or returning your rental. They have another Yaletown location, which also rents electric bikes (from $28 for 1.5 hours), and a branch near Granville Island.

MAP 3: 110 Davie St., 604/648-2600, www.reckless.ca, 9:30am-7pm daily, 1.5 hours $18.50, all-day $44.50

SPECTATOR SPORTS
✪ Vancouver Canucks

Vancouver is wild for hockey, particularly the city's National Hockey League team, the Vancouver Canucks, whose regular season runs from October-April. The Canucks take to the ice at Rogers Arena (604/899-7400, http://rogersarena.com) on False Creek.

Games are always packed with fans wearing blue Canucks jerseys, but in years when the team is playing well, tickets are in particularly high demand. Expect larger crowds when the Canucks face off against their rivals, including the Calgary Flames, Chicago Blackhawks, and Los Angeles Kings. Rogers Arena has a place in Olympic hockey history. In the 2010 Winter Olympics, the Canadian men's team beat their U.S. rivals here in the gold medal game, a 3-2 overtime cliffhanger, and Canada's women's team took gold on the same ice, winning 2-0 over the United States.

Behind-the-scenes tours (60-75 minutes, generally 10:30am, 12:15pm, and 2pm Wed.-Sat., noon, 1:30pm, and 3pm Sun., adults $18, seniors, students, and ages 4-12 $12) of Rogers Arena are a guided walk through the facility; access to some areas, particularly the locker rooms, isn't guaranteed. On the Game Day tours (10:15am and 11:35am, $25 pp), offered on hockey game days only, you can watch one of the teams who'll play later that day practice for 30 minutes, with an arena tour afterward. Book the 10:15am tour for the best chance to see the Canucks on the ice, although the arena emphasizes that they can't confirm which team will be practicing when. Book your tour online and meet at the Canucks Team Store (Gate 6, Pat Quinn Way at Pacific Blvd.) at least 10 minutes before the scheduled tour time.

MAP 3: 800 Griffiths Way, 604/899-7440 or 800/745-3000, http://canucks.nhl.com, Oct.-Apr., tickets $55-300

BC Lions

Curious about how professional Canadian football differs from its U.S. cousin? Watch the BC Lions run the field at BC Place (604/669-2300, www.bcplace.com). Both the U.S.

and Canadian versions of the sport got their start back in the 1800s, but they've diverged with a few different rules.

The nine-team Canadian Football League (CFL) plays on a longer and wider field than the National Football League (NFL), making passing more important to the game. Canadian teams have 12 players on the field, compared to 11 in the States, and have three downs rather than four to move the ball 10 yards forward. The CFL season begins in late June-July, and the Canadian equivalent of the Super Bowl, called the Gray Cup, is played in late November. While the CFL isn't the mega-business that the sport has become for the NFL, and its popularity pales in comparison to hockey, plenty of orange-shirted BC Lions fans turn out for their local team's games.

MAP 3: 777 Pacific Blvd., 604/589-7627, www.bclions.com, late June-Nov., tickets $35-130

Vancouver Whitecaps

Vancouver's professional Major League Soccer team, the Vancouver Whitecaps, also plays at BC Place (604/669-2300, www.bcplace.com). The regular season runs March-October. Since many Vancouver youth, both boys and girls, play soccer, families often bring kids to Whitecaps games.

The Whitecaps played their first match in 1974 in what was then known as the North American Soccer League. In 2011 the Vancouver club launched its first season as a Major League Soccer team.

MAP 3: 777 Pacific Blvd., 604/669-9283, www.whitecapsfc.com, Mar.-Oct., tickets $30-80

Arts and Culture

GALLERIES
Contemporary Art Gallery
The Contemporary Art Gallery shows eclectic works by modern artists. Even if you just walk by the small Yaletown exhibit space, check out the windows, where there's often an unusual or thought-provoking display.

MAP 3: 555 Nelson St., 604/681-2700, www.contemporaryartgallery.ca, noon-6pm Tues.-Sun., donation

Equinox Gallery
Several contemporary art galleries cluster in The Flats district, near the intersection of Main Street and East 2nd Avenue, close to the Olympic Village. The largest is the 14,500-square-foot (1,347-square-m) Equinox Gallery, in a bright orange building that once housed a tractor company, which mounts regular exhibitions of work by established Canadian artists.

The Equinox Gallery and adjacent Monte Clark Gallery may have to relocate when construction of a subway line extension through this neighborhood begins in 2020; check with the galleries for updates.

MAP 3: 525 Great Northern Way, 604/736-2405, www.equinoxgallery.com, 10am-5pm Tues.-Sat., free

Monte Clark Gallery

Monte Clark Gallery, in the same former industrial building as the Equinox Gallery, shows work by contemporary Canadian artists. Among the creatives that the gallery represents are Vancouver artist Roy Arden, Toronto-based Scott McFarland, and textile artist Colleen Heslin.

MAP 3: 525 Great Northern Way, 604/730-5000, www.monteclarkgallery.com, 10am-5:30pm Tues.-Sat., free

THEATER

Goldcorp Stage at the BMO Theatre Centre

The Arts Club Theatre Company, Vancouver's leading repertory theater, performs on three stages, presenting their more experimental works in the Olympic Village at the Goldcorp Stage at the BMO Theatre Centre. This striking contemporary building features a multistory glass-walled lobby. Recent productions in the 250-seat theater have included *Blind Date*, Rebecca Northan's creation where an audience member is chosen for an on-stage blind date, and *Forget About Tomorrow*, Vancouver playwright Jill Daum's work about her husband's early-onset Alzheimer's disease.

MAP 3: 162 W. 1st Ave., 604/687-1644, www.artsclub.com, $29-53

DANCE

Scotiabank Dance Centre

A variety of dance events, from ballet and modern to flamenco and Bollywood, take place throughout

Contemporary Art Gallery

the year at Scotiabank Dance Centre, a Yaletown theater and rehearsal complex, opened in 2001, with seven studio spaces. The Discover Dance! series includes one-hour lunchtime performances by a varied range of BC-based companies, while the Global Dance Connections series showcases contemporary works by local and international performers.

Recent events have featured the indigenous Dancers of Damelahamid; African dancer Jacky Essombe; and Vancouver's Wen Wei Dance, led by dancer and choreographer Wen Wei Wang, who formerly performed with Ballet BC.

MAP 3: 677 Davie St., 604/606-6400, www.thedancecentre.ca, $15-37

Festivals and Events

Talking Stick Festival

The 10-day Talking Stick Festival, in late February, typically produces more than two dozen theater, dance, storytelling, and music events by indigenous performers or featuring indigenous themes. The Roundhouse Community Arts & Recreation Centre (181 Roundhouse Mews) in Yaletown and the Vancouver East Cultural Centre (1895 Venables St.) near Commercial Drive stage many of the productions.

Various locations: http://fullcircle. ca, Feb.

TD Vancouver International Jazz Festival

With nearly two weeks of concerts around the city, from big-name big-ticket shows to free music in the park, the TD Vancouver International Jazz Festival has tunes for jazz, Latin, funk, and world music lovers. The festival runs during the last half of June and early July at venues downtown, in Yaletown, on Granville Island, and elsewhere across town, with popular outdoor concerts in Yaletown's David Lam Park (Pacific Blvd. at Drake St.).

Various locations: www.coastaljazz. ca, June-July

Vancouver International Film Festival

Movie lovers line up at the Vancouver International Film Festival to see the latest releases from Canadian, U.S., and international filmmakers. Yaletown's Vancity Theatre (1181 Seymour St.) is the festival's main venue, but films are shown at other theaters downtown, in Gastown, and elsewhere around the city. The two-week festival runs late September-mid-October.

Various locations: www.viff.org, Sept.-Oct.

Shops

CLOTHING AND ACCESSORIES

⊙ Fine Finds Boutique

You'll likely unearth some fine finds at Fine Finds Boutique, a Yaletown shop stocked with casually stylish women's clothing, hats, jewelry, and handbags, mixing local labels and global brands. They carry a large selection of vegan leather wallets, purses, and packs from Canadian maker Matt & Nat, plus cards and gift items, all attractively displayed in this window-lined storefront.

MAP 3: 1014 Mainland St., 604/669-8325, http://finefindsboutique.com, 10am-7pm Mon.-Sat., 11am-6pm Sun.

Global Atomic Designs

Hidden down a narrow corridor in a restored brick building, this surprisingly spacious boutique outfits millennial men and women in everything from funky T-shirts, hoodies, and denim to spangled club wear from Canadian and international designers, like Naked & Famous, Religion, and John Varvatos. In the center of this shop, which was one of the first boutiques to open in Yaletown in 1998, is a coffee bar where you can pull up a stool and consider your purchases over an espresso and a cookie.

MAP 3: 1144 Mainland St., 604/806-6223, www.globalatomic.com, 11am-7pm daily

Woo To See You

Inside Woo To See You, a tiny white-walled Yaletown boutique that gets its distinctive name from owner Hans Woo, you'll find jeans, blouses, jackets, and other fashionably casual women's clothing, primarily mid-priced garments from smaller or independent labels. Prepare for winter with handmade hats by Vancouver's Hendrik.Lou, and check out the cases along the wall displaying original jewelry, including Vancouver designer Carli Marie Sita's "famous fingers" series, necklaces inspired by American Sign Language (and other hand gestures). There's another location on Main Street.

MAP 3: 1062 Mainland St., 604/559-1062, http://wootoseeyou.com, 10am-7pm Mon.-Sat., 11am-6pm Sun.

OUTDOOR GEAR

MEC

One of the city's largest outdoor gear stores, MEC, as Mountain Equipment Co-op is known, is slated to relocate in 2020 to this shiny new building near the Olympic Village. This branch of the Canadian chain stocks its own label and other brands of clothing, backpacks, and gear for hiking, bicycling, rock climbing, kayaking, and other sports, as well as camping supplies. You must be a co-op member to purchase anything at MEC; a lifetime membership, which you can include with your first purchase, is $5.

The Vancouver MEC store organizes a variety of events, listed on the website, such as free group runs, hikes, and cycles as well as backcountry adventure planning workshops and bike maintenance clinics.

MAP 3: 111 E. 2nd Ave., 604/872-7858, www.mec.ca, 10am-7pm Mon.-Wed., 10am-9pm Thurs.-Fri., 9am-6pm Sat., 10am-5pm Sun.

VINTAGE AND SECONDHAND
My Sister's Closet
Shopping at this Yaletown "eco-thrift" boutique supports a good cause. At My Sister's Closet, which the local Battered Women's Support Services organization operates, proceeds from sales help fund violence prevention and intervention services. Allow some time to browse; this corner store is crammed with racks of women's secondhand clothing, from pants to coats to formal wear, along with some jewelry, shoes, bags, and a small selection of men's garments.

MAP 3: 1092 Seymour St., 604/687-0770, www.bwss.org, 10am-6pm Mon.-Thurs., 10am-7pm Fri., 11am-7pm Sat., noon-6pm Sun.

SPECIALTY FOOD AND DRINK
Legacy Liquor Store
British Columbia's largest privately owned liquor store, Legacy Liquor Store, in the Olympic Village, has an excellent selection of BC wines from more than 80 wineries around the province. The knowledgeable staff can help you choose, whether you're looking for a gift or for a bottle to sip with your bread-and-cheese picnic. In this 8,600-square-foot (800-square-m) store, they stock plenty of BC craft spirits, and their selection of 1,000-plus beers includes many local microbrews. It holds periodic wine-tastings and other special events.

MAP 3: 1633 Manitoba St., 604/331-7900, http://legacyliquorstore.com, 10am-11pm daily

Granville Island   Map 4

This former industrial district, across False Creek from downtown, is one of Vancouver's most popular attractions. Technically a peninsula, the 38-acre (15-ha) island is home to more than 300 businesses, including **art galleries** and **theaters,** as well as the popular **Granville Island Public Market.** A few industrial elements remain, including Ocean Concrete, whose brightly painted cement trucks chug around the island.

The island and the Public Market get packed with visitors in the afternoons and on weekends, especially on sunny summer days. Take a ferry from downtown, cycle, or walk onto the island rather than driving, if you can.

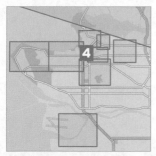

TOP SIGHTS

- Most Photogenic Food Destination: **Granville Island Public Market** (page 114)
- Best Hidden Art Spot: **Railspur Alley** (page 115)

TOP NIGHTLIFE

- Best Way to Laugh Yourself Silly: **Vancouver Theatre Sports League** (page 119)

TOP ARTS AND CULTURE

- Where to Find Eagles, Ravens, and Other Creatures: **Eagle Spirit Gallery** (page 121)
- Best Variety of Canadian Art: **Federation of Canadian Artists Gallery** (page 121)

TOP SHOPS

- Where to Channel Harry Potter: **Granville Island Broom Co.** (page 124)

GETTING THERE AND AROUND

- Bus lines: 50
- Ferries: Aquabus, False Creek Ferries

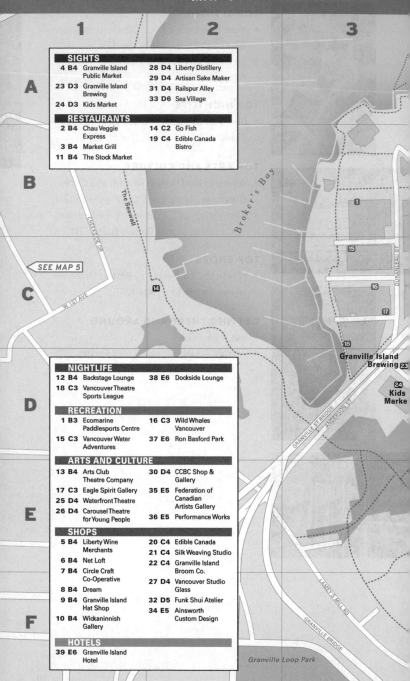

1   **2**   **3**

SIGHTS
4 B4	Granville Island Public Market	**28 D4**	Liberty Distillery
23 D3	Granville Island Brewing	**29 D4**	Artisan Sake Maker
		31 D4	Railspur Alley
24 D3	Kids Market	**33 D6**	Sea Village

RESTAURANTS
2 B4	Chau Veggie Express	**14 C2**	Go Fish
3 B4	Market Grill	**19 C4**	Edible Canada Bistro
11 B4	The Stock Market		

A

B

Broker's Bay

The Seawall

CREEKSIDE DR

← SEE MAP 5

C

W 1ST AVE

14

DURANLEAU ST

1

15

16

17

18

Granville Island Brewing **23**

24 Kids Marke

NIGHTLIFE
12 B4	Backstage Lounge	**38 E6**	Dockside Lounge
18 C3	Vancouver Theatre Sports League		

RECREATION
1 B3	Ecomarine Paddlesports Centre	**16 C3**	Wild Whales Vancouver
15 C3	Vancouver Water Adventures	**37 E6**	Ron Basford Park

ARTS AND CULTURE
13 B4	Arts Club Theatre Company	**30 D4**	CCBC Shop & Gallery
17 C3	Eagle Spirit Gallery	**35 E5**	Federation of Canadian Artists Gallery
25 D4	Waterfront Theatre		
26 D4	Carousel Theatre for Young People	**36 E5**	Performance Works

SHOPS
5 B4	Liberty Wine Merchants	**20 C4**	Edible Canada
		21 C4	Silk Weaving Studio
6 B4	Net Loft	**22 C4**	Granville Island Broom Co.
7 B4	Circle Craft Co-Operative		
8 B4	Dream	**27 D4**	Vancouver Studio Glass
9 B4	Granville Island Hat Shop	**32 D5**	Funk Shui Atelier
10 B4	Wickaninnish Gallery	**34 E5**	Ainsworth Custom Design

HOTELS
39 E6	Granville Island Hotel	

D

E

F

GRANVILLE ST BRIDGE

ANDERSON ST

LAMEY'S MILL RD

GRANVILLE BRIDGE

Granville Loop Park

4

5

2

3

**Granville Island
Public Market**

4

12

13

5

11

7 9 8 10

20

19

21

99

**GRANVILLE
ISLAND**

George
Wainborn
Park

The Seawall

SEE MAP 3

False Creek

22

27

**Liberty
Distillery**

**Artisan Sake
Maker**

26

28

29

**Railspur
Alley**

31

32

30

33 Sea Village

34

35

38

39

36

37

Sutcliffe
Park

Ron Basford
Park

The Seawall

Alder Bay

FAIRVIEW

SEE MAP 6

© MOON.COM

0   100 yds

0   100 m

DISTANCE ACROSS MAP
Approximate: 0.6 mi or 1 km

...attraction is the year-round indoor Granville Island Public Market. It's a food lover's heaven, where artistically arranged fruits garnish the produce stalls, and you can nibble on charcuterie, cheeses, pastries, fudge, and other treats. While food vendors predominate among the nearly 50 stands, some stalls sell jewelry, leather goods, and other locally made crafts. There's no particular order to the merchandise, though, so plan to wander, browse, and snack.

Granville Island was once known as Industrial Island for the sawmills, factories, and other businesses that operated here. The buildings that house the market were converted from their former uses in the 1970s.

Start at **Blue Parrot Espresso Bar** (604/688-5127, www.blueparrotcoffee.com) for java with a water view. Sample the unexpectedly addictive **salmon candy** (cured, salty-sweet fish snacks) at any of the seafood counters, or line up with the locals for house-made charcuterie at **Oyama Sausage** (604/327-7407, www.oyamasausage.ca) or nut-studded grape loaves at **Terra Breads Bakery Café** (604/685-3102, www.terrabreads.com). You might hope that the kids won't notice

Granville Island Public Market

Granville Island Public Market

Ecomarine Paddlesports Centre

Granville Island Hat Shop

Eagle Spirit Gallery

Backstage Lounge

Edible Canada Bistro

False Creek

GRANVILLE ST BRIDGE

DURANLEAU ST

ANDERSON ST

OLD BRIDGE ST

JOHNSTON ST

© MOON.COM

longtime favorite **Lee's Donuts** (604/685-4021, www.leesdonuts.ca), at least until it's time for dessert.

In summer, the **Granville Island Farmers Market** (11am-4pm Thurs. June-Sept.) sets up once a week in front of the Public Market, bringing more local farmers and artisans to the island. At any time, musicians and other entertainers might perform outside the market.

You can pick up picnic fixings or prepared foods in the Public Market and eat outdoors behind the market building. If it's too crowded there, take your picnic to the opposite end of the island and enjoy it on the grass overlooking the water in **Ron Basford Park.**

For a behind-the-scenes look at the Public Market, book the two-hour Granville Island Market Tour with **Vancouver Foodie Tours** (http://foodietours.ca, 10:30am daily, check for additional tour times, $65). You'll learn the stories of many of the vendors and their products and sample 20 different foods and drinks.

The Public Market is located along False Creek, facing the downtown skyline. As you walk onto the island on Anderson Street, continue till the road forks, then bear left;

the market is one block ahead. The market is busiest on weekend afternoons, especially when the weather is nice.

MAP 4: 1689 Johnston St., 604/666-6655, http://granvilleisland.com, 9am-7pm daily, free

NEARBY:

- Eat your way across the country at **Edible Canada Bistro** (page 117).
- Check out the local music scene at the **Backstage Lounge** (page 119).
- Kayak around the island with **Ecomarine Paddlesports Centre** (page 120).
- Browse museum-quality indigenous art at **Eagle Spirit Gallery** (page 121).
- Find almost anything you'd wear on your head at the **Granville Island Hat Shop** (page 123).

Railspur Alley

✪ Railspur Alley

Explore this pedestrian-only cobblestone lane near the center of Granville Island for its artist studios and shops. Go inside the petite studios, where many of the artists welcome you to watch and chat while they work. Look for textile weavers,

115

leather crafters, woodworkers, and even a sake maker in the lane's low buildings.

MAP 4: Between Cartwright St. and Old Bridge St.

Liberty Distillery

Liberty Distillery brews small batches of vodka, gin, and whiskey in their 140- and 220-liter (36- and 58-gallon) copper-pot stills. Sample their handcrafted products in the cocktail lounge with its elaborately carved bar. Listen for the sound of a steam whistle announcing the start of happy hour (3pm-6pm Mon.-Thurs.). On weekends, Liberty offers a tour (11:30am and 1:30pm Sat.-Sun., $10) of their facilities, where you can learn about the processes of mashing, fermenting, and distilling—with samples, of course. Tours are limited to 10 people, so reserve ahead.

MAP 4: 1494 Old Bridge St., 604/558-1998, www.thelibertydistillery. com, 11am-9pm daily

Artisan Sake Maker

At the tiny shop that houses Artisan Sake Maker, Vancouver's only local producer of Japanese rice wine, step up to the counter, where the staff explain how sake is brewed. They offer tastings of a single sake ($2) or samples of three ($5). In business since 2007, the company that Japan-born sake maker Masa Shiroki founded brews several varieties of sake, including sparkling sakes. Shiroki works with local farmers to grow the rice for his sakes here in British Columbia.

MAP 4: 1339 Railspur Alley, 604/685-7253, www.artisansakemaker. com, 11:30am-6pm daily

Sea Village

Sea Village is a community of colorful floating homes, each set on its own dock on False Creek. They're private residences, but you can look at the area from the walkway above and imagine what it would be like to live here on the water. The entrance to Sea Village is off Johnston Street, on the west side of the Granville Island Hotel.

MAP 4: Off Johnston St., near intersection with Cartwright St.

Kids Market

On Granville Island, youngsters have their own marketplace, the multilevel Kids Market, a family-friendly mini mall where two dozen cute shops sell toys, games, candy, and clothing. Note the children's-only doorway at the entrance, then walk around to the back of the bright yellow building and notice the painted eyes looking down at you from a mural above. The kids can run around in the Adventure Zone, an indoor playground, or outside in the splash park (late May-early Sept.).

MAP 4: 1496 Cartwright St., 604/689-8447, www.kidsmarket.ca, 10am-6pm daily, free

Granville Island Brewing

Granville Island Brewing started producing craft beers in 1984. They make a wide variety, including their Island Lager and English Bay Pale Ale, but good choices to try are the more limited small batch series, like the Belgian-style Saison, Kellerbier Unfiltered, and West Coast Pale Ale.

Although most of their beer is now made in other locations, you can take the 30-minute tour

(11:30am, 1:30pm, 2:30pm, 4pm, and 5:30pm daily, $12) of the original island brewery, which provides an education in beer making. The tour wraps up with 5-ounce (140-ml) samples of three of the beers. You can also have a drink in their taproom (11am-9pm daily), or pick up beer to go, along with brewery-themed merchandise, in the retail store (10am-9pm daily).

MAP 4: 1441 Cartwright St., 604/687-2739, www.gib.ca, 11am-9pm daily

Restaurants

PRICE KEY

$ Entrées less than CAD$15
$$ Entrées CAD$15-25
$$$ Entrées more than CAD$25

Edible Canada Bistro

MODERN CANADIAN
Edible Canada Bistro $$

Opposite the Public Market, Edible Canada Bistro creates contemporary dishes with ingredients from around British Columbia and across Canada. It's always busy with tourists, but locals appreciate the Canadian menu. At midday, try duck confit poutine or eggs Benedict with boar belly bacon. For supper, find plates like tagliatelle with braised lamb or wild salmon with fresh peas. The restaurant regularly partners with Canadian chefs to host special dinners. Adjacent to the window-lined restaurant, which has an open kitchen and seasonal patio seating, the retail outlet sells Canadian-made gourmet products.

MAP 4: 1596 Johnston St., 604/682-6681, www.ediblecanada.com, 11am-8:30pm Mon.-Fri., 9am-8:30pm Sat.-Sun.

SEAFOOD
Go Fish $

Like seafood? Then go fish—at Go Fish, a busy waterfront takeout shack. Choose fish-and-chips made from cod, salmon, or halibut; a wild salmon sandwich; an oyster po' boy; or fish tacos. Expect line-ups on sunny days. It's a five-minute walk along the Seawall from Granville Island; look for the dockside sign that says "Public Fish Sales." Go Fish is opposite the docks.

MAP 4: 1505 W. 1st Ave., 604/730-5040, 11:30am-7pm Tues.-Fri., noon-7pm Sat.-Sun.

VIETNAMESE
Chau Veggie Express $

Chau Veggie Express serves Vietnamese-inspired vegetarian and vegan dishes. The short menu at this to-go counter inside the Granville Island Public Market features several soups, fresh spring rolls, and noodle or rice bowls layered with different combinations of vegetables, tofu, and sauces, from vegan "fish" sauce to spicy peanut satay.

MAP 4: Granville Island Public Market, 1689 Johnston St., 778/379-9508, www.chowatchau.ca, 9am-7pm daily

QUICK BITES
Market Grill $

A takeout stall facing the water at the back of the Granville Island Public Market, the friendly Market Grill cooks up burgers with beef, chicken, and veggie options. The local favorite is the salmon burger, with sockeye piled high on a homemade bun. Simple but good, the burgers come with either thick-cut fries or Caesar salad. Market Grill also serves hot dogs and breakfast options (bacon and eggs, breakfast sandwiches).

MAP 4: Granville Island Public Market, 1689 Johnston St., 604/689-1918, 8am-7pm daily

The Stock Market $

Inside the Granville Island Public Market, the Stock Market prepares three kinds of homemade soup daily. On the rotating menu, one soup is fish-based (like the tasty wild salmon chowder), one is meat-based, and the third is vegetarian. Each bowl is served with a slab of bread and makes for a quick lunch. Although the stall has no seating, you can sit at tables nearby or take your food to a bench outdoors.

MAP 4: Granville Island Public Market, 1689 Johnston St., 604/687-2433, http://thestockmarket.ca, 8am-7pm daily

Nightlife

CRAFT BEER
Dockside Lounge

At the east end of Granville Island, connected to the Granville Island Hotel, Dockside Brewing Company has been making craft beer since 2001. Among their long-running classics are the Cartwright Pale Ale and Johnston Street Pilsner. For brews with water views, take a seat in their Dockside Lounge, which looks out across False Creek, a perfect spot for drinks on a sunny afternoon. Even if you sit inside, you can check out the vistas through the expansive windows.

MAP 4: Granville Island Hotel, 1253 Johnston St., 604/685-7070, www.docksidevancouver.com, 11:30am-11pm Sun.-Thurs., 11:30am-midnight Fri.-Sat.

the patio at Dockside Lounge

LIVE MUSIC
Backstage Lounge

In the same building as the Granville Island Stage, next to the Public Market, the Backstage Lounge overlooks the water and city skyline. Several nights a week, this cozy pub hosts an eclectic lineup of live music, featuring local artists performing everything from indie rock to world music to open-mic jams.

MAP 4: 1585 Johnston St., 604/687-1354, www. thebackstagelounge.com, noon-2am Tues.-Sat., noon-midnight Sun.-Mon., cover $5-15

COMEDY
✪ Vancouver Theatre Sports League

Established in 1980, the popular Vancouver Theatre Sports League performs always-entertaining improv shows at their cabaret-style waterside theater on Granville Island. Among recent productions are *Firecracker!* with an all-women improv cast; *OR Tinder—Swipe Right Comedy*, a send-up of Vancouver's dating scene; and *Laugh Till Your Face Hurts,* a two-team improv competition. Most shows have mature themes and aren't appropriate for kids. Prices vary depending on the day and time of the show, with the most expensive performances on Friday-Saturday evenings. Have a drink before or after the performance in the lounge overlooking False Creek.

MAP 4: 1502 Duranleau St., 604/738-7013, www.vtsl.com, showtimes vary Tues.-Sun., adults $16-27, seniors and students $11-21

Recreation

PARKS
Ron Basford Park

The grassy green space known as Ron Basford Park occupies a hilly knoll at the eastern end of Granville Island, between the Granville Island Hotel and Performance Works Theatre. Take a break to sit on the lawn and enjoy the views of False Creek and the city skyline. The park's outdoor amphitheater hosts occasional concerts.

The park is named for the Honorable Stanley Ronald Basford, a Member of Parliament and cabinet minister. Basford was instrumental in transforming the island into its current lively collection of studios, shops, markets, and theaters, earning him the nickname "Mr. Granville Island."

MAP 4: Eastern end of Cartwright St. and Johnston St., dawn-dusk daily

WHALE-WATCHING
Wild Whales Vancouver

Wild Whales Vancouver offers whale-watching trips leaving from Granville Island spring-fall. Depending on where the whales are swimming on a particular day, the boats will take you from False Creek into English Bay and the Strait of Georgia, heading either for the Gulf

Islands or the San Juan Islands in Washington State, on trips lasting 3-7 hours. The on-board guides will help you spot orcas, Pacific gray whales, humpback whales, and minke whales; you might see seals and various birds along the way. While regulations limit how close you can get to the whales, you'll usually come near enough to see them swimming and spouting. A telephoto lens will help you get the best photos. Boats typically carry 23-35 passengers and have restroom facilities. They also offer tours on more adventurous inflatable Zodiacs.

MAP 4: 1806 Mast Tower Rd., 604/699-2011, www.whalesvancouver. com, Apr.-Oct., standard tours adults $145, seniors and students $120, ages 3-12 $95, ages 0-2 $30, Zodiac tours $160 pp

KAYAKING AND STAND-UP PADDLEBOARDING

Ecomarine Paddlesports Centre

From the sheltered waters around Granville Island you get great views of the downtown skyline, making it a good spot to set out in a kayak or on a stand-up paddleboard (SUP). Ecomarine Paddlesports Centre rents kayaks and SUPs and offers guided kayak and SUP tours. Their last rentals on Granville Island typically go out at 6pm (5pm in Sept.); call to confirm seasonal hours. Be alert for boat traffic.

MAP 4: 1668 Duranleau St., 604/689-7575 or 888/425-2925, www. ecomarine.com, 10am-8pm daily mid-May-Aug., 11am-7pm Tues.-Sun. Sept., paddleboard rental 1-3 hours $25-45, kayak rental 2 hours-all day $45-99

kayak rental on Granville Island

Vancouver Water Adventures

Vancouver Water Adventures rents kayaks and SUPs, offers tours, and rents Jet Skis. One of the most popular tours is "Light the Night," a 90-minute excursion where you explore at dusk by glowing lighted paddleboard ($75) or kayak (single $85, double $105). In addition to this branch on Granville Island, seasonal rental locations are on English Bay Beach and Kitsilano Beach.

MAP 4: 1812 Boatlift Ln., 604/736-5155, www.vancouverwateradventures. com, hours vary by season May-Sept., paddleboard rental $20 per hour, kayak rental $25-35 per hour

Arts and Culture

GALLERIES

✪ Eagle Spirit Gallery

The large museum-like Eagle Spirit Gallery specializes in Northwest Coast indigenous art. Stone carvings, sculptures, totem poles, wood carvings, masks, and paintings by First Nations and Inuit artists are among the original high-quality works on view.

MAP 4: 1803 Maritime Mews, 604/801-5277 or 888/801-5277, www. eaglespiritgallery.com, 11am-5pm daily, free

Federation of Canadian Artists Gallery

✪ Federation of Canadian Artists Gallery

Founded in 1941 by several noted Canadian landscape painters from the Group of Seven, the Federation of Canadian Artists now has more than 2,000 members, including both established and emerging artists. In a large corner space at the east end of Cartwright Street, their Granville Island gallery exhibits work by member artists from across Canada.

MAP 4: 1241 Cartwright St., 604/681-8534, www.artists.ca, 10am-5pm Mon.-Sat., 10am-3pm Sun. May-Sept., 10am-4pm Tues.-Sun. Oct.-Apr., free

CCBC Shop & Gallery

Located in a cute little house, the CCBC Shop & Gallery shows work by members of the Craft Council of British Columbia. Look for pieces in ceramic, glass, wood, textiles, and other media. They stock a large selection of handcrafted jewelry.

MAP 4: 1386 Cartwright St., 604/687-7270, www.craftcouncilbc. ca, 10am-6pm daily May-Aug., 10:30am-5:30pm daily Sept.-Apr., free

THEATER

Arts Club Theatre Company

Vancouver's top repertory theater and the largest theater company in western Canada, the Arts Club Theatre Company performs on three stages around the city. On Granville Island, their shows are held at the Granville Island Stage, next to the Public Market. At this 440-seat venue, the Arts Club produces new plays, contemporary works, and eclectic musicals. Recent productions have included *Mom's the Word* (from a Vancouver-based playwrights' collective), Morris Panych's *The Shoplifters*, and *Avenue Q*, the racy puppet musical.

MAP 4: 1585 Johnston St., 604/687-1644, www.artsclub.com, $29-53

Carousel Theatre for Young People

If you're traveling with kids, see what's on stage at Granville Island's Carousel Theatre for Young People, a theater and troupe that produces shows for toddlers through teens. Some productions take place on their own small stage, while others are held in the larger Waterfront Theatre across the street or at other nearby venues; confirm the location when you buy your tickets. Recent productions have included *Sultans of the Street*, by Indo-Canadian playwright Anusree Roy; *The Rainbow Fish*, adapted from the popular children's book; and *Dr. Seuss' The Cat in the Hat*.

MAP 4: 1411 Cartwright St., 604/685-6217, www.carouseltheatre. ca, adults $25-35, seniors and students $21-29, ages 17 and under $12.50-18

Performance Works

The building that houses Performance Works, a theater space used by a variety of performers and companies, including the Vancouver Fringe Festival in September, was once a machine shop, built in the 1920s. Nowadays, it no longer resembles its industrial origins; the performance area can be configured for auditorium or cabaret-style seating for 150-200 people.

MAP 4: 1218 Cartwright St., 604/687-3020, http://gitd.ca, prices vary

Waterfront Theatre

Confusingly, the Waterfront Theatre isn't actually located on the waterfront, but this 224-seat auditorium-style performance space hosts festivals, theater events, and other performances throughout the year. It's a mainstage venue for the annual Vancouver Fringe Festival in September.

MAP 4: 1412 Cartwright St., 604/685-1731, http://gitd.ca, prices vary

Festivals and Events

Vancouver Fringe Festival

For the first two weeks in September, the Vancouver Fringe Festival takes over Granville Island and other stages around town with innovative, quirky, and often surprising theater, comedy, puppetry, and storytelling performances. The Waterfront Theatre and Performance Works on Granville Island host some of the larger performances.

Various locations: www. vancouverfringe.com, Sept.

Vancouver Writers Fest

The Vancouver Writers Fest, a week of readings, lectures, and other literary events, features more than 100 authors from across Canada and abroad. Most of the festival events, held the third week of October, take place on Granville Island.

Granville Island: www.writersfest. bc.ca, Oct.

Shops

SHOPPING MALLS

Net Loft

Opposite the Public Market is the Net Loft, an indoor mini mall in a former warehouse building. Explore its hallways, a warren of tiny shops and art galleries, for gifts and unique souvenirs, including jewelry, kitchenware, hats, and indigenous art.

MAP 4: 1666 Johnston St., no phone, 10am-7pm daily Apr.-Dec., 10am-6pm daily Jan.-Mar.

CLOTHING AND ACCESSORIES

Funk Shui Atelier

In this light and open Railspur Alley studio, the textile artists at Funk Shui Atelier craft handmade hats, scarves, and other wearable or decorative fabric items. You can often watch the artists as they work.

MAP 4: 1375 Railspur Alley, 604/684-5327, www.funkshuifelt. com, 10:30am-5:30pm daily May-Sept., 11am-5pm daily Oct.-Apr.

Granville Island Hat Shop

At the Granville Island Hat Shop, inside the Net Loft building, you can find almost anything to wear on your head, for both men and women. Stacks and stacks of hats line the shelves, and the staff can help you find your best style. They craft custom hats and do hat repair and restoration.

MAP 4: Net Loft, 1666 Johnston St., 604/683-4280, www.thehatshop.ca, 10am-7pm daily Apr.-Dec., 10am-6pm daily Jan.-Mar.

Dream

Dream carries an eclectic assortment of locally made fashions, jewelry, and accessories for women in its compact Net Loft shop. Crafted by Vancouver designers, their distinctive clothing, which ranges from casual to dressy, isn't on the racks at your standard suburban mall.

MAP 4: Net Loft, 1666 Johnston St., 604/683-6930, www.dreamvancouver. com, 10am-7pm daily Apr.-Dec., 10am-6pm daily Jan.-Mar.

Silk Weaving Studio

It's worth hunting for Silk Weaving Studio, hidden in a corrugated metal-clad bungalow near the waterfront, between the Public Market and Ocean Concrete. You can frequently watch the weavers at work, creating handwoven scarves, shawls, and other garments and textile pieces on their sizable looms.

MAP 4: 1531 Johnston St., 604/687-7455, www.silkweavingstudio. com, 10am-5pm daily

Silk Weaving Studio

DESIGN AND GIFTS

✪ Granville Island Broom Co.

Harry Potter and his Quidditch team would covet the handmade sweepers from the Granville Island Broom Co. Mary and Sarah Schwieger, the sisters who own the shop, craft brooms using traditional Shaker methods. Check out the "marriage brooms" with their entwined brushes, or the only-in-Canada versions with handles made of hockey sticks.

MAP 4: 1406 Old Bridge St., 604/629-1141, www.broomcompany.com, 10am-6pm daily

Ainsworth Custom Design

Part metalworking studio (specializing in furniture) and part gift shop, Ainsworth Custom Design carries whimsical one-of-a-kind items such as magnets, cards, prints, and T-shirts.

MAP 4: 1243 Cartwright St., 604/682-8838, www.ainsworthcustomdesign.com, 10am-6pm Mon.-Fri., noon-6pm Sat., noon-5pm Sun.

Circle Craft Co-Operative

In the Net Loft, spacious Circle Craft Co-Operative is a good place to browse for handmade jewelry, leatherwork, ceramics, and other work by more than 150 BC craftspeople, with items attractively displayed on wooden tables and shelves.

MAP 4: Net Loft, 1666 Johnston St., 604/669-8021, www.circlecraft.net, 10am-7pm daily Apr.-Dec., 10am-6pm daily Jan.-Mar.

Granville Island Broom Co.

Circle Craft Co-Operative

Vancouver Studio Glass

Watch the glassblowers at work at Vancouver Studio Glass, a glass-blowing studio and shop that sells colorful glass pieces of various sizes. If you're interested in learning about glassblowing yourself, ask about their 30-60-minute workshops, offered by appointment only, for adults and teens ages 14 and up.

MAP 4: 1440 Old Bridge St., 604/681-6730, http://vancouverstudioglass.com, 10am-6pm Mon.-Sat., 11am-5pm Sun.

Wickaninnish Gallery

The compact Wickaninnish Gallery sells cards, prints, scarves, and other moderately priced items with First Nations designs.

MAP 4: Net Loft, 1666 Johnston St., 604/681-1057, www.wickaninnishgallery.com, 10am-7pm daily Apr.-Dec., 10am-6pm daily Jan.-Mar.

SPECIALTY FOOD AND DRINK

Edible Canada

Looking for a souvenir for a foodie friend or an edible memory from your Vancouver visit? Edible Canada, opposite the Granville Island Public Market and connected to the restaurant of the same name, stocks locally produced salts, jams, vinegars, and more from around British Columbia and across Canada. The shop is decorated with canoes and other Canadiana.

MAP 4: 1596 Johnston St., 604/682-6675, www.ediblecanada.com, 10am-6pm Mon.-Fri., 10am-7pm Sat.-Sun.

Liberty Wine Merchants

A good source of wines from BC and elsewhere is Liberty Wine Merchants, near the Granville Island Public Market. The staff can introduce you to the region's wines and advise you about local labels. They have additional locations in the Point Grey neighborhood and on the East Side.

MAP 4: 1660 Johnston St., 604/602-1120, www.libertywinemerchants.com, 9:30am-8pm Mon.-Thurs., 9:30am-8:30pm Fri., 9am-8:30pm Sat., 9am-8pm Sun.

Kitsilano   Map 5

Across the Burrard Bridge from downtown and within walking distance of Granville Island, Kitsilano (aka "Kits") was Vancouver's hippie community in the 1960s and 1970s, and where the environmental organization Greenpeace got its start. Today, this upscale neighborhood, with a mix of residential and commercial areas, has a **great beach** and a large saltwater pool, both with views of the city skyline. The district has several museums in waterfront Vanier Park, including the well-designed **Museum of Vancouver,** and lots of **shops,** restaurants, and cafés, particularly along **West 4th Avenue,** between Burrard and Balsam Streets.

TOP SIGHTS
- Best Way to Time-Travel: **Museum of Vancouver** (page 130)

TOP RECREATION

- Sportiest Stretch of Sand: **Kitsilano Beach** (page 136)
- Most Scenic Spot to Swim: **Kitsilano Pool** (page 137)

TOP SHOPS
- Best Bookstore for Kids and Teens: **Kidsbooks** (page 139)
- Easiest Way to Make Friends with Cheese: **Les Amis du Fromage** (page 140)
- Best Travel Store: **Wanderlust** (page 141)

GETTING THERE AND AROUND
- Bus lines: 2, 4, 7, 9, 14, 16, 84, 99
- Ferries: Aquabus, False Creek Ferries

1 2 3

0   300 yds
0   300 m
DISTANCE ACROSS MAP
Approximate: 2.6 mi or 4.2 km

A

English Bay

B

Jericho Beach Park

POINT GREY RD

SEE MAP 6

Tat
P...

W 4TH AVE

Mcbride Park

C

HIGHBURY ST
ALMA ST
DUNBAR ST
COLLINGWOOD ST
WATERLOO ST
BLENHEIM ST
TRUTCH ST
BALACLAVA ST

13 W BROADWAY

W 10TH AVE

COURTENAY ST
CAMOSUN ST
CROWN ST
WALLACE ST

D

Almond Park

DUNBAR ST

POINT GREY

W 16TH AVE

Carnarvon Park

E

F

**DUNBAR-
SOUTHLANDS**

© MOON.COM

4   **5**   **6**

Vancouver Maritime Museum

Vanier Park

Kitsilano Beach

MCNICOLL AVE

Museum of Vancouver

Kitsilano Beach Park

H. R. MacMillan Space Centre

WHYTE AVE

CREELMAN AVE

CHESTNUT ST

ARBUTUS ST

POINT GREY RD

BURRARD ST

CORNWALL AVE

SEE MAP 4

YORK AVE

Arbutus Greenway

W 1ST AVE

KITSILANO

W 2ND AVE

MAPLE ST

W 3RD AVE

W 4TH AVE

BURRARD ST

PINE ST

FIR ST

W 5TH AVE

CYPRESS ST

W 6TH AVE

STEPHENS ST

TRAFALGAR ST

W 7TH AVE

VINE ST

YEW ST

ARBUTUS ST

W 8TH AVE

W BROADWAY

W 10TH AVE

Connaught Park

W 12TH AVE

W 13TH AVE

W 14TH AVE

VALLEY DR

W 15TH AVE

W 16TH AVE

ARBUTUS RIDGE

W 18TH AVE

W 19TH AVE

W 20TH AVE

W 21ST AVE

W 22ND AVE

W 23RD AVE

Trafalgar Park

OLIVER CRESCENT

ARBUTUS ST

W KING EDWARD AVE

SIGHTS

1	A6	Vancouver Maritime Museum	3	A6	H. R. MacMillan Space Centre
2	A6	Museum of Vancouver			

RESTAURANTS

9	B5	Mak N Ming	21	C5	Turf
10	B5	Café Zen	24	C5	Maenam
12	B6	AnnaLena	28	C6	Beaucoup Bakery & Café
16	C5	Au Comptoir	30	D4	Mr. Red Café
18	C5	O5 Tea Bar	31	D4	Kitsilano Farmers Market
19	C5	Bishop's			

NIGHTLIFE

8	B5	Local Public Eatery	13	C2	The Wolf and Hound
11	B5	Corduroy			

RECREATION

6	B5	Kitsilano Pool	25	C5	Arbutus Greenway
7	B5	Kitsilano Beach			

ARTS AND CULTURE

4	A6	Bard on the Beach	

SHOPS

14	C3	The Travel Bug	23	C5	Wanderlust
15	C4	Kidsbooks	26	C6	Les Amis du Fromage
17	C5	Gravity Pope	27	C6	Comor Sports
20	C5	Silk Road Tea	29	D4	Pulp Fiction Books
22	C5	Two of Hearts			

HOTELS

5	B4	Corkscrew Inn	

Sights

✪ Museum of Vancouver

Its building resembles a flying saucer that might have landed in Kitsilano's Vanier Park, but this city museum's unique structure, created by architect Gerald Hamilton, was actually designed to recall a traditional hat of the Haida First Nations people. Inside the Museum of Vancouver, the exhibition spaces are no less distinctive.

The permanent galleries take you through Vancouver's past, from its indigenous heritage to early settlement days to the hippie era of the 1960s, with participatory activities that bring the city's history to life. Listen to recordings of First Nations people discussing their families, punch up some tunes on the 1950s jukebox, or dress for the Summer of Love in macramé. The sometimes controversial temporary exhibitions explore social phenomena from happiness to sex. The museum hosts lectures, workshops, and social events that are as engaging as the exhibits themselves.

The **Vanier Park Explore Pass** (adults $42.50, seniors, students, and ages 5-18 $36.50) includes admission to the Museum of Vancouver and the adjacent H. R. MacMillan Space Centre, as well as the nearby Vancouver Maritime Museum.

It's a half-mile (0.8-km) walk along the Seawall from Kitsilano Beach to the museum; from

Museum of Vancouver

Granville Island, it's just over a mile (1.6 km) along the water and through Vanier Park. Either route is a lovely seaside stroll. To reach the museum by bus, take bus 2 from Burrard Street downtown into Kitsilano; get off at the corner of Cornwall Avenue and Chestnut Street, where it's a short walk toward the water to the museum. Or take False Creek Ferries (604/684-7781, www.granvilleislandferries.bc.ca) to Vanier Park from Granville Island or downtown.

MAP 5: 1100 Chestnut St., 604/736-4431, www.museumofvancouver.ca, 10am-5pm Sun.-Wed., 10am-8pm Thurs., 10am-9pm Fri.-Sat., adults $20.50, seniors and students $17.25, ages 11-18 $13.75, ages 5-11 $9.75

H. R. MacMillan Space Centre

In the same building as the Museum of Vancouver, the H. R. MacMillan Space Centre, the city's planetarium, has galleries of space exhibits to explore and astronomy (and other space-themed) shows throughout the day. Presentations might let you experience "A Day in Space," explore "Seven Wonders of the Universe," or take a virtual expedition by "Surfing the Solar System."

On Saturday evenings, the Space Centre's Gordon MacMillan Southam Observatory (604/738-2855; Sat.; adults $14, seniors and students $11, ages 5-11 $8.50) is also open for a planetarium show (7:30pm and 9pm) and guided stargazing (7:30pm-11:30pm) through the 20-inch (50-cm) telescope. If you come only for the stargazing, admission is by donation.

MAP 5: 1100 Chestnut St., 604/738-7827, www.spacecentre.ca, 10am-5pm daily late June-early Sept., 10am-3pm Mon.-Fri., 10am-5pm Sat., noon-5pm Sun. early Sept.-late June, adults $19.50, seniors and ages 12-18 $16.50, ages 5-11 $14

Vancouver Maritime Museum

Vancouver Maritime Museum

Built in BC in the 1920s, the historic Arctic-exploring schooner *St. Roch* is now the centerpiece of the family-friendly Vancouver Maritime Museum, an A-frame building on the waterfront in Vanier Park. The *St. Roch* was the first to sail the Northwest Passage from west to east and the first to circumnavigate North America, when it traveled from Vancouver to Halifax via the Panama Canal in 1950.

Climb aboard the *St. Roch* and learn more about its Arctic adventures. You can clamber around the wooden decks, explore the ship's compact cabins, and even get behind the captain's wheel as you discover the boat's story. The museum has other hands-on exhibits designed for kids, from piloting a submersible to talking with a model shipbuilder while he works, as well as changing exhibitions about the Pacific Northwest and Arctic maritime history.

Outside the museum is a 100-foot (30-m) **totem pole** that Kwakwaka'wakw First Nations artist Mungo Martin carved to mark British Columbia's centennial in 1958.

To get to the museum, take bus 2 from Burrard Street downtown to the corner of Cornwall Avenue and Chestnut Street in Kitsilano. Or take **False Creek Ferries** (604/684-7781, www.granvilleislandferries.bc.ca) to Vanier Park from Granville Island or downtown.

MAP 5: 1905 Ogden St., 604/257-8300, www.vancouvermaritimemuseum. com, 10am-5pm Fri.-Wed., 10am-8pm Thurs. late May-early Sept., 10am-5pm Tues.-Wed. and Fri.-Sat., 10am-8pm Thurs., noon-5pm Sun. early Sept.-late May, adults $13.50, seniors and students $11, ages 6-18 $10, by donation 5pm-8pm Thurs.

Restaurants

PRICE KEY

$ Entrées less than CAD$15
$$ Entrées CAD$15-25
$$$ Entrées more than CAD$25

MODERN CANADIAN

AnnaLena $$$

Though it's named for the chef's grandmothers, there's nothing old-fashioned about AnnaLena, a smart Kitsilano bistro with white walls, black banquettes, and west coast wood trimmings. The modern menu, designed to share, might include smoked tuna with blood orange ponzu, buttermilk fried chicken, and halibut with hazelnut miso and fermented green garlic. Sip local microbrews, BC wines, and fun cocktails.

MAP 5: 1809 W. 1st Ave., 778/379-4052, www.annalena.ca, 5pm-midnight daily

Bishop's $$$

Chef-owner John Bishop helped pioneer Vancouver's farm-to-table movement long before the 100-mile diet was on the lips of every locavore. At Bishop's namesake classy, white-tablecloth restaurant, adorned with works by local artists, the polished staff can guide you to seasonal suppers that might start with seared scallops served with a beet and bulgur salad, before continuing with sea bass with tomato marmalade or pork tenderloin with prawns, peas, and polenta. Finish with black tea ice cream paired with a shortbread biscuit or "death by chocolate" with sour cherry coulis.

MAP 5: 2183 W. 4th Ave., 604/738-2025, www.bishopsonline.com, 5:30pm-11pm Tues.-Sat.

Mak N Ming $$$

Mak N Ming is the brainchild of Chef Makoto (Mak) Ono and pastry

artistic plating at Mak N Ming

chef Amanda Cheng (her Chinese name is Ming). With fewer than 30 seats in a spare space up the hill from Kitsilano Beach, the duo concocts ambitious fixed-price menus nightly, mixing Asian flavors and regional ingredients. Look for inventions like velvety sweet-pea *chawanmushi* (custard), wild salmon with morels and roe, and rice with azuki beans and summery greens. Even a simple cornbread served with honeycomb butter might hold a surprise (a *shishito* pepper hidden inside). Sunday brunch is less formal yet still creative.

MAP 5: 1629 Yew St., 604/737-1155, www.maknming.com, 5pm-10pm Tues.-Sat., 10am-2pm Sun.

THAI
Maenam $$

Serving modern Thai cuisine in a minimalist Kitsilano space, Maenam brightens Vancouver's dark nights with banana blossom salad, grilled fermented sausage with crispy rice, and flavorful curries. Asian-inspired cocktails, like the "Siam Sunburn" (chili-infused tequila, butterscotch, lime, passionfruit, and egg white), or the alcohol-free house-made ginger beer pair well with the brightly flavored dishes.

MAP 5: 1938 W. 4th Ave., 604/730-5579, www.maenam.ca, 5pm-10pm Sun.-Mon., noon-2pm and 5pm-10pm Tues.-Sat.

VIETNAMESE
Mr. Red Café $

This family-run eatery in Kitsilano, decked out with bamboo paneling and a tropical feel, specializes in dishes from Hanoi and northern Vietnam. Recommended choices include the turmeric fish with dill, mango salad with shrimp, and *pho ga* (chicken noodle soup). To drink, try a traditional sweet Vietnamese coffee with condensed milk. The restaurant's original location is a smaller storefront on the East Side;

the same owners operate another East Side eatery called Hanoi Old Quarter.

MAP 5: 2680 W. Broadway, 604/559-6878, www.mrredcafe.ca, 11am-9pm daily

FRENCH
Au Comptoir $$$

With its copper bar and copper-rimmed tables, the setting at classic French bistro Au Comptoir declares "Paris." Try croissants and omelets in the morning, *croque-monsieur* and grilled chicken at midday, and steak frites, wild salmon with fennel tagliatelle, or duck breast paired with melon and charred onions in the evenings. On a warm day, the windows open to the outdoors, as they might in a traditional Parisian café, to take in the surrounding Kitsilano streetscape.

MAP 5: 2278 W. 4th Ave., 604/569-2278, www.aucomptoir. ca, 8am-10pm Mon. and Wed.-Sat., 8am-9:30pm Sun.

VEGETARIAN
Turf $

You don't have to work out in the adjacent fitness studio to enjoy a coffee, smoothie, salad, or rice bowl at Turf, a hip vegetarian-friendly Kitsilano café. Start your day with toast topped with cashew ricotta and mushrooms, grilled veggies and hummus, or classic avocado, or try the morning greens bowl layered with roasted broccoli, avocado, sautéed greens, and brown rice. Later, you might find a Thai-style green curry with tofu or a "plant power" salad of kale, spinach, roasted beets, and quinoa. And because even

athletes need to chill, you can order a BC microbrew or glass of wine too.

MAP 5: 2041 W. 4th Ave., 604/428-9970, www.ourturf.com, 7am-8pm Mon.-Fri., 8am-6pm Sat.-Sun.

BREAKFAST AND BRUNCH
Café Zen $

Popular with local families, old-favorite Café Zen fuels you up with breakfast classics, like plate-size pancakes or more than a dozen varieties of eggs Benedict, from spinach and mushroom to shrimp and avocado, before you flop down in the sand at nearby Kits Beach. Behind the sunny yellow facade, the hard-working staff keeps your coffee hot, and the long menu also features omelets, crepes, waffles, burgers, and a few sandwiches.

MAP 5: 1631 Yew St., 604/731-4018, www.cafezenonyew.com, 7am-2:30pm Mon.-Thurs., 7am-4pm Fri.-Sun.

BAKERIES AND CAFÉS
Beaucoup Bakery & Café $

With classic French pastries like croissants or buttery *kouign-amann*, and other baked treats like the kid-pleasing peanut butter sandwich cookies, petite Beaucoup Bakery & Café makes a sweet stop for Kitsilano or South Granville shoppers. It's a short walk from Granville Island too.

MAP 5: 2150 Fir St., 604/732-4222, www.beaucoupbakery.com, 7am-5pm Tues.-Fri., 8am-5pm Sat.-Sun.

FARMERS MARKETS
Kitsilano Farmers Market $

Operating on Sunday spring-fall, the Kitsilano Farmers Market sets up behind the Kitsilano Community

Centre with more than 50 vendors selling fresh produce, baked goods, and other local treats. Among the highlights are freshly made crepes from Chouchou Crepes, Asian-flavored chocolates from Coconama, and vegan fare from the Chickpea food truck.

MAP 5: Kitsilano Community Centre, 2690 Larch St., 604/879-3276, www. eatlocal.org, 10am-2pm Sun. early May-late Oct.

COFFEE AND TEA
O5 Tea Bar $
When you step into this serene Asian-style tea salon, you leave the bustle of West 4th Avenue far behind and enter the space of the tea masters. O5 Tea Bar specializes in rare, single-origin teas from around the world, the majority of which they purchase directly from the growers. Take a seat at the long bar, made of reclaimed Douglas fir, and linger over a cup of tea, or do a traditional tea tasting. They also have house-brewed kombucha on tap, which you can sip in the shop or take to go.

MAP 5: 2208 W. 4th Ave., 604/558-0500, http://o5tea.com, 10am-10pm daily

Nightlife

PUBS
Corduroy
Looking for an offbeat way to spend an evening? Corduroy, an eclectic pub near Kitsilano Beach, is best known for its Rock Paper Scissors tournaments that take place on Monday nights, popular with local university students and 20-somethings. Part game night and part comedy show, the fun starts at 10pm, but plan to arrive by 9pm or earlier to nab a seat. If you laugh so hard that you work up an appetite, you can munch on burgers, wings, and poutine.

MAP 5: 1943 Cornwall Ave., 604/733-0162, www. corduroyrestaurant.com, 4pm-2am Mon.-Sat., 4pm-midnight Sun.

Local Public Eatery
Although it's not actually local to Vancouver (it's part of a Canada-wide chain), the Local Public Eatery is a lively spot to grab a beer and a bite to eat, with a beach bar vibe. They offer a rotating selection of beer on tap, with a mix of commercial and craft varieties, while the food runs to burgers and other pub fare. The sunny umbrella-lined patio seats opposite Kitsilano Beach are packed with beachgoers and sun-seekers all summer. There's another location in Gastown that's also great for people-watching.

MAP 5: 2210 Cornwall Ave., 604/734-3589, http://localkits.com, 11am-1am Mon.-Thurs., 11am-2am Fri., 10am-2am Sat., 10am-1am Sun.

The Wolf and Hound

A traditional Irish pub, The Wolf and Hound has a classic wooden bar and pours a proper pint from its changing selection of local and Irish taps. Thursday-Saturday evenings, starting around 8:30pm, there are live bands playing folk, Celtic, and other tunes. **MAP 5:** 3617 W. Broadway, 604/738-8909, www.wolfandhound.ca, 4pm-midnight Mon., noon-midnight Tues.-Thurs., noon-1am Fri.-Sat., 11am-11pm Sun.

Recreation

BEACHES

✪ Kitsilano Beach

Popular Kitsilano Beach, aka Kits Beach, is a good swimming and people-watching spot. In summer, serious beach volleyball players flock here, and you can rent kayaks or stand-up paddleboards. Adjacent to the sandy beach is a children's playground, along with public tennis courts and a grassy lawn for lounging and picnicking.

Around the start of the 20th century, Kits Beach, then known as Greer's Beach after one of its first nonnative settlers, was a popular tent camping area, with many holidaymakers making their way across the water from the fashionable West End. While overnight camping is no

volleyball game on Kitsilano Beach

longer permitted, you can perch on a log or spread your blanket on the sand to watch the beach action.

Bus 2 from Burrard Street downtown stops directly in front of the beach; get off on Cornwall Avenue at Yew Street. From Kits Beach, you can follow the Seawall path east around Vanier Park (popular with kite-flyers and home to the Museum of Vancouver and the Vancouver Maritime Museum) to Granville Island.

MAP 5: Off Cornwall Ave. between Arbutus St. and Vine St., http://vancouver.ca, 6am-10pm daily, free

Kitsilano Pool

CYCLING
Arbutus Greenway
Along a former rail line, the paved, relatively flat Arbutus Greenway currently extends 5.25 miles (8.5 km) from Kitsilano south to the Fraser River, traveling through several West Side residential

neighborhoods. From downtown, you can cycle over the Burrard Bridge and turn west onto the greenway at West 6th Avenue. The city has announced plans to expand this greenway; check the city website for a greenway map.

MAP 5: From Burrard St. at W. 6th Ave. to Milton St. south of SW Marine Dr., http://vancouver.ca

SWIMMING
✪ Kitsilano Pool
Kitsilano Pool, next to Kitsilano Beach, is a 450-foot-long (135-m) outdoor saltwater swimming pool with three waterslides to entertain the kids. As you lounge on the pool deck, you can take in views of the city skyline, the North Shore mountains, and the sea. The pool gets wildly busy, particularly with families; expect lines on hot-weather weekends. Many people pair a swim in the pool with a picnic at the beach. When the original pool opened here in 1931, it was the first saltwater pool in Canada.

MAP 5: 2305 Cornwall Ave., 604/731-0011, http://vancouver.ca, 11:30am-8:30pm Mon.-Fri., 9am-8:30pm mid-May-early June, 7am-8:30pm Mon.-Fri., 9am-8:30pm Sat.-Sun. early June-early Aug., 7am-7pm or later Mon.-Fri., 9am-7pm or later early Aug.-early Sept., adults $6, seniors and ages 13-18 $4.27, ages 5-12 $3

Arts and Culture

THEATER

Bard on the Beach

June-September, the Bard on the Beach Shakespeare Festival performs several of Shakespeare's plays under billowing white tents in Kitsilano's Vanier Park. Established in 1990, this professional theater company has a dramatic performance space; the back of the mainstage tent is open to views of the waterfront and North Shore mountains.

MAP 5: Vanier Park, Whyte Ave., 604/739-0559, http://bardonthebeach. org, adults $26-77, ages 6-22 $26-38.50

Bard on the Beach

Festivals and Events

Vancouver International Children's Festival

Bring the kids to Kitsilano's Vanier Park when the weeklong Vancouver International Children's Festival offers family-friendly concerts, circus performers, crafts, and other activities in late May-early June.

Kitsilano: Vanier Park, Whyte Ave., www.childrensfestival.ca, May-June

Shops

SHOPPING DISTRICTS

West 4th Avenue

On Vancouver's West Side, the Kitsilano neighborhood mixes North American chains and local boutiques, centered along West 4th Avenue. There's a collection of ski and snowboard gear shops on 4th at Burrard Street.

MAP 5: W. 4th Ave., between Burrard St. and Vine St.

CLOTHING AND ACCESSORIES

Two of Hearts

For women's clothing and accessories by emerging Canadian designers, check out Two of Hearts, a friendly boutique in Kitsilano. They carry their own made-in-Vancouver label, Cici, as well as designs from other independent companies, stocking both moderately priced casual clothes and dressier wear. In the center of the shop, look for displays of jewelry.

MAP 5: 1986 W. 4th Ave., 604/428-0998, www.twoofhearts. ca, 11am-6pm Mon.- Wed. and Sat., noon-7pm Thurs.-Fri., noon-5pm Sun.

SHOES

Gravity Pope

Kitsilano's Gravity Pope sells upscale style-conscious shoes for men and women, including brands like Camper, Cydwoq, Vans, and their own in-house line. Park yourself on one of the curved banquettes while you see what fits. Their next-door boutique, Gravity Pope Tailored Goods (2203 W. 4th Ave., 604/731-7647, 10am-8pm Mon.-Fri., 10am-7pm Sat., 11am-6pm Sun.), carries high-end women's clothing that ranges from funky to fine, from labels like Comme des Garçons, Naked & Famous, and Alexander Wang.

MAP 5: 2205 W. 4th Ave., 604/731-7673, www.gravitypope.com, 10am-9pm Mon.-Fri., 10am-7pm Sat., 11am-6pm Sun.

BOOKS

✪ Kidsbooks

Kidsbooks is Vancouver's best place to find reading matter for toddlers to teens. The Kitsilano shop stocks a large selection of titles by Canadian authors and books with multicultural themes, plus games, crafts, science projects, and audiobooks. This spacious store has nooks for young readers, middle grades, and teenagers to browse. If you're shopping for a gift or want some suggestions, ask the knowledgeable staff for ideas.

MAP 5: 2557 W. Broadway, 604/738-5335, www.kidsbooks.ca, 9:30am-6pm Mon.-Thurs. and Sat., 9:30am-9pm Fri., 10:30am-6pm Sun.

Pulp Fiction Books

One of the city's long-established booksellers, Pulp Fiction Books carries both new and used books on the sturdy pine shelves at its Kitsilano location. The store also has two East Side shops: one on Main Street, another on Commercial Drive.

MAP 5: 2754 W. Broadway, 604/873-4311, http:// pulpfictionbooksvancouver.com, 11am-7pm daily

SPECIALTY FOOD AND DRINK

✪ Les Amis du Fromage

The friendly cheesemongers at Les Amis du Fromage will help you pick the perfect wedge, whether you're looking for locally made brie or a pungent *époisses* from France. Sampling is encouraged. The Kitsilano storefront, where you can peruse the cheese-filled display cases and coolers, is a short walk from Granville Island; there's a second location on the East Side.

MAP 5: 1752 W. 2nd Ave., 604/732-4218, www.buycheese.com, 9am-6pm Sat.-Wed., 9am-6:30pm Thurs.-Fri.

Silk Road Tea

Based in Victoria, local leaf expert Silk Road Tea runs a spacious store in Kitsilano, where you can browse and sample from their extensive inventory of tea, tea-related products, and cosmetics. They also offer tea classes and workshops.

MAP 5: 2066 W. 4th Ave., 778/379-8481, www.silkroadteastore. com, 10am-6pm Mon.-Sat., 11am-5pm Sun.

OUTDOOR GEAR

Comor Sports

Along West 4th Avenue at Burrard Street in Kitsilano, several shops sell gear for skiing, snowboarding, surfing, and cycling. Comor Sports is a well-stocked outdoor gear store with helpful staff. In their large warehouse-like location, they carry skis, snowboards, winter accessories, and bicycles, as well as clothing for outdoor sports. It runs a seasonal discount outlet nearby (1766 W. 4th Ave., 604/734-4231), where you can often find good deals.

Les Amis du Fromage

MAP 5: 1787 W. 4th Ave., 604/736-7547, www.comorsports.com, 10am-6pm Mon.-Wed. and Sat., 10am-8pm Thurs.-Fri., 11am-5pm Sun.

TRAVEL

✪ Wanderlust

Wander into Wanderlust, a well-stocked Kitsilano travel store, for a large selection of guidebooks, maps, luggage, and other travel gear. One room is full of books, while the second is stocked with useful gadgets and bags of all shapes and sizes. The staff know their stock, whether it's what kind of plug adapter you need or which backpacks fit different body shapes, and they're quick to make recommendations.

MAP 5: 1929 W. 4th Ave., 604/739-2182, www.wanderlustore.com, 10am-7pm Mon.-Fri., 10am-6pm Sat., noon-5pm Sun.

The Travel Bug

The Travel Bug has a cozy nook filled with travel books, and this compact but well-stocked storefront carries luggage, bags, and travel supplies as well.

MAP 5: 2865 W. Broadway, 604/737-1122, www.thetravelbug.ca, 9:30am-6pm Mon.-Sat., 11am-5pm Sun.

UBC and Point Grey   Map 6

On the city's far west side, surrounded by forests and sea, the University of British Columbia (UBC) is worth visiting for its stellar **Museum of Anthropology** and for several gardens and smaller museums. Also on campus are a modern **concert hall** and one of the few working farms within the city of Vancouver. On the shore near the university is Vancouver's clothing-optional **Wreck Beach.**

Point Grey, between the university and Kitsilano, is a leafy residential area with several family-friendly **sandy beaches** along its northern shore. **Pacific Spirit Regional Park,** Vancouver's largest park, with miles of hiking trails through the rainforest, is also located here.

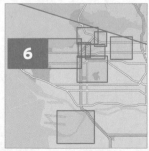

TOP SIGHTS

- Best Place to Explore Indigenous Culture: **Museum of Anthropology** (page 146)
- Quickest Trip to Japan: **Nitobe Japanese Garden** (page 147)

TOP RECREATION

- Best Beach for Water Sports and a Beer: **Jericho Beach** (page 151)
- Where to Wander in the Rainforest: **Pacific Spirit Regional Park** (page 153)

TOP ARTS AND CULTURE

- Best Performance Space: **Chan Centre for the Performing Arts** (page 154)

GETTING THERE AND AROUND

- Bus lines: 4, 14, 25, 49, 84, 99

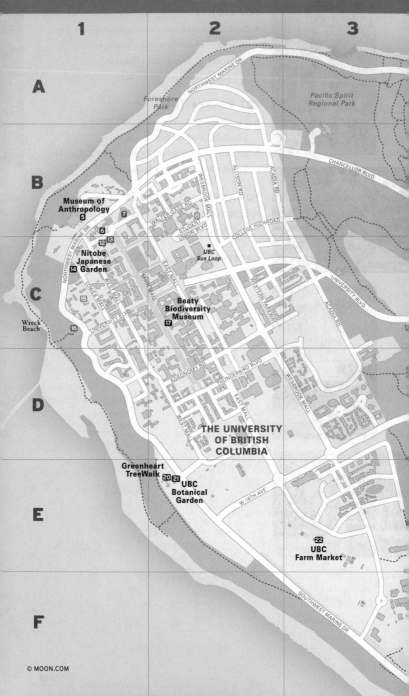

1
2
3

A

Foreshore
Park

Pacific Spirit
Regional Park

NORTHWEST MARINE DR

CHANCELLOR BLVD

B

Museum of
Anthropology
5

7

WESBROOK MALL

ALLISON RD

ACADIA RD

WALKER GAGE RD

6

STUDENT
UNION BLVD

8

COLLEGE HIGHROAD

12 **13**

Nitobe
Japanese
Garden

14

UBC
Bus Loop

UNIVERSITY BLVD

C

NORTHWEST MARINE DR

LOWER MALL

WEST MALL

15

MAIN MALL

EAST MALL

Beaty
Biodiversity
Museum
17

WESTERN PARKWAY

ACADIA RD

Wreck
Beach

16

AGRONOMY RD

THUNDERBIRD BLVD

WESBROOK MALL

D

WEST MALL

EAST MALL

**THE UNIVERSITY
OF BRITISH
COLUMBIA**

Greenheart
TreeWalk
20 **21**
UBC
Botanical
Garden

W. 16TH AVE

E

22
UBC
Farm Market

SOUTHWEST MARINE DR

F

© MOON.COM

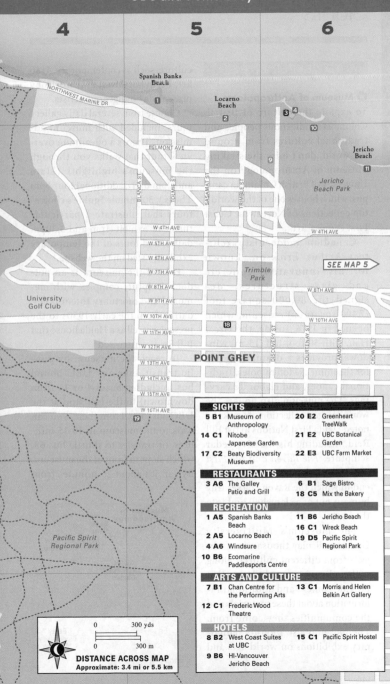

UBC and Point Grey

4 **5** **6**

Spanish Banks Beach

Locarno Beach

Jericho Beach

Jericho Beach Park

NORTHWEST MARINE DR

BELMONT AVE

BLANCA ST
TOLMIE ST
SASAMAT ST
TRIMBLE ST

W 4TH AVE
W 4TH AVE

W 5TH AVE
W 6TH AVE
W 7TH AVE

Trimble Park

W 8TH AVE
W 8TH AVE

W 9TH AVE

University Golf Club

W 10TH AVE
W 10TH AVE

W 11TH AVE
DISCOVERY ST
COURTENAY ST
CAMOSUN ST
CROWN ST

POINT GREY

W 12TH AVE
W 13TH AVE
W 14TH AVE
W 15TH AVE
W 10TH AVE

SEE MAP 5

Pacific Spirit Regional Park

SIGHTS

5 B1	Museum of Anthropology	**20 E2**	Greenheart TreeWalk
14 C1	Nitobe Japanese Garden	**21 E2**	UBC Botanical Garden
17 C2	Beaty Biodiversity Museum	**22 E3**	UBC Farm Market

RESTAURANTS

3 A6	The Galley Patio and Grill	**6 B1**	Sage Bistro
		18 C5	Mix the Bakery

RECREATION

1 A5	Spanish Banks Beach	**11 B6**	Jericho Beach
2 A5	Locarno Beach	**16 C1**	Wreck Beach
4 A6	Windsure	**19 D5**	Pacific Spirit Regional Park
10 B6	Ecomarine Paddlesports Centre		

ARTS AND CULTURE

7 B1	Chan Centre for the Performing Arts	**13 C1**	Morris and Helen Belkin Art Gallery
12 C1	Frederic Wood Theatre		

HOTELS

8 B2	West Coast Suites at UBC	**15 C1**	Pacific Spirit Hostel
9 B6	HI-Vancouver Jericho Beach		

0   300 yds
0   300 m

DISTANCE ACROSS MAP
Approximate: 3.4 mi or 5.5 km

Sights

✪ Museum of Anthropology

To explore the culture of British Columbia's indigenous peoples and traditional cultures from around the world, don't miss the striking Museum of Anthropology on the University of British Columbia campus, which houses one of the world's top collections of Northwest Coast First Peoples' art.

Canadian modernist architect Arthur Erickson, known for his innovative concrete and glass structures, designed the 80,000-square-foot (7,400-square-m) museum, which opened in 1976. Inside, the Great Hall, with 50-foot-tall (15-m) windows, provides a dramatic home for the immense totem poles, traditional canoes, and elaborate carvings. The museum also houses the world's largest collection of works by noted Haida First Nations artist Bill Reid, including his massive cedar sculpture, *The Raven and the First Men*, which depicts a creation legend in which the Raven coaxes tiny humans out of a clamshell and into the world.

The museum's Multiversity Galleries display thousands of objects from different cultures, along with audio, video, and photos that provide context and additional information about these materials and the communities they come from. The museum also mounts temporary exhibitions on world arts and culture, such as contemporary Arab art, Peruvian silver, and works by present-day indigenous artists.

Choose from several daily gallery tours, included with museum admission. There's a 60-minute overview tour that walks you through the museum's highlights (11am and 2pm daily, additional tour 6pm Thurs.), 30-minute "guide's choice" tours that illustrate a particular theme or exhibit (1pm and 3:30pm daily), and tours of the temporary exhibits, listed on the website.

Behind the museum is an outdoor sculpture complex with memorial and mortuary totem poles, dating from the early 1950s to the present, as well as a Haida house that Bill Reid constructed.

To reach the museum by public transit, take any UBC-bound bus (including buses 4 or 14 from downtown) to the last stop at the UBC bus loop. From there, you can walk to the museum in 10-15 minutes, or transfer to shuttle bus 68, which stops in front of the museum. By car, it's about 25 minutes from

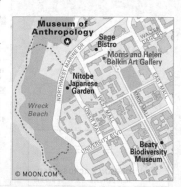

© MOON.COM

downtown to the museum, which has a public parking lot.

MAP 6: 6393 NW Marine Dr., 604/822-5087, http://moa.ubc.ca, 10am-9pm Thurs., 10am-5pm Fri.-Wed. mid-May-mid-Oct., 10am-9pm Thurs., 10am-5pm Fri.-Sun. and Tues.-Wed. mid-Oct.-mid-May, adults $18, seniors, students, and over age 6 $16, 5pm-9pm Thurs. $10

the Museum of Anthropology

NEARBY:

- Stroll among the flowers and koi ponds of the serene Nitobe Japanese Garden (page 147).
- Explore the natural world, from a blue whale skeleton to tiny fossils, at the Beaty Biodiversity Museum (page 148).
- Dine alongside UBC professors at Sage Bistro (page 150).
- Check out the modern art collection at the Morris and Helen Belkin Art Gallery (page 154).

✪ Nitobe Japanese Garden

You could be in Japan as you stroll among the flowers, waterfalls, and koi ponds at the serene Nitobe Japanese Garden, one of the most authentic traditional Japanese gardens in North America. Several stone lanterns decorate the paths;

another feature is the Island of Eternity, a collection of rocks shaped like a turtle, which symbolizes longevity. Many of the plants, from azaleas and irises to maple and cherry trees, came from Japan. The garden is particularly scenic in April-May, when the cherry blossoms bloom.

The 2.5-acre (1-ha) garden is named for Dr. Inazo Nitobe, a professor, author, and advocate for East-West relations who served as Japan's representative to the League of Nations in the 1920s. The garden's 77-log bridge symbolizes Nitobe's goal of being "a bridge over the Pacific." The garden features five other bridges that crisscross its streams. For an extra fee, participate in a traditional Japanese tea ceremony (May-Sept., $10) in the garden's teahouse, a classical structure in which you pass through exterior and interior gardens before entering the tearoom itself. Ceremonies are held on the hour 11am-3pm the last Saturday of the month. Reservations are advised.

The garden is a short walk from

Nitobe Japanese Garden

the Museum of Anthropology. From the UBC bus loop, you can walk or take shuttle bus 68.

MAP 6: 1895 Lower Mall, 604/822-6038, www.botanicalgarden. ubc.ca, 10am-4:30pm daily Apr.-Oct., 10am-2pm Mon.-Fri. Nov.-Mar., adults $7, seniors and students $6, ages 6-12 $4, Nov.-Mar. by donation

Beaty Biodiversity Museum

Beaty Biodiversity Museum

An 85-foot (26-m) blue whale skeleton, the largest on display in Canada, greets visitors to the Beaty Biodiversity Museum, a modern natural history gallery. The museum has more than two million specimens of bugs, fish, plants, fossils, and more, many of which come from BC and the surrounding regions. In this family-friendly museum, many of the items are set at kids' eye level for youngsters to check out; in the interactive Discovery Lab, children can learn to use a microscope, compare different types of fossils, and participate in other hands-on activities.

At 10:30am most weekdays, a museum staffer leads a 30-minute hands-on presentation about specific specimens. The museum also offers 30-minute tours (11:30am

and 3pm daily) highlighting particular aspects of the collections.

The museum is near the center of the UBC campus, a short walk from the UBC bus loop.

MAP 6: 2212 Main Mall, 604/827-4955, www.beatymuseum.ubc.ca, 10am-5pm Tues.-Sun., adults $14, seniors, students, and children ages 13-17 $12, ages 5-12 $10

UBC Botanical Garden

A garden of native BC plants, a woodland garden, a traditional Asian garden: These are just a few groupings of the more than 50,000 trees and plants that thrive at the 70-acre (28-ha) UBC Botanical Garden, where walking paths wend through the woods and grounds.

Explore the BC Rainforest Garden, with its tall western red cedars, several varieties of maple trees, and bushes of blackberries, blueberries, and huckleberries. In the Alpine Garden, you can travel the world of mountain-region plants, grouped geographically, while in the Food Garden, you can check out vegetables, fruits, and herbs that grow locally. The David C. Lam Asian Garden blossoms with rhododendrons, magnolias, dogwood, hydrangeas, lilies, and other plants native to China, Korea, Japan, and the Himalayas that also thrive in Vancouver's temperate climate. The garden's two oldest trees, Douglas firs that are more 400 years old, are also in the Asian Garden.

The Botanical Garden is on the south side of the UBC campus. By public transit, the fastest way to reach it from downtown is to take the Canada Line south to the Langara-49th Avenue station and transfer to bus 49 UBC, which stops near the garden. By car, it's about 25 minutes from downtown to the gardens, which have a public parking lot.

MAP 6: 6804 SW Marine Dr., 604/822-4208, www.botanicalgarden. ubc.ca, 10am-4:30pm daily, adults $10, seniors $8, ages 5-12 $5, Nov.-Mar. by donation

Greenheart TreeWalk

An adventurous way to explore the UBC Botanical Garden is on the Greenheart TreeWalk, a 1,000-foot (310-m) aerial trail system that takes you high into the rainforest canopy. Cross a series of swinging bridges to eight increasingly higher viewing platforms mounted among the Douglas firs, cedars, and other lofty trees. The tallest platform is 75 feet (23 m) above the forest floor. To protect the trees, the platforms were constructed without using nails or bolts; a cable tension system suspends them from the tree trunks.

Explore the walkway on your own or on a 45-minute **guided tour,** included with your walkway ticket, where your guide tells you about the surrounding second-growth forest. Though the area was once logged, many trees are more than a century old. You'll also learn how First Nations people use various trees and plants, from carving canoes to traditional medicine. Each tour can accommodate up to 20.

The Greenheart TreeWalk is located within the UBC Botanical Garden. From the garden's main entrance, follow the signs to the TreeWalk. Your TreeWalk ticket lets you explore the rest of the botanical gardens too.

MAP 6: 6804 SW Marine Dr., 604/822-4208, www.botanicalgarden. ubc.ca, 10am-4pm daily Apr.-Oct., adults $23, seniors $17, ages 5-12 $10, includes admission to UBC Botanical Garden

Greenheart TreeWalk

UBC Farm Market

The University of British Columbia operates a 60-acre (24-ha) organic farm on the south side of the campus. You can purchase produce grown on-site at the weekly UBC Farm Market, held Saturday mornings on the farm grounds. The market also sells produce from other local growers, including indigenous farmers, plus baked goods, locally made honey, soaps, prepared foods, and crafts. The farm is a good place for kids, who can explore the fields and see what's growing.

During the Saturday market, you can take a 30-minute family-friendly **farm tour** (noon Sat. June-Nov., free). Reservations aren't required for the farm tours; meet at the farm about five minutes in advance.

From the UBC bus loop in the

center of campus, catch bus 70, UBC Exchange/Wesbrook Mall, to the farm. Get off on Ross Drive at Birney Avenue.

MAP 6: 3461 Ross Dr., 604/822-5092, http://ubcfarm.ubc.ca, 9am-1pm Sat. June-Nov.

Restaurants

PRICE KEY

$ Entrées less than CAD$15
$$ Entrées CAD$15-25
$$$ Entrées more than CAD$25

MODERN CANADIAN
Sage Bistro $$

One of the more upscale dining options on the UBC Campus, overlooking the gardens with views of the North Shore mountains beyond, Sage Bistro serves weekday lunches in the Leon and Thea Koerner University Centre, a short walk from the Museum of Anthropology. The menu draws on local ingredients in dishes like a Niçoise-style salad with gin-cured salmon gravlax, olive tapenade, and tomatoes, smoked tofu steak with mushroom pâté and baby vegetables, or pan-seared sablefish paired with Dungeness crab and corn fritters. While the bistro is popular with university faculty, you won't be graded on whether you finish your meal.

MAP 6: 6331 Crescent Rd., UBC, 604/822-0968, http://sage.ubc.ca, 11:30am-2pm Mon.-Fri.

PUB FARE
The Galley Patio and Grill $$

Overlooking the sea from the 2nd floor of the Jericho Sailing Centre at Jericho Beach, The Galley Patio and Grill cooks simple, beach-friendly bites, including burgers, grilled steelhead, and sweet potato fries, served on a deck with ocean views. Local beer is on tap. If you can't find a seat, take your food outside and picnic. Tip for morning beachcombers: The Galley serves breakfast on weekends.

MAP 6: 1300 Discovery St., 604/222-1331, www.thegalley.ca, 11am-10pm Mon.-Fri., 9am-10pm Sat.-Sun. June-Sept., hours vary Oct.-May

BAKERIES AND CAFÉS
Mix the Bakery $

On your way to or from UBC, stop at Mix the Bakery, a homey Point Grey neighborhood café, for coffee, baked goods, or sandwiches. For breakfast, there's always a selection of muffins, scones, and toast with homemade jam. Among the sandwich choices, look for the Granny Gobbler (smoked turkey, cheddar cheese, spinach, and apple) or a vegetarian option, with grilled zucchini, pan-fried onions, roasted tomatoes, and swiss cheese. Staff set up enticing displays of fruit tarts, cakes, and pastries along the counter.

MAP 6: 4430 W. 10th Ave., 604/221-4145, www.mixthebakery.com, 7am-5pm Mon.-Sat., 8am-4pm Sun.

Recreation

Jericho Beach

BEACHES
✪ Jericho Beach

West of Kitsilano, three connected beaches draw families with sandy swimming areas and grassy stretches for picnicking and playing. The easternmost of these Point Grey beaches is Jericho Beach, divided into two sections. One section, where Point Grey Road ends west of Alma Street, has a long crescent of sand backed by a grassy lawn. The other section of the beach is to the west, at the foot of Discovery Street, with a smaller sandy beach, a pier where you can often see fishers at work, and the Jericho Sailing Centre, a public water-sports facility where you can go kayaking or windsurfing, or enjoy a burger and a beer in The Galley, the water-view pub.

You can also cycle along a waterside path that connects Point Grey's beaches. The Seaside Cycling Route continues west from Kitsilano Beach along Point Grey Road and onto a flat gravel pathway along Jericho, Locarno, and Spanish Banks Beaches.

To reach Jericho Beach by public transit from downtown, take bus 4 toward UBC. For the eastern section, get off along West 4th Avenue at Alma Street. Walk north on Alma to Point Grey Road and turn west toward the beach. To the Jericho Sailing Centre and the western area, get off the bus at West 4th Avenue and Northwest Marine Drive. Follow Northwest Marine toward the water, and turn right onto Discovery Street, which leads to the sailing facility.

There's a public parking lot ($3.50 per hour, $13 per day Apr.-Sept., free Oct.-Mar.) adjacent to the Jericho Sailing Centre.

MAP 6: NW Marine Dr. and Discovery St. to Point Grey Rd. and Alma St., http://vancouver.ca, 6am-10pm daily, free

Locarno Beach

A sandy shore with evergreens beyond, Locarno Beach, west of Jericho, is a city-designated "quiet" beach, which means that amplified music is not allowed. There's plenty of space for sunning, swimming, and picnicking, and the beach has a snack bar and restrooms. Bus 4 between downtown and UBC stops on West 4th Avenue at Trimble Street; walk north on Trimble down the hill to the beach. Alternatively, late June-early September, you can transfer to Bus 42 at Alma Street; this bus runs along Northwest Marine Drive to Spanish Banks Beach, stopping at Locarno en route.

There's a small free parking area adjacent to Locarno Beach. Parking is also permitted along Northwest Marine Drive.

MAP 6: Northwest Marine Dr. at Trimble St., http://vancouver.ca, 6am-10pm daily, free

Spanish Banks Beach

Spanish Banks, the westernmost of the three Point Grey beaches, has sandy stretches, an expansive grassy lawn with picnic tables, an off-leash dog park, and a launch site for kite-boarders. Vancouverites heading for Spanish Banks Beach often suggest "Let's meet at *The Anchor,*" a massive concrete sculpture that BC artist Christel Fuoss-Moore created in 1986. Designed to mark the 1791 arrival of Spanish explorer José María Narváez, reportedly the first European to arrive in this harbor, this anchor-shaped artwork is installed toward the beach's western end. Spanish Banks has a snack bar, restrooms, and a large public parking area ($3.50 per hour, $13 per day Apr.-Sept., free Oct.-Mar.).

Bus 4 between downtown and UBC can drop you on West 4th Avenue at Tolmie Street. It's a steep walk down the hill on Tolmie to the beach. To avoid the hill, you can walk to or from the bus stop at West 4th Avenue and Northwest Marine Drive; it's about a third of a mile (0.5 km) longer, but much flatter. Alternatively, late June-early September, you can transfer to Bus 42 at Alma Street; this bus runs along Northwest Marine Drive to Spanish Banks.

MAP 6: NW Marine Dr. at Tolmie St., http://vancouver.ca, 6am-10pm daily, free

Wreck Beach

Vancouver's clothing-optional Wreck Beach is located along the shore below the far west end of the UBC campus. Extending nearly 5 miles (7.8 km), it's among Canada's longest naturist beaches. You don't have to get naked on the sand, but it's considered poor etiquette to gawk.

On temperate days, vendors sell snacks, sandwiches, and crafts at the main section of the beach, near Trail 6. Their schedules can be erratic, so come prepared with your own water and food.

Several trails lead down to Wreck Beach from the campus. From the UBC bus loop, the most direct route is to walk west on University Boulevard to Northwest Marine Drive and look for Trail 6. It's more than 400 steps down to the sand.

Another option is to walk along the shore from Spanish Banks. Wear running shoes or sport sandals that will protect your feet from rocks and logs, and allow at least an hour if you're heading toward the Trail 6 section of the beach. Do this walk only at low tide, or you can be stranded as the tide comes in.

MAP 6: Off NW Marine Dr., on the west side of the UBC campus, www.wreckbeach.org, dawn-dusk daily, free

KAYAKING

Ecomarine Paddlesports Centre

From its location behind the sailing center at Jericho Beach, Ecomarine Paddlesports Centre rents kayaks and offers guided kayak tours. One popular tour is the guided nature sunset kayak tour (2.5 hours, $79), offered Friday evenings June-August, where you'll explore the shoreline looking for bald eagles and other birds and even the occasional harbor seal, enjoying views of the setting sun reflecting off the city skyline. You don't need prior kayaking experience; your guide will provide brief paddling instructions and safety information before you launch. Tour rates include all gear; reservations are required. If you're renting a kayak, you can take out a boat until two hours before sunset. Check ahead to verify specific rental hours.

MAP 6: Jericho Sailing Centre, 1300 Discovery St., 604/689-7575 or 888/425-2925, www.ecomarine.com, 10am-8pm daily mid- May-early Sept., single kayak $45-99, double kayak $65-125

WINDSURFING
Windsure

If you have experience windsurfing, you can rent a board and related gear from Windsure at Jericho Beach. If you're keen to try windsurfing for the first time, sign up (at least 48 hours in advance) for one of their lessons, such as the 2.5-hour group beginner class. They also rent stand-up paddleboards. Windsure is generally open daily April-September, but hours can vary in spring and fall or if the weather is questionable; call ahead.

MAP 6: Jericho Sailing Centre, 1300 Discovery St., 604/224-0615 or 604/728-7567, http://windsure. com, generally 8:30am-8:30pm daily Apr.-Sept., rentals $22-24 per hour

HIKING
✪ Pacific Spirit Regional Park

Although it's less well known than downtown's Stanley Park, Pacific Spirit Regional Park, in Vancouver's Point Grey neighborhood near the UBC campus, is actually larger, measuring more than 1,800 acres (760 ha). More than 40 miles (70 km) of hiking trails wend through dense rainforest. Most are gentle forest strolls, and some steeper routes lead from the park to Spanish Banks Beach.

Access several park trails off West 16th Avenue between Discovery Street and Acadia Road; several others start from Chancellor Boulevard west of Blanca Street. Another park entrance is on West 29th Avenue at Camosun Street. Maps are posted at the start of most trails. For an online map, see the website of the **Pacific Spirit Park Society** (www. pacificspiritparksociety.org).

Don't hike alone here. You're close to the city, but many trails quickly lead deep into the forest and feel quite remote.

MAP 6: Central section bounded by W. 16th Ave., Camosun St., SW Marine Dr., and Binning Rd., north section between NW Marine Dr. and University Blvd., west of Blanca St. and east of Acadia Rd., 604/224-5739, www.metrovancouver. org, dawn-dusk daily, free

Pacific Spirit Regional Park

Arts and Culture

GALLERIES

Morris and Helen Belkin Art Gallery

The Morris and Helen Belkin Art Gallery on the UBC campus mounts several exhibitions every year, highlighting Canadian and international contemporary art. Shows emphasize Canadian avant-garde artists of the 1960s and 1970s as well as emerging artists. In its boxy modernist building, the gallery also exhibits works from the 2,500-object University Art Collection, including collages, drawings, paintings, and prints by BC's Jack Shadbolt. Works by Emily Carr, Lawren Harris (a founding member of the famed Group of Seven early-20th-century Canadian landscape artists), and First Nations artist Lawrence Paul Yuxweluptun are also among their collections. The gallery is closed between exhibitions, so check ahead.

MAP 6: 1825 Main Mall, 604/822-2759, www.belkin.ubc.ca, 10am-5pm Tues.-Fri., noon-5pm Sat.-Sun., free

THEATER

Frederic Wood Theatre

The well-regarded UBC Theatre Department produces several plays every year with all-student casts. The season might include works from Shakespeare's era to modern times; recent productions have included Guillermo Calderón's *Goldrausch* and *Lion in the Streets* by Canadian playwright Judith Thompson. Most performances are held Wednesday-Saturday evenings late September-April in the Frederic Wood Theatre on campus; some productions take place in the Telus Studio Theatre, inside the Chan Centre for the Performing Arts.

MAP 6: 6354 Crescent Rd., 604/822-2678, http://theatrefilm.ubc.ca, adults $24.50, seniors $16.50, students $11.50

the Chan Centre for the Performing Arts

MUSIC

✪ Chan Centre for the Performing Arts

On the UBC campus, the modern Chan Centre for the Performing Arts hosts jazz, blues, and world music performers, as well as early music and chamber concerts. The wide-ranging events calendar might feature a student musical group one day and an internationally known artist the next, including jazz musician Herbie Hancock, Mongolian throat singers Anda Union, and Portuguese *fado* star Mariza. The

Vancouver Symphony performs here periodically. Opened in 1997, the curvaceous contemporary building, surrounded by evergreens, has an 1,185-seat concert hall and several smaller performance spaces. **MAP 6:** 6265 Crescent Rd., 604/822-2697, www.chancentre.com, prices vary

Festivals and Events

Vancouver Folk Festival

It's not just folk music at the long-established Vancouver Folk Festival. This musical extravaganza draws world beat, roots, blues, and folk musicians from across Canada and around the world to Jericho Beach for three days of always-eclectic music on multiple outdoor stages. Held the 3rd weekend of July, it's great fun for all ages.

UBC and Point Grey: Jericho Beach, http://thefestival.bc.ca, July

Vancouver Folk Festival at Jericho Beach

Cambie Corridor   Map 7

Cambie Street runs between downtown Vancouver and the Fraser River, bisecting the city's east and west sides; the Canada Line Sky-Train operates along Cambie. The notable **VanDusen Botanical Garden** is located west of Cambie, and a little farther west, the South Granville district boasts **high-end art galleries.**

To the east, browse **funky Main Street** for its **vintage clothing shops, independent fashion boutiques,** and **locavore restaurants.** You can always discover something new in this fast-changing neighborhood.

TOP SIGHTS

- Best Place to Stop and Smell the Flowers:
  VanDusen Botanical Garden (page 160)

TOP RESTAURANTS

- Where to Eat Hyper-Locally:
  Burdock & Co (page 161)
- How to Channel Tropical Asia:
  Anh & Chi (page 163)

TOP ARTS AND CULTURE

- Where to See What's New in Canadian
  Art: **Bau-Xi Gallery** (page 167)
- Top Spot to Buy a Totem Pole: **Douglas
  Reynolds Gallery** (page 168)
- Best Place for Indigenous Art and
  Gifts: **Hill's Native Art** (page 168)

TOP SHOPS

- Where to Find Frilly, Flouncy Frocks:
  Barefoot Contessa (page 170)
- Most Fashion-Forward Vintage Shop:
  Front and Company (page 170)

GETTING THERE AND AROUND

- SkyTrain lines: Canada Line
- SkyTrain stops: Broadway-
  City Hall, King Edward
- Bus lines: 3, 9, 10, 15, 17, 99

To [2] [SEE MAP 4]　1　　　2　　　3

[1] Farmer's
Apprentice

W 8TH AVE

W BROADWAY [5]

[6]

W 10TH AVE

A

W 11TH AVE

FAIRVIEW

W 12TH AVE

W 13TH AVE

W 14TH AVE

B [15]

W 15TH AVE

WOLFE AVE

W 16TH AVE

Shaughnessy
Park

Heather
Park

C

Douglas
Park

SOUTH
CAMBIE

D

E KING EDWARD AVE

Braemar
Park

E

SIGHTS

| 29 F2 | VanDusen Botanical Garden | 30 F4 | Queen Elizabeth Park |

RESTAURANTS

1 A1	Farmer's Apprentice	12 A5	Chicha
3 A1	Rangoli	14 A5	Burdock & Co
5 A2	Tojo's	17 B4	Vij's
6 A2	Salmon n' Bannock	18 B5	49th Parallel Coffee Roasters
7 A3	Dynasty Seafood	19 C5	Anh & Chi
8 A3	Shao Lin Noodle House	24 D5	The Acorn
		25 E5	Chickpea

NIGHTLIFE

10 A5	The Sunday Service	26 E5	The Shameful Tiki Room
13 A5	The Cascade Room		
16 B4	Yuk Yuk's Vancouver Comedy Club		

RECREATION

| 28 E5 | Vancouver Canadians | | |

ARTS AND CULTURE

2 A1	Douglas Reynolds Gallery	11 A5	Hill's Native Art
4 A1	Arts Club Theatre Company	15 B1	Bau-Xi Gallery
		27 E5	The Flame

SHOPS

9 A5	Sports Junkies	22 D5	Front and Company
20 C5	Vancouver Special	23 D5	The Regional Assembly of Text
21 C5	Barefoot Contessa		

0 ——— 300 yds
0 ——— 300 m

DISTANCE ACROSS MAP
Approximate: 2.4 mi or 3.9 km

F

VanDusen
Botanical
Garden

W 33RD AVE

VanDusen
Botanical Garden [29]

Oak Meadows
Park

SEE MAP 8

Sights

✪ VanDusen Botanical Garden

Wander the plant world without leaving Vancouver at the 55-acre (22-ha) VanDusen Botanical Garden. With more than 250,000 plants, the garden contains varieties native to the Pacific Northwest, other parts of Canada, the Himalayas, the Mediterranean, and South America. Different flowers and plants are highlights at different times of year, like cherry trees and dogwood in the spring, roses and lilies in summer, colorful trees in the autumn, and evergreens in winter. You can find your way through an Elizabethan maze too. A one-hour **guided tour** (10:30am and 1pm Wed., 1pm Thurs.-Tues. Apr.-mid-Oct., 1pm Sun. mid-Oct.-Mar.) helps you explore what's growing.

From downtown, bus 17 for Oak Street stops at West 37th Avenue at the garden entrance.

MAP 7: 5251 Oak St., 604/257-8335, www.vandusengarden.org, 9am-8pm daily June-Aug., 9am-6pm daily Sept., 10am-5pm daily Oct. and Mar., 10am-3pm daily Nov.-Feb., 9am-6pm daily Apr., 9am-7pm daily May, adults $11.25, seniors and ages 13-18 $8.45, ages 4-12 $5.50, Oct.-Mar. discounted admission

Queen Elizabeth Park

At Queen Elizabeth Park, at the highest point in Vancouver, you

a maze at the VanDusen Botanical Garden

can explore several gardens, have a picnic on its manicured grounds, or take photos of the city skyline and mountains.

In a geodesic dome near the center of the park, the Bloedel Conservatory (604/873-7000, www.vancouver.ca, 10am-8pm May-Aug., 10am-6pm daily Sept.-Oct. and Apr., 10am-5pm daily Nov.-Mar., adults $6.50, seniors and students $4.35, ages 4-12 $3.15) houses three different ecosystems, including a tropical rainforest, subtropical rainforest, and desert environment, with native plants and more than 200 free-flying birds. It's a warm destination for a cold or rainy day. Also in the park are tennis courts, a pitch-and-putt golf course, and a lawn bowling green.

To get to the park by public transit, take the Canada Line to King Edward station. Then either transfer to bus 15 southbound on Cambie Street to West 33rd Avenue, or walk south on Cambie Street to the park entrance. Follow the trails through the trees or walk along the park road to reach the conservatory; it's a short but uphill climb.

MAP 7: 4600 Cambie St., www.vancouver.ca, dawn-dusk daily

Restaurants

PRICE KEY

$ Entrées less than CAD$15
$$ Entrées CAD$15-25
$$$ Entrées more than CAD$25

MODERN CANADIAN
✪ Burdock & Co $$

Chef-owner Andrea Carlson runs this relaxed neighborhood bistro, delivering a creative hyperlocal menu to customers seated at Burdock & Co's rustic wooden tables. Dishes like risotto with aged miso and crispy quinoa, pine mushrooms paired with steamed egg custard, or fettuccini with pork and fennel ragout change with the harvest; the house-made kimchi and crispy fried chicken with buttermilk mashed potatoes are well-loved staples. The short but distinctive wine list includes bottles from BC, Oregon, France, Italy, and even Lebanon. Weekend brunch, which might bring a vegan avocado "smash" with cashew curd or tomato baked eggs with feta, will put you in the mood for some Main Street shopping.

MAP 7: 2702 Main St., 604/879-0077, www.burdockandco.com, 5pm-10pm Mon.-Fri., 10am-2pm and 5pm-10pm Sat.-Sun.

Farmer's Apprentice $$$

Imaginative creations inspired by local products bring adventurous diners to Farmer's Apprentice, a petite South Granville dining room. Cucumber cashew terrine with kombu puree? Ling cod with corn curry and Thai farro salad? You won't find these creations on any other tables around town. The same team runs the more casual wine and tapas bar Grapes and Soda (1541

UKRAINIAN CHURCH SUPPERS

Every month since 1995, the Holy Trinity Ukrainian Orthodox Cathedral (154 E. 10th Ave., 604/876-4747, http://uocvancouver.com, 5pm-8pm 1st Fri. of the month) has been hosting a moderately priced family-style supper that's open to all, in the church hall just off Main Street. Dinners feature stick-to-your-ribs classics like pierogi, cabbage rolls, *koubassa* (sausage), and borscht (beet vegetable soup) that church volunteers prepare. The ambience is a cross between a traditional church supper and a hipster hangout, with apron-clad women serving from the buffet line, and everyone from kids to seniors sharing the communal tables.

W. 6th Ave., 604/336-2456, www.grapesandsoda.ca) next door.

MAP 7: 1535 W. 6th Ave., 604/620-2070, www.farmersapprentice.ca, 11am-2pm and 5:30pm-10pm Tues.-Sun.

FIRST NATIONS
Salmon n' Bannock $$

To explore First Nations cuisine, visit Salmon n' Bannock. This modern indigenous bistro uses traditional ingredients in its elk burgers, game sausages, and slow-roasted bison—and yes, there's plenty of salmon and bannock, a traditional bread, on the menu. Wines come from Nk'Mip Cellars and Indigenous World Winery, indigenous-owned wineries based in BC's Okanagan region. Desserts might include bannock bread pudding or homemade fruit pies.

MAP 7: 1128 W. Broadway, 604/568-8971, www.salmonandbannock.net, 5pm-9pm Mon.-Sat.

CHINESE
Dynasty Seafood $$

Dynasty Seafood serves some of Vancouver's best dim sum, a sophisticated mix of traditional and creative dumplings, buns, and other small bites. Highlights include lemony baked barbecue pork buns, steamed black truffle dumplings, and sweet sago pudding, a tapioca dessert. The busy 2nd-floor dining room, with views of the downtown skyline and North Shore mountains, is a short walk west of the Broadway-City Hall Canada Line station. Reservations are recommended for dim sum, especially on Saturday-Sunday.

MAP 7: 777 W. Broadway, 604/876-8388, www.dynasty-restaurant.ca, 10am-3pm and 5pm-10pm daily

Shao Lin Noodle House $

Watch the noodle makers stretch, pull, and toss their lumps of dough at the Shao Lin Noodle House, a casual eatery near the Broadway-City Hall Canada Line station that specializes in dishes from northern China. Order a bowl of the handmade noodles, choosing from different shapes and adding your choice of meat or vegetable toppings, but don't neglect the steamed or pan-fried dumplings or the side dishes, like the spicy fried green beans.

MAP 7: 656 W. Broadway, 604/873-1618, www.shalinnoodlehouse.com, 11am-9:30pm Sun.-Thurs., 11am-10pm Fri.-Sat.

JAPANESE
Tojo's $$$

Long considered Vancouver's top Japanese dining room, Tojo's, which takes its name from chef-owner

Hidekazu Tojo, is known for the high quality of its sushi and sashimi. Chef Tojo arrived in Vancouver in the early 1970s, when North Americans were not very familiar with Japanese food. He reportedly created a roll made from cooked crabmeat and fresh avocado—widely known today as the California roll. For a special evening, sit at the sushi bar and order *omakase* (chef's choice, $80-200 pp), a parade of traditional and creative dishes. Sip rice wines and order small plates at The Sake Bar, adjacent to the main restaurant, when you don't want a full meal.

MAP 7: 1133 W. Broadway, 604/872-8050, www.tojos.com, 5pm-10pm Mon.-Sat.

INDIAN
Vij's $$

Celebrated for its innovative riffs on Indian cuisine, Vij's became equally famous for its no-reservations lineups. Relocating the restaurant to a larger space, six blocks from the Broadway City Hall Canada Line station, and introducing limited online reservations has helped tame the crowds, who still come for dishes like jackfruit in black cardamom curry, rainbow trout in coconut-fenugreek masala, and the signature lamb "Popsicles."

MAP 7: 3106 Cambie St., 604/736-6664, www.vijsrestaurant.ca, 5:30pm-10:30pm daily

Rangoli $

Under the same ownership as Vij's, the more casual Rangoli serves interesting Indian dishes in a South Granville café. Many of the choices are vegetarian, like the kale, jackfruit, and cauliflower curry or the chickpeas in fenugreek curry with grilled eggplant, while meat lovers might opt for the cumin lamb or the beef short ribs served with naan. To drink, try a salty or sweet *lassi* (yogurt drink), which is also available in a dairy-free coconut-mango version.

MAP 7: 1480 W. 11th Ave., 604/736-5711, www.vijsrangoli.ca, 11:30am-1am Sun.-Thurs., 11:30am-2am Fri.-Sat.

VIETNAMESE
✪ Anh & Chi $$

Fresh, updated Vietnamese dishes and a breezy outdoor patio bring steady lineups to Main Street's Anh & Chi. Among the menu standouts are *chả cá thăng long* (cod spiced with turmeric and dill), *cà tím tay cầm* (eggplant with okra and pickled radish), and *gỏi xoài* (a salad of fresh mango, roasted peanuts, and herbs). Ask the servers to recommend favorite dishes. Even the restrooms have admirers; the smartly

the patio of Anh & Chi

designed, gender-neutral facilities have been recognized as one of the top restrooms in Canada.

MAP 7: 3388 Main St., 604/874-0832, www.anhandchi.com, 11am-11pm daily

colorful Peruvian fare at Chicha

LATIN AMERICAN
Chicha $$

This lively storefront west of Main Street takes you to Peru by way of the Pacific Northwest, incorporating regional ingredients into classic Peruvian dishes. Start your sipping with a traditional pisco sour or with the restaurant's nonalcoholic namesake, *chicha morada*, a sweet beverage made from purple corn. Among the sharing-style plates, order one of the ceviches or opt for the addictive *palitas de yuca* (cassava-root fries). Other good choices include empanadas filled with butternut squash, corn, kale, and cheese, and any of the *causas*, whipped potatoes topped with seafood or vegetables.

MAP 7: 136 E. Broadway, 604/620-3963, www.chicharestaurant.com, 4pm-1pm Mon.-Thurs., noon-midnight Fri., 10:30am-midnight Sat., 10:30am-11pm Sun.

VEGETARIAN
The Acorn $$

At The Acorn, plant-based food shakes off its crunchy-granola reputation with ambitious plates that would enhance any upscale table: beer-battered halloumi cheese with zucchini-potato pancakes or sourdough cavatelli with corn, chanterelles, and crispy corn nuts. The dining space isn't much larger than the restaurant's namesake, and they don't take reservations (except for parties of 6-8), so you might chill at the bar with an Oma'sake (made from Granville Island sake, flowering currant, green strawberry bitters, and soda) or a craft cider. The Arbor (www.thearborrestaurant.ca), a more casual dining spot run by the same team, is down the street.

MAP 7: 3995 Main St., 604/566-9001, www.theacornrestaurant. ca, 5:30pm-10pm Mon.-Thurs., 5:30pm-11pm Fri., 10am-2:30pm and 5:30pm-11pm Sat., 10am-2:30pm and 5:30pm-10pm Sun.

chickpeas at Chickpea

Chickpea $$

Launched as a downtown food truck (which is still operating), this laid-back café on Main Street, with the slogan "The world needs more chickpeace," serves an all-vegan

Middle Eastern menu. You might opt for falafel, *sabich* (eggplant), or tofu schnitzel served as a sandwich, atop a salad, or as a platter with hummus, chickpea fries, vegetables, and pickles, or choose all day breakfast: tofu scrambles, potato-zucchini pancakes, or almond-milk French toast. To drink, there are fresh juices, kefir on tap, local beer and cider, and refreshing cocktails like the "Ginger Balagan," your choice of spirit topped with ginger beer, rosemary, and lemon.

MAP 7: 4298 Main St., 604/620-0602, www.ilovechickpea.ca, 9am-11pm Sun.-Thurs., 9am-midnight Fri.-Sat.

COFFEE AND TEA
49th Parallel Coffee Roasters $
This airy coffeehouse is perpetually packed with friends catching up over an espresso or freelancers tapping away at their laptops. The shop's popularity is partly because they make Lucky's Donuts fresh throughout the day, in flavors like classic old-fashioned, salted caramel, and white chocolate-matcha. The team at Vancouver-based 49th Parallel Coffee Roasters is serious about their coffee too, sourcing beans from small producers and brewing top-notch cups. In addition to this Main Street location, they have branches downtown and in Kitsilano.

MAP 7: 2902 Main St., 604/420-4900, http://49thcoffee.com, 7am-10pm Mon.-Sat., 7:30am-10pm Sun.

Nightlife

COCKTAIL BARS AND LOUNGES
The Cascade Room
A comfortable neighborhood lounge with exposed wood beams and a garage door-style front window, The Cascade Room specializes in creative cocktails, including many variations on the gin and tonic. Like any good Main Street watering hole, they serve a selection of local microbrews too, with a rotating roster of guest taps, along with plenty of BC wines by the glass. You won't go hungry here either, with a cascade of updated pub fare like burgers, chickpea fritters, or Scotch eggs sharing the table with larger plates that range from Pacific rockfish to steak.

MAP 7: 2616 Main St., 604/709-8650, www.thecascade.ca, 4pm-midnight Sun.-Tues., 4pm-1am Wed.-Thurs., 4pm-2am Fri.-Sat.

The Shameful Tiki Room
If you're longing for a holiday in the Polynesian islands or a drink in a classic tiki bar, there's no shame in spending an evening at The Shameful Tiki Room, Main Street's homage to kitschy tiki lounges. In the dimly lit space, adorned with palm fronds, masks, and tapa cloth, you can sip a Singapore sling, a zombie, or other vintage cocktail while

grazing on pupus like Hawaiian-style ribs or teriyaki chicken wings. MAP 7: 4362 Main St., no phone, www.shamefultikiroom.com, 5pm-midnight Sun.-Thurs., 5pm-1am Fri.-Sat.

COMEDY
The Sunday Service

No, it's not like going to church. Held in the Fox Cabaret, a former adult theater turned alternative club, The Sunday Service, by the comedy group of the same name, is a weekly improv show. The five performers typically mix short improv games with a longer comedic improvisation. Guest comedians occasionally share the stage with the regular troupe.

MAP 7: Fox Cabaret, 2321 Main St., www.thesundayservice.ca, 9pm Sun., $10

Yuk Yuk's Vancouver Comedy Club

At this local branch of a national chain of comedy venues, you can chuckle through stand-up shows by local and visiting comedians in this 170-seat cabaret-style club. The two weekend evening shows generally run 90 minutes to two hours and include a warm-up host, an opening act, and the featured performer. Amateur nights are 8pm Wednesday, when newer comics can get their start.

MAP 7: 2837 Cambie St., 604/696-9857, www.yukyuks.com, showtimes vary, $7-30

Recreation

SPECTATOR SPORTS
BASEBALL
Vancouver Canadians

The city's minor league baseball team, the Vancouver Canadians, plays June-early September at family-friendly Nat Bailey Stadium, a historic outdoor venue built in 1951 near Queen Elizabeth Park. The Canadians are affiliated with Major League Baseball's Toronto Blue Jays. Several nights during the season, the skies light up with postgame fireworks at the stadium.

By public transit from downtown, take the Canada Line to King Edward station. From there, you can walk to the stadium in about 15-20 minutes, or catch bus 33 toward 29th Avenue and ride it three stops to Midlothian Avenue at Clancy Loranger Way, opposite the stadium.

MAP 7: 4601 Ontario St., 604/872-5232, www.canadiansbaseball.com, June-early Sept., adults $16-27

Dude Chilling Park

Until one day in 2012, Guelph Park, near Main Street, was just one of Vancouver's many small neighborhood parks. Then, on an otherwise ordinary November day, a sign appeared in a corner of the park. Looking like other official Vancouver Park Board signage, the sign made it seem that the park's name had been changed. The new name? Dude Chilling Park.

Local artist Victor Briestensky created and erected the sign in jest. Though many people assumed the new name was a play on the neighborhood's hipster community, the artist was actually referring to a sculpture, *Reclining Figure* by Michael Dennis, which was installed in the park in 1991. City staff promptly removed Briestensky's fake sign, but not before it circulated widely on social media.

Local media picked up the story, and the community rallied around the artist, submitting a petition with more than 1,500 signatures requesting that the sign be permanently reinstalled. The artist offered to donate the work, and the Park Board agreed to reinstall it as part of the city's public art program. Officially, the park's name remains Guelph Park. But at the corner of East 8th Avenue and Brunswick Street, where this unique artwork is now installed, it's Dude Chilling Park.

Arts and Culture

GALLERIES
✪ Bau-Xi Gallery

See what's on view at Bau-Xi Gallery, which features regular showings of contemporary fine art in an airy white South Granville space. Established in 1965, the gallery represents a wide range of Canadian painters, photographers, sculptors, and other artists.

MAP 7: 3045 Granville St., 604/733-7011, www.bau-xi.com, 10am-5:30pm Mon.-Sat., 11am-5:30pm Sun., free

✪ Douglas Reynolds Gallery

Stop in to Douglas Reynolds Gallery, a white-walled two-level space in the South Granville district, to explore the museum-quality exhibits of historic and contemporary Northwest Coast First Nations art, from masks, jewelry, and sculpture to totem poles. The gallery shows works by Bill Reid, Robert Davidson, and other notables, along with pieces by emerging indigenous artists.

MAP 7: 2335 Granville St., 604/731-9292, www. douglasreynoldsgallery.com, 10am-6pm Mon.-Sat., noon-5pm Sun., free

✪ Hill's Native Art

Lloyd and Frances Hill first began showing and selling indigenous art after they acquired the Koksilah General Store on Vancouver Island's east coast in 1946. The business has grown to several locations, housing one of North America's largest collections of Northwest Coast native art. Hill's Native Art, near Main Street, carries a large range of First Nations and Inuit works, from souvenir-style items (T-shirts, jewelry, books, and cards) to high-quality artworks, carvings, and more by noted indigenous artists.

MAP 7: 120 E. Broadway, 604/685-4249, www.hills.ca, 10am-7pm daily, free

THEATER

Arts Club Theatre Company

Vancouver's top repertory theater and the largest theater company in western Canada, the Arts Club Theatre Company, established in 1958, now performs on three stages. The main stage shows are at the 650-seat Stanley Industrial Alliance Stage, a historic theater in the South Granville district, and include crowd-pleasing musicals, entertaining comedies, and thought-provoking dramas; recent seasons have included *The Curious Incident of the Dog in the Night-Time, Matilda: The Musical,* and *Angels in America.*

MAP 7: 2750 Granville St., 604/687-1644, http://artsclub.com, $29-99

Stanley Industrial Alliance Stage

The Flame

The Flame is Vancouver's home-grown storytelling series, modeled after the U.S.-based storytelling organization and National Public Radio show *The Moth*. The Flame hosts monthly storytelling evenings at Hood 29 (formerly the Cottage Bistro) on Main Street. The 8-10 preselected performers in each show must abide by The Flame's three rules: Stories must be true, about you, and "told in a few" (typically under 10 minutes). The Flame is held on the first Wednesday of the month September-November and January-June, but check the "flamevancouver" Facebook page to confirm. Shows start at 7pm, but arrive 6pm-6:30pm if you want a seat.

Festivals and Events

Festival of Lights

The VanDusen Botanical Garden marks the holiday season with its annual Festival of Lights, illuminating its garden paths with thousands of sparkling lights. The festival runs early December-early January.

Cambie Corridor: VanDusen Botanical Garden, http://vandusengarden.org, Dec.

Vancouver Mural Festival

Artists from Vancouver and around the world paint the walls on and near Main Street during the annual Vancouver Mural Festival. Events encompass guided walks through the artworks and a lively street party with free live music featuring local bands. Although the festival runs for 10 days in August, you can view most of the murals year-round. The greatest concentration is on Main Alley (half a block west of Main St.,

Festival of Lights at the VanDusen Botanical Garden

between 2nd Ave. and Broadway) and on 7½ Lane (between 7th Ave. and 8th Ave. from Main Alley west to Manitoba St.).

Various locations: www.vanmuralfest. ca, Aug.

Chutzpah! Festival

At the monthlong Chutzpah! Festival, which showcases contemporary and traditional Jewish arts and culture, internationally recognized theater artists, dancers, musicians, and comedians perform in a diverse collection of shows mid-October-mid-November. The Norman Rothstein Theatre at the Jewish Community Centre of Greater Vancouver (950 W. 41st Ave.) is the festival's home base— and just south of the VanDusen Botanical Garden—although events take place at venues around the city.

Various locations: http:// chutzpahfestival.com, Oct.-Nov.

Shops

SHOPPING DISTRICTS
Main Street

Looking for clothes you won't find at the local mall? Main Street is lined with independent boutiques, many carrying clothing by local and Canadian designers.

MAP 7: Main St., between E. 20th Ave. and 30th Ave.

CLOTHING AND ACCESSORIES
✪ Barefoot Contessa

The motto of this Main Street boutique is "all things lovely," and with their stock of frilly, flouncy, feminine styles, it's hard to dispute that claim. At Barefoot Contessa (which has no connection to cooking guru Ina Garten), you can find a perfect dress to wear to a garden party or a flowery frock to brighten a rainy day. Check out the vintage-inspired jewelry and other sparkly baubles. Their second location is on Commercial Drive.

MAP 7: 3715 Main St., 604/879-8175, www.thebarefootcontessa.com,

Barefoot Contessa

11am-6pm Mon.-Sat., noon-5pm Sun.

✪ Front and Company

For vintage, designer consignment, and smart new clothing, the fashion-conscious frequent Front and Company. While it can take some hunting to unearth the stylish finds from this jam-packed Main Street shop, the selection of men's and women's garments is generally high quality. They also stock jewelry, handbags, shoes, and fun gift items.

MAP 7: 3772 Main St., 604/879-8431, www.frontandcompany.com, 11am-6:30pm daily

BOOKS AND STATIONERY

The Regional Assembly of Text

Remember the days when writing meant pen and paper or perhaps a typewriter? Even if you don't, you can journey back to the pre-digital era at The Regional Assembly of Text, a Main Street stationer that stocks cards, journals, and anything to do with correspondence.

Even cooler is their Letter Writing Club, held at 7pm on the first Thursday of every month, where you can gather to send notes to your friends and family. The shop provides supplies for this free event; all you need to do is show up and write. Your mom will thank you.

MAP 7: 3934 Main St., 604/877-2247, www.assemblyoftext.com, 11am-6pm Mon.-Sat., noon-5pm Sun.

DESIGN AND GIFTS

Vancouver Special

If you need a retro-styled Bluetooth clock radio, a guide to Canadian cocktails, or vibrantly colored nesting measuring cups, stop into this emporium of cool design stuff. At Vancouver Special on Main Street, you'll find shelves and tables piled with art books, cookbooks, Scandinavian textiles, Japanese ceramics, and a few Vancouver-made objects, as well as a second room with a selection of home furnishings.

The shop shares its name (though not its design) with a type of house built across the city in the 1960s and 1970s. Resembling a ranch house atop a box, many of these two-story homes sheltered multigenerational families.

MAP 7: 3612 Main St., 604/568-3673,

Vancouver Special

http://shop.vanspecial.com, 11am-6pm Mon.-Sat., noon-5pm Sun.

OUTDOOR GEAR

Sports Junkies

Sports Junkies has good deals on new and used sports equipment and clothing for both kids and adults. The jam-packed store, between Cambie and Main Streets, can feel a little disorganized, but if you take the time to hunt, you can frequently find bargains.

MAP 7: 102 W. Broadway, 604/879-6000, www.sportsjunkies. com, 10am-7pm Mon.-Wed., 10am-8pm Thurs.-Fri., 10am-6pm Sat., 10am-5pm Sun.

Commercial Drive   Map 8

Funky Commercial Drive runs north-south through the city's East Side. Once the heart of Vancouver's Italian community, the neighborhood is now home to a diverse collection of residents. Along The Drive, you'll find **pubs, cafés,** and a multicultural mix of casual places to eat.

The up-and-coming **East Village** district is along East Hastings Street, between Victoria Drive and Renfrew Street. Nearby, Powell Street is a center of Vancouver's booming **craft brewery** scene.

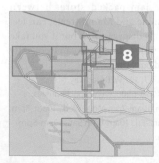

TOP SIGHTS

- Best Place to Start (or End) a Craft Beer Crawl: **Parallel 49 Brewing Company** (page 176)
- Best Spot to Sample Local Spirits: **Odd Society Spirits** (page 176)

TOP RESTAURANTS

- Where to Find the Best Treats in a Crust: **The Pie Shoppe** (page 180)

TOP NIGHTLIFE

- Best Place for a Geeky Good Time: **Storm Crow Tavern** (page 181)

TOP ARTS AND CULTURE

- Most Offbeat Theater Offerings: **Vancouver East Cultural Centre** (page 183)

GETTING THERE AND AROUND

- SkyTrain lines: Expo Line
- SkyTrain stops: Commercial-Broadway
- Bus lines: 4, 7, 9, 14, 16, 20, 95, 99

COMMERCIAL DRIVE

173

1　　2　　3

Powell Street Craft Brewery
❶
POWELL ST

A

FRANKLIN ST

Callister Brewing ❷

JACKSON AVENUE
PRINCESS AVENUE
HEATLEY AVENUE
HAWKS AVENUE
CAMPBELL AVENUE

EAST HASTINGS ST ❻

EAST PENDER ST

CLARK DR

FRANCES ST

B

MacLean Park

E GEORGIA ST

Woodland Park

◀ SEE MAP 2

ADANAC ST

VENABLES ST

PARKER ST

C

Strathcona Park

NAPIER ST

WILLIAM ST

CHARLES ST

GRANT ST

D ⑬

GRAVELEY ST

Central Valley Greenway

E 1ST AVE

E 2ND AVE

E 3RD AVE

E 4TH AVE

E

◀ SEE MAP 3

VCC-Clark Ⓜ ⑲

Monument for East Vancouver

CLARK DR

F

E 8TH AVE

E BROADWAY

© MOON.COM

4 · **5** · **6**

Odd Society Spirits **3**

Parallel 49 Brewing Company **5**

COMMERCIAL DR · SALSBURY DR · VICTORIA DR · SEMLIN DR · LAKEWOOD DR · TEMPLETON DR

Pandora Park

8

GARDEN DR

NANAIMO ST

Templeton Park

7

10

9

COMMERCIAL DR

11

12

Grandview Park

14

15

Victoria Park

16

17

18

McSpadden Park

COMMERCIAL DR · VICTORIA DR · SEMLIN DR · LAKEWOOD DR

20

21

Ⓜ *Commercial Drive*

Ⓜ *Broadway*

SIGHTS

1	A3	Powell Street Craft Brewery	5	A5	Parallel 49 Brewing Company
2	A3	Callister Brewing	19	E3	Monument for East Vancouver
3	A4	Odd Society Spirits			

RESTAURANTS

4	A4	The Pie Shoppe	17	E4	La Grotta del Formaggio
8	B5	The Red Wagon	18	E4	Prado Café
9	C4	Kin Kao Thai Kitchen	20	F4	Jamjar
14	D4	Turks Coffee House			

NIGHTLIFE

| 12 | C4 | Havana | 16 | D4 | La Mezcaleria |
| 15 | D4 | Storm Crow Tavern | 21 | F4 | St. Augustine's |

RECREATION

| 13 | D1 | Central Valley Greenway |

ARTS AND CULTURE

| 7 | B4 | York Theatre | 10 | C4 | Vancouver East Cultural Centre |

SHOPS

| 6 | B3 | Gourmet Warehouse | 11 | C4 | Still Fabulous |

0 — 300 yds
0 — 300 m

DISTANCE ACROSS MAP
Approximate: 2.1 mi or 3.4 km

Sights

✪ Parallel 49 Brewing Company

The tasting room at Parallel 49 Brewing Company, one of the more established East Side breweries, is a beer tasting hall, a pubby small-plates restaurant dubbed Street Kitchen, and a spirited neighborhood gathering place. Three of the brewery's founders grew up nearby in East Van. These days, the company is known for their Ruby Tears red ale, the Tricycle Grapefruit Radler (blended from lager and red grapefruit juice), and a changing array of seasonal brews. Stop in for a tasting flight to see what's on tap. Free tours (on the hour noon-5pm Sun.) are offered.

MAP 8: 1950 Triumph St., 604/558-2739, http://parallel49brewing. com, tasting room 11am-11pm daily, restaurant 11am-midnight Sun.-Thurs., 11am-1am Fri.-Sat.

Callister Brewing

Billing themselves as "Canada's first collaborative brewery," Callister Brewing not only sells and serves their own beer in their East Side tasting room, but every year they also team up with three additional brewers who use the facilities in Callister's red stucco brewery to make their own beers. Along with a changing selection of Callister's own brews, which might include Field Day Farmhouse Ale, Sweater Weather Belgian Amber, and 1 Hop Mind Pale Ale, you can sample these partners' creations in the tasting room. Four-ounce samplers start at $2 each. The tasting room is teeny, with a long communal table and a few stools at the counter, so you're likely to strike up a conversation with fellow beer aficionados.

MAP 8: 1338 Franklin St., 604/569-2739, www.callisterbrewing.com, 2pm-9pm Mon.-Thurs., 2pm-10pm Fri., 1pm-10pm Sat., 1pm-8pm Sun.

Powell Street Craft Brewery

A husband-and-wife team manages Powell Street Craft Brewery in a small East Side warehouse on busy Powell Street. Old Jalopy Pale Ale and Ode to Citra (also a pale ale) are two well-regarded brews. Try a glass or a flight in the tasting room, where you can perch at a blond-wood bar-height table and look through the window into the brewery. Glasses start at $2.30 for a five-ounce sampler; a flight of four is $7.50.

MAP 8: 1357 Powell St., 604/558-2537, www.powellbeer.com, 2pm-9pm Mon.-Thurs., noon-10pm Fri.-Sat., noon-9pm Sun.

✪ Odd Society Spirits

Standing out amid the East Side beer makers, Odd Society Spirits is a small-batch distillery in a former motorcycle garage, where they make their signature East Van Vodka, along with gin, a "moonshine" whiskey, crème de cassis, amaro, and a distinctive bittersweet vermouth. Tasting flights (three samples for $7) and mixed drinks are available in their front room, an old-time cocktail lounge with marble-top tables and a long bar. In the lounge, floor-to-ceiling windows showcase the

CRAFT BREWERIES

Vancouver's first microbreweries launched in the 1980s, but more recent changes in BC's provincial liquor laws paved the way for a craft brewery boom that has been growing exponentially since 2010. Two East Side neighborhoods have become the center

flight at Callister Brewing

of Vancouver's craft brewery scene. The city's eastern districts are locally known as "East Van," but the increasing number of microbreweries in this area has earned it the nickname "Yeast Van."

One center of local craft beer production is in the Mount Pleasant neighborhood, around Main Street between 2nd and 8th Avenues, a short walk from the Olympic Village, where several breweries with tasting rooms are within strolling distance of each other. Even more craft breweries have set up shop farther east, between Hastings and Powell Streets, east of Clark Drive. This partly industrial, partly residential neighborhood isn't the most picturesque, but with lots of excellent beer to sample, it's perfect for a brewery crawl. Most brewery tasting rooms here open around midday or early afternoon and remain open into the evening.

Many of Vancouver's craft breweries are too small for formal tours, but some offer regularly scheduled tours, and at others, staff are happy to show you around if you call ahead. If you want to learn more about the brewing process and the local beer industry, another option is to take a tour with **Vancouver Brewery Tours** (604/318-2280, http://vancouverbrewerytours.com, $70-90). Each of their three-hour excursions visits three different breweries. Their website details the tour schedule and which breweries each tour visits on which day.

The drinking age in British Columbia is 19, and you may be asked to show identification to verify your age. Here are some spots to incorporate into your Vancouver brewery crawl. Cheers!

- **33 Acres Brewing:** Raise a glass of 33 Acres of Sunshine (a blond ale) or 33 Acres of Darkness (a malty dark beer) at this Main Street tasting room, or see what new brews they're concocting at the 33 Brewing Experiment next door. Tip: On weekends, there are waffles (page 100).

- **Brassneck Brewery:** At this casual Main Street brewery popular with craft-brew connoisseurs, enjoy a glass of the signature Brassneck Ale, or sample seasonal creations (page 100).

- **Granville Island Brewing:** Tour the original brewery at one of the city's first craft brewers, conveniently located on Granville Island (page 116).

- **Parallel 49 Brewing Company:** At this well-established East Side gathering spot, you can hang out over a Tricycle Grapefruit Radler or sample a seasonal brew (page 176).

- **Callister Brewing:** There's always something new to try at Canada's first "collaborative brewery," which serves its own beers and those of a changing line-up of beer makers who share their East Side facilities (page 176).

distilling room in back, which you can visit on a free tour (by reservation). You'll learn about the distilling process and how they use their two 92-gallon (350-liter) German-made copper-pot stills and their 15-foot (4.5-m) "vodka column," which removes impurities from the vodka. MAP 8: 1725 Powell St., 604/559-6745, www.oddsocietyspirits.com, 1pm-11pm Thurs.-Sat., 1pm-7pm Sun., tours by reservation

Monument for East Vancouver

This illuminated cross with the words "EAST VAN" nested inside isn't for a religious venue. Rather, it's a public art piece, *Monument for East Vancouver,* created by Vancouver-born artist Ken Lum.

Lum has written that the inspiration for the 57-foot (17-m) sculpture, which lights up after dark, came from a graffiti symbol that circulated on the city's East Side as early as the 1940s. Its origin is unknown, although Lum notes that it may derive from the large Catholic community that lived in the area at that time, when many Italian, Greek, and Eastern European immigrants settled in East Van.

East Vancouver was once considered the poorer cousin to the city's well-to-do West Side neighborhoods. As real estate prices escalated across the region and East Van lost some of its working-class image, Lum's artwork has become a symbol of local pride for many East Siders. Look for images of this "monument" on T-shirts around town.

MAP 8: Clark Dr. and E. 6th Ave.

Restaurants

PRICE KEY

$ Entrées less than CAD$15
$$ Entrées CAD$15-25
$$$ Entrées more than CAD$25

MIDDLE EASTERN
Jamjar $$

Casual Jamjar serves traditional Lebanese dishes, updated with local ingredients, in a space that mixes pendant lights, white subway tiles, and other industrial elements with homey wooden tables and jars of their own hummus, dips, and sauces on display. From *fattoush* salad to *makdous* (pickled eggplant stuffed with chili and walnuts) to *makali* (fried cauliflower with pomegranate molasses), plates are designed to share, with lots of vegetarian options. Additional locations are in South Granville, on the UBC campus, and in North Vancouver's Shipyards District.

MAP 8: 2280 Commercial Dr., 604/252-3957, www.jam-jar.ca, 11:30am-10pm daily

THAI
Kin Kao Thai Kitchen $$

Convenient for a bite before a show at the Vancouver East Cultural Centre or the York Theatre, Kin Kao Thai Kitchen serves Thai dishes with contemporary twists in a modern minimalist space, where you can

pork ribs and salad at Kin Kao Thai Kitchen

perch at the counter or line up for seats at one of the light wood tables (it's a small spot). Don't miss the tangy sour cured pork ribs. Other recommended dishes include papaya salad, steak salad or any curry dish. Craft beers from neighborhood breweries are on tap. **MAP 8:** 903 Commercial Dr., 604/558-1125, www.kinkao.ca, 5pm-10pm Mon., 11:30am-3pm and 5pm-10pm Tues.-Sat.

DINERS
The Red Wagon $

What brings the all-day breakfast crowds of families, East Side hipsters, and other neighborhood denizens to The Red Wagon, a homey diner in the heart of the East Village? First are pulled pork pancakes—buttermilk pancakes layered with tender pork and Jack Daniels-laced maple syrup. Beyond this specialty, the menu starts with eggs, bacon, and other morning classics, but gets creative with a Vietnamese-influenced breakfast banh mi, vegetarian tofu scramble, and goat cheese and basil frittata. If you're in a lunch mood, opt for a burger, soups, salads, or sandwiches. **MAP 8:** 2296 E. Hastings St., 604/568-4565, www.redwagoncafe. com, 8am-3pm Mon.-Tues., 8am-9pm Wed.-Sun.

QUICK BITES
La Grotta del Formaggio $

A delicious reason to visit Italian grocer La Grotta Del Formaggio is the Italian sandwiches this Commercial Drive shop makes to order. Load up your fresh bread or focaccia with salami, prosciutto, or other cured meats, along with cheeses, peppers, olives, and various condiments. The shop has a couple of seats out on the sidewalk, but a better plan is to take your meal to a nearby park. The shop also sells imported pastas, anchovies, and a large selection of cheeses.

MAP 8: 1791 Commercial Dr., 604/255-3911, www.lgdf.ca, 9am-6pm Mon.-Thurs. and Sat., 9am-7pm Fri., 10am-6pm Sun.

MAP 8: 1875 Powell St., 604/338-6646, http://thepieshoppe.ca, 11am-6pm Wed.-Thurs., 11am-7pm Fri.-Sat., 11am-5pm Sun.

BAKERIES AND CAFÉS
✪ The Pie Shoppe $

The Pie Shoppe turns out a seasonally changing array of sweet things in a crust. The proprietors of this cheerful East Side bakery, with a common table and handcrafted pine counter, down the street from several craft breweries, also run Panoramic Roasting Company, a small-batch coffee roaster, and pair their blueberry, nectarine-cardamom, chocolate pecan, or other slices with pour-overs, espressos, and cappuccinos from their own beans. They sell whole pies and savory options too.

COFFEE AND TEA
Prado Café $

A hip Commercial Drive coffee spot that's expanded to several locations across the city, window-lined Prado Café serves its brews in turquoise mugs to clients who settle at the wooden tables to chat or get some work done. Staff use locally roasted 49th Parallel beans and bake their pastries in-house.

MAP 8: 1938 Commercial Dr., 604/255-5537, http://pradocafevancouver.com, 7am-8pm Mon.-Fri., 8am-6pm Sat.-Sun.

The Pie Shoppe

Turks Coffee House $

As the first independent coffee bar on Commercial Drive, Turks Coffee House may claim that they've been "non-conforming since 1992," but it conforms to seriously high coffee standards, serving Italian-style brews sourced primarily from small, fair trade, and organic producers. Sip your drip, pour over, or espresso-style java at the long communal counter, a sunny window table, or out on the pocket-size sidewalk patio.

MAP 8: 1276 Commercial Dr., 604/255-5805, www.milanocoffee.ca, 6:30am-10pm Mon.-Sat., 7am-10pm Sun.

Nightlife

CRAFT BEER

St. Augustine's

To find out whether your favorite beer is in stock before heading to this easygoing Commercial Drive pub, check the St. Augustine's website, which lists their 60 beer taps and how much of each variety is remaining. The friendly beer-loving staff dispense a vast selection of local craft beer and cider, as well as other brews from the Pacific Northwest and farther afield. Pizzas, burgers, and other bar snacks round out the menu.

MAP 8: 2360 Commercial Dr., 604/569-1911, http://staugustinesvancouver.com, 11am-1am Sun.-Thurs., 11am-2am Fri.-Sat.

PUBS

✪ Storm Crow Tavern

Consider yourself a nerd? Then this Commercial Drive pub, which bills itself as "Vancouver's Original Nerd Bar," is your place. Its walls decorated with ray guns and science fiction photos, Storm Crow Tavern hosts nerd trivia nights (1st and 3rd Tuesday of the month) and Saturday morning cartoon brunches (11am-2pm Sat.), provides stacks of board games to play, and shows sci-fi (never sports!) on their TVs. To pair with locally made craft beer, the nerd-themed munchies include Rebel X-Wings (chicken wings), Teenage Mutant Deep-fried Pickles, and the Dungeon Burger, a chef's choice mystery. A second location, Storm Crow Alehouse, is on West Broadway near Granville.

MAP 8: 1305 Commercial Dr., 604/566-9669, www.stormcrowtavern.com, 11am-1am Mon.-Sat., 11am-midnight Sun.

Havana

Open since 1996, this Commercial Drive fixture is a pub, restaurant, art gallery, and performance space. Havana serves Cuban-inspired cocktails and Latin-influenced bar food on the heated watch-the-world-go-by patio and in the cozy interior. An eclectic lineup performs on a small backroom stage several nights a week—comedy, magic, fringe theater, and more.

MAP 8: 1212 Commercial Dr., 604/253-9119, www.havanarestaurant.ca, 11am-midnight Mon.-Fri., 10am-midnight Sat.-Sun.

La Mezcaleria

The front door of La Mezcaleria proclaims: *"Para Todo Mal Mezcal, Para Todo Bien Tambien"* ("For everything bad, mescal, and for everything good too.") If that's your philosophy, then raise a glass at this lively Mexican pub that pours a large selection of mescal, tequila, and south-of-the-border cocktails. Nibble some ceviche or guacamole while you sip. There's a second location in Gastown.

MAP 8: 1622 Commercial Dr., 604/559-8226, www.lamezcaleria.ca, 5pm-10pm Mon.-Thurs., 11am-11pm Fri., 10am-11pm Sat., 10am-10pm Sun.

the sunny patio at Havana

Recreation

CYCLING
Central Valley Greenway

A 15-mile (24-km) urban cycling route, the Central Valley Greenway takes you through Vancouver's eastern districts, beginning near Science World and the Olympic Village and continuing east to Commercial Drive and beyond, through the suburbs of Burnaby and New Westminster. Part of the route runs along neighborhood streets; other sections follow a paved path under or alongside the SkyTrain line. Some of the greenway feels more industrial than "green," while other sections are naturally scenic, particularly the area near Burnaby Lake Regional Park (www.burnaby.ca), where you can stop to walk a trail along the lake.

The Greenway's easternmost point is near the River Market (810 Quayside Dr., New Westminster, 604/520-3881, http://rivermarket.ca), where you can take a break at several food stalls like Longtail Kitchen (http://longtailkitchen.com) for street food-inspired Thai fare. River Market is one block south of the New Westminster SkyTrain station.

If you don't want to ride the Greenway all the way out of town and back, or if you get tired along the way, you and your bike can board the SkyTrain to return downtown. Bikes are allowed on the Expo Line, except during weekday rush hours (7am-9am westbound toward downtown, 4pm-6pm eastbound).

MAP 8: From Quebec St. near Terminal Ave. to Quayside Dr. in New Westminster, http://vancouver.ca

Arts and Culture

THEATER
✪ Vancouver East Cultural Centre

The Vancouver East Cultural Centre, known locally as "The Cultch," hosts an eclectic season of theater, dance, and musical events, showcasing local, Canadian, and international performers. Among their recent shows are *Little Dickens,* provocative puppetry by Toronto-based Ronnie Burkett and his 40-plus marionettes; *A Vancouver Guldasta,* a drama about a local South Asian family, set in the 1980s; and *The Ones We Leave Behind,* from the Vancouver Asian Canadian Theatre. Their main East Side building houses two performance spaces: the 200-seat Historic Theatre and the smaller black-box Vancity Culture Lab. Off-site, they also produce shows at the nearby York Theatre.

MAP 8: 1895 Venables St., 604/251-1363, http://thecultch.com, prices vary

the York Theatre

York Theatre

The Vancouver East Cultural Centre produces music, dance, theater, and other events at the restored 355-seat York Theatre, down the street from their main building. Built in 1913, the York started life as the Alcazar Theatre, and over the years was a movie house and a concert venue (Nirvana played here). More recent productions have included *Elbow Room Café: The Musical,* an original musical based on a Vancouver breakfast joint; *Children of God,* a world premiere about an Oji-Cree family whose children are sent to a residential school in northern Ontario; and a show from storyteller Edgar Oliver, often featured on the U.S. public radio show *The Moth.*

MAP 8: 639 Commercial Dr., 604/251-1363, http://thecultch.com, prices vary

Festivals and Events

Eastside Culture Crawl

East Vancouver artists open their studios to visitors during the popular Eastside Culture Crawl. Whether you're in the market for artwork or just like to browse, most artists are interested in chatting with visitors during this mid-November weekend. Most of the open studios are located between Gastown and Commercial Drive.

Various locations: www.culturecrawl. ca, Nov.

Shops

VINTAGE AND SECONDHAND
Still Fabulous

Commercial Drive thrift shop Still Fabulous carries good-quality secondhand women's and men's clothing. It's a small shop, but the packed racks may hold bargains, and your purchases are for a good cause. Proceeds from the shop benefit BC Children's Hospital and BC Women's Hospital. There's another location on Main Street.

MAP 8: 1124 Commercial Dr., 604/620-6110, www.stillfabulousthrift. com, 10:30am-5:30pm Tues.-Sat. and noon-5:30pm Sun. Apr.-Sept., 10:30am-5pm Tues.-Sat. and noon-5pm Sun. Oct.-Mar.

Still Fabulous thrift shop

SPECIALTY FOOD AND DRINK
Gourmet Warehouse

Vancouver's best kitchen supply store is the cavernous East Side Gourmet Warehouse, which carries a vast stock of small appliances, kitchenware, and food items from spices to snacks to chocolates. If you can eat it or cook with it, they have it, and the accommodating staff can help you find what you need, whether you're looking for the Pacific Northwest's best dried cherries, Vancouver-made snack crackers, or ingredients for a molecular gastronomy project. They'll make up gift baskets for your foodie friends, and they offer periodic cooking workshops and other events.

MAP 8: 1340 E. Hastings St., 604/253-3022, www. gourmetwarehouse.ca, 10am-6pm daily

Richmond

Map 9

Vancouver is now considered the most Asian metropolis outside Asia. Many of its Asian residents have settled in Richmond, a city of more than 200,000 on Vancouver's southern boundaries, where more than half the population is of Asian descent, with most from mainland China, Taiwan, or Hong Kong.

Richmond has several multicultural attractions to explore, including a popular **night market** and some of the best **Chinese restaurants** in North America. The city's waterfront **Steveston Village** was important in the region's fishing history and still houses a bustling fish market and numerous seafood restaurants. It's also a departure point for **whale-watching** cruises.

TOP SIGHTS

- Tastiest Place to Graze Outdoors: **Richmond Night Market** (page 190)

TOP RESTAURANTS

- Top Cantonese Dining: **Bamboo Grove** (page 193)
- Best Shanghainese: **Su Hang Restaurant** (page 193)
- Where to Eat Lamb, and Lots of It: **Hao's Lamb Restaurant** (page 194)
- Best Dim Sum: **Chef Tony Seafood Restaurant** (page 196)

GETTING THERE AND AROUND

- SkyTrain lines: Canada Line (Richmond-Brighouse branch)
- SkyTrain stops: Bridgeport, Aberdeen, Lansdowne, Richmond-Brighouse

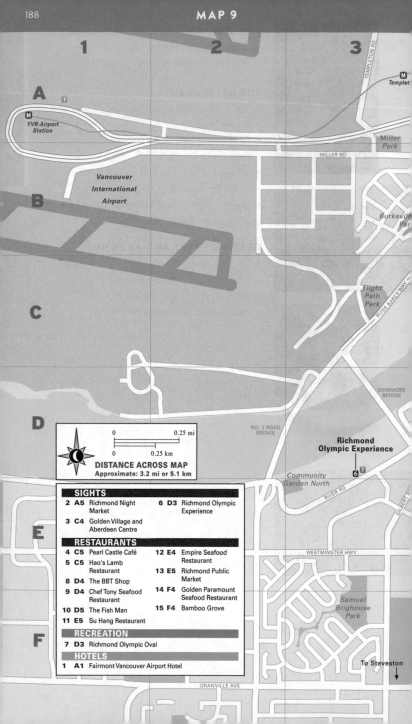

1　　　　**2**　　　　**3**

TEMPLETON RD

A

🚇 YVR-Airport Station

Ⓜ Templet

Vancouver International Airport

Miller Park

MILLER RD

B

Burkevill Par

C

Flight Path Park

RUSS BAKER WAY

DINSMORE BRIDGE

D

NO. 2 ROAD BRIDGE

Richmond Olympic Experience

Ⓖ🅖

Community Garden North

RIVER RD

GILBERT R

0   0.25 mi
0   0.25 km
DISTANCE ACROSS MAP
Approximate: 3.2 mi or 5.1 km

E

WESTMINSTER HWY

Samuel Brighouse Park

F

To Steveston

GRANVILLE AVE

SIGHTS
2 A5	Richmond Night Market	
3 C4	Golden Village and Aberdeen Centre	
6 D3	Richmond Olympic Experience	

RESTAURANTS
4 C5	Pearl Castle Café	
5 C5	Hao's Lamb Restaurant	
8 D4	The BBT Shop	
9 D4	Chef Tony Seafood Restaurant	
10 D5	The Fish Man	
11 E5	Su Hang Restaurant	
12 E4	Empire Seafood Restaurant	
13 E5	Richmond Public Market	
14 F4	Golden Paramount Seafood Restaurant	
15 F4	Bamboo Grove	

RECREATION
7 D3	Richmond Olympic Oval	

HOTELS
1 A1	Fairmont Vancouver Airport Hotel	

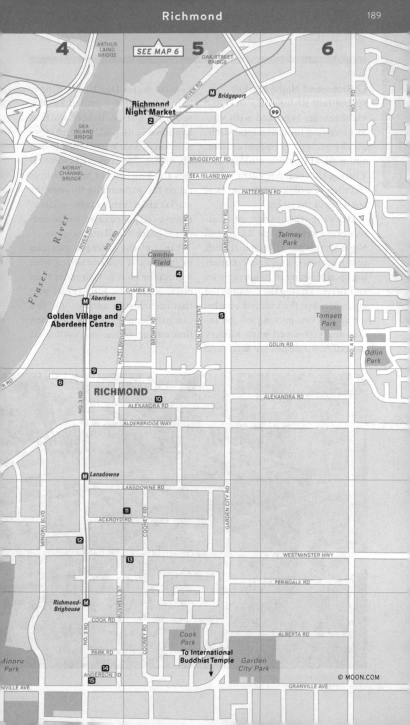

4

SEE MAP 6

5

6

ARTHUR
LAING
BRIDGE

OAK STREET
BRIDGE

RIVER RD

M Bridgeport

99

SEA
ISLAND
BRIDGE

**Richmond
Night Market**
2

MORAY
CHANNEL
BRIDGE

BRIDGEPORT RD

SEA ISLAND WAY

PATTERSON RD

RIVER RD

NO. 3 RD

SEXSMITH RD

GARDEN CITY RD

Talmey
Park

Fraser River

*Cambie
Field*
4

CAMBIE RD

M *Aberdeen*

**Golden Village and
Aberdeen Centre**
3

HAZELBRIDGE WAY

BROWN RD

ODLIN CRESCENT

5

Tomsett
Park

ODLIN RD

NO. 4 RD

Odlin
Park

NO. 3 RD

9

8

RICHMOND

10

ALEXANDRA RD

ALEXANDRA RD

ALDERBRIDGE WAY

M *Lansdowne*

LANSDOWNE RD

GARDEN CITY RD

MINORU BLVD

11

ACKROYD RD

COONEY RD

12

13

WESTMINSTER HWY

FERNDALE RD

**Richmond-
Brighouse** M

RUSSELL ST

COOK RD

NO. 3 RD

COONEY RD

Cook
Park

ALBERTA RD

PARK RD

14

*Minoru
Park*

ANDERSON RD

15

**To International
Buddhist Temple**
↓

Garden
City Park

NVILLE AVE

GRANVILLE AVE

© MOON.COM

Sights

RICHMOND

SIGHTS

✪ Richmond Night Market

Spring-fall, Richmond's weekend night market is packed with visitors enjoying the Asian food stalls, quirky shopping opportunities, and general carnival atmosphere. Visiting this outdoor event is like traveling to a night market in Asia, but without the jet lag.

Drawing thousands of visitors every weekend, the Richmond Night Market has 120 vendors, with row upon row of snack sellers offering up all manner of Asian savories and sweets. During the evening, the aisles between the outdoor booths, set up in a vast parking lot, get increasingly jammed with hungry patrons; most dishes are small and easy to share. Don't have dinner before you go; try grilled kebabs, squid on a stick, bubble waffles, handmade tofu pudding, and other Asian-style snacks; most dishes cost $10 or less. The market has some tables and benches, but many visitors eat on the go, wending through the market aisles. Vendors also sell inexpensive cell phone cases, socks, electronic gadgets, and more.

Lines at the entrance gate can be lengthy. If you're visiting with a group or plan to visit more than once, purchase a $28 express pass that includes six admissions. You can use them all at once or at any time during the season. Pass holders

Richmond Night Market

INTERNATIONAL BUDDHIST TEMPLE

To explore another aspect of Richmond's Asian culture, detour to the International Buddhist Temple (9160 Steveston Hwy., 604/274-2822, www.buddhisttemple.ca, 9:30am-5pm daily, free), one of the largest Chinese Buddhist temples in North America.

A serene traditional Chinese garden with two fountains acts as the gateway to the temple complex. As you enter the main courtyard, on your right is the Seven Buddha Hall, where the gold Avalokitesvara Bodhisattva stands, with its thousand arms and thousand eyes.

Continue through the courtyard and up the stairs to the gold-roofed Main Gracious Hall, constructed in

International Buddhist Temple

1983, where a massive gold Buddha dominates, flanked by several towering statues. Behind the main temple, the Thousand Buddha Hall is filled with miniatures of the deity. On the lower level, vegetarian restaurant Zen Kitchen serves lunch (11:30am-3pm Sat.-Sun.).

At the back of the complex, the Meditation Hall, another gold-roofed structure, is used primarily for meditation classes and lectures. The temple offers weekly two-hour classes on Buddhism and meditation in English (9am Sat.) that are open to visitors.

To reach the temple by public transit from downtown Vancouver, take the Canada Line to Bridgeport Station, then transfer to bus 403, Three Road. After the bus turns east onto Steveston Highway, get off at Mortfield Gate, in front of the temple complex. If you're making other stops in Richmond's Golden Village en route to or from the temple, you can board bus 403 along No. 3 Road outside the Aberdeen, Lansdowne, or Richmond-Brighouse stations.

enter through a separate gate that bypasses the main queue.

The Richmond Night Market is easy to reach by public transit. Take the Canada Line from downtown to Bridgeport Station. From there, it's a 15-minute walk to the market. Just follow the crowds.

MAP 9: 8351 River Rd., 604/244-8448, www.richmondnightmarket.com, 7pm-midnight Fri.-Sat., 7pm-11pm Sun. mid-May-mid-Oct., adults $4.75, seniors and under age 8 free

Golden Village and Aberdeen Centre

The Richmond branch of the Canada Line follows No. 3 Road through the district known as the Golden Village, the region's new Chinatown. You'll know you've arrived when the Chinese-language signs outnumber those in English, and Asian restaurants, markets, and shops line the strip malls and surrounding streets.

A good place to start exploring is Aberdeen Centre, a glitzy Hong Kong-style shopping mall with shops selling tea, electronics, clothing, Asian-language books, and more. Hunt for all kinds of quirky (but useful) housewares and gadgets at **Daiso** (604/295-6601, www.daisocanada.com, 9:30am-9pm daily), the local branch of a Japanese discount chain; at the Richmond location, most products cost just $2. On the mall's 3rd floor, stop for excellent Cantonese, Sichuan, Japanese, and Korean fare in the busy **food court.**

Aberdeen Centre has several good sit-down restaurants too, including **Fisherman's Terrace Seafood Restaurant** (604/303-9739, dim sum 10am-3pm daily, dinner 5:30pm-10pm daily, dim sum $4-15, mains $15-35) for dim sum, and **Chef Hung Taiwanese Beef Noodle** (604/295-9357, www.chefhungnoodle.com, 11am-9pm Sun.-Thurs., 11am-9:30pm Fri.-Sat., $8-13) for noodle soup.

Aberdeen Centre is one block from the Canada Line's Aberdeen Station, at the corner of Cambie Road and Hazelbridge Way. **MAP 9:** Aberdeen Centre, 4151 Hazelbridge Way, 604/270-1234, www.aberdeencentre.com, 11am-7pm Sun.-Wed., 11am-9pm Thurs.-Sat.

Richmond Olympic Experience

Want to swish down an Olympic bobsled track, pilot a race car, or test your mettle on a ski jump? At the Richmond Olympic Experience, aka "The ROX," an interactive Olympic sports museum, you can try out simulators of several Olympic and Paralympic events. Among the activities, which are best suited for older kids and adults, there are games to test your reaction time and see how high you can jump. For Olympic trivia buffs, the multimedia

Slide down a virtual Olympic bobsled track at the Richmond Olympic Experience.

exhibits have thousands of facts about the Games through the decades. Actual Olympic medals and torches are on display.

The ROX is inside the Richmond Olympic Oval, a sports facility that was a venue for the 2010 Winter Olympic Games. Most exhibits are on the 3rd floor. On the main level, you can watch an eight-minute film about pursuing Olympic dreams. Stop on the 2nd floor to see another small exhibition space that includes *Athlete*, a fascinating photograph by Howard Schatz that portrays the "ideal" male and female body types for a wide variety of sports: a jockey next to a sumo wrestler next to a football player, a boxer next to a gymnast next to a shot-putter, and many more.

To reach The ROX by public transit from Vancouver, take the Canada Line (Richmond branch) to Richmond-Brighouse Station. Change to bus 414, which stops directly in front of the Richmond Olympic Oval. The 414 runs only every 35 minutes, and there's no service on Sunday, so check the schedule online (www.translink.ca) before you set out.

You can also walk along a riverfront path to The ROX from the Canada Line's Aberdeen Station. After exiting the station, walk one block west on Cambie Road to River Road. Turn left (south) onto the path that hugs the Fraser River. From here, it's 1.25 miles (2 km) to the Olympic Experience.

MAP 9: 6111 River Rd., Richmond, 778/296-1400, http://therox.ca, 10am-5pm Tues.-Sun., adults $20, seniors $16, ages 13-18 $13, ages 6-12 $5

Restaurants

PRICE KEY
$ Entrées less than CAD$15
$$ Entrées CAD$15-25
$$$ Entrées more than CAD$25

CANTONESE
✪ Bamboo Grove $$$
From the front, Bamboo Grove looks like a nearly abandoned old-time Asian eatery. But go around back, enter through the parking lot, and you'll find a high-end Cantonese restaurant with white tablecloths, black-suited waiters, and an elaborate menu. Any fresh fish dish is a good option, as is the eggplant with tiger prawns, fried rice with cod roe, and the unusual pork stomach with ginkgo soup, a pale, creamy, rich broth. If you have a big budget and adventurous tastes, try the succulent geoduck clam sautéed with velvety scrambled eggs; check the current price before ordering, as geoduck can often run $50 a pound. Reservations are recommended.

MAP 9: 6920 No. 3 Rd., 604/278-9585, 4:30pm-10:30pm daily, subway: Richmond-Brighouse

SHANGHAINESE
✪ Su Hang Restaurant $$
Su Hang Restaurant, in a Richmond strip mall, specializes in dishes from

rack of lamb at Hao's Lamb Restaurant

the Shanghai region, from delicate *xiao long bao* (pork-filled soup dumplings) to fresh fish or crab to meaty pork ribs. To sample their signature dish, Hangzhou beggar chicken, order a day in advance. At lunchtime, they serve Shanghai-style dim sum. Make a reservation; the restaurant is small.

MAP 9: 8291 Ackroyd Rd., Suite 100, 604/278-7787, www.suhang. ca, 11am-3pm and 5pm-10pm daily, subway: Lansdowne

SICHUAN
The Fish Man $$
Every table has a whole fish swimming in a selection of spicy sauces at The Fish Man, an upscale Sichuan-style seafood restaurant. To order, choose a type of fish, your preferred sauce, and a selection of accompaniments; even the small fish are large, so it's best to bring hungry friends. Other excellent options are the spicy clams, grilled squid, or the chili-laden "water-boiled" fish.

194

MAP 9: 8391 Alexandra Rd., 604/284-5393, 5pm-midnight Sun.-Thurs., 5pm-1am Fri.-Sat., subway: Lansdowne

XI'AN STYLE
✪ Hao's Lamb Restaurant $$
Sesame flatbread stuffed with sliced lamb, steamed lamb dumplings, creamy lamb soup with hand-pulled noodles, cumin-spiced lamb stir-fry—Hao's Lamb Restaurant specializes in lamb dishes from western China's Xi'an region. The kitchen uses every part of the sheep (yes, you can even order lamb penis). Accompany your meat with refreshing cold plates, including pickled radishes or garlicky cucumbers, from the display case at the counter, or with vegetable options like the crisp and creamy fried eggplant. Reservations are recommended.

MAP 9: 8788 McKim Way, Suite 1180, 604/270-6632, 11am-9:30pm Fri.-Wed., subway: Aberdeen

CHINESE FOOD

More than 40 percent of the population in metropolitan Vancouver is of Asian descent. These strong Asian influences permeate the city, from business culture to food. In particular, the Vancouver region has hundreds of Chinese restaurants, many serving high-end cuisine that rivals the fare in Hong Kong, Taipei, and Beijing. Near the city center, Chinatown was once a vibrant immigrant community. While it still has Chinese markets, bakeries, and restaurants, the best place for traditional Asian meals is Richmond, the region's new Chinatown, where dozens of restaurants serve cuisines from across China.

eggplant with tiger prawns at Bamboo Grove

Whether you're looking for spicy Sichuan fare, handmade noodles and dumplings like you'd see in Shanghai, delicately seasoned Cantonese seafood, or the hearty lamb dishes of China's western provinces, you'll find it in Richmond. Cafés serving bubble tea and shaved ice desserts draw a young crowd, while families pack the round tables of countless dim sum houses. Richmond's Alexandra Road, which runs for several blocks east from No. 3 Road, has so many restaurants that it's known locally as "Food Street."

The center of Richmond's Asian food scene is the Golden Village, along No. 3 Road from Cambie Road south toward Granville Avenue. Most restaurants are located in shopping centers or mini malls, so don't hesitate to explore. The city even has a Dumpling Trail (www. visitrichmondbc.com), which highlights where to eat pot stickers, *xiao long bao* (soup dumplings), and other delectable stuffed dough dishes.

IF YOU'RE LOOKING FOR . . .

CANTONESE:
Head to Bamboo Grove for high-end Hong Kong-style cuisine.

SHANGHAINESE:
Try Su Hang Restaurant, on Richmond's "Dumpling Trail," which is known for *xiao long bao* (soup dumplings) and other Shanghai specialties.

SICHUAN-STYLE SEAFOOD:
Make your way to "Food Street," where The Fish Man serves fresh fish in a variety of spicy preparations.

DIM SUM:
Book at table at Chef Tony Seafood Restaurant.

HAND-PULLED NOODLES:
Look for tiny Xi'an Cuisine, a stall inside the Richmond Public Market, which makes excellent hand-pulled noodles fresh to order.

DIM SUM

✪ Chef Tony Seafood Restaurant $$

Glitzy Chef Tony is one of the area's best spots for dim sum, with classics like *har gow* (shrimp dumplings) or more innovative creations like pumpkin in black bean sauce or spicy clams. One specialty is the slightly sweet "salty egg bun," charcoal-hued dough that almost explodes with lava-like egg custard. Reservations are recommended.
MAP 9: Empire Centre, 4600 No. 3 Rd., 604/279-0083, www.cheftonycanada. com, 10:30am-3pm and 5pm-10pm Mon.-Fri., 10am-3pm and 5pm-10pm Sat.-Sun., subway: Aberdeen

Golden Paramount Seafood Restaurant $$

Golden Paramount Seafood Restaurant is a first-rate spot for Hong Kong-style dim sum. Try the pan-fried oysters, congee (rice porridge), and steamed dumplings filled with pork and crab, or survey what other tables are eating and politely point. Reservations are recommended, particularly on weekends.
MAP 9: 8111 Anderson Rd., 604/278-0873, www.goldenparamount. com, 9am-3pm and 5pm-10pm daily, subway: Richmond-Brighouse

Empire Seafood Restaurant $

For dim sum classics, like *har gow* (delicate steamed shrimp dumplings), *siu mai* (pork and shrimp dumplings topped with fish roe), and barbecue pork buns, Empire Seafood Restaurant is a good choice. Other items to sample include scallop and shrimp dumplings, pan-fried turnip cakes, and steamed egg-yolk buns. To find the entrance, head for the 2nd floor of the Richmond complex that also houses a London Drugs store. Arrive before 11am or book ahead for dim sum.
MAP 9: London Plaza, 5951 No. 3 Rd., Suite 200, 604/249-0080, www. empirerestaurant.ca, 9am-3pm and 5:30pm-10:30pm daily, subway: Richmond-Brighouse

bubble tea at Pearl Castle Café

QUICK BITES

The BBT Shop $

Hidden in the parking garage underneath a Richmond grocery superstore, The BBT Shop not only makes tasty bubble tea but is also known for eggy bubble waffles, which you can sample plain or with a variety of sweet toppings, including fresh strawberries with whipped cream or matcha ice cream with red beans. A seasonal specialty is the "super mango" version, piled high with mango ice cream, fresh mango, and mango sauce; bring a friend and share. There's another location in the West End.
MAP 9: 4651 No. 3 Rd., 604/285-8833, noon-9:30pm Sun.-Thurs., noon-11:30pm Fri.-Sat., subway: Aberdeen

Pearl Castle Café $

Modern Pearl Castle Café has long been a favored destination for young Richmond residents to meet up over bubble tea, from classic milk tea to fresh fruit slush to their own creations. Accompany your drinks with Taiwanese snacks like spiced fried chicken, pork and kimchi fried rice, or thick toast slathered with condensed milk. You'll find a second smaller branch inside the Richmond Centre Mall.

MAP 9: Continental Centre, 3779 Sexsmith Rd., Suite 1128, 604/270-3939, www.pearlcastle.com, 11am-12:30am Sun.-Thurs., 11am-1am Fri.-Sat., subway: Aberdeen

Richmond Public Market $

When you need a quick lunch or early supper, wander past the vegetable sellers and other stalls on the main level of the Richmond Public Market and find your way to the 2nd-floor food court. At Xi'an Cuisine, which serves dishes from western China, try a lamb dish with hand-pulled noodles or the pan-fried pot stickers. To drink, get a bubble tea from Peanuts, which also makes a sweet round waffle-like pastry known as a "car wheel cake," filled with your choice of coconut, peanuts, sweet red beans, even radish. Other stalls sell Chinese regional specialties. Although not every vendor is open every day, you'll always have several options during the market's regular hours.

MAP 9: 8260 Westminster Hwy., no phone, 10am-8pm daily, subway: Richmond-Brighouse

food stalls in the Richmond Public Market

Recreation

ICE-SKATING
Richmond Olympic Oval

During the 2010 Winter Olympic Games, the Richmond Olympic Oval hosted the speed-skating events. You can practice your own skating moves on the indoor Olympic-size rink during the Oval's public skating hours. Most skating sessions run 90 minutes, and rentals are available (skates $3, helmets $2.25). The Oval also has a large fitness center, a climbing wall, an indoor track, and other activities, included in the drop-in prices. Tip: Admission rates are only $8 9am-2:30pm and 9:30pm-11pm Monday-Friday.

MAP 9: 6111 River Rd., Richmond, 778/296-1400, www.richmondoval.ca, hours vary, adults $20, seniors $16.50, ages 13-18 $13, ages 6-12 $5

Festivals and Events

Lunar New Year

With its large Asian population, Vancouver hosts plenty of festivities to mark the Lunar New Year, including parades, lion dances, music, fireworks, and other special events in Chinatown and throughout Richmond. In Richmond, Aberdeen Centre hosts a week of performances and New Year's events, and on the eve of the Lunar New Year itself, many people welcome the coming year at the International Buddhist Temple.

Chinatown and Richmond: www.cbavancouver.ca, http://vancouverchinesegarden.com and www.visitrichmondbc.com, Jan.-Feb.

orca whale

WHALE-WATCHING

Where the Fraser River meets the Pacific Ocean, the village of Steveston has long been a launching point for fishing boats, and it remains among Canada's largest commercial fishing ports. Steveston Harbour is also a departure point for whale-watching tours.

Most whale-watching trips that depart from Steveston head out through the Strait of Georgia toward the Gulf Islands and San Juan Islands, where you'll most often spot orcas. You might see humpback whales, minke whales, or gray whales, as well as sea lions, bald eagles, and other wildlife. Whale-watching excursions run April-October.

Steveston Seabreeze Adventures (12551 No. 1 Rd., Richmond, 604/272-7200, www.seabreezeadventures.ca, semi-enclosed vessel adults $145, seniors and students $125, ages 3-12 $85, Zodiac tours $150 pp) operates whale-watching trips and provides a shuttle (round-trip $10) from downtown Vancouver hotels. In the spring, they also offer 90-minute sea lion tours (Apr.-mid-May, adults $32, seniors and students $25, children $20) to view migrating California sea lions.

Vancouver Whale Watch (210-12240 2nd Ave., Richmond, 604/274-9565, www.vancouverwhalewatch.com, $145-150) offers whale-watching tours with a shuttle (round-trip $15) between Steveston and several downtown Vancouver hotels.

Also in Steveston are a few cultural attractions. Steveston once had more than 15 salmon canneries lining its waterfront. The largest is now the Gulf of Georgia Cannery National Historic Site (12138 4th Ave., Richmond, 604/664-9009, www.gulfofgeorgiacannery.org, 10am-5pm daily, adults $12, seniors $10, under age 18 free). Inside, see what it was like to work the canning line. To see how Steveston's community lived, visit the Britannia Shipyards National Historic Site (5180 West-water Dr., Richmond, 604/718-8050, http://britanniashipyard.ca, 10am-5pm daily May-Sept., noon-5pm daily Oct.-Apr., free). This collection of restored homes and shops housed Chinese, Japanese, European, and First Nations people.

To get a bite to eat before heading back downtown, stop by Pajo's (12351 3rd Ave., Richmond, 604/272-1588, www.pajos.com, 11am-7pm daily Feb.-June and Sept.-Oct., 11am-8pm daily July-Aug., $11-19), a simple waterfront spot known for its fish-and-chips, which you can order with cod, salmon, or halibut.

To reach Steveston by public transit, take the Canada Line to Richmond-Brighouse Station, then change to any Steveston-bound bus (401, 402, 406, or 407).

The North Shore   Map 10

Ready to get outdoors? Across Burrard Inlet, the North Shore mountains provide the backdrop for the waterfront cities of North Vancouver and West Vancouver. In any season, you can find plenty of adventures here, whether swinging across the Capilano Suspension Bridge, exploring the rainforest in **Lighthouse Park,** or **kayaking** in Deep Cove. Visit **Grouse Mountain** to learn about local wildlife, climb "Mother Nature's Stairmaster," or head down the ski trails. Several other peaks offer **hiking, snowshoeing,** and **skiing**—all a short trip from the city center.

Explore the redeveloping **Shipyards District,** a five-minute walk

from **Lonsdale Quay,** where the Polygon Gallery shows off contemporary art and a summer night market draws crowds with live music and an array of international food trucks.

TOP SIGHTS

- Top Mountain Escape: **Grouse Mountain** (page 204)
- Best Place to Swing over a Gorge: **Capilano Suspension Bridge** (page 206)

TOP RESTAURANTS

- Best North Shore Adventure Breakfast: **Lift Breakfast Bakery** (page 210)

TOP RECREATION

- Most Scenic Paddle: **Deep Cove Kayaks** (page 211)
- Mother Nature's Stairmaster: **Grouse Grind** (page 211)
- Where to Find Ancient Trees and Skyline Views: **Lighthouse Park** (page 212)

GETTING THERE AND AROUND

- Ferries: SeaBus
- Bus lines: 211, 228, 229, 230, 236, 241, 246, 250, 257

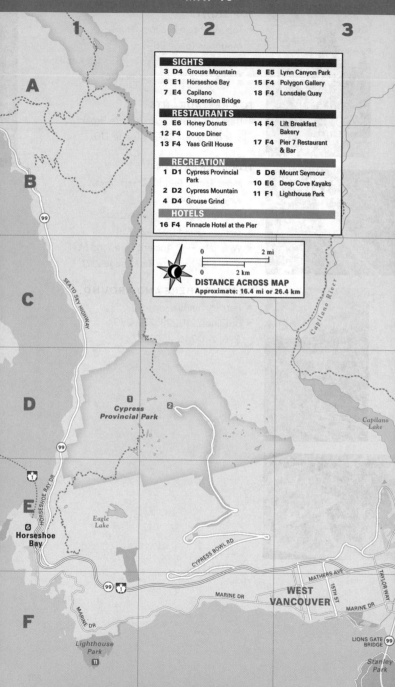

SIGHTS

3	D4	Grouse Mountain	8	E5	Lynn Canyon Park
6	E1	Horseshoe Bay	15	F4	Polygon Gallery
7	E4	Capilano Suspension Bridge	18	F4	Lonsdale Quay

RESTAURANTS

9	E6	Honey Donuts	14	F4	Lift Breakfast Bakery
12	F4	Douce Diner			
13	F4	Yaas Grill House	17	F4	Pier 7 Restaurant & Bar

RECREATION

1	D1	Cypress Provincial Park	5	D6	Mount Seymour
2	D2	Cypress Mountain	10	E6	Deep Cove Kayaks
4	D4	Grouse Grind	11	F1	Lighthouse Park

HOTELS

16	F4	Pinnacle Hotel at the Pier

0 ———— 2 mi
0 ———— 2 km
DISTANCE ACROSS MAP
Approximate: 16.4 mi or 26.4 km

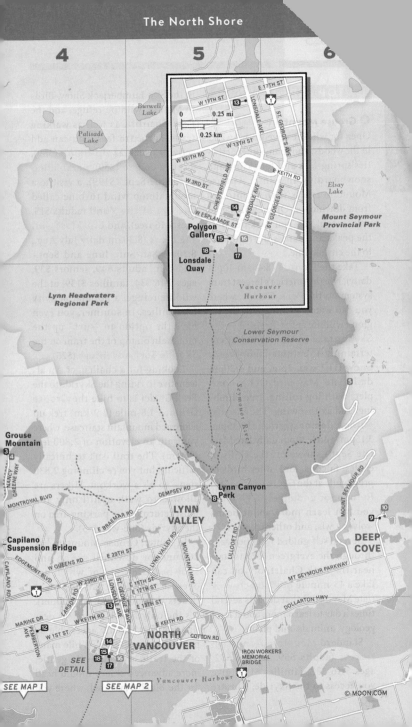

4　　　　　　　5　　　　　　　6

Burwell Lake

Palisade Lake

W 17TH ST
13
E 17TH ST
1
LONSDALE AVE.
ST. GEORGE'S AVE.
W 13TH ST

W KEITH RD
E KEITH RD
W 3RD ST
CHESTERFIELD AVE
LONSDALE AVE
ST. GEORGE'S AVE

W ESPLANADE ST
14

Polygon Gallery
15
16
18
17

Lonsdale Quay

Vancouver Harbour

0   0.25 mi
0   0.25 km

Elsay Lake

Mount Seymour Provincial Park

Lynn Headwaters Regional Park

Lower Seymour Conservation Reserve

Seymour River

5

Grouse Mountain
3
4
NANCY GREENE WAY

MONTROYAL BLVD

Capilano Suspension Bridge

EDGEMONT BLVD

CAPILANO RD

1

MARINE DR
PEMBERTON AVE
12
W 1ST ST

W 73RD ST

E BRAEMAR RD

E 29TH RD

E QUEENS RD

LARSON RD

LONSDALE AVE

DEMPSEY RD

LYNN VALLEY

Lynn Canyon Park
8

LYNN VALLEY RD

MOUNTAIN HWY

LILLOOET RD

MT SEYMOUR PARKWAY

MOUNT SEYMOUR RD

DEEP COVE
10
9

ST GEORGE'S AVE
E 15TH ST
13
E 13TH ST

W KEITH RD

NORTH VANCOUVER

COTTON RD

E KEITH RD

14

SEE DETAIL
18
15
16
17

IRON WORKERS MEMORIAL BRIDGE
1

DOLLARTON HWY

Vancouver Harbour

SEE MAP 1

SEE MAP 2

© MOON.COM

ain

Open for wildlife adventures, walks in the woods, and many other activities spring-fall, and for skiing and snowboarding in winter, Grouse Mountain is less than 40 minutes from downtown. On a clear day in any season, you can look out over the peaks and across Burrard Inlet to the city skyline.

Take the Skyride (8:45am-10pm daily), North America's largest tram system, to the Peak Chalet, where you can watch a film about the region's wildlife at the Theatre in the Sky, or take in the corny but entertaining 45-minute Lumberjack Show (11:15am, 2pm, and 4:30pm daily late May-mid-Oct.), complete with log rolling, tree climbing, and ax throwing. The Birds in Motion demonstration (12:45pm, 3:15pm, and 5:30pm daily late May-late Sept.) shows off the skills of eagles, falcons, and other birds of prey, while at the Grouse Mountain Refuge for Endangered Wildlife, you can learn more about bears, wolves, owls, and other creatures.

Several self-guided walking trails through the evergreen forests start near the Peak Chalet, or you can take a 45-minute guided eco-walk (late May-Sept.) that departs several times a day to learn more about local geology, animals, and plants.

Standard Mountain Admission tickets (adults $59, seniors $52, ages 5-16 $32, families $159) give you access to the Skyride, Theatre in the Sky, Lumberjack Show, Birds in Motion, wildlife refuge, and the Peak Chairlift, as well as walking trails. For extra fees, you can add activities such as zip-lining ($89), a ropes course ($39), paragliding (late June-Sept., $199), a visit to a mountaintop wind turbine called The Eye of the Wind (adults $15, ages 5-16 free), and breakfast with the bears (8:30am daily July-Aug., 8:30am Sat.-Sun. June and Sept.-mid-Oct., adults $49, seniors $39, ages 5-16 $34, families $139) at the wildlife refuge, a popular activity for families. In summer, you even have the option to "surf" up the mountain on top of the tram on the Skyride Surf Adventure ($25).

Looking for a challenge? An alternative to riding the Skyride to the Peak Chalet is to hike the Grouse Grind, a 1.8-mile (2.9-km) trek up a forested mountain staircase, where you gain an elevation of 2,800 feet (850 m). The trail isn't technically difficult, but you're climbing 2,830 steps, so it's a workout. Hikers are allowed to walk uphill only and must return to the parking area on the Skyride (one-way $15).

In winter, Grouse Mountain has 26 runs for downhill skiing and snowboarding, 14 of which are open at night (you can buy night tickets that are valid 4pm-10pm). It's the only North Shore ski destination that's easily accessible by public transportation. While many of the trails are relatively gentle, more advanced skiers should head for the Blueberry Bowl, where you

zip-lining at Grouse Mountain

can access more challenging runs from the Olympic Express and Peak Chairs. If you've arrived in Vancouver without proper winter clothes, you can rent jackets, snow pants, helmets, and gloves, as well as ski and snowboard gear. Lift tickets (adults full-day $69, night $49, seniors and ages 13-18 full-day $49, night $40, ages 5-12 full-day $25, night $23, ages 0-4 free) include access to the Standard Mountain activities along with the ski and snowboard runs.

Other winter activities include snowshoeing on four groomed trails or ice-skating on the mountaintop rink. For these activities, if you're not already buying a lift ticket to ski or snowboard, you need to purchase a Standard Mountain access ticket.

The mountain's fine-dining restaurant, The Observatory (604/998-5045, www.observatoryrestaurant. ca, 5pm-10pm daily, $28-45), in the Peak Chalet, serves seafood, steak, and other west coast fare. Make dinner reservation in advance to obtain a complimentary Mountain Access ticket for each member of your party. There are several casual eateries and snack shops on the mountain as well.

You don't need a car to get to Grouse Mountain. May-early October, a free shuttle takes you between Canada Place and the mountain every 30 minutes 9am-12:30pm and 2pm-6pm. Year-round, you can take public transit between downtown and Grouse; take the SeaBus from Waterfront Station to Lonsdale Quay and change to bus 236 for Grouse Mountain, which will drop you at the mountain's base.

MAP 10: 6400 Nancy Greene Way, North Vancouver, 604/980-9311, www. grousemountain.com, 9am-10pm daily

NEARBY:

- Get your thrills swaying high above the ground on the Capilano Suspension Bridge (page 206).
- Work up a sweat by hiking up the Grouse Grind, known as "Mother Nature's Stairmaster" (page 211).

✪ Capilano Suspension Bridge

Built in 1889, the 450-foot (137-m) Capilano Suspension Bridge sways 230 feet (70 m) above the Capilano River in a rainforest park. And yes, it does swing! Before you cross the bridge, follow the Cliffwalk, a series of boardwalks and stairways cantilevered out over the river. If you're feeling brave, stand on the glass platform and look down (way down!) into the canyon where the river rushes below.

After you've made your way over the suspension bridge, explore the Treetops Adventure, a 700-foot (213-m) network of gently swaying wooden bridges linking eight treehouse platforms. Many of the surrounding Douglas firs are up to 300 feet (90 m) tall. Back on the ground, gentle walking trails lead through the rainforest.

Particularly in the summer high season, the least crowded times to visit the bridge are before 10am or after 5pm. Take a free shuttle to the suspension bridge from several locations downtown, including Canada Place, Hyatt Hotel (Melville St. at Burrard St.), Blue Horizon Hotel (1225 Robson St.), and Library Square (Homer St. at Robson St.). Call or check the website for seasonal schedules. By public transportation, take the SeaBus from Waterfront Station to Lonsdale Quay and change to bus 236 for Grouse Mountain. Get off at Ridgewood Avenue, a block from the bridge park.

Cliffwalk at the Capilano Suspension Bridge

MAP 10: 3735 Capilano Rd., 604/985-7474, www.capbridge.com, 8am-8pm daily late May-early Sept., 9am-6pm daily early Sept.-mid-Oct. and mid-Mar.-late Apr., 9am-5pm daily mid-Oct.-late Nov. and early Jan.-mid-Mar., 11am-9pm daily late Nov.-early Jan., 9am-7pm daily late Apr.-late May, adults $54, seniors $49, students $40, ages 13-16 $30, ages 6-12 $17

Lynn Canyon Park

The 617-acre (250-ha) Lynn Canyon Park is a little farther from downtown than the Capilano bridge, but it has its own suspension bridge, built back in 1912—and it's free.

Hiking trails wend through the park, including the 30 Foot Pool Trail and the Twin Falls Trail, which both lead to popular swimming areas (bring your bathing suit); both trails are easy and are 0.6 mile (1 km) long, starting from the suspension bridge. The Ecology Centre (3663 Park Rd., North Vancouver, 604/990-3755, www.lynncanyonecologycentre.ca, 10am-5pm daily June-Sept., 10am-5pm Mon.-Fri., noon-4pm Sat. Sun. Oct.-May, donation $2) has kid-friendly exhibits about the region's plants and animals.

To get to the park by public transit, take the SeaBus from Waterfront Station to Lonsdale Quay, then change to bus 228 or 229 for Lynn Valley. Get off the bus at Lynn Valley Center, a 15-minute walk from the park entrance.

MAP 10: Park Rd., North Vancouver, www.lynncanyon.ca, 7am-8pm daily spring, 7am-9pm daily summer, 7am-7pm daily fall, 7am-6pm daily winter, free

Lonsdale Quay

A food and shopping complex overlooking the water adjacent to the SeaBus terminal in North Vancouver, Lonsdale Quay is like a small-scale Granville Island Public Market. Vendors sell fruit, vegetables, seafood, sandwiches, and other prepared foods. Green Leaf Brewing (604/984-8409, www.greenleafbrew.com) makes craft beer; the Artisan Wine Shop (604/264-4008, www.artisanwineshop.ca) does complimentary wine-tastings. On Friday evenings (May-Sept.), a lively summer night market takes over the Shipyards District, a five-minute walk east of Lonsdale Quay.

The easiest way to get to Lonsdale Quay from downtown Vancouver is to take the SeaBus from Waterfront Station, a 12-minute ride.

MAP 10: 123 Carrie Cates Court, North Vancouver, 604/985-6261, www.lonsdalequay.com, 9am-7pm daily

Polygon Gallery

In a striking silver building on the North Vancouver waterfront, a short walk east of Lonsdale Quay, Polygon Gallery exhibits contemporary art, specializing in photography and

Lonsdale Quay

works by Canadian artists. The museum has a first-rate view of the downtown Vancouver skyline from the 1st-floor glass atrium and the 2nd-floor waterside terrace.

To reach the museum from downtown Vancouver, catch the SeaBus from Waterfront Station to Lonsdale Quay.

MAP 10: 101 Carrie Cates Court, North Vancouver, 604/986-1351, www.thepolygon.ca, 10am-5pm Tues.-Sun., donation

Polygon Gallery

Horseshoe Bay

The seaside village of Horseshoe Bay, 12.5 miles (20 km) northwest of downtown Vancouver, is a departure point for BC Ferries' routes to Bowen Island, Nanaimo (on Vancouver Island), and the Sunshine Coast. It's a pretty spot for a picnic by the shore or for a quick break when you're driving between Vancouver and Whistler.

Another reason to visit Horseshoe Bay is to take a two-hour Sea Safari from Sewell's Marina (6409 Bay St., West Vancouver, 604/921-3474, www.sewellsmarina.com, 11am, 1:30pm, and 4:30pm Apr.-Oct., adults $93, seniors and ages 13-18 $83, ages 5-12 $60). These scenic guided wildlife cruises in 30-foot (10-m) Zodiac-style boats take you through the waters of Howe Sound, where you'll spot seals and a variety of seabirds. The company offers a shuttle ($19 pp round-trip) from downtown Vancouver hotels.

By public transit from downtown Vancouver to Horseshoe Bay, catch bus 257 (Vancouver/Horseshoe Bay Express), along West Georgia Street, which takes you to the Horseshoe Bay Ferry Terminal in 45 minutes. The ferry terminal is in the village.

You can generally make the drive from downtown to Horseshoe Bay in 30-35 minutes. Allow extra time if you're catching a ferry, since traffic congestion can cause delays. Returning to the city can take longer, since traffic often backs up on the West Vancouver side of the Lions Gate Bridge entrance.

MAP 10: Off Hwy. 1 west, West Vancouver

Restaurants

PRICE KEY

$ Entrées less than CAD$15
$$ Entrées CAD$15-25
$$$ Entrées more than CAD$25

SEAFOOD

Pier 7 Restaurant & Bar $$

Near Lonsdale Quay in North Vancouver, Pier 7 Restaurant & Bar perches over the water with views across Burrard Inlet to the downtown skyline. While the menu emphasizes simple fresh seafood and casual pub fare, the waterfront setting makes the room feel more special. It's a nice spot for sunset drinks too. The restaurant is a five-minute walk from the SeaBus terminal, so you can start and end your evening with a 12-minute cruise between Waterfront Station and the North Shore.

MAP 10: 25 Wallace Mews, North Vancouver, 604/929-7437, http://pierseven.ca, 11:45am-11pm Mon.-Fri., 10:30am-11pm Sat.-Sun.

Pier 7 Restaurant & Bar

PERSIAN

Yaas Grill House $

Vancouver's North Shore has a large Persian community, and one of the best places to sample the food of this region is at Yaas Grill House. This cafeteria-style eatery is not especially atmospheric, but order at the counter, find a seat in the cramped storefront, and the staff will pile your table high with platters of kebabs, stews, and freshly grilled breads that are nearly as large as the tabletops. You'll particularly appreciate the hearty portions if you've been adventuring in the nearby mountains. For dessert, have a piece of classic baklava.

MAP 10: 1629 Lonsdale Ave., North Vancouver, 604/990-9099, http://yaasgrill.com, 11:30am-10pm daily

DINERS

Douce Diner $$

With chic black-and-white tiles, pastel accents, and repurposed lunch counter stools, North Vancouver's Douce Diner feels like a fashionable little hangout. And that's before you get to chef-owner Dawn Doucette's modern takes on typical diner fare. She's pairing eggs with French white beans and romesco sauce and layering her "Double Douce Burger," with aged cheddar and house-made zucchini and onion pickles on a toasted brioche bun. For the kids (of all ages), there are old-style milk shakes in flavors ranging from vanilla and chocolate to the banana-caramel banoffee.

MAP 10: 1490 Pemberton Ave., North Vancouver, 604/980-2510, http://doucediner.com, 7am-3pm Mon.-Fri., 8am-4pm Sat.-Sun.

milkshake at Douce Diner

BAKERIES AND CAFÉS
✪ Lift Breakfast Bakery $$

It's worth the short walk up the hill from Lonsdale Quay in North Vancouver for the locally sourced, thoughtfully made breakfast and lunch plates at Lift Breakfast Bakery. At this cozy bakery-café, you might start your morning with eggs Benedict on a potato rosti layered with salty-sweet maple bacon or smoked trout, or a breakfast sandwich on a house-made English muffin. Breads like the country sourdough are excellent as a slice of toast or to back up a BLT. The eatery stays open for weekend suppers of salads and handmade pastas.

Tip: If you want a cookie or other treat to go, avoid the line-ups and walk to Lift Production Bakery (700 Copping St., North Vancouver, www.liftproductionbakery.com, 8am-4pm Mon.-Fri., 9am-4pm Sat.-Sun.). Hidden in an industrial park, it's where the restaurant's baking magic happens, and there's a small take-out café.

MAP 10: 101 Lonsdale Ave., North Vancouver, 778/388-5438, www.liftonlonsdale.ca, 7am-5pm Mon.-Thurs., 7am-10pm Fri., 9am-10pm Sat., 9am-3pm and 5pm-10pm Sun.

Honey Donuts $

For many Vancouverites, a day kayaking at Deep Cove isn't complete without a stop for an old-fashioned freshly made doughnut at North Shore institution Honey Donuts. Besides the doughnuts—honey is the classic flavor—you can fuel up with eggs and bacon, hot soup, or a selection of sandwiches.

MAP 10: 4373 Gallant Ave., Deep Cove, North Vancouver, 604/929-4988, http://honeydoughnuts.com, 6am-5pm daily

Recreation

kayaks at Deep Cove

transit from downtown Vancouver, take bus 211 from Burrard Station (Burrard St. at Dunsmuir St.). It's a 50-60-minute ride. This bus doesn't run early in the morning or in the evening.

MAP 10: 2156 Banbury Rd., Deep Cove, North Vancouver, 604/929-2268, www.deepcovekayak.com, weather permitting 10am-dusk Sat.-Sun. Mar., 10am-dusk daily Apr., 10am-dusk Mon.-Fri. and 9am-dusk Sat.-Sun. May, 9am-dusk Mon.-Fri. and 8:30am-dusk Sat.-Sun. June, 9am-dusk Mon.-Fri. and 8am-dusk Sat.-Sun. July, 9am-dusk daily Aug., 10am-6pm Mon.-Fri. and 9am-6pm Sat.-Sun. Sept., 10am-6pm daily early-mid-Oct., 2 hour-full-day rentals $39-135

KAYAKING AND STAND-UP PADDLEBOARDING
✪ Deep Cove Kayaks

For a water-based excursion just outside the city, head for the North Shore village of Deep Cove, where you can explore the scenic 11-mile (18-km) Indian Arm fjord, ringed with forests, mountains, and rocky shores. Deep Cove Kayaks rents single and double kayaks as well as stand-up paddleboards and surf skis (open-cockpit kayaks). They offer lessons and run a number of kayak tours, including the three-hour beginner-friendly Deep Cove Explorer tour (Apr.-Nov., adults $89, ages 12 and under $50). Another popular option is the Full Moon Evening tour (Apr.-Sept., $75), scheduled on the two or three evenings closest to the full moon.

To reach Deep Cove by public

HIKING
✪ Grouse Grind

You can't call yourself a Vancouverite until you've hiked the Grind, or so say the many who've made the trek up Vancouver's best-known trail. Nicknamed "Mother Nature's Stairmaster," the Grouse Grind is only 1.8 miles (2.9 km) long, but it's essentially a mountain staircase that you climb straight up, gaining an elevation of 2,800 feet (850 m). Along most of the trail, you're hiking in the forest. The reward comes at the top, with vistas across the city.

Active hikers can complete the Grouse Grind, which has 2,830 steps, in about 90 minutes, but plenty of people need at least two hours. Hikers are allowed to walk uphill only. To return to the parking

the Grouse Grind

area, you ride down on the Skyride (one-way $15), the Grouse Mountain tram. Check the trail status if you're planning a spring or fall hike; there can be snow on the trail even when it's warm in the city.

The mountain runs a free shuttle (May-Sept.) from Canada Place. By public transportation, take the SeaBus from Waterfront Station to Lonsdale Quay and change to bus 236 for Grouse Mountain, which will drop you at the mountain's base. MAP 10: 6400 Nancy Greene Way, North Vancouver, 604/980-9311, www. grousemountain.com, Skyride $15 one-way

✪ Lighthouse Park

There are beautiful views across the water toward downtown Vancouver from Lighthouse Park, a seaside recreation area in West Vancouver. Perched on a point between Burrard Inlet and Howe Sound, the 185-acre (75-ha) park has several easy trails through old-growth forests that lead

to dramatic lookout points. Some of the park's trees, which include Douglas fir, western hemlock, and western red cedar, are 500 years old and grow as tall as 200 feet (60 m).

The park's lighthouse, which is a national historic site, is not open to the public. The original lighthouse was built here in 1874, and the current structure dates to 1912. A nearby viewpoint has expansive water vistas. The Beacon Lane trail is the most direct route from the parking area to the lighthouse viewpoint.

On the east side of the park, the Valley of the Giants trail takes you among the towering trees to a lookout at Eagle Point. On the park's west side, follow the Juniper Loop to the Juniper Point Trail, which leads to a viewpoint facing Howe Sound and the Gulf Islands.

Pack a picnic if you plan to stay a while. The park has restrooms but no other services. Lighthouse Park is 12.5 miles (20 km) northwest of downtown Vancouver. By public transit, catch bus 250 (toward Horseshoe Bay) along West Georgia Street and get off on Marine Drive at Beacon Lane. It's a 45-minute ride. Walk south on Beacon Lane to the park.

MAP 10: Beacon Ln., West Vancouver, 604/925-7275, www.lighthousepark.ca, dawn-dusk daily, free

Cypress Provincial Park

In winter, you can ski, snowboard, cross-country ski, or snowshoe at Cypress Mountain, located within Cypress Provincial Park. After the snow melts, it's a close-to-the-city hiking destination. Encompassing three peaks—Black Mountain, Mount Strachan, and Hollyburn Mountain—Cypress is known for its spectacular views across Howe Sound, to the Gulf Islands, and toward downtown Vancouver.

A popular trail for day hikers is the Hollyburn Peak Trail, which starts at the Nordic ski area base and gradually ascends 1,300 feet (400 m) to the top of Hollyburn Mountain. Your reward for hiking this 5-mile (8-km) round-trip trail is expansive vistas over the peaks and forests. Another option with excellent views over Howe Sound is the shorter trail to the Bowen Lookout, which begins at the alpine ski area base. With an elevation change of 325 feet (100 m), the trail is 3 miles (5 km) round-trip.

The best time to hike the Cypress area is June or July to October, since snow can cover the trails at higher elevations the rest of the year.

MAP 10: 6000 Cypress Bowl Rd., West Vancouver, 604/926-5612, www.cypressmountain.com or www.env.gov.bc.ca, dawn-dusk daily, free

SKIING, SNOWBOARDING, AND SNOWSHOEING

Ski season on metro Vancouver's North Shore mountains normally runs December-March. Grouse Mountain (page 204) is closest to downtown and the only North Shore peak that's easily accessible by public transportation. Two hours north of the city, the much larger Whistler-Blackcomb resort is typically open for skiing and snowboarding late November-April.

Cypress Mountain

The largest of the North Shore mountains, Cypress Mountain hosted several events during the 2010 Winter Olympics. You can ski and snowboard on the mountain's 53 downhill trails. You can buy tickets for a full day, afternoon only (12:30pm-closing), or night (5pm-closing), and you get a discount if you purchase them online in advance. Check the Cypress website on the day you plan to ski or snowboard, since they offer a changing "daily discount" coupon, which might save you money on gear rentals, food in the on-site cafeteria, or purchases in the mountain shop. You can rent equipment and clothing on the mountain, and lessons are offered for both kids and adults.

Cypress has a separate Nordic area with trails for cross-country skiing and snowshoeing. Of the 12 miles (19 km) of cross-country trails, nearly five miles (7.5 km) stay

WHAT TO DO IN WINTER

When it's raining in Vancouver—and if you're visiting in winter, it will—you can head for a museum, take refuge in a café, or simply put up your umbrella and keep exploring. Even during the city's dampest months, typically November-February, there's plenty to do to brighten cloudy days, as long as you pack good raingear and waterproof footwear. Here's how to make the most of the winter in Vancouver.

HEAD FOR THE MOUNTAINS

Good news: If it's raining in the city, it's often snowing in the mountains. Three mountains on Vancouver's North Shore, within easy day-tripping distance of downtown, are typically open December-March for skiing, snowboarding, and snowshoeing.

You can get to Grouse Mountain (page 204), which offers lots of activities year-round, by public transit from downtown, and both Cypress Mountain (page 213)—the largest of the North Shore ski areas—and family-friendly Mount Seymour (page 215) run winter-season shuttles from the city. Occasionally, these peaks sit above the clouds that blanket the city, offering dramatic cloudscape views from sunny ski runs.

EXPLORE THE RAINFOREST

What's a rainforest without rain? Don't let a few showers stop you from exploring Stanley Park (page 46), particularly the walking trails in the park's interior, where the woods remain green throughout the year and the tall leafy trees offer some shelter from the drizzle. You can also hike year-round in the rainforest at Pacific Spirit Regional Park (page 153) on the city's west side.

GO ICE SKATING

Take a break from the weather with a spin or two around the ice at the Robson Square Ice Rink (page 57), which is open for free ice-skating December-February. This downtown rink is semi-enclosed and covered, so you're protected from the rain.

CELEBRATE ARTS AND CULTURE

Throughout the winter months, Vancouver's cultural calendar is full of festivals, concerts, theatrical productions, and other special events. Check out events like the holiday Festival of Lights at the VanDusen Botanical Garden (page 169), the eclectic PuSh International Performing Arts Festival (page 62), or the Talking Stick Festival (page 107), which celebrates indigenous culture. See what's on stage at the Arts Club Theatre Company (page 121) or the Vancouver East Cultural Centre (page 183). Or see a performance by the Vancouver Symphony Orchestra (page 60) or Ballet BC (page 60).

GET AWAY TO THE TROPICS

Inside the always warm and humid Bloedel Conservatory (page 161), a glass-domed greenhouse high on a hill in Queen Elizabeth Park, are hundreds of tropical flowers and plants, along with more than 100 birds. A walk amid the colorful flora is a great way to forget about winter's cloudy skies.

open for night skiing. If you're snowshoeing, unless you're with a guide, you need to be off the trails before sunset. Several guided snowshoe tours are available, from a two-hour introductory tour to an evening excursion that wraps up with chocolate fondue.

Cypress also has a snow tube park, where both adults and kids over age 5 can slide down six chutes and let a tube tow pull you back up to the top. Tickets are good for two hours of tubing fun.

There is no public transportation to Cypress, but you can catch the **Cypress Coach Lines shuttle bus** (604/637-7669, http://cypresscoachlines.com) between the city and the mountain during the winter ski season. The website has schedules and pickup and drop-off locations. Purchase round-trip tickets (adults $25, seniors and ages 13-18 $20) from the driver when you board (cash only). On the mountain, you can buy one-way tickets (adults $13, seniors and ages 13-18 $10) from the Guest Relations office in the downhill area or from the Nordic area ticket office. Up to two kids (ages 6-12) ride free with a paying adult.

MAP 10: 6000 Cypress Bowl Rd., West Vancouver, 604/926-5612, www. cypressmountain.com, hours vary, downhill: adults $89, seniors and ages 13-18 $62, ages 6-12 $40, under age 6 $6-8, cross-country: adults $27, seniors and ages 13-18 $16, ages 6-12 $13, under age 6 $5, snowshoeing: adults $14, seniors and ages 13-18 $9, ages 6-12 $6, under age 6 $4, snow tube park: $25-26

Mount Seymour

Family-friendly Mount Seymour, the North Shore's smallest ski area, has five lifts serving 40 downhill runs, with tickets for a full day, afternoon (2:30pm-10pm), or evening (6pm-10pm) skiing or snowboarding. It's a good spot for snowshoeing, with easy trails through the forest, and there's a snow tube park.

A shuttle bus (check the website for schedules, round-trip $15) can take you between Mount Seymour and the Rupert SkyTrain station in East Vancouver. Buy a ticket from the shuttle driver when you board (cash only). From downtown to Rupert Station, catch the Expo Line to Commercial-Broadway Station, where you change to the Millennium Line for Rupert.

MAP 10: 1700 Mt. Seymour Rd., North Vancouver, 604/986-2261, www. mountseymour.com, downhill trails 10am-10pm Mon.-Fri., 9am-10pm Sat.-Sun. Dec.-Mar., snowshoe and snow tube park hours vary, downhill: adults $69, seniors and ages 13-18 $48, ages 5-12 $26, under age 5 free, snowshoeing: adults $11, seniors $9.50, ages 13-18 $10, ages 5-12 $9.50, under age 5 free, snow tube park: $25

Cypress Mountain

WHERE TO STAY

Most Vancouver accommodations are on the downtown peninsula, with a few B&Bs and smaller hotels in other parts of the city. Rates peak and availability is limited July-August, so book early if you're planning a summer visit. At other times, especially during the slower winter season, hotel rates drop significantly from the high-season prices listed here.

Fairmont Pacific Rim hotel

CHOOSING WHERE TO STAY

When you stay **downtown**, you're in the center of everything, close to sights, restaurants, clubs, and theaters. If you prefer a more residential neighborhood that's still convenient to downtown attractions and close to Stanley Park, choose accommodations in the **West End.**

Gastown buzzes late into the night with innovative restaurants and lively bars and lounges; stay here if you love nighttime action. Expect street noise in this neighborhood. **Yaletown** is a center of dining and nightlife, so the streets are busy till the wee hours. You're close to the Seawall (great for morning or evening jogs) and most downtown attractions. There's just one hotel on **Granville Island,** but it's located on the waterfront a short stroll from the Public Market. To get downtown, you can hop on a mini ferry; just note that ferries don't run late at night.

Kitsilano has a few B&Bs in Victorian-era homes and numerous short-term rentals, available from sites like Airbnb.com and VRBO.com. As long as you're near a major thoroughfare, like West 4th Avenue or Broadway, you can catch a bus from Kits to downtown, Granville Island, or UBC. Budget travelers, take note: On the **University of British Columbia** campus, close to attractions like the Museum of Anthropology, you can stay

HIGHLIGHTS

✪ **BEST SPLURGE:** Vancouver's most elegant modern hotel is the **Fairmont Pacific Rim,** a luxurious Asian-influenced tower near the waterfront (page 219).

✪ **BEST HOTEL FOR CLASSIC GLAMOUR:** Originally built in the 1920s, the classy restored **Rosewood Hotel Georgia** has upscale guest rooms, excellent eateries, and stylish lounges (page 220).

✪ **MOST RETRO MOTEL:** The **Burrard Hotel,** an old-time motor hotel downtown, has been converted into a fun retro-chic lodging (page 222).

✪ **MOST ARTISTIC SLEEPING SPOT:** Original contemporary art distinguishes the low-rise **Listel Hotel,** with a prime perch on Vancouver's main downtown shopping street (page 223).

✪ **BEST WAY TO SUPPORT THE ARTS WHILE YOU SLEEP:** One-of-a-kind works by First Nations artists adorn the rooms at **Skwachàys Lodge,** Canada's first indigenous arts hotel (page 225).

✪ **COOLEST HOTEL:** At **Opus Hotel Vancouver,** many of the vibrantly hued rooms have windows into the baths. Don't be shy (page 226)!

PRICE KEY

$	Less than CAD$150 per night
$ $	CAD$150-300 per night
$ $ $	More than CAD$300 per night

room at Skwachàys Lodge

WHERE TO STAY IF . . .

YOU'RE ONLY HERE FOR A WEEKEND:
Stay downtown, where you're within walking distance of many attractions, restaurants, bars, and outdoor activities.

YOU LOVE GETTING OUTDOORS IN AN URBAN SETTING:
Choose a lodging in the West End, and you'll have Stanley Park, the Seawall, and English Bay at your door.

YOU PLAN YOUR DAYS AROUND YOUR NEXT MEAL:
Look for accommodations in or near Gastown to stay in the center of Vancouver's food and drink scene.

YOU WANT TO EXPERIENCE LIFE AS A LOCAL:
Imagine yourself living in Vancouver when you sleep amid the condos and lofts in Yaletown, where you're a short stroll from False Creek and from plenty of restaurants and bars.

YOU WANT TO FEEL LIKE A STUDENT AGAIN:
Stay in dorm-style suites or a hostel on the UBC campus.

in simple hotel-style suites or, May-mid-August, bunk hostel-style in a residence hall. The downside of campus life? Dining options tend toward student-centered fast food, and you're a 30-minute ride from downtown.

Sleeping in Richmond, where the airport is located, is handy if you're arriving late or have an early flight out, and you'll be in the heart of the Asian dining scene. Choose a hotel near a Canada Line station, and you can get downtown in less than 25 minutes. Since far more attractions are located in Vancouver proper, however, you'll spend more time in transit.

Staying on the North Shore means being close to the mountains and all their outdoor activities. The drawback is that getting downtown means crossing an often-congested bridge (or taking a ferry); touring other parts of the city will be easier if you have a car.

ALTERNATIVE LODGING OPTIONS
Online Lodging Services

Online lodging services like Airbnb.com and VRBO.com are huge in Vancouver, offering listings for apartments on the downtown peninsula and for houses, basement suites, apartments, and condo buildings throughout the rest of the city. The city of Vancouver has implemented regulations to manage the proliferation of short-term rentals, requiring that owners be licensed and limiting rentals of many units to 30 days or more. The result is that availability can be tight, particularly in the peak months of July-August; book early.

Get to know these Canadian real estate terms if you're looking for a short-term rental. A suite is another word for an apartment; a bachelor suite is a studio (one-room) apartment. A strata unit is a condominium, and a parkade is a parking garage. And a "garburator?" That's a garbage disposal.

Camping

Recreational vehicles and other campers should plan to stay outside the city proper; RVs and other large vehicles are not allowed to park on Vancouver streets 10pm-6am. The closest private campgrounds are in West Vancouver at the Capilano River RV Park (www.capilanoriverrvpark.com), which is almost directly under the Lions Gate Bridge, and in suburban Burnaby at the Cariboo RV Park & Campground (http://bcrvpark.com). RVs can also stay south of the city at the Peace Arch RV Park (www.peacearchrvpark.ca) in Surrey and north of Vancouver at Paradise Valley Campground (http://paradisevalleycampground.net) in Squamish.

Several provincial parks within an easy drive of Vancouver offer a more scenic setting for campers, including Alice Lake Provincial Park (http://seatoskyparks.com) in Squamish, Cultus Lake Provincial Park (http://seatoskyparks.com) near Chilliwack, east of Vancouver, and Golden Ears Provincial Park (www.env.gov.bc.ca), also east of Vancouver, near the city of Maple Ridge.

Airport Hotels

The posh Fairmont Vancouver Airport Hotel is the only lodging right at the Vancouver International Airport; the lobby sits above the U.S. departures hall. Many other Richmond lodgings advertise themselves as "airport hotels" and provide shuttles for guests. Of these off-airport accommodations, the Pacific Gateway Hotel (3500 Cessna Dr., Richmond, 604/278-1241 or 866/382-3474, www.pacificgatewayhotel.com) is closest to the terminals, a five-minute ride on the hotel's complimentary shuttle.

Downtown and West End Map 1

✪ Fairmont Pacific Rim $$$

High-tech, Asian-inspired Fairmont Pacific Rim is one of the city's most luxurious lodgings. Stearns & Foster beds topped with Italian linens, plush robes, and marble baths with soaker tubs make the 377 contemporary guest rooms feel like urban oases. And that's before you open the electronically controlled drapes to check out the city and harbor views, or head for the rooftop to lounge around the secluded swimming pool. When you're ready to venture out, the hotel's bicycle butler can outfit you with two-wheeled transportation, or you can book the complimentary car service for downtown outings. As at all Fairmont properties, Wi-Fi is included for members of the hotel's frequent-stay program. Chic Botanist is equal parts cocktail "lab" (for its inventive drinks), garden eating space, and high-end dining room.

MAP 1: 1038 Canada Pl., 604/695-5300 or 877/900-5350, www.fairmont.com

✪ Rosewood Hotel Georgia $$$

Originally built in the 1920s and still channeling that era's glamour, the Rosewood Hotel Georgia downtown has 156 classy guest rooms and suites done in blues, creams, and chocolate browns with Italian linens and luxe baths with heated floors. Make time to exercise in the indoor saltwater lap pool or the 24-hour fitness center, since the hotel's **Hawksworth Restaurant** is among the city's top special-occasion dining spots and **Bel Café** is an upscale place for a pastry or quick lunch. Room service is available around the clock, and when you need to go out, the hotel's car service can chauffeur you around town.

MAP 1: 801 W. Georgia St., 604/682-5566 or 888/767-3966, www. rosewoodhotels.com

EXchange Hotel Vancouver $$$

In the early 20th-century downtown building that once housed the Vancouver Stock Exchange, the EXchange Hotel Vancouver pairs heritage elements with sustainable design and high-tech features to draw both business and leisure travelers. The 202 guest rooms have distinctive wallpapers, Italian coffee machines, and tablets that act as electronic concierges; in the baths, with gray marble vanities, the floors are heated. The street-level **Hydra Café** serves breakfast, lunch, and daytime coffee, transforming into an evening *mezze* bar. Upstairs, **Hydra Estiatorio Mediterranean Restaurant** features Greek-inspired specialties.

MAP 1: 475 Howe St., 604/563-4693 or 833/381-7623, www.exchangehotelvan.com

room at EXchange Hotel Vancouver

room at Loden Hotel

Fairmont Hotel Vancouver $$$

At the oldest of the chain's downtown properties, the green copper roof and stone gargoyles of the 1939 Fairmont Hotel Vancouver make it a recognizable landmark amid the city's glass-and-steel towers. The least expensive of the 507 guest rooms are small, but all have been updated with a mix of traditional and more contemporary furnishings, air-conditioning, and flat-screen TVs, as well as the classic Fairmont service. The indoor pool is in a window-lined greenhouse space, and on the lower level, Absolute Spa at the Fairmont caters to men, although women are welcome. Settle in for a drink or a bite at Notch8 Restaurant & Bar, which oozes modern-day elegance. For Wi-Fi access, sign up for the hotel's complimentary frequent-stay program.

MAP 1: 900 W. Georgia St., 604/684-3131 or 866/540-4452, www.fairmont.com

Loden Hotel $$$

Health-conscious guests at the Loden Hotel can tool around the city on complimentary electric bikes, work out in the window-lined gym, or tune in to the 24-hour yoga channel in your room, which comes with a yoga mat. The 77 guest rooms in this skinny 15-story West End boutique lodging have earth-tone furnishings, dark granite baths, and floor-to-ceiling windows. Recover from all this activity with a drink or a meal at Tableau Bar Bistro, which serves updated French classics.

MAP 1: 1177 Melville St., 604/669-5060 or 877/225-6336, http://theloden.com

Pan Pacific Hotel Vancouver $$$

Above the cruise ship terminal at Canada Place downtown, the 23-story Pan Pacific Hotel Vancouver is especially convenient if you're starting or ending your Vancouver stay on a boat, though even land-lubbers appreciate the panoramic views of the harbor and North Shore mountains. Enjoy the vistas from the heated saltwater pool and from many of the 503 nautical-style guest rooms, outfitted with padded white-leather headboards, white duvets trimmed with navy piping, and maple furniture. Have a drink in the Coal Harbour Bar or the Patio Terrace for more sea-to-sky views.

MAP 1: 999 Canada Pl., 604/662-8111 or 800/663-1515, www.panpacific.com

Wedgewood Hotel & Spa $$$

You don't hear much buzz about the Wedgewood Hotel & Spa, but guests at this fashionable downtown hideaway seem to like it that way. The 83 traditional rooms and suites feature deluxe amenities like plush robes and slippers, twice-daily housekeeping, and homemade bedtime cookies. You can work out in the up-to-date fitness facility and relax in the eucalyptus steam room; there's also a full-service spa. Elegant Bacchus Restaurant and Lounge serves French-accented cuisine with west coast ingredients.

MAP 1: 845 Hornby St., 604/689-7777 or 800/663-0666, www.wedgewoodhotel.com

West End Guest House $$$

This colorfully painted 1906 Victorian on a quiet residential block is a short stroll from Robson Street. It's a classic B&B, where guests mingle over afternoon sherry and sit around the dining table for a full hot breakfast. The owners have lined the hallways with historic Vancouver photos and furnished the eight guest rooms, all with Wi-Fi, TVs, and en suite baths, with antiques and period pieces, though the updated linens and upholstery give them a more contemporary feel. Bonus: The inn offers free parking for guests.

MAP 1: 1362 Haro St., 604/681-2889, www.westendguesthouse.com

✪ Burrard Hotel $$

Built in 1956, the four-story Burrard Hotel is an old-time motor hotel gone glam. The best feature of this retro-chic mid-century-modern lodging downtown is the courtyard garden, with palm trees and a fire pit, hidden from the surrounding city hum. The 72 guest rooms are small (baths are particularly petite), but they're well designed with espresso makers, mini fridges, and flat-screen TVs. Rates include Wi-Fi, North American phone calls, a pass to a nearby health club, and use of the hotel's bicycles. Off the lobby, Elysian Coffee serves pastries, coffee, and local beer.

MAP 1: 1100 Burrard St., 604/681-2331 or 800/663-0366, www.theburrard.com

Burrard Hotel

❂ Listel Hotel $$

Original artworks adorn the lobby, corridors, and guest rooms at the low-rise 129-room Listel Hotel on Vancouver's main downtown shopping street. The "museum" rooms feature works by First Nations artists, while staff from a local gallery decorated the eclectic "gallery" rooms. The retro-designed standard units on the 2nd floor are simpler but less expensive. You can work out in the small fitness center or request a complimentary pass to a nearby health club. Overall, the hotel is a comfortable and classy choice. On-site restaurant Forage, which emphasizes BC ingredients, is a bonus. The Listel charges an additional 6 percent fee to cover Wi-Fi and North American phone calls.

MAP 1: 1300 Robson St., 604/684-8461 or 800/663-5491, www.thelistelhotel.com

Barclay House B&B $$

Each of the six guest rooms at the Barclay House B&B, in a yellow 1904 Victorian home in the midst of urban Vancouver, is decorated differently. The bay-windowed turquoise-accented Beach room has a queen bed and a cozy sitting area, while the Peak room, under the eaves on the top floor, has skylights and a claw-foot tub. Guests can mingle in the lounge or games room, both furnished with a mix of contemporary and antique pieces. Rates at this West End inn include parking, Wi-Fi, and a full breakfast.

MAP 1: 1351 Barclay St., 604/605-1351 or 800/971-1351, www.barclayhouse.com

Hotel Belmont $$

It's all about the party at this funky lodging in the heart of the Granville Street nightlife district, from the lobby ceiling papered with wacky faces to the on-site pub where DJs spin tunes to the lively basement nightclub serving boozy popsicles. Upstairs in the revamped heritage building, the 82 guest rooms, while not huge, feel cool, with dark-blue headboards, black and white baths, one-cup coffeemakers, and complimentary Wi-Fi. Pack ear plugs if you need to drown out the late-night revelry.

MAP 1: 654 Nelson St., 604/605-4333 or 888/936-5676, www.hotelbelmont.ca

Moda Hotel $$

In a restored 1908 building downtown, the boutique Moda Hotel has 67 cozy rooms. The smallest measure just 150 square feet (14 square m), while standard doubles are 300-350 square feet (28-32 square m), but they're smartly designed, with red accents, updated baths, air-conditioning, and free Wi-Fi and North American phone calls. You don't have to go far to eat and drink: Uva Wine & Cocktail Bar, Red Card Sports Bar, and Cibo Trattoria are all on the lobby level.

MAP 1: 900 Seymour St., 604/683-4251 or 877/683-5522, www.modahotel.ca

Sunset Inn and Suites $$

On a residential West End block, steps from lively Davie Street, the Sunset Inn and Suites, in a 1970s former apartment building, has 50 unpretentious studios and one-bedroom units (with sofa beds), all with full kitchens and handy features like multiple outlets and USB

Sylvia Hotel

ports by the beds. Rates include lots of extras: Wi-Fi, a light continental breakfast, and free parking. The cheapest units overlook the back alley; the priciest have views toward False Creek. The tiny fitness room has just three cardio machines, but get outdoors: you're a short stroll from the Seawall.

MAP 1: 1111 Burnaby St., 604/688-2474, http://sunsetinn.com

Sylvia Hotel $$

Sure, the ivy-covered Sylvia Hotel, constructed as a West End apartment building in 1912, is a little old-fashioned. But all 120 units, from basic queens and kings to larger family suites, have free Wi-Fi and flat-screen TVs; some have kitchens, and the best rooms have million-dollar views of English Bay. Even if your room doesn't, you can walk out the front door to the beach, Stanley Park, and plenty of dining spots.

MAP 1: 1154 Gilford St., 604/681-9321 or 877/681-9321, www.sylviahotel.com

✪ Skwachàys Lodge $$

At Skwachàys Lodge, Canada's first indigenous arts and culture hotel, indigenous artists worked with hotel designers to craft 18 distinctive guest rooms in an early-20th-century brick Victorian. In the Poem Suite, poems and pencil drawings dance across walls; in the Moon Suite, artists painted a golden moon face on the ceiling watching over the bed below. An indigenous-owned company created the hotel's bath products; rates include Wi-Fi and both local and international calls. Guests can participate in sweat lodge or smudging ceremonies with an indigenous elder, with advance reservations. An added benefit: Hotel profits help subsidize housing for First Nations artists.
MAP 2: 31 W. Pender St., 604/687-3589 or 888/998-0797, http:// skwachays.com

Victorian Hotel $$

The 47-room Victorian Hotel is a European-style boutique property in two brick buildings, dating to 1898 and 1908. While the least expensive rooms are tiny and share hallway baths, others are more spacious and have private baths. All tastefully mix period pieces and modern furnishings, with pillow-top mattresses, robes, and flat-screen TVs. Rates include Wi-Fi and continental breakfast.
MAP 2: 514 Homer St., 604/681-6369, www.victorianhotel.ca

Skwachàys Lodge

✪ Opus Hotel Vancouver $$$

A clear contender for the title of "Vancouver's coolest hotel," the boutique Opus Hotel Vancouver outfitted its 96 guest rooms in eye-popping lime greens, magentas, purples, and vibrant oranges. Many of the spacious baths have a window into the bedroom, while in others, bath windows face outside (don't be shy!). Rooms aren't huge, though they come with high-tech toys like flat-screen TVs, one-cup coffee-makers, and iPads that you can use throughout your stay (with free Wi-Fi, of course). Staff greet guests with a complimentary glass of sparkling wine; to get around town, book the hotel's complimentary car service or borrow a gratis mountain bike.

MAP 3: 322 Davie St., 866/642-6787, http://vancouver.opushotel.com

Opus Hotel Vancouver

Parq Vancouver $$$

One block from the False Creek waterfront, adjacent to BC Place arena, copper-clad Parq Vancouver houses a casino, numerous food and drink outlets, and two upscale hotels. The lodgings share the window-lined fitness facilities and spa, as well as "The Park," the 6th-floor green space and outdoor lounge that gives the complex its name. The Douglas (604/676-0889 or 888/236-2427, www.thedouglasvancouver.com) is styled with boutique ambiance in its 188 rooms, designed like cabins with dark walnut furniture, concrete ceilings, plaid throws on the pillow-top beds, and quirky amenities including retro pencil sharpeners. In the larger JW Marriott Parq Vancouver (604/676-0888 or 888/236-2427, www.marriott.com), the 329 rooms in two towers feel light and airy if more corporate, though both business and leisure travelers will appreciate the floor-to-ceiling windows, colorful artwork, espresso makers, and marble baths. Note that parking at Parq Vancouver is $40-45 per day.

MAP 3: 39 Smithe St., 604/683-7277, www.parqvancouver.com

Hotel BLU $$

This contemporary 75-room lodging sits at the foot of Robson Street, within shouting distance of BC Place, and at Hotel BLU, there's plenty to keep you active: an indoor pool with a courtyard patio, 24-hour fitness room, and complimentary bicycles. Guest rooms are technology-friendly, with tablet computers, free Wi-Fi, handy USB ports, and plenty of electrical outlets. Other amenities include mini fridges, microwaves, teakettles, and one-cup espresso makers, and many

of the modern bathrooms have glass walls into the showers. The building also has a self-service guest laundry.
MAP 3: 177 Robson St., 604/620-6200 or 855/284-2091, www. hotelbluvancouver.com

YWCA Hotel Vancouver $

One of Vancouver's best options for travelers on a budget is the modern YWCA Hotel Vancouver. The 155 rooms range from basic singles with either a hall bath or a semiprivate bath (shared between two rooms) or doubles with hall, semiprivate, or private baths to larger units that accommodate three to five people. All have air-conditioning, flat-screen TVs, mini fridges, and Wi-Fi included. Guests can prep meals in one of the three common kitchens or grab a snack in the lobby café.
MAP 3: 733 Beatty St., 604/895-5830 or 800/663-1424, www.ywcavan.org

Granville Island

Map 4

Granville Island Hotel $$$

To stay right on Granville Island, book a room at the waterfront Granville Island Hotel. The 82 guest rooms and suites are all furnished differently; the nicest ones take advantage of the island location with balconies and water views. Wi-Fi is included, and the hotel has a small fitness room—but for a more interesting workout, you can run or walk along the Seawall.
MAP 4: 1253 Johnston St., 604/683-7373 or 800/663-1840, www. granvilleislandhotel.com

Kitsilano

Map 5

Corkscrew Inn $$

Glass artist Sal Robinson has outfitted the Corkscrew Inn, the B&B that she co-owns with her husband, Wayne Meadows, in a 1912 Craftsman-style Kitsilano home, with her original art deco-inspired wine-themed stained glass. You'll see her work in the sitting areas, dining room, and the five guest rooms, which also have custom-designed baths. The inn also takes its name from Meadows's collection of antique corkscrews, which he displays in a tiny "museum" on the lower level. Rates include a family-style hot breakfast, which might feature a wild salmon frittata or lemon ricotta pancakes.
MAP 5: 2735 W. 2nd Ave., 604/733-7276 or 877/737-7276, www. corkscrewinn.com

West Coast Suites at UBC $$

On the University of British Columbia campus, West Coast Suites at UBC are modern one-bedroom apartment-style suites. Units have a king bed in the bedroom, a living room with a small dining table and a sofa bed, and a full kitchen. Other amenities include flat-screen TVs, Wi-Fi, and U.S. and Canadian phone calls. Open year-round, the suites are located a short walk from the UBC bus loop.

MAP 6: 5959 Student Union Blvd., 604/822-1000 or 888/822-1030, http://suitesatubc.com

HI-Vancouver Jericho Beach $

Fancy a cheap sleep by the beach? Hostelling International runs this seasonal hostel in a former military barracks, a short walk from the shore in Point Grey. The dorms remain true to their origins, with each room sleeping 14 to 18 people in curtained-off four-person "quads," each with two bunk beds. Updated private rooms, with shared baths down the hall, accommodate 2-4. There's also a private room with a queen bed and an en suite bath, as well as two family rooms, each sleeping 2-4 and sharing a kitchen and bath.

The hostel has a kitchen for guests' use, complimentary Wi-Fi, laundry facilities, bike rentals, and a small café. The nearest commercial district, with a grocery store, liquor store, and several restaurants, is along West 4th Avenue near Alma Street, a 20-minute walk from the hostel. Buses run along West 4th Avenue toward downtown (20-25 minutes) and the UBC campus (10 minutes).

MAP 6: 1515 Discovery St., 604/224-3208 or 778/328-2220, www.hihostels.ca, May-mid-Sept.

Pacific Spirit Hostel $

More student dormitory than classic travelers' hostel, Pacific Spirit Hostel offers summer-only budget accommodations in a UBC residence hall. Sleeping options include basic private single or double rooms; you get a bed, a desk, and a storage cabinet, but not much else. There are shared baths and a TV lounge on each floor. Although complimentary Wi-Fi is available in the lobby, for in-room access, you need to rent a router ($2 per day).

The hostel is open only during the university's summer break, May-mid-August. From the UBC bus loop, walk west on University Boulevard and turn right onto Lower Mall; it's about a 10-minute walk.

MAP 6: 1935 Lower Mall, 604/822-1000 or 888/822-1030, http://suitesatubc.com, May-mid-Aug.

Richmond — Map 9

Fairmont Vancouver Airport Hotel $$$

You can't stay closer to the departure gates than at this luxury lodging inside the terminal at Vancouver International Airport. At the Fairmont Vancouver Airport Hotel, the lobby sits above the U.S. departures hall, yet despite the bustle below, this contemporary property feels surprisingly quiet. The floor-to-ceiling windows in the 392 guest rooms, many of which overlook the runways, are triple-glazed to keep out the airplane noise; pillow-top mattresses and white duvets cover the king or queen beds. To unwind before or after your travels, swim in the lap pool, work out in the fitness facility, or book a treatment at the spa.

Even if you're not staying at the hotel, head for the Jetside Bar for refreshments. You can watch the planes come and go over drinks and light meals while waiting for your flight.

MAP 9: 3111 Grant McConachie Way, subway: YVR Airport, 604/207-5200 or 866/540-4441, www.fairmont.com

The North Shore — Map 10

Pinnacle Hotel at the Pier

Pinnacle Hotel at the Pier $$

Convenient to mountain activities, eight-story Pinnacle Hotel at the Pier has panoramic views across the water to the Vancouver skyline. Of the 106 modern guest rooms, with Wi-Fi included, those on the harbor side have small step-out balconies, and if you open the bath blinds, you can take in the vistas while you soak in the tub. City-side rooms glimpse the mountains. In the health club, you can enjoy the seascape from the cardio and weight machines, waterside sundeck, or indoor Olympic-size pool. The hotel is a five-minute walk from Lonsdale Quay and a 12-minute ride on the SeaBus to downtown Vancouver.

MAP 10: 138 Victory Ship Way, North Vancouver, 604/986-7437 or 877/986-7437, http://pinnaclepierhotel.com

VICTORIA AND VANCOUVER ISLAND

Vancouver Island offers lots of ways to relax, from enjoying a cup of tea or a glass of wine to watching whales and catching waves.

At the southern tip of Vancouver Island, across the Strait of Georgia from the city of Vancouver, British Columbia's capital, Victoria, mixes historic and hip. You can easily spend a day or more taking in the sights along the Inner Harbour, venturing offshore for whale-watching, or enjoying traditional afternoon tea. A boom in contemporary restaurants, craft breweries, and cool cocktail bars means that you'll eat and drink well too. Near Victoria, both the agricultural Cowichan Valley and the Saanich Peninsula are wine- and cider-making regions, where you can sample what's new at the winery tasting rooms.

Fairmont Empress in Victoria

North of Victoria, Nanaimo is an alternate ferry port between Vancouver and the island; it's the most convenient route between Vancouver and Tofino on the island's west coast. Besides an attractive waterfront and historic sites, Nanaimo is worth a stop to sample a sweet Nanaimo bar.

Vancouver Island's striking west coast is the region's ocean playground. Explore the beaches and rainforest trails in the Pacific Rim National Park Reserve and unwind in the sand-and-surf communities of Tofino and Ucluelet. Day-trip to remote hot springs, kayak to a First Nations island, or go on a whale- or bear-watching excursion. Oceanfront resorts and fine casual restaurants (seafood is a specialty) keep you comfortable when you come in from the sea.

HIGHLIGHTS

✪ **VICTORIA'S INNER HARBOUR:** Buskers, ferries, floatplanes, and travelers converge on Victoria's waterfront, where the city's major sights are located (page 234).

✪ **ROYAL BRITISH COLUMBIA MUSEUM:** Trace British Columbia's roots at this museum of cultural and natural history (page 235).

✪ **BUTCHART GARDENS:** Elaborate floral displays and holiday lights make these gardens one of Vancouver Island's most popular year-round attractions (page 245).

✪ **WHALE-WATCHING:** You may spot orcas, humpbacks, or gray whales from the whale-watching boats that depart from Victoria (page 249).

✪ **PACIFIC RIM NATIONAL PARK RESERVE:** Explore the rainforest and beaches in this lush oceanfront national park (page 268).

✪ **TOFINO:** This funky town on Vancouver Island's far west coast has beautiful beaches, great restaurants, and a chill surfer vibe, plus lots of on-the-water excursions (page 271).

flowers at Butchart Gardens

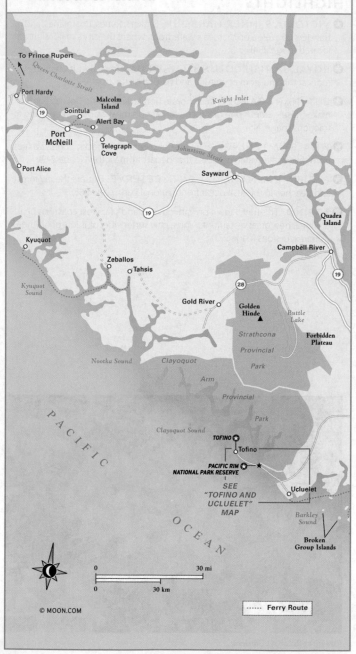

Vancouver Island

To Prince Rupert

Queen Charlotte Strait

Port Hardy

(19)

Sointula

Malcolm Island

Alert Bay

Port McNeill

Telegraph Cove

Johnstone Strait

Port Alice

Sayward

(19)

Knight Inlet

Quadra Island

Kyuquot

Zeballos

Tahsis

Campbell River

(19)

Kyuquot Sound

(28)

Gold River

Golden Hinde ▲

Buttle Lake

Strathcona Provincial Park

Forbidden Plateau

Nootka Sound

Clayoquot Arm Provincial Park

PACIFIC

Clayoquot Sound

TOFINO ✪

Tofino

PACIFIC RIM NATIONAL PARK RESERVE ✪ ★

SEE "TOFINO AND UCLUELET" MAP

Ucluelet

Barkley Sound

OCEAN

Broken Group Islands

0 _____ 30 mi

0 _____ 30 km

© MOON.COM

······· Ferry Route

232

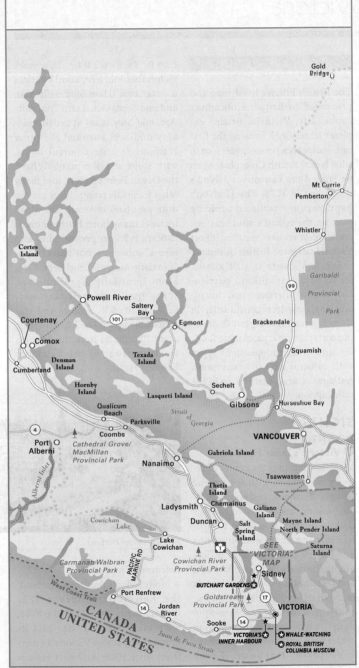

Gold Bridge

Mt Currie

Pemberton

Whistler

Cortes
Island

Powell River

Saltery
Bay

Egmont

Brackendale

99

Garibaldi

Provincial

Park

Courtenay

Comox

Denman
Island

Cumberland

Texada
Island

Sechelt

Squamish

Hornby
Island

Lasqueti Island

Qualicum
Beach

Gibsons

Horseshoe Bay

Parksville

Strait
of
Georgia

4

Coombs

Cathedral Grove/
MacMillan
Provincial Park

VANCOUVER

Port
Alberni

Alberni Inlet

Nanaimo

Gabriola Island

Tsawwassen

Thetis
Island

Chemainus

Galiano
Island

Cowichan
Lake

Ladysmith

Duncan

Salt
Spring
Island

Mayne Island
North Pender Island

SEE
"VICTORIA"
MAP

Saturna
Island

Lake
Cowichan

1

Cowichan River
Provincial Park

Sidney

Carmanah Walbran
Provincial Park

PACIFIC
MARINE RD

BUTCHART GARDENS ★

West Coast Trail

Port Renfrew

14

Goldstream
Provincial Park

17

VICTORIA

Jordan
River

CANADA
UNITED STATES

Sooke

14

Juan de Fuca Strait

★

VICTORIA'S
INNER HARBOUR

★ **WHALE-WATCHING**

★ **ROYAL BRITISH**
COLUMBIA MUSEUM

233

Victoria

The British Empire lived long and prospered in British Columbia's capital city, Victoria. British explorer James Cook became the first non-indigenous person to set foot in what is now British Columbia, when he landed on Vancouver Island's west coast in 1778. The Hudson's Bay Company established a trading post on the island's southeastern corner 65 years later, naming it Fort Victoria, after the British queen.

While Victoria is still known for its British traditions, particularly elegant afternoon tea, this increasingly modern community in Canada's warmest region is drawing entrepreneurs, passionate foodies, and other independent types with cultural attractions, vibrant restaurants, and plenty to do in the mild outdoors.

SIGHTS
DOWNTOWN
✪ Victoria's Inner Harbour

Victoria's harbor is the center of activity downtown, with ferries and floatplanes coming and going, buskers busking, and plenty of tourists soaking up the scene. Many companies offering whale-watching tours and other excursions have offices along the waterside promenade, and **Destination Greater Victoria** (812 Wharf St., 250/953-2033, www.tourismvictoria.com, 9am-5pm daily) runs a visitor information center here, with public restrooms.

Victoria Harbour Ferry (250/708-0201, www.victoriaharbourferry.com) operates a water taxi (11am-5pm daily Mar. and mid-Sept.-Oct., 11am-7pm daily Apr.-mid-May, 10am-9pm daily mid-May-mid-Sept.) around the Inner Harbour in cute colorful boats, with stops at Fisherman's Wharf, the Ocean Pointe Resort, and many other waterside points. Fares vary by distance; a basic one-zone trip, which includes many Inner Harbour destinations, is $6 per person. They also offer 45-minute harbor tours (11am-5pm daily Mar. and mid-Sept.-Oct., 11am-7pm daily Apr.-mid-May, 10am-9pm daily mid-May-mid-Sept., adults $30, seniors and students $28, ages 1-11 $20), departing every 20 minutes from the Empress Dock in front of the Fairmont Empress Hotel.

Victoria's Inner Harbour

Fairmont Empress

A landmark on the Inner Harbour, the **Fairmont Empress** (721 Government St., 250/384-8111, www.fairmont.com) has cast its grand visage across Victoria's waterfront since 1908. Architect Francis

Mawson Rattenbury designed and built the hotel as one of the Canadian Pacific Railway's majestic château-style lodgings. British royals have slept here, including Prince Charles and Camilla, as have U.S. presidents and numerous celebrities, including Katharine Hepburn, Bob Hope, John Travolta, Harrison Ford, and Barbra Streisand.

Even if you're not staying at the Empress, you can walk through its public spaces, dine in its restaurants and lounges, or take afternoon tea (a Victoria tradition). On the front lawn, check out the beehives where Fairmont staff harvest honey to use in the property's kitchen.

Royal British Columbia Museum

✪ Royal British Columbia Museum

Tracing British Columbia's cultural and natural history, the **Royal British Columbia Museum** (675 Belleville St., 250/356-7226, http://royalbcmuseum.bc.ca, 10am-5pm Sun.-Thurs., 10am-10pm Fri.-Sat. late May-mid-Oct., 10am-5pm daily mid-Oct.-late May, adults $27, seniors and students $19, ages 6-18 $17) was founded in 1886. A highlight is the First Peoples Gallery, with totem poles, masks, regalia,

and other indigenous objects, along with exhibits that illuminate the lives of Canada's first inhabitants. Also check out the multimedia Living Languages gallery, where you can listen to some of BC's indigenous languages.

You can take a one-hour **guided tour** (included with museum admission); check the calendar on the museum's website or in the lobby for tour times and topics. To spread out your museum meanderings over two consecutive days, buy a discounted **two-day ticket** (adults $41, seniors and students $29, ages 6-18 $26).

The museum has an **IMAX Theatre** (IMAX only adults $12, seniors and ages 6-18 $9.75, students $10.75, with museum admission adults $37, seniors $29, students $30, ages 6-18 $27), showing a changing selection of movies on the big screen.

Adjacent to the museum, several totem poles stand in **Thunderbird Park.** Also outside is the 1852 **Helmcken House,** the oldest public building in BC still on its original site; the Hudson's Bay Company built the cabin for Dr. John Sebastian Helmcken and his wife, Cecilia Douglas. A physician and politician, Helmcken helped bring BC into the Canadian Confederation, though he allegedly once said that Canada would eventually be absorbed into the United States.

BC Parliament Building

Although Vancouver, on the mainland, is a much larger city, Victoria has been the provincial capital since British Columbia joined the Canadian Confederation in 1871. The seat of the provincial

Victoria

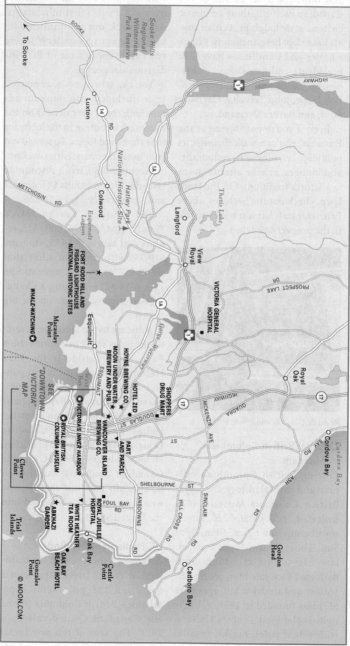

To Sooke

Sooke Hills
Regional
Wilderness
Park Reserve

HIGHWAY

SOOKE RD

Luxton

14

RD

Colwood

METCHOSIN RD

Hatley Park
National Historic Site

1A

Thetis
Lake

Langford

View
Royal

Esquimalt
Lagoon

Colwood

FORT RODD HILL AND
FISGARD LIGHTHOUSE
NATIONAL HISTORIC SITES

WHALE-WATCHING ○

Macaulay
Point

Esquimalt

VICTORIA GENERAL
HOSPITAL

PROSPECT LAKE DR

1A

Gorge Waterway

Royal
Oak

17

HOYNE BREWING CO.
MOON UNDER WATER
BREWERY AND PUB.

HOTEL ZED

SHOPPERS
DRUG MART

ESQUIMALT

West Bay

"DOWNTOWN"
MAP

SEE
"DOWNTOWN"
MAP

VICTORIA'S INNER HARBOUR

ROYAL BRITISH
COLUMBIA MUSEUM

Clover
Point

VANCOUVER ISLAND
BREWING CO.

DOUGLAS ST

HIGHWAY

MCKENZIE AVE

QUADRA

17

Cordova Bay

PART
AND PARCEL

ST

SHELBOURNE ST

LANSDOWNE RD

HILL CROSS RD

SINCLAIR RD

ASH RD

BAY RD

Cordova Bay

Gordon
Head

ROYAL JUBILEE
HOSPITAL

FOUL BAY RD

WHITE HEATHER
TEA ROOM

AKHAZI
GARDEN

Trial
Islands

Gonzales
Point

OAK BAY
BEACH HOTEL

Oak Bay

Cattle
Point

Cadboro Bay

© MOON.COM

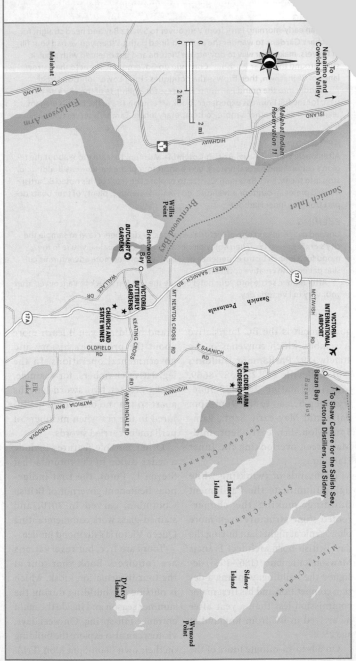

To Nanaimo and
Cowichan Valley

To
Nanaimo and
Cowichan Valley

Malahat

ISLAND

ISLAND

Finlayson Arm

Malahat Indian
Reservation 11

HIGHWAY 1

Willis
Point

Brentwood Bay

Saanich Inlet

0   2 km
0   2 mi

Brentwood
Bay

BUTCHART
GARDENS

VICTORIA
BUTTERFLY
GARDENS

CHURCH AND
STATE WINES

WALLACE DR

KEATING CROSS RD

WEST SAANICH RD

MT NEWTON CROSS RD

Saanich
Peninsula

17A

17A

Elk
Lake

OLDFIELD
RD

E SAANICH
RD

PATRICIA BAY
RD

MARTINDALE RD

CORDOVA

SEA CIDER FARM
& CIDERHOUSE

HIGHWAY

MCTAVISH
RD

VICTORIA
INTERNATIONAL
AIRPORT

Bazan Bay

To Shaw Centre for the Salish Sea,
Victoria Distillers, and Sidney

Cordova Channel

James
Island

Sidney Channel

Sidney
Island

Miners Channel

D'Arcy Island

Wymond
Point

g ferry from Vancouver to Swartz Bay and head straight for
vander the blossom-lined paths. When you've had your fill
way to downtown Victoria and get oriented with a quick
Harbour. Continue up Government Street to the narrow
n browse the boutiques along Lower Johnson Street.
d Fairmont Empress for a glimpse of the city's Victorian
the full Empress experience, book afternoon tea in the hotel's elegant
tearoom. If you'd rather a more contemporary lunch, Zambri's serves fine Italian
fare.

AFTERNOON

After lunch, visit the Royal British Columbia Museum to learn more about the region's cultural and natural history, take a short tour of the Parliament Building, or stop into the Robert Bateman Centre to explore the work of this noted BC artist. If you'd prefer an outdoor adventure, go whale-watching; plenty of tour boats depart from the Inner Harbour.

EVENING

Unwind over drinks in one of Victoria's lounges, or do a beer crawl to sample the city's craft breweries. Then enjoy dinner at Brasserie L'Ecole if you're in the mood for a French bistro experience or OLO if you prefer more adventurous cuisine paired with creative cocktails.

After dinner, settle into your hotel or take the late ferry back to Vancouver, after your very full Victoria day.

government is the BC Legislative Assembly, which convenes in the stately 1897 **Parliament Building** (501 Belleville St., 250/387-8669, tour information 250/387-3046, www.leg.bc.ca, tours 9am-5pm daily mid-May-early Sept., 9am-5pm Mon.-Fri. early-Sept.-mid-May, free), overlooking the Inner Harbour.

Thousands of twinkling white lights illuminate the Parliament Building, making the copper-roofed stone structure even more photogenic at night than during the day. British-born architect Francis Mawson Rattenbury (1867-1935) designed the building, winning a design competition and his first major commission less than a year after he arrived in BC from England at age 25.

On 30- to 45-minute tours of the

grand building, you'll learn more about the province's history and governmental operations. In the legislative chambers, for example, desks are set two sword-lengths apart so that no one would get injured in the era when members of parliament carried swords.

Other notable features include a cedar canoe in the rotunda that Steven L. Point, the first indigenous lieutenant governor of British Columbia, carved in 2010, and stained-glass work commemorating Queen Victoria's diamond jubilee.

Tours are free, but **reservations are required.** Book your tour at the tour information kiosk, which is outside the building during the summer season and inside the main entrance fall-spring. On weekdays, visitors can also explore the building on their own (9am-5pm Mon.-Fri.).

Robert Bateman Centre

Artist and naturalist Robert Bateman is a notable Canadian wildlife painter. Born in Ontario in 1930, he made an epic round-the-world journey in a Land Rover before returning to Canada to teach and paint, eventually relocating to BC's Salt Spring Island. View his paintings and learn more about his interesting life at the Robert Bateman Centre (470 Belleville St., 250/940-3630, http://batemancentre.org, 10am-5pm daily, adults $10, seniors and students $8.50, under age 19 free), in the 1924 beaux arts Steamship Terminal on the Inner Harbour.

Victoria Bug Zoo

If you're not afraid of ants, tarantulas, and other crawling, flying, or wriggling insects, visit this fascinating little museum devoted to the world of bugs. The Victoria Bug Zoo (631 Courtney St., 250/384-2847, www.victoriabugzoo.ca, 11am-4pm Mon.-Fri., 11am-5pm Sat.-Sun., adults $14, seniors and students $10, ages 5-17 $8) houses more than 40 insect species, as well as Canada's largest ant colony, which you can view through a clear wall. Guides are on hand to share fun bug facts.

Fisherman's Wharf

Can you imagine yourself living on the water? With your house *in* the water? The residents of the 30 compact floating houses in the Float Home Village at Fisherman's Wharf (1 Dallas Rd., www.fishermanswharfvictoria.com) do exactly that. Wander the docks and envision life in this colorful waterfront community; these are private homes, so do respect residents' privacy.

Fisherman's Wharf has several outdoor eateries, including ever-popular Barb's Fish 'n' Chips, touristy shops, and kayak rentals. From the Inner Harbour, it's a lovely walk along the waterfront on the David Foster Harbour Pathway, or you can catch a Victoria Harbour Ferry (www.victoriaharbourferry.com).

Emily Carr House

Known for her paintings of British Columbia's landscape and its indigenous people, artist Emily Carr (1871-1945) is considered one of Canada's most important early-20th-century painters. Unusually for a woman of her era, she made several solo trips to remote First Nations communities, where she wanted to document what she believed was the disappearing indigenous culture. She didn't begin seeing commercial success until late in her life, after a 1927 National Gallery of Canada exhibit featured some of her work; the now-famous artist managed a Victoria apartment building for 15 years to support herself.

Set in a Victorian home in Victoria's James Bay neighborhood where she was born and spent her childhood, Emily Carr House (207 Government St., 250/383-5843, www.emilycarr.com, 11am-4pm Tues.-Sat. May-Sept., adults $8, seniors and students $7, ages 6-18 $5) is a museum about her life and work and about BC society during her era.

Beacon Hill Park

Established in 1882, the 200-acre (81-ha) Beacon Hill Park (bounded by Douglas, Southgate, and Cook

Downtown Victoria

STORE ST

JAM CAFÉ

BRASSERIE L'ECOLE

CHINATOWN

VENUS SOPHIA TEA ROOM & VEGETARIAN EATERY

SWIFT ST

GATE OF HARMONIOUS INTEREST

Upper Harbour

FISHHOOK AT MERMAID WHARF

OLO

SILK ROAD TEA

FAN TAN ALLEY

SWANS BREWPUB

PANDORA ST

HARBOUR RD

Market Square

STILL LIFE FOR HIM

BAGGINS SHOES

STILL LIFE FOR HER

SUASION

MEC

JOHNSON ST BRIDGE

JOHNSON ST

GOVERNMENT ST

WADDINGTON ALLEY

STORE ST

WHARF ST

LULULEMON

YATES ST

0   200 yds
0   200 m

COMMERCIAL ALLEY

LANGLEY ST

REBAR

SPRINGTIDE WHALE WATCHING

LITTLE JUMBO

MUNRO'S BOOKS

Laurel Point

Centennial Park

RED FISH BLUE FISH

VICTORIA INNER HARBOUR CENTRE

ORCA SPIRIT ADVENTURES

WHALE-WATCHING ✕

COURTNEY ST

DESTINATION GREATER VICTORIA INFORMATION CENTRE

Inner

Harbour

PRINCE OF WHALES

INN AT LAUREL POINT

VICTORIA'S INNER HARBOUR

GOVERNMENT ST

QUEBEC ST

PENDRAY ST

THE PEDALER

Quadra Park

OSWEGO ST

BELLEVILLE ST

VICTORIA STEAMSHIP TERMINAL

NOURISH KITCHEN & CAFÉ

ROBERT BATEMAN CENTRE

To Orca Spirit Adventures, Eagle wing Tours, Barb's Fish 'N' Chips, and Fisherman's Wharf

QUEBEC ST

BRITISH COLUMBIA PARLIAMENT BUILDING

KINGSTON ST

OSWEGO HOTEL

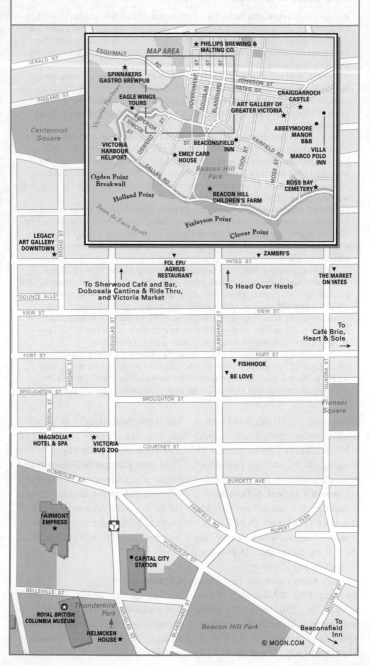

TWO SCANDALS AND A MURDER

Architect Francis Mawson Rattenbury became one of British Columbia's most notable architects at the turn of the 20th century, designing Victoria's Parliament Building, the Empress Hotel, and the Vancouver Court House, which now houses the
Vancouver Art Gallery. Yet Rattenbury became enmeshed in two marital scandals
that tarnished his reputation and eventually led to his grisly murder.

In 1898, not long after he completed work on the Parliament Building, Rattenbury married Florence Nunn, and they had two children. As his professional stature
grew, his personal life deteriorated, and by the early 1920s he and Florence were
living in different sections of their Oak Bay home, communicating only through
their daughter.

At a reception at the Empress Hotel in 1923, Rattenbury met a young musician,
Alma Pakenham, nearly 30 years his junior, and they began a very public affair.
Florence initially refused Rattenbury's request for a divorce, agreeing only after
he moved Alma into their home, where Florence still lived. Rattenbury's indiscreet
behavior scandalized Victoria society. Even after he and Alma married in 1925, they
were never accepted in the community.

In 1929, they moved to England to start fresh. Instead, they became embroiled
in another scandal. Rattenbury had begun drinking, and when they settled in England, his alcoholism worsened, triggering depression and, reportedly, impotence.
After they hired 18-year-old George Stoner as a chauffeur, Alma began an affair
with the teenager.

Apparently jealous that Alma had any relationship at all with her husband,
Stoner attacked Rattenbury in their home, hitting him repeatedly on the head with
a mallet. When Rattenbury died not long after the attack, both Alma and Stoner
were charged with murder. After a public trial at London's Old Bailey that mes-
merized the city, Alma was found innocent and Stoner guilty, sentenced to die by
hanging. Four days later, apparently distraught by the scandal and by her lover's
sentence, Alma committed suicide by stabbing herself to death.

Despite the trial's verdict, Alma became the villain in the court of public opin-
ion, accused of corrupting an innocent boy. Stoner's death sentence was com-
muted to life in prison. For the murder of the eminent BC architect whose life
deteriorated into scandal, George Stoner served only seven years in jail.

Streets and the Dallas Road waterfront, www.beaconhillpark.ca, free)
is Victoria's urban green space, with
flower gardens, walking paths, and
several attractions, including one of
the **world's tallest totem poles,**
measuring 128 feet (39 m) tall, and
the **Mile 0 marker,** in the park's
southwest corner, which denotes the
start of the 5,000-mile (8,000-km)
Trans-Canada Highway.

Near the center of the park,
Beacon Hill Children's Farm
(Circle Dr., 250/381-2532, www.
beaconhillchildrensfarm.ca, 10am-
4pm daily Mar.-Apr. and early
Sept.-mid-Oct., 10am-5pm daily

May-early Sept., free) has wander-
ing peacocks, furry alpacas, and
a petting zoo. A highlight is the
daily **goat stampede** (10:10am and
5:10pm daily summer, 10:10am and
4:10pm daily spring and fall), when
the farm's goats race between their
sleeping barn and the petting area.
It's one of those things you just have
to see!

Chinatown

Settled in the 1850s, Victoria's
Chinatown (Fisgard St. at
Government St.) is the oldest in
Canada. Although it has shrunk to
a couple of blocks around Fisgard

Gate of Harmonious Interest in Chinatown

Street, where the neighborhood's gateway, the **Gate of Harmonious Interest,** stands, the district was once Canada's largest Chinese settlement.

After BC's gold rush drew the first Chinese immigrants, the community really began to grow as Chinese workers arrived in Victoria on their way to jobs on the Canadian Pacific Railway. More than 17,000 Chinese immigrants came to Canada between 1881 and 1884.

Today, you'll find a few Chinese-run shops and restaurants and many non-Asian boutiques and eateries. One remaining landmark is narrow **Fan Tan Alley** (between Fisgard St. and Pandora Ave.), a lane only 3-6 feet (1-2 m) wide, where, somehow, several shops have managed to squeeze in.

Breweries

Victoria's craft beer scene has bubbled up in recent years, with a cluster of breweries in an industrial district north of the downtown core, and other microbreweries and brewpubs scattered around the city. Here's where to find the suds:

Lively Victoria old-timer **Swans Brewpub** (506 Pandora Ave., 250/361-3310, http://swanshotel. com, 11am-1am Mon.-Fri., 9am-1am Sat., 11am-midnight Sun.) has a central location, pub fare, and even a hotel if you can't move on after a night of beer-tasting.

At **Phillips Brewing & Malting Co.** (2010 Government St., 250/380-1912, www.phillipsbeer.com, tasting room noon-10pm daily, store 10am-7pm daily), you can sample its beers as well as hand-crafted sodas in the tasting room overlooking its packaging facility.

Vancouver Island Brewing Co. (2330 Government St., 250/361-0005, http://vanislandbrewery.com, 11am-6pm Sun.-Thurs., 11am-7pm Fri.-Sat., tours 3pm Fri.-Sat., $7, reserve in advance) was the island's first craft brewery when it launched in 1984. It brews staples like the Victoria Lager and Faller Northwest Pale Ale.

Moon Under Water Brewery and Pub (350 Bay St., 250/380-0706, www.moonunderwater.ca, 11:30am-11pm Mon.-Sat., 11:30am-8pm Sun.) draws inspiration from European brewing traditions and craft beers like Creepy Uncle Dunkel, a dark lager.

West of downtown, **Spinnakers Gastro Brewpub** (308 Catherine St., 250/386-2739, www.spinnakers. com, 11am-11pm daily) has waterfront views and is known as much for its farm-to-table fare as for its craft brews, which include a cask special every weekday afternoon.

EAST OF DOWNTOWN
Abkhazi Garden

The story of this manicured garden is a love story between a British woman born in Shanghai and an erstwhile prince from the Republic of Georgia. Marjorie Pemberton-Carter, known as Peggy, first met Prince Nicholas Abkhazi in Paris in the 1920s. Although they wrote to each other over the years, circumstances kept them apart; during World War II, each spent time in prisoner-of-war camps—Nicholas in Germany and Peggy in Shanghai.

En route from China to Britain in 1945, Peggy stopped to see friends in Victoria. Her visit turned more permanent when she purchased an overgrown lot and decided to build a summer home. Peggy had lost contact with Nicholas, but he wrote to her in early 1946; they met later that year in New York, and by November, they had returned to Victoria and married.

The home and garden that the newlyweds built on Peggy's property, and where they lived for more than 40 years, became Abkhazi Garden (1964 Fairfield Rd., 778/265-6466, http://conservancy. bc.ca, 11am-5pm daily Apr.-Sept., 11am-5pm Wed.-Sun. Oct.-Mar., last admission 1 hour before closing, $10). The compact garden, slightly over 1 acre (0.4 ha), features a rhododendron woodland with large Garry oak trees, a winding path known as the Yangtze River, and a variety of other plantings around the site's natural rock formations.

Peggy's 1947 summer home is now The Teahouse at Abkhazi Garden (778/265-6466, www. abkhaziteahouse.com, 11am-5pm daily May-Sept., 11am-5pm Wed.-Sun. Oct.-Apr., $13-22), which serves soups, salads, and light meals as well as traditional afternoon tea ($38-48).

From downtown Victoria, take BC Transit bus 7 for UVIC (one-way $2.50) from Douglas and View Streets and get off on Fairfield Road at Foul Bay Road, opposite the garden.

Craigdarroch Castle

Like any good British-inspired city, Victoria has a castle—a grand stone Romanesque revival structure complete with turrets, stained glass, and Victorian-era artifacts. Robert Dunsmuir, a Scottish immigrant who made his fortune mining coal on Vancouver Island, built this 39-room mansion, Craigdarroch Castle (1050 Joan Cres., 250/592-5323, www.thecastle.ca, 9am-7pm daily mid-June-early Sept., 10am-4:30pm daily early Sept.-mid-June, adults $14.60, seniors $13.60, students $9.50, ages 6-12 $5.10), in the late 1880s.

Sadly, Dunsmuir died before the castle was finished. His wife Joan lived here with three of her unmarried daughters (the Dunsmuirs had 10 children) from the castle's

Craigdarroch Castle

completion in 1890 until she died in 1908. With more than 20,000 square feet (1,880 square m) of floor space, the castle, now a national historic site, is decorated as it would have been in the Dunsmuirs' time, with lavish Victorian appointments, including sculptures, paintings, books, and period furnishings.

From downtown Victoria, any of the Fort Street buses (one-way $2.50), including BC Transit bus 14 or 15 for UVIC, will drop you near the castle. On foot, allow 30-35 minutes from the Inner Harbour.

Art Gallery of Greater Victoria

Built around an 1899 Victorian mansion, the Art Gallery of Greater Victoria (1040 Moss St., 250/384-4171, www.aggv.ca) has a significant collection of work by Victoria-born painter Emily Carr and extensive Asian art holdings. The gallery's changing exhibitions typically showcase Canadian or Asian works. The Art Gallery is slated to close in 2020 for a multi-year renovation project but plans to organize events and exhibits at temporary locations during this construction period.

Ross Bay Cemetery

Many notable Victorians are buried in the historic Ross Bay Cemetery (Fairfield Rd. at Stannard Ave., dawn-dusk daily, free), which stretches between Fairfield Road and the Dallas Road waterfront. The Victorian-era cemetery's most visited grave is that of artist Emily Carr (1871-1945), near the intersection of Fairfield Road and Arnold Avenue. The cemetery is also the final resting place of Sir James Douglas,

who served as British Columbia's first governor from 1858 to 1864, and Robert Dunsmuir, who built Craigdarroch Castle. The cemetery includes sections for different Christian denominations, with separate areas for First Nations and Chinese people, and a potter's field, where the poor were buried.

Get a cemetery map online from the Old Cemeteries Society of Victoria (250/598-8870, www. oldcem.bc.ca), which runs tours ($5) focusing on different aspects of the cemetery's history. Tours are offered at 2pm every Sunday in July-August, and generally on the first and third Sunday September-June.

From Douglas Street in downtown Victoria, BC Transit bus 3 or 7 (onc-way $2.50) will take you along Fairfield Road to the cemetery. It's a 35- to 40-minute walk from the Inner Harbour.

THE SAANICH PENINSULA

The Saanich Peninsula extends north of downtown Victoria to the communities of Saanich, North Saanich, Sidney, and Brentwood Bay. Partly suburban and partly a rural landscape of farms, forests, and fields, the peninsula is worth exploring for one major attraction—the popular Butchart Gardens—and for several smaller sights; it's also home to several wineries and distilleries. The Swartz Bay Ferry Terminal, with boats to Vancouver and several of the Gulf Islands, is at the northern tip of the Saanich Peninsula.

✪ Butchart Gardens

How did a cement factory and limestone quarry become one of

Vancouver Island's most popular garden attractions? Jennie Butchart and her husband, Robert, moved to the island from Ontario in the early 1900s, where Robert established a quarry and cement business, and Jennie became the company's chemist. The Butcharts built a large manor nearby and began planting flowers around it.

The Butcharts named their estate Benvenuto, Italian for "welcome," and by the 1920s, more than 50,000 people were visiting their gardens every year. Now, more than one million visitors annually come to ogle the floral displays at the 55-acre (22-ha) **Butchart Gardens** (800 Benvenuto Ave., Brentwood Bay, 250/652-5256, www.butchartgardens.com, 8:45am-10pm daily June-Aug., 8:45am-5pm daily early-late Sept., 9am-4pm daily Oct., 9am-3:30pm daily Nov., 9am-9pm daily Dec.-early Jan., 9am-3:30pm daily early Jan.-Feb., 9am-4pm daily Mar., 9am-5pm daily Apr.-May, adults $34, ages 13-17 $17, ages 5-12 $3 June-Sept., reduced rates Oct.-May).

When the company limestone quarry was exhausted, Jennie had the former pit transformed into what is now known as the Sunken Garden. Other highlights include the Rose Garden, the Italian Garden, and the serene Japanese Garden. On summer Saturday nights (July-early Sept.), **fireworks shows** are choreographed to music. During the winter holidays, the pathways twinkle with thousands of lights.

The Butchart Gardens are 14 miles (23 km) north of Victoria and 12.5 miles (20 km) south of the Swartz Bay Ferry Terminal. From downtown Victoria, **BC Transit bus 75** (one-way $2.50) can take you to the gardens in about 45 minutes during weekday rush hours and on the weekends. At other times, bus 75 doesn't start or end its route downtown; instead, take **bus 30** or **31** north to Royal Oak Exchange, where you can connect to bus 75.

Victoria Butterfly Gardens

Don't be surprised if a common Mormon or a blue morpho lands on your head inside this tropical greenhouse. More than 3,000 butterflies dart and flutter around the palm trees and exotic plants at the family-friendly **Victoria Butterfly Gardens** (1461 Benvenuto Ave., Brentwood Bay, 250/652-3822 or 877/722-0272, www.butterflygardens.com, 9:30am-6pm daily July-Aug., 10am-4pm daily early Mar.-June and Sept., 10am-3:30pm daily Oct.-early Mar., extended hours late Dec., last admission 1 hour before closing, adults $16.50, seniors and ages 13-17 $12.50, ages 5-12 $6.50), which houses about 75 different species from around the world.

The Butterfly Gardens are 12 miles (20 km) north of Victoria

Butchart Gardens

and 11 miles (18 km) south of the Swartz Bay Ferry Terminal, near the Butchart Gardens. BC Transit bus 75 (one-way $2.50) can take you from downtown Victoria in about 40 minutes during weekday rush hours and on weekends. At other times, when bus 75 doesn't start or end its route downtown, take bus 30 or 31 north to Royal Oak Exchange, where you can connect to bus 75.

Shaw Ocean Discovery Centre

A small modern aquarium on the waterfront in the town of Sidney, the Shaw Ocean Discovery Centre (9811 Seaport Pl., Sidney, 250/665-7511, www.salishseacentre.org, 10am-5pm daily mid-June-early Sept., 10am-4:30pm daily early Sept.-mid-June, last admission 30 minutes before closing, adults $17.50, seniors $14, ages 13-18 $12, ages 4-12 $8) focuses on the marine life of the Salish Sea, the waters surrounding southern Vancouver Island. More than 3,500 creatures, representing 150 different species, are typically on view. On Saturday-Sunday, marine-themed games, crafts, and other special activities add to the fun for kids.

Off Highway 17, the aquarium is 17 miles (28 km) north of downtown Victoria and four miles (6.5 km) south of the Swartz Bay Ferry Terminal. BC Transit buses 70 and 72 (one-way $2.50) stop in Sidney en route between Victoria and the ferry terminal. Get off at 5th Street and Beacon Avenue, and walk down Beacon to the aquarium.

Wineries and Distilleries

You don't have to go far from Victoria to go wine-tasting, with several wineries and distilleries across the Saanich Peninsula.

One of the region's more established wineries, Church and State Wines (1445 Benvenuto Ave., Central Saanich, 250/652-2671, www.churchandstatewines.com, 11am-6pm Wed.-Sun., tastings $8) launched with 10 acres (4 ha) on the island and now has a winery and vineyards in the Okanagan Valley as well. Try their wines at the tasting bar or with lunch in the Bistro (11am-3pm Wed.-Sun. May-Dec., $17-21).

On a 10-acre (4-ha) farm with more than 1,300 apple trees, Sea Cider Farm & Ciderhouse (2487 Mt. St. Michael Rd., Saanichton, 250/544-4824, www.seacider.ca, 11am-4pm daily May-Sept., 11am-4pm Wed.-Sun. Oct.-Apr., tastings $3-9) produces traditional fermented artisanal ciders, including special seasonal releases.

cider tasting at Sea Cider Farm & Ciderhouse

The master distillers at Victoria Distillers (9891 Seaport Pl., Sidney, distillery 250/544-8218, lounge and tour bookings 250/544-8217, http://victoriadistillers.com, lounge 2pm-7pm Sun.-Wed., 2pm-9pm

Thurs.-Sun., reduced hours winter, tours 1pm-4pm Thurs.-Sun., tastings $7) infuse their signature Victoria Gin with a custom blend of botanicals. They make an aged Oaken Gin and an unusual hemp vodka too. In the lounge, order a gin and tonic with the deep-blue Empress 1908 Gin. It's infused with butterfly pea flowers and tea from the Fairmont Empress Hotel; when you add citrus or tonic, the drink turns a soft pinkish lavender. To take a 45-minute tour, which includes tastings, phone to reserve in advance.

WEST OF DOWNTOWN

Wend your way through the suburbs west of the city center to reach a historic lighthouse and fort and another of Victoria's famous castles.

Fort Rodd Hill and Fisgard Lighthouse National Historic Sites

The Fort Rodd Hill and Fisgard Lighthouse National Historic Sites (603 Fort Rodd Hill Rd., 250/478-5849, www.pc.gc.ca, 10am-5pm Wed.-Sun. Mar.-mid-May, 10am-5pm daily mid-May-mid-Oct., 10am-4pm Sat.-Sun. mid-Oct.-Feb., adults $4, seniors $3.40) combine two historic venues at one location.

Constructed in 1860 at the entrance to Victoria's Esquimalt Harbor, Fisgard Lighthouse was the first on Canada's west coast. Inside, exhibits explain the light station's historic role and illustrate the lives of its light keepers, who staffed the facility until 1929. Fort Rodd Hill was built in the 1890s to protect the harbor and waterways around Victoria. Nearly all the fort's structures, including the stone fortifications, underground ammunition storage, and soldiers' barracks, are original. Occasional special programs help bring these sites to life.

These national historic sites are 7.5 miles (12 km) west of the Inner Harbour, easiest to reach by car.

Hatley Park National Historic Site

Given that his father, Robert, built Craigdarroch Castle, perhaps it's no surprise that James Dunsmuir (1851-1920) and his wife, Laura, wanted a castle of their own, particularly as the parents of 12 children. The 1908 Edwardian stone manor that they constructed, now known as Hatley Castle at the Hatley Park National Historic Site (2005 Sooke Rd., 250/391-2511, www.hatleypark. ca), has 40 rooms, including 22 bedrooms and eight baths.

The only way to visit the castle, on the campus of Royal Roads University, is on a one-hour guided tour (10:30am, 11:45am, 1:30pm, and 2:45pm daily mid-May-early Sept., adults $18.50, seniors $15.75, ages 6-17 $10.75, families $51) that takes you through the grounds, gardens, and main-floor rooms while offering details about the Dunsmuir family's history. The castle's upper floors, used as university offices, aren't part of the tour. Alternatively, you can visit only the manicured gardens (10:15am-3pm daily, adults $9.75, seniors $8.75, ages 6-17 $6.75, families $30) or wander the 9 miles (15 km) of walking paths through the property.

Hatley Park is 7.5 miles (12 km) west of the Inner Harbour. While it's possible to get here by public transit, it's much faster to come by car.

RECREATION
✪ WHALE-WATCHING

The waters off Vancouver Island, the Gulf Islands, and Washington's San Juan Islands are home to several pods of resident orcas (also known as killer whales), particularly during the summer. Pods of transient orcas as well as Pacific gray whales, humpback whales, and minke whales migrate through the region.

whale watching boats

Numerous Victoria-based companies offer 3-5-hour whale-watching tours April-October; summer (July-Aug.) is peak season for both whales and tourists. Some operators use inflatable Zodiacs, which give you a rougher but more exhilarating ride. Others use larger boats for a calmer trip and more shelter from the weather, a better choice on rainy days or choppy seas. Victoria's whale-watching tour companies include:

- Orca Spirit Adventures (250/383-8411 or 888/672-6722, www.orcaspirit.com, adults $120, ages 13-17 $90, ages 3-12 $80), with departures from two Inner Harbour locations: 950 Wharf Street, at the Harbour Air Terminal, or 146 Kingston Street, at the Coast Harbourside Hotel
- Prince of Whales (812 Wharf St., 250/383-4884 or 888/383-4884, www.princeofwhales.com, adults $130, ages 13-17 $105, ages 5-12 $95)
- Eagle Wing Tours (Fisherman's Wharf, 12 Erie St., 250/384-8008 or 800/708-9488, www.eaglewingtours.com, adults $135, seniors $122, ages 13-17 $105, ages 3-12 $85)
- SpringTide Whale Watching (1119 Wharf St., 250/384-4444 or 800/470-3474, www.victoriawhalewatching.com, adults $119, seniors $109, ages 13-18 $99, ages 3-12 $89)

HOT TUB BOATING

Want to explore Victoria's waterways—in a hot tub? Hot Tub Boat Canada (Canoe Marina, 450 Swift St., 250/880-1366, http://hottubboatcanada.ca, from $65 pp) offers self-guided cruises in small boats that are essentially floating hot tubs. You can book the hot tub boats, which accommodate 2-6 people and are powered by an electric motor, for 1.5-hour excursions.

FESTIVALS AND EVENTS

Honoring Victoria's namesake queen, the city's Victoria Day festivities (www.tourismvictoria.com, May) include a parade downtown. Indigenous dancers, singers, and musicians perform at Victoria's three-day Indigenous Cultural Festival (www.indigenousbc.com, June), which also showcases works by First Nations artists.

The annual Victoria Symphony Splash (www.victoriasymphony.ca, Aug.) includes a live performance by the Victoria Symphony from a floating stage moored in the Inner Harbour. The Victoria Fringe Fest (http://victoriafringe.com, Aug.) is a 12-day festival of weird and often wonderful theater, comedy, and storytelling performances.

SHOPPING

Shops line Government Street, stretching north from the Inner Harbour, many selling T-shirts, Canadian flag patches, and other souvenirs. Lower Johnson Street in Chinatown and Fort Street east of downtown have more distinctive local clothing, jewelry, and shoes.

CLOTHING AND ACCESSORIES

In Chinatown, Lower Johnson Street between Government and Wharf is a mix of trend-conscious chains like yoga-wear maker Lululemon (584 Johnson St., 250/383-1313, www.lululemon.com, 9:30am-8pm Mon.-Sat., 10am-7pm Sun.) and locally run boutiques, including Still Life for Her (550 Johnson St., 250/386-5658, http://stilllifeboutique.com, 10:30am-6pm Mon.-Sat., 11am-5pm Sun.) and its companion store Still Life for Him (560 Johnson St., 250/386-5655, http://stilllifeboutique.com, 10:30am-6pm Mon.-Sat., 11am-5pm Sun.), and Suasion (552 Johnson St., 250/995-0133, http://shopsuasion.com, 10:30am-6pm Mon.-Sat., 11am-5pm Sun.).

Sneaker fans run into Baggins Shoes (580 Johnson St., 250/388-7022, http://bagginsshoes.com, 10am-6pm Mon.-Sat., 11am-5pm Sun.), which has one of the world's largest selections of Converse styles. In the Atrium Building, Head Over Heels (1323 Blanshard St., 250/590-5154, www.headoverheelsvictoria.ca, 10:30am-5:30pm Mon.-Sat., noon-4pm Sun.) sells fashion-forward shoes. The shoes, boots, and bags at Heart & Sole (1023 Fort St., 250/920-7653, www.heartandsoleshoes.ca, 10am-6pm Mon.-Sat., 11am-5pm Sun.) mix practicality and style.

BOOKS

Nobel prize-winning author Alice Munro and her former husband Jim opened Munro's Books (1108 Government St., 250/382-2464, www.munrobooks.com, 9am-6pm Mon.-Wed., 9am-9:30pm Thurs.-Sat., 9:30am-6pm Sun.) in 1963. Although the writer is no longer involved in its management, this well-stocked old-school bookstore in a grand 1909 former bank carries titles by Canadian authors and other books of local interest.

Silk Road Tea

GOURMET FOOD AND DRINK

Stocking a mind-boggling variety of teas, with helpful labels about their ingredients, flavors, and

VICTORIA'S CHOCOLATE PROJECT

David Mincey is passionate about chocolate. The owner and resident chocolate obsessive at the Chocolate Project (Victoria Public Market, 1701 Douglas St., www. chocolateproject.ca) is on a mission to improve the chocolate that is produced around the world and that we eat closer to home.

In his stall at the Victoria Public Market, Mincey carries single origin, sustainably produced chocolate from many different countries. If you stop to chat, he'll tell you about the horrors of conventional chocolate production; he says that most commercial chocolate comes from West African plantations where enslaved people provide the labor, which is how companies can produce chocolate bars selling for $3 or less. He can tell you about the small businesses and individual growers across the globe who produce the chocolate he sells, many of whom he has visited personally.

You can generally find Mincey at his stand during market hours, offering tastings and preaching the chocolate gospel. His chocolate bars start around $10 each, and he'll convince you that they're worth it.

---

caffeine content, Silk Road Tea (1624 Government St., 250/704-2688, www.silkroadteastore.com, 10am-6pm Mon.-Sat., 11am-5pm Sun.) also carries tea-related products and cosmetics. Take a seat at the tea bar to rest your shopping-weary feet over a freshly brewed cup, or book a massage in the on-site spa. The shop has a small branch in the Victoria Public Market.

FOOD

AFTERNOON TEA

The Fairmont Empress (721 Government St., 250/384-8111, www.teaattheempress.com, 11am-5:45pm daily, reservations recommended, adults $82, under age 13 $42) has been offering afternoon tea since the hotel opened in 1908. Upholding that tradition, the regal tea lounge still serves an estimated 500,000 cups of tea every year, along with tiered trays of finger sandwiches, scones with jam and clotted cream, and assorted pastries.

The Dining Room at Butchart Gardens (800 Benvenuto Ave., Brentwood Bay, 250/652-8222, www. butchartgardens.com, 11am-4pm daily, $41 pp) serves traditional afternoon tea with a mix of sweet and savory items. A vegetarian version of afternoon tea is available.

In the traditionally British neighborhood of Oak Bay, the White Heather Tea Room (1885 Oak Bay Ave., 250/595-8020, www.whiteheather-tearoom.com, 11:30am-5pm Tues.-Sat., last seating 3:45pm) offers a traditionally British afternoon tea in several sizes, from the Wee Tea ($26 pp) to the Not-So-Wee Tea ($37) to the Big Muckle Giant Tea For Two ($80 for 2, each additional person $40).

For a less formal (and meat-free) tea, visit Venus Sophia Tea Room & Vegetarian Eatery (540 Fisgard St., 250/590-3953, www.venussophia. com, afternoon tea 11am-4:30pm daily, adults $45, under age 13 $35), a pretty Chinatown storefront. Choose among their signature teas to pair with a seasonally changing assortment of sandwiches, baked goods, and sweets.

MODERN CANADIAN

✪ Little Jumbo (506 Fort St., 778/433-5535, www.littlejumbo.

ca, 5pm-11pm Sun.-Thurs., 5pm-midnight Fri.-Sat., $16-35) feels like a secret speakeasy, set at the end of a narrow hallway. In the cozy narrow room with exposed brick walls and green lights illuminating the banquettes, the well-stocked bar and hardworking bartenders draw cocktail connoisseurs (they'll make you delicious "mocktails" too, if you're keeping with the Prohibition theme), but the kitchen is serious as well. Graze on plates like a summery tomato-burrata salad with ancho-honey puree or steamed clams with dill cream, or dig into the burger with smoked gouda and onion-bacon jam.

Taking its name from a Chinook word meaning "hungry," ✪ OLO (509 Fisgard St., 250/590-8795, www.olorestaurant.com, 5pm-10pm Sun.-Thurs., 5pm-11pm Fri.-Sat., $20-36) doesn't just satisfy your hunger. This fashionably relaxed Chinatown restaurant, decorated with woven wooden light fixtures that dangle from the ceiling like outsized birds' nests, delights guests with its innovative seasonal fare, from shrimp toast with smelt roe and pickled seaweed to poached halibut paired with octopus and dashi butter.

The owners of Fol Epi bakery expanded their operations into Agrius Restaurant (732 Yates St., 778/265-6312, www.agriusrestaurant.com, 9am-2pm Sun.-Mon., 9am-2pm and 5pm-10pm Tues.-Sat., brunch $9-18, dinner $15-21), where organic ingredients feature in creative daily brunches, like a fried cauliflower sandwich with crispy chickpeas and a salsa verde of mint and pumpkin seeds, or the ham hock hash with kale chimichurri. In the evenings,

you might try beet salad with huckleberries and hazelnuts, wild ling cod with mussels, or pork belly with sauerkraut and golden turnips.

Café Brio (944 Fort St., 250/383-0009 or 866/270-5461, www.cafe-brio.com, 5:30pm-9pm Tues.-Thurs., 5:30pm-9:30pm Fri.-Sat., $23-36) is an old favorite with a modern Mediterranean menu. Look for dishes like seared scallops with roasted pepper and fennel risotto, pan-roasted salmon in a broth of red wine and beets, or venison loin with chanterelles. Note to grazers, or those with small appetites: You can order most dishes in full or half portions. The wine list is strong on BC labels.

An unassuming order-at-the-counter eatery, Part and Parcel (2656 Quadra St., 778/406-0888, www.partandparcel.ca, 11:30am-9pm Mon.-Sat., $10-16) surprises with the first-rate quality of its straightforward but innovative dishes. On the changing menu that leans heavily on salads and sandwiches, super-fresh greens might be topped with spring rhubarb, feta cheese and roasted broccoli might come sandwiched with pickled shallots, and pillowy gnocchi might be dressed with a cauliflower puree and pecans. In the Quadra Village neighborhood, not quite 2 miles (3 km) north of the Inner Harbour, this local joint is an easy pit stop on the way to or from the Swartz Bay ferry.

SEAFOOD

It's a little hard to find, but that hasn't stopped the hordes from lining up at the wharf-side shipping container housing Red Fish Blue Fish (1006 Wharf St., 250/298-6877, www.redfish-bluefish.com, 11am-9pm daily late May-early Sept., 11am-7pm daily Apr.-late May and early Sept.-early Oct., 11am-3pm daily Feb.-Mar. and early-late Oct., $6-26), a busy seafood takeaway at the foot of Broughton Street. Choose tempura-battered Pacific cod, wild salmon, BC halibut, or oysters for your fish-and-chips. The hand-rolled fish tacos and salmon sandwich with pickled cucumbers are other popular picks.

Reel in a quick bite at Fishhook (805 Fort St., 250/477-0470, www.fishhookvic.com, 11am-9pm daily, $8-15), which specializes in seafood *tartines,* open-faced sandwiches topped with cured, broiled, or smoked fish. Try the smoked squid with shrimp and harissa or the tuna melt with cheddar and caramelized broccoli. This casual café also makes an array of fish curries. There's a newer branch on the waterfront at Mermaid Wharf, with a bigger menu of Indian-influenced seafood dishes.

ASIAN

Dobosala Cantina & Ride Thru (760 Pandora Ave., 250/590-6068, www.dobosala.com, 11am-9pm Mon.-Thurs., 11am-10pm Fri., noon-10pm Sat., $7-17) has a take-out window along a bike path, so as the name suggests, you could ride thru (or stroll by) to pick up your meal. Inside or out, this smart-casual dining spot creates fun plates like adobo-gochujang chicken thighs served with sticky rice balls, *pling pling* (duck and pork dumplings with tomatillo salsa verde), and tikka masala-braised brisket *tacones*—a mash-up of flavors from India, the Pacific Rim, and the Pacific Northwest. To drink, you might try a house-made lime-ade or a "GinGinger," a fizzy blend of Vancouver Island's Merridale gin and ginger syrup.

FRENCH

A long-standing French bistro on the edge of Chinatown, ✪ Brasserie L'Ecole (1715 Government St., 250/475-6260, www.lecole.ca, 5:30pm-10pm Tues.-Thurs., 5:30pm-11pm Fri.-Sat., $20-40) continues to charm with its warm welcome and its just-classic-enough menu. You might find local trout paired with beets and a green tomato relish or a stew of duck confit, sausage, and cannellini beans. The restaurant stocks a long list of Belgian beers and French wines. Reservations are not taken.

ITALIAN

The modern Italian fare at ✪ Zambri's (820 Yates St., 250/360-1171, www.zambris.ca, 11:30am-3pm and 5pm-9pm Mon.-Thurs., 11:30am-3pm and 5pm-10pm Fri., 10:30pm-2pm and 5pm-10pm Sat., 10:30am-2pm and 5pm-9pm Sun., $17-34), in the equally modern Atrium Building, makes one of Victoria's best meals, Italian or otherwise. The pastas, like penne with gorgonzola and peas or orecchiette with house-made sausages and rapini, are always good choices, as are the pizzas, or try more elaborate mains like crispy pork shoulder with greens, potatoes, grapes, and radishes or beef tenderloin paired with polenta. Save room for desserts like panna cotta or chocolate *budino.*

VEGETARIAN

Order a local craft beer or a "super-food" cocktail (perhaps the Sombrio made with island gin, mead, algae, and kelp) at cool laid-back Be Love (1019 Blanshard St., 778/433-7181, http://beloverestaurant.ca, 11am-9:30pm Sun.-Thurs., 11am-10pm Fri.-Sat., $9-23), a bright vegetarian café where veggie-friendly doesn't mean ascetic. Try a salad combining kale, avocado, cucumber, and cashew parmesan, or go for the Ganesha Bowl, a mix of curried chickpeas, spinach, and roasted squash served over quinoa with huckleberry chutney.

An old favorite among plant-eaters and their omnivorous dining companions, Rebar (50 Bastion Square, 250/361-9223, www.rebarmodernfood.com, 11am-9pm Mon.-Fri., 9:30am-9pm Sat., 9:30am-8pm Sun., $12-18) serves vegetarian comfort food like curries, enchiladas, and stir-fries, along with a few seafood dishes. Their almond burger is a classic. Save room for a sweet, like a homey ginger molasses cookie or gooey carrot cake.

DINERS

A favorite joint for breakfast or brunch is funky Jam Café (542 Herald St., 778/440-4489, www.jamcafes.com, 8am-3pm daily, $8-15), where the hip takes on diner classics include fried oatmeal, red velvet pancakes, and chicken and waffles. Come hungry, and be prepared to line up; they don't take reservations.

Who doesn't love an old-school diner, where you can sit at the polished metal counter or a red vinyl booth? And when that

old-fashioned-looking eatery—Paul's Diner by Fol Epi (1900 Douglas St., 250/590-6586, www.paulsdiner.ca, 7am-9pm Tues.-Sat., 8am-3pm Sun.-Mon., $9-18), from the team behind Agrius Restaurant and Fol Epi Bakery—serves up new-style food, from a kale- and mushroom-filled breakfast sandwich to a cauliflower tempeh bowl, alongside enduring favorites like eggs Benedict, liver and onions, and lemon pie with mile-high meringue, all the better.

BAKERIES AND CAFÉS

Pick up a croissant, *pain au chocolate,* or fruit danish from Fol Epi (732 Yates St., 778/265-6311, www.folepi.ca, 7am-6pm Mon.-Fri., 8am-6pm Sat.-Sun.), a petite patisserie that uses organic ingredients in its French-style baked goods.

brunch at Sherwood Café and Bar

The Sherwood Café and Bar (710 Pandora Ave., 250/590-3255, www.sherwoodvictoria.com, 7am-11pm Mon.-Fri., 8am-11pm Sat., 8am-3pm Sun., $8-17) morphs from a breakfast café to a casual lunch spot to an after-work bar. Try the Dutch Baby, a puffy, sweet-savory pancake with berries and Swiss cheese, or graze your way through a breakfast board, with smoked trout, creamy ricotta, egg, ham, and fruit. The same owners run the excellent coffee shop Habit (www.habitcoffee.com), with nearby locations in Chinatown (552 Pandora Ave., 250/294-1127, 7am-6pm Mon.-Fri., 8am-6pm Sat.-Sun.) and the Atrium Building (808 Yates St., 250/590-5953, 7am-10pm Mon.-Fri., 8am-10pm Sat., 8am-6pm Sun.).

Homey Nourish Kitchen & Café (225 Quebec St., 250/590-3426, www.nourishkitchen.ca, 9am-3pm daily, $8-18), set in an 1888 Victorian house, has a full-service dining room on the main floor and an order-at-the-counter living room-style café upstairs. Throughout the space, there's local art on the walls and veggie-friendly breakfasts and lunches on the plates. A popular dish is "Benny Gone Nuts," a vegetarian eggs Benedict with turmeric-cashew hollandaise that will nourish you for a day of sightseeing.

GROCERIES AND MARKETS

In a historic building that once housed the Hudson's Bay department store, the Victoria Public Market (1701 Douglas St., 778/433-2787, http://victoriapublicmarket.com, 10am-6pm Mon.-Sat., 11am-5pm Sun.) draws foodies with stalls selling cheeses, chocolate, tea, olive oil, pie, and other goodies.

To buy groceries close to downtown, head for The Market on Yates (903 Yates St., 250/381-6000, www.themarketstores.com, 7am-11pm daily), a well-stocked local food store.

ACCOMMODATIONS AND CAMPING

Victoria's hotels are clustered around the Inner Harbour. In some surrounding neighborhoods, you'll find B&Bs and other good-value lodgings.

UNDER CAD$150

An old motel given new life as a funky retro lodging, Hotel Zed (3110 Douglas St., 250/388-4345 or 800/997-6797, www.hotelzed.com, $109-269), decorated in vibrant oranges, turquoises, fuchsias, and purples, is Victoria's most fun place to stay. The 63 rooms have rotary phones (with free local calls), comic books in the baths, and complimentary Wi-Fi. The indoor-outdoor pool has a bubblegum-pink waterslide. A hip diner-style restaurant, The Ruby (http://therubyvictoria.com), cooks big breakfasts and roasts free-range chicken; downstairs, there's a Ping-Pong lounge. It's 2 miles (3 km) north of the Inner Harbour, but the hotel runs a free shuttle downtown in their vintage VW bus.

CAD$150-300

In a 1912 Victorian home in the residential Rockland neighborhood, Abbeymoore Manor B&B (1470 Rockland Ave., 250/370-1470 or 888/801-1811, www.abbeymoore.com, $169-299) looks formal, with polished woodwork, oriental rugs, and period furnishings, but the owners keep things comfortable with help-yourself coffee, tea, soft drinks, and snacks, a book-and game-filled guest library, and hearty morning meals. The five guest rooms are all traditionally appointed, while the three suites (two on the garden level and one on the top floor) are more modern. Wi-Fi and local calls are included.

To capture Victoria's traditional ambience, stay at the Beaconsfield Inn (998 Humboldt St., 250/384-4044 or 888/884-4044, www.beaconsfieldinn.com, $169-279), a nine-room B&B in a 1905 Edwardian manor furnished with antiques, stained-glass windows, and chandeliers. Most guest rooms have fireplaces and whirlpool tubs; all have down comforters and Wi-Fi. Rates include full breakfast, afternoon tea and cookies, and evening sherry. No children under 12 are allowed.

OVER CAD$300

A landmark on the Inner Harbour, the ✪ Fairmont Empress (721 Government St., 250/384-8111 or 800/441-1414, www.fairmont.com, $339-869, parking $33) charms with its polished staff and stately public spaces. Blending classic and contemporary furnishings, the 464 guest rooms vary from petite to grand, but you're here for the heritage and gracious service as much as the physical space. An indoor pool and well-equipped health club keep you busy, while the Willow Stream Spa keeps you pampered. Decorated with royal portraits, Q at the Empress serves breakfast, lunch, and dinner, offering contemporary fare with produce from the rooftop garden and around the island, paired with classic cocktails and craft beers. The Empress is also famous for its traditional afternoon tea. Join the hotel's complimentary frequent-stay program to get Wi-Fi access; otherwise it's $15 per day.

Inn at Laurel Point

Noted Canadian architect Arthur Erickson designed one wing of the art-filled ✪ Inn at Laurel Point (680 Montreal St., 250/386-8721 or 800/663-7667, www.laurelpoint. com, $274-419, parking $17), where most of the Zen-like contemporary suites are angled to take advantage of the property's waterfront views. The Laurel Wing units are more conventional, but the harbor vistas from these rooms aren't bad either. A short walk from the busy Inner Harbour, the Pacific Rim-style lodging has an indoor pool and a sundeck facing a Japanese garden. Wi-Fi is included. The well-regarded Asian-influenced Aura Restaurant features lots of local produce and seafood.

✪ Magnolia Hotel & Spa (623 Courtney St., 250/381-0999 or 877/624-6654, www.magnoliahotel. com, $229-529, parking $30), a well-managed boutique lodging two blocks from the Inner Harbour, caters to both business and leisure travelers. The 64 rooms are decorated in soothing grays and creams, with mini fridges, single-cup coffeemakers, included Wi-Fi, and flat-screen TVs. The best rooms are on the 6th and 7th floors above the surrounding buildings; from the corner units, you can see the Parliament Building, illuminated at night. Work out in the compact gym or borrow a complimentary bike to go touring. The staff are quick with a greeting or to offer assistance, from directions to restaurant recommendations. The hotel's restaurant, The Courtney Room, pairs regional products with French style from morning through evening.

Oak Bay Beach Hotel

A stay at the ✪ Oak Bay Beach Hotel (1175 Beach Dr., 250/598-4556 or 800/668-7758, www.oakbaybeachhotel.com, $297-669) feels like an escape to a seaside resort, particularly when you swim or soak in the heated mineral pools fronting the ocean. The 100 sizeable suites have electric fireplaces, flat-screen TVs, kitchen facilities, and deluxe baths. The panoramic vistas from the water-facing rooms are spectacular. Rates include Wi-Fi, local calls, and parking. The 34-seat main Dining Room overlooks the gardens and the ocean beyond. The Snug, a British-style pub, serves classics like fish-and-chips and

bangers and mash with a cold pint; Kate's Café keeps guests and locals supplied with coffee and pastries. The hotel is in the residential Oak Bay district, east of downtown.

Removed from the Inner Harbour's fray, but still an easy stroll from the sights, the condo-style Oswego Hotel (500 Oswego St., 250/294-7500 or 877/767-9346, www.oswegohotelvictoria.com, $209-499 d, 2-bedroom unit $359-759, parking $15) has 80 stylish and urban studio, one-bedroom, and two-bedroom units. All have kitchens with granite counters, stainless-steel appliances, and French-press coffeemakers, as well as large baths with soaker tubs. The upper-floor suites have expansive city views. Wi-Fi is included.

The five romantic guest suites at the deluxe Villa Marco Polo Inn (1524 Shasta Pl., 250/370-1524, www.villamarcopolo.com, $249-349), an upscale 1923 Italian Renaissance manor in the Rockland district, entice with European linens, Persian carpets, fireplaces, and plush Silk Road style. Breakfasts feature homemade breads or muffins and organic produce from the region. Lounge in the garden or the wood-paneled library, checking your email if you must (Wi-Fi and local calls are included), or laze with your beloved in your double soaker tub. No children under 14 are allowed.

CAMPING

At the Fort Rodd Hill and Fisgard Lighthouse National Historic Sites (603 Fort Rodd Hill Rd., 250/478-5849, www.pc.gc.ca), west of the city center, you can camp in an oTENTik (mid-May-Sept., $120), a family-friendly canvas-walled platform tent that sleeps up to six. The five tents sit in a clearing in the middle of the fort grounds, a short walk from the lighthouse and a small rocky beach. A building with flush toilets and running water is nearby, although there are no showers on the grounds. Bring your own bedding and food; you can cook your meals on a propane barbecue. Book through Parks Canada reservations (877/737-3783, www. reservation.parkscanada.gc.ca).

INFORMATION AND SERVICES

VISITOR INFORMATION

Destination Greater Victoria (812 Wharf St., 250/953-2033, www. tourismvictoria.com, 9am-5pm Sun.-Thurs., 8:30am-8:30pm Fri.-Sat.) runs a year-round information center on the Inner Harbour, with helpful staff who can assist you in booking tours and accommodations. The building has public restrooms too. Tourism Vancouver Island (www.vancouverisland. travel) publishes a guide to things to do across the island, available online and in print from area visitors centers.

MEDICAL SERVICES

Victoria General Hospital (1 Hospital Way, 250/727-4212 or 877/370-8699, www.islandhealth.ca) and Royal Jubilee Hospital (1952 Bay St., 250/370-8000 or 877/370-8699, www.islandhealth.ca) provide emergency medical services. The pharmacy at Shoppers Drug Mart (3511 Blanshard St., 250/475-7572, www.shoppersdrugmart.ca) is open 24 hours daily.

GETTING THERE

AIR

The fastest way to travel between Vancouver and Victoria is by floatplane or helicopter. Both take off and land from the city centers, making this option convenient for a car-free day trip. It's more expensive than taking the ferry, but the scenery over the Gulf Islands and Strait of Georgia is impressive. Check the carriers' websites for schedules and occasional fare discounts.

Harbour Air (604/274-1277 or 800/665-0212, www.harbourair. com, 35 minutes, one-way adults $159-254) flies frequently throughout the day between the Vancouver Harbour Flight Centre (1055 Canada Pl., behind the Vancouver Convention Centre, 604/274-1277) and the Victoria Inner Harbour Centre (1000 Wharf St., 250/384-2215).

Helijet (800/665-4354, www. helijet.com, 35 minutes, one-way adults $189-325) departs frequently throughout the day between Vancouver Harbour Heliport (455 Waterfront Rd., near Waterfront Station, 604/688-4646) and Victoria Harbour Heliport (79 Dallas Rd., 250/386-7676), between the Breakwater District Cruise Ship Terminal and Fisherman's Wharf. It offers passengers landing in Victoria a complimentary shuttle to downtown destinations. One child (ages 2-12) flies free with each adult; additional one-way children's fares are $99.

A number of airlines serve Victoria International Airport (YYJ, 1640 Electra Blvd., Sidney, 250/953-7533, www.victoriaairport. com), which is north of downtown. Air Canada (www.aircanada.

com) flies between Victoria and Vancouver, Calgary, Montreal, Toronto, and San Francisco. WestJet (www.westjet.com) has flights between Victoria and Vancouver, Calgary, Edmonton, Kelowna (BC), and Toronto. Canadian discount carrier Flair Air (www.flairair.ca) connects Victoria and Edmonton. Alaska Air (www.alaskaair.com) makes the quick hop between Victoria and Seattle.

CAR AND FERRY

BC Ferries (888/223-3779, www.bcferries.com) provides frequent service between the Vancouver metropolitan area on the mainland and Vancouver Island. Ferries transport foot passengers, bicycles, cars, trucks, and recreational vehicles. Reservations ($10 at least 7 days in advance, $17 1-6 days in advance, $21 same-day travel) are recommended for vehicles, particularly if you're traveling on summer weekends or during holiday periods. Reservations are not available for walk-on passengers or bicycles.

Metropolitan Vancouver's two ferry docks are both outside the city center. Tsawwassen Terminal (1 Ferry Causeway, Delta), the departure point for ferries to Victoria, is 24 miles (38 km) south of Vancouver. The Tsawwassen-Swartz Bay Ferry (one-way adults $17.20, ages 5-11 $8.60, cars $57.50, bikes $2) takes you between the mainland and Victoria in 1.5 hours.

To drive from Vancouver to Tsawwassen, head south on Oak Street, following the signs for Highway 99 south, and cross the Oak Street Bridge into Richmond. Stay on Highway 99 through the George Massey Tunnel. Exit onto Highway 17 south toward the Tsawwassen ferry terminal. Allow about 45 minutes to drive from downtown Vancouver to Tsawwassen, with extra time during the morning and evening rush hours.

Late June-early September, ferries between Tsawwassen and Swartz Bay generally run every hour 7am-9pm daily, and every two hours the rest of the year; because there are frequent variations, check the schedule on the BC Ferries website (www.bcferries.com) before you travel.

The Swartz Bay Terminal (Hwy. 17) is 20 miles (32 km) north of Victoria at the end of Highway 17, about a 30-minute drive. After you exit the ferry at Swartz Bay, follow Highway 17 south, which goes directly into downtown Victoria, where it becomes Blanshard Street.

DIRECT BUS AND FERRY

Another car-free way to travel between Vancouver and Victoria is to take a direct bus service that picks up passengers at several points downtown, takes you onto the ferry at BC Ferries' Tsawwassen terminal, and continues to downtown Victoria.

BC Ferries Connector (604/428-9474 or 888/788-8840, www.bcfconnector.com, one-way bus adults $50.50, BC seniors or students $37, ages 5-11 $26), operated by Wilson's Transportation, transports passengers between downtown Vancouver and downtown Victoria. The bus takes you to the Tsawwassen Ferry Terminal and drives onto the ferry. At Swartz Bay, you reboard the bus and travel to downtown Victoria. Trips depart several times daily in each direction, and reservations are required; the entire trip takes about four hours.

In Vancouver, the BC Ferries Connector bus originates at Pacific Central Station (1150 Station St.). For a slightly higher fare (one-way bus adults $60.50, BC seniors or students $47, ages 5-11 $36), you can schedule a pickup from many downtown Vancouver hotels. In Victoria, the coach takes you to the Capital City Station (721 Douglas St.), behind the Fairmont Empress Hotel, one block from the Inner Harbour.

The BC Ferries Connector fare does not include a ferry ticket (one-way adults $17.20, ages 5-11 $8.60), which you must purchase in addition to your bus ticket.

PUBLIC TRANSIT

If you don't have a lot of luggage, it's possible to take public transit between downtown Vancouver and the Tsawwassen Ferry Terminal and from the Swartz Bay Ferry Terminal to downtown Victoria. It's much cheaper than the BC Ferries Connector option, but it takes a little longer.

In Vancouver, take the Canada Line to Bridgeport Station, where you change to bus 620 for Tsawwassen Ferry (www.translink. ca, one-way adults $5.75, seniors, students, and ages 5-13 $4). The total trip takes about an hour.

After taking the Tsawwassen-Swartz Bay Ferry (www.bcferries. com, 1 hour and 35 minutes, one-way adults $17.20, ages 5-11 $8.60), catch BC Transit bus 70 for Swartz Bay/Downtown Express (www. bctransit.com/victoria, 50 minutes, one-way $2.50 pp) to downtown Victoria.

GETTING AROUND

Victoria's Inner Harbour is compact and walkable, easy to navigate without a car. It's possible to reach sights outside the city center on the region's public buses, although to explore farther afield on Vancouver Island, having your own vehicle is more convenient.

BUS

BC Transit (250/382-6161, http:// bctransit.com/victoria, one-way $2.50) runs buses around Victoria, to Butchart Gardens, and to the Swartz Bay Ferry Terminal. Hours vary by bus route, but major routes typically begin service 6am-7am and stop service 11pm-midnight. Service to the Swartz Bay ferry begins at 5:30am Monday-Saturday and 6am Sunday.

FERRY

Victoria Harbour Ferry (250/708-0201, www.victoriaharbourferry. com, 11am-5pm daily Mar. and mid-Sept.-Oct., 11am-7pm daily Apr.-mid-May, 10am-9pm daily mid-May-mid-Sept.) can take you around the Inner Harbour in their cute colorful boats, stopping at Fisherman's Wharf, the Ocean Pointe Resort, and other waterside points. Fares vary by distance; a basic one-zone trip is $6 per person.

TAXI

You can usually find taxis near the Inner Harbour and the Fairmont Empress Hotel. Victoria taxi rates start at $3.30, plus $1.93 per km. Local cab companies include Bluebird Cabs (250/382-2222, www.taxicab.com) and Yellow Cab of Victoria (250/381-2222, www.yellowcabvictoria.com).

CAR

Victoria's downtown sights are all clustered around the Inner Harbour, so if you've driven downtown, park your car and do your exploring on foot. Having a car is handy to visit attractions outside downtown, on the Saanich Peninsula, or in the Cowichan Valley.

Parking

Pay for downtown on-street parking (9am-6pm Mon.-Sat. $1.50-3 per hour) at the nearby pay stations with cash, credit cards, or the ParkVictoria app. Parking is free in the evenings and on Sunday.

The city has five centrally located public parking garages (1st hour free, 2nd and 3rd hours $2 per hour, 4th and subsequent hours $3 per hour, $16 per day) open 24 hours daily: Bastion Square Parkade (575 Yates St.), Broughton Street Parkade (745 Broughton St., below the Central Library), Centennial Square Parkade (645 Fisgard St.), Johnson Street Parkade (750 Johnson St.), and View Street Parkade (743 View St.). Rates are in effect 8am-6pm Monday-Saturday; parking is free in the evening and on Sunday.

You can also park in these city-run surface lots ($2.50 per hour, $15 per day): 900 Wharf Street (near the Harbour Air terminal) and 820 Courtney Street. There's no free parking in these lots; pay rates are in effect 24 hours daily.

Car Rentals

Avis (800/879-2847, www.avis.ca), Budget (250/953-5300 or 800/668-9833, www.budget.ca), Hertz (800/263-0600, www.hertz.ca), and National (250/656-2541 or 800/227-7368, www.nationalcar.ca) have rental desks at Victoria International Airport. Enterprise (250/655-7368, www.enterprise.com) has a nearby off-airport location. Both Budget and National also have rental offices downtown, near the Inner Harbour.

BICYCLE

Victoria is a bike-friendly city. Among the scenic routes for visitors on bikes are Dallas Road, which skirts the seashore on the city's southern edge, and Fairfield Road, which passes Ross Bay Cemetery.

Running along a former rail line, the 35-mile (55-km) Galloping Goose Trail takes you from Victoria west to the town of Sooke. The 18-mile (29-km) Lochside Regional Trail, another rail trail, connects Swartz Bay and Victoria.

The Pedaler (321 Belleville St., 778/265-7433, http://thepedaler.ca, 9am-6pm daily mid-Mar.-Oct., call for off-season hours) has a fleet of modern bikes for rent (1 hour $13, 2 hours $19, full-day $35). They also run fun guided cycling tours, including the two-hour Castles, Hoods & Legends (adults $55, youth $50), a short tour of Victoria's major sights; the four-hour Eat.Drink.Pedal ($110), which takes you through several Victoria neighborhoods with stops for coffee, pastries, ice cream, and lots of other snacks; and the three-hour Hoppy Hour Ride ($95), sampling Victoria's craft breweries.

The Cowichan Valley

The agricultural Cowichan Valley, along Highway 1 on the way to Nanaimo from Victoria, is known for its wineries and cider makers, and it has other artisanal offerings as well. Wineries cluster around the small towns of Cobble Hill, Cowichan Bay, and Duncan.

WINERIES

Start your Cowichan explorations with stops at some of these well-regarded winemakers; most charge a small fee for tastings, which they'll waive if you make a purchase. For more winery ideas, check out the **British Columbia Wine Institute** (www.winebc.com).

Unsworth Vineyards (2915 Cameron Taggart Rd., Mill Bay, 250/929-2292, www.unsworthvineyards.com, 11am-5pm Mon.-Tues., 11am-6pm Wed.-Sun. mid-May-mid-Oct., 11am-4pm Mon.-Tues., 11am-5pm Wed.-Sun. mid-Oct.-mid-May, tastings $5), a family-owned winery, has an upscale restaurant (11am-close Wed.-Sun., $15-39) in a restored 1907 farmhouse overlooking the vineyards.

Merridale Ciderworks (230 Merridale Rd., Cobble Hill, 250/743-4293, www.merridalecider.com, 11am-5pm daily, tastings $5) makes sparkling cider, brandies, fortified wines, and spirits. Its bistro (noon-3pm Mon.-Fri., 11am-3pm Sat.-Sun.) serves casual comfort food.

Another family-owned winemaker, **Venturi-Schulze Vineyards** (4235 Vineyard Rd., Cobble Hill, 250/743-5630, www.venturischulze.com, 10am-4:30pm Wed.-Sun. Apr.-Aug., 10am-4pm Wed.-Sun. Sept.-Dec., tastings $5) produces organic wines from estate-grown grapes.

Known for its sparkling wines and pinot gris, **Blue Grouse Estate Winery** (2182 Lakeside Rd., Duncan, 250/743-3834, www.bluegrouse.ca, 11am-5pm Fri.-Sun. Feb., 11am-5pm Wed.-Sun. Mar.-Apr., 11am-5pm daily May-Sept., 11am-5pm Wed.-Sun. Oct.-Dec., tastings $5), has a striking contemporary tasting room with a vineyard-view terrace and upper-level lounge.

Averill Creek Vineyard (6552 North Rd., Duncan, 250/709-9986, www.averillcreek.ca, 11am-5pm daily, tastings complimentary) has a patio where you can bring a picnic to enjoy with your wine.

COWICHAN BAY

The scenic seaside town of Cowichan Bay is worth a stop between winery visits. Check out **Wild Coast Perfumery** (1721 Cowichan Rd., 250/701-2791, www.wildcoastperfumes.com, 10:30am-4:30pm Tues.-Sat., 11am-4pm Sun. mid-May-late Dec.), which crafts scents from natural botanicals, and pack a picnic with provisions from **Hilary's Cheese** (1725 Cowichan Rd., 250/748-5992, www.hilarycheese.ca, 10am-4pm Mon.-Fri., 9am-6pm Sat.-Sun.) and **True Grain Bread** (1725 Cowichan Rd., 250/746-7664, www.truegrain.ca, 8am-6pm daily).

WESTHOLME TEA FARM

Canada's first tea growers, Westholme Tea Farm (8350 Richards Trail, Westholme, 250/748-3811, www.westholmetea.com, 10am-5pm Wed.-Sun. Feb.-Dec.), north of Duncan, sells several varieties of its own tea, along with others sourced from smaller farms and estates. Staff can tell you about the different types, and you can pair a pot with a selection of sweets in the tearoom or garden. Co-owner Margit Nellemann makes ceramics that she displays in the on-site gallery; your tea may be served in one of her creations.

FOOD AND ACCOMMODATIONS

On a small family-run farm off Highway 18 between Duncan and Lake Cowichan, the Farm Table Inn (6755 Cowichan Lake Rd., Lake Cowichan, 250/932-3205, www.farmtableinn.ca, $19-32) is a relaxing spot for a meal or overnight stop. Locally raised meats and Pacific seafood might turn up in plates like braised lamb shank with barley risotto or halibut with dill-caper sauce, alongside fresh *yu choy* (a type of leafy green), roasted squash, and other produce from nearby farms. Two cozy rooms ($150-170), with private terraces and a shared kitchen, are in the farmhouse behind the restaurant. Call for restaurant reservations and to confirm seasonal hours.

GETTING THERE

Most people tour the Cowichan Valley as a day trip from Victoria. The easiest way to go wine touring in the area is with your own car; public transit isn't a viable option. The Cowichan Valley is about 30 miles (48 km) from Victoria, an hour's drive north. From downtown Victoria, follow Douglas Street north to Highway 1, which turns west and then north through the wine region.

If you don't want to drive yourself, contact one of the companies offering Cowichan Valley wine tours from Victoria, including Canadian Craft Tours (www.canadiancrafttours.ca, $136 pp), Cheers Cowichan Tours (www.cheerscowichan.com, $137-169 pp), and Vancouver Island Wine Tours (www.vancouverislandwinetours.com, $109-119 pp).

Nanaimo

This city of 90,000 on Vancouver Island's east coast, 70 miles (110 km) north of Victoria, is an alternate ferry port between the city of Vancouver and the island, convenient if you're traveling to Tofino on the island's west coast. British Columbia's third oldest city, Nanaimo is worth a stop for its pretty waterfront and historic sites. Be sure to sample a Nanaimo bar, the local signature sweet.

SIGHTS AND RECREATION

NANAIMO MUSEUM

The modern Nanaimo Museum (100 Museum Way, 250/753-1821, www.nanaimomuseum.ca, 10am-5pm daily mid-May-early Sept., 10am-5pm Mon.-Sat. early Sept.-mid-May, adults $2, seniors and students $1.75, ages 5-12 $0.75) tells the stories of the city's development, from its First Nations communities to its days as a mining hub, when the Hudson's Bay Company established a coal mine nearby. Other exhibits focus on the city's quirkier traditions, like its annual summer bathtub race.

THE BASTION

Built in 1853 by the Hudson's Bay Company, The Bastion (95 Front St.), on the Nanaimo waterfront, is the city's oldest structure and North America's only original wooden bastion (fortified tower). The 1st-floor exhibits (10am-3pm daily mid-May-early Sept., donation) talk about the Hudson's Bay Company and its trading activities; the upper floors illustrate the building's military uses.

Outside the Bastion, stop to watch the midday cannon firing ceremony (noon daily mid-May-early Sept.), with a local bagpiper and a really big bang.

FOOD

Start your day with pastries and coffee from Mon Petit Choux (120 Commercial St., 250/753-6002, www.monpetitchoux.ca, 8am-5pm Mon.-Sat., 9am-5pm Sun., $8-15), a sunny French-style café downtown. Beyond the sweets, they serve breakfasts (including scrambled eggs with smoked salmon or a *croque-madame* on house-made brioche) and light lunches, from quiche to sandwiches on their own baguettes.

vegetable hash at Gabriel's Gourmet Cafe

In a cheerful downtown space decorated with colorful artwork and lots of plants, Gabriel's Gourmet Café (39A Commercial St., 250/741-0271, www.gabrielscafe.ca,

ON THE NANAIMO BAR TRAIL

The city of Nanaimo has its own name-sake dessert: the Nanaimo bar. This sweet treat, which became popular in the 1950s, has three layers: a nutty base of coconut, cocoa, and graham cracker crumbs with a custard filling and a thick dark chocolate coating on top. You can find Nanaimo bars at bakeries all around town.

You can get more adventurous with your Nanaimo bars if you follow the city's Nanaimo bar trail. At more than 30 stops, you can sample numerous variations on the Nanaimo bar theme. There's a rich, creamy vegan version at Powerhouse Living Foods (200 Commercial St., 250/571-7873, www.powerhouseliving.ca)

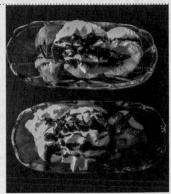
deep-fried Nanaimo bars at Pirate Chips

and a whipped cream-slathered deep-fried wonder at Pirate Chips (1-75 Front St., 250/753-2447). The Modern Café (page 265) even serves a Nanaimo bar martini.

Get a guide to the Nanaimo bar trail on the website of Tourism Nanaimo (www.tourismnanaimo.com) or pick up a copy at the Nanaimo Visitor Centre.

8am-7pm daily, $7-15) uses locally sourced meats, eggs, and produce in its breakfasts (available till 3pm) and lunches. Coconut pancakes with roasted apples, omelets filled with oyster mushrooms and kale, or eggs with black bean corncakes kick off the morning; chicken curry wraps, lemongrass beef sandwiches with pickled vegetables, and rice bowls with tofu and peanut sauce round out the menu from midday on.

Despite its name, the Modern Café (221 Commercial St., 250/754-5022, www.themoderncafe.ca, 8am-9pm Sun.-Mon., 8am-10pm Tues.-Thurs., 8am-midnight Fri.-Sat., breakfast $8-14, lunch $10-21, dinner $15-30) is one of Nanaimo's oldest restaurants, serving food and drinks in its pub-style space downtown since 1946. Burgers, sandwiches, salads, and macaroni and cheese are the lunchtime draws, while the dinner menu adds heartier

plates like braised lamb shank or grilled steak. To drink? A Nanaimo bar martini!

ACCOMMODATIONS

If you're going to stay over in Nanaimo, the friendly Buccaneer Inn (1577 Stewart Ave., 250/753-1246 or 877/282-6337, www.buccaneerinn.com, $80-200) is the closest place to sleep near the Departure Bay ferry terminal. In this basic but well-maintained family-run motel, many of the nautical-themed rooms and suites have kitchens. Rates include parking, Wi-Fi, and local phone calls. The inn is on a busy road, although traffic typically quiets at night.

The waterside setting overlooking a peaceful mile-long pond elevates three-story Inn on Long Lake (4700 N. Island Hwy., 250/758-1144 or 800/565-1144, www.innonlonglake.com, $150-300) beyond an ordinary motel. In summer, you can rent kayaks, pedal boats, and stand-up paddleboards to cruise around the lake. The family-friendly rooms with lake-view patios or terraces come with fridges, microwaves, one-cup coffeemakers, and Wi-Fi. Rates include a simple continental breakfast, which you can eat on the lakeside terrace. The inn, which also has a guest laundry, is off the Island Highway (Hwy. 1), north of the city center 5.5 miles (9 km).

Oh, the views! At MGM Seashore B&B (4950 Fillinger Cres., 250/729-7249, www.mgmbandb.com, $229-325), with three guest rooms in a residential neighborhood north of town, the panoramas stretch across the water, particularly out on the mammoth deck, where you can soak in the hot tub. Owners Marilyn and Glenn McKnight start guests' stays with a welcome Nanaimo bar, serve a full breakfast, and stock a guest lounge with espresso, tea, books, and movies. The Honeymoon Suite has a whirlpool tub positioned toward the ocean vistas, while the Sunset Room, with a round king bed, opens to the deck. The more basic King Room could accommodate a family, with a king bed and two singles.

INFORMATION AND SERVICES

Tourism Nanaimo (www. tourismnanaimo.com) runs the year-round Nanaimo Visitor Centre (2450 Northfield Rd., 250/751-1556 or 800/663-7337, 9am-6pm daily May-mid.-Sept., 9am-5pm Mon.-Sat. mid-Sept.-Apr.), off Highway 19 northwest of the city

center, and provides lots of information about the area.

GETTING THERE
AIR
Harbour Air (604/274-1277 or 800/665-0212, www.harbourair. com, 20 minutes, one-way adults $92-129) flies regularly between the Vancouver Harbour Flight Centre (1055 Canada Pl., 604/274-1277) and Nanaimo's Pioneer Waterfront Plaza (90 Front St., 250/714-0900).

Helijet (800/665-4354, www. helijet.com, 20 minutes, one-way adults $129-149) buzzes across the water several times a day between Vancouver Harbour Heliport (455 Waterfront Rd., near Waterfront Station, 604/688-4646) and Nanaimo Harbour Heliport (Port of Nanaimo Welcome Centre, 100 Port Dr.). One child (ages 2-12) flies free with each adult; additional one-way children's fares are $99.

CAR AND FERRY
Via Horseshoe Bay
BC Ferries' Horseshoe Bay Terminal (6750 Keith Rd., West Vancouver), where the most direct ferries leave for Nanaimo, is on the North Shore, 12 miles (20 km) northwest of downtown Vancouver. The Horseshoe Bay-Departure Bay Ferry (one-way adults $17.20, ages 5-11 $8.60, cars $56.45, bikes $2) takes one hour and 40 minutes.

From downtown Vancouver to Horseshoe Bay, take West Georgia Street to the Lions Gate Bridge. Watch the signs carefully as you approach Stanley Park en route to the bridge to stay in the proper lane. The center lane on the three-lane bridge

THE ISLAND'S BIGGEST TREES

Heading west from Nanaimo toward Vancouver Island's west coast, you'll pass through a section of old-growth rainforest, with massive trees that began their lives more than 800 years ago. In Cathedral Grove, which is part of MacMillan Provincial Park (Hwy. 4, 250/474-1336, www.env.gov.bc.ca, dawn-dusk daily, free), you can follow two short trails through these forests of giants.

Cathedral Grove

The biggest trees—colossal Douglas firs—are on the south side of the highway. The largest measures more than 30 feet (9 m) around. On the north side of the road, the trail passes through groves of ancient western red cedars and along the shore of Cameron Lake.

Cathedral Grove is 40 miles (65 km) west of Nanaimo and 10 miles (16 km) east of Port Alberni. Highway 4 runs directly through the park; there's a parking lot near the big trees.

reverses its travel direction at different times of the day, typically creating two travel lanes into the city in the morning and two travel lanes toward the North Shore during the afternoon rush hour.

After you cross the Lions Gate Bridge, bear left toward Marine Drive west/Highway 1/Highway 99. Enter Marine Drive and stay in the far right lane to take the first right onto Taylor Way (the sign says "Whistler"). Follow Taylor Way up the hill, and exit left onto Highway 1 west. Continue on Highway 1 to the ferry terminal. The drive from downtown to Horseshoe Bay generally takes about 30 minutes, but allow extra time during the morning and afternoon commute times.

Late June-early September, ferries between Horseshoe Bay and Departure Bay generally make 8-9 trips daily, with 6-7 daily runs the rest of the year; check the BC Ferries website (www.bcferries.com) for the seasonal schedule.

The Departure Bay Terminal (680 Trans-Canada Hwy., Nanaimo) is 2 miles (3 km) north of downtown Nanaimo.

Via Tsawwassen

Another route between the mainland and Nanaimo is the Tsawwassen-Duke Point Ferry (one-way adults $17.20, ages 5-11 $8.60, cars $56.45, bikes $2). The ferry ride is two hours. Ferries run 6-8 times per day. Consider this route if you are traveling to the Nanaimo area from points south of Vancouver.

The Duke Point Terminal (400 Duke Point Hwy., Nanaimo) is off Highway 1, south of downtown Nanaimo 9 miles (16 km).

PUBLIC TRANSIT

From downtown Vancouver, bus 257 for Horseshoe Bay Express (www.translink.ca, 45 minutes, one-way adults $4.25, seniors, students, and ages 5-13 $3) runs to the Horseshoe Bay Ferry Terminal from several stops along West Georgia Street. The slightly slower bus 250 for Horseshoe Bay (www.translink.ca, 55 minutes, one-way adults $4.25, seniors, students, and ages 5-13 $3) follows a similar route.

After taking the Horseshoe Bay-Departure Bay Ferry (www.bcferries.com, 1 hour and 40 minutes, one-way adults $17.20, ages 5-11 $8.60), catch BC Transit bus 2 (www.bctransit.com/nanaimo, 25 minutes, one-way adults $2.50) from the Departure Bay Ferry Terminal to downtown Nanaimo.

The West Coast

Vancouver Island's west coast can feel like the edge of the world. After you climb the winding road up and over the spines of mountains in the center of the island, you finally reach the west shore, where the Pacific waves crash along the beach. Here are the ocean sands and peaceful coastal rainforests of the island's first national park, along with two easygoing west coast towns, larger Tofino to the north and Ucluelet to the south. These peninsula communities have whale-watching tours, First Nations canoe trips, and plenty of other outdoor adventures, as well as good restaurants and beachfront lodges.

The weather on the west coast can be cooler, damper, and more changeable than elsewhere on the island. Bring layers, rain gear, and shoes or boots that can get wet. Whatever the weather, the west coast is a laid-back region where local surfers carry their boards on their bikes, and cocktail hour can seem like a sacred ritual. And it's hugely popular with travelers: Tofino's population of 2,000 can swell to more than 20,000 on weekends in July-August.

Don't worry, though. Even in midsummer, it's still worth a visit to this edge of the world.

✪ PACIFIC RIM NATIONAL PARK RESERVE

With 14 miles (22 km) of sandy beaches and dunes backed by coastal rainforest, the reserve protects a wide swath of Vancouver Island's west coast. Established in 1970, it was the island's first national park.

VISITING THE PARK

The Pacific Rim National Park Reserve has three geographically separate components. Most visitors head directly to the park's Long Beach Unit (Pacific Rim Hwy., 250/726-3500, www.pc.gc.ca), north of the Tofino-Ucluelet junction. The park visitors center is here, as is the longest beach on the island's west coast. You can camp here, although you can easily day-trip to the park from Tofino or Ucluelet.

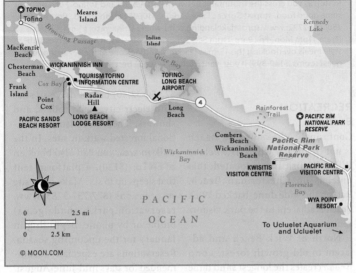

Tofino and Ucluelet

TOFINO
Tofino
Meares Island
Browning Passage
MacKenzie Beach
Chesterman Beach
WICKANINNISH INN
Frank Island
Cox Bay
TOURISM TOFINO INFORMATION CENTRE
Point Cox
Radar Hill
PACIFIC SANDS BEACH RESORT
LONG BEACH LODGE RESORT
Indian Island
Grice Bay
Kennedy Lake
TOFINO-LONG BEACH AIRPORT
Long Beach
4
Rainforest Trail
PACIFIC RIM NATIONAL PARK RESERVE
Combers Beach
Wickaninnish Beach
Wickaninnish Bay
Pacific Rim National Park Reserve
KWISITIS VISITOR CENTRE
PACIFIC RIM VISITOR CENTRE
Florencia Bay
WYA POINT RESORT

PACIFIC OCEAN

To Ucluelet Aquarium and Ucluelet →

0   2.5 mi
0   2.5 km

© MOON.COM

You can reach the park's **Broken Islands Group,** offshore in Barkley Sound, only by boat. The park website recommends tour operators who organize guided kayaking or sailing tours to the islands. Also part of the park is the 47-mile (75-km) **West Coast Trail** (May-Sept.), a rugged backpacking route.

Park Passes and Fees

Purchase a **day pass** (adults $7.80, seniors $6.80, families $15.70) for the Pacific Rim National Park Reserve at the **Pacific Rim Visitor Centre** (2791 Pacific Rim Hwy., Ucluelet), at the park's **Kwisitis Visitor Centre** (Wick Beach, off Pacific Rim Hwy.), or from vending machines at parking lots within the park.

Buying a Parks Canada **annual discovery pass** (adults $68, seniors $58, families $137), valid for a year, is a good deal if you're spending at

least a week in one or more parks. It's good at more than 100 national parks and national historic sites across Canada. Buy annual passes online from Parks Canada or at any park visitors center. For both day and annual passes, family passes cover up to seven people in a single vehicle.

Visitors Center

Start your park visit at the **Kwisitis Visitor Centre** (485 Wick Rd., off Pacific Rim Hwy., 250/726-3524, www.pc.gc.ca, 10am-5pm daily June-early Oct., reduced hours off-season). The park encompasses the traditional territory of the Nuu-chah-nulth First Nation, and you can get an introduction to their culture through the center's exhibits.

REST STOP: SPROAT LAKE

When you're driving to or from Vancouver Island's west coast, there are few places to stop as you cross the mountains between Port Alberni and Tofino. For a break or some good food, stop at Sproat Lake Landing (10695 Lakeshore Rd., Port Alberni, 250/723-2722, www.sproatlakelanding.com), where Drinkwaters Social House (11am-11pm Mon.-Fri., 9am-11pm Sat.-Sun., call for off-season hours) serves pub-style meals overlooking the 15-mile (25-km) lake. Book one of the seven modern guest rooms ($149-399) if you want a longer rest; the best have lake views.

RECREATION
Beaches

Confusingly, Wickaninnish Beach is not the beach where the deluxe Wickaninnish Inn is located; that hotel is on Chesterman Beach. Rather, the wide dune-backed Wick Beach is adjacent to the park visitors center.

North of Wick Beach and adjacent to old-growth forest, Long Beach creates the longest sand dune on Vancouver Island, more than 9 miles (16 km) long.

Hiking

Several gentle hiking trails start from the park's Kwisitis Visitor Centre. The 3-mile (5-km) Nuu-chah-nulth Trail is an easy loop with interpretive panels about First Nations culture. You can branch from this trail onto the 0.5-mile (800-m) South Beach Trail, which leads to a pebble beach with often spectacular waves; don't swim here, though, due to the strong currents. The gentle Shorepine Bog Trail, a 0.5-mile (800-m) loop, takes you through an old-growth temperate rainforest.

CAMPING

Above the beach, 7.5 miles (12 km) north of the Tofino-Ucluelet junction, Green Point Campground (www.pc.gc.ca, May-early Oct., $23.50-32.30) has 94 drive-in sites with electricity, flush toilets, and showers. There are also 20 additional forested walk-in sites. In the walk-in area, you can also book an oTENTik ($120), a platform tent that sleeps up to six. Make campsite reservations (877/737-3783, www.reservation.parkscanada.gc.ca) online or by phone, beginning in January for the upcoming season. Reservations are especially recommended for stays mid-June-August.

Wickaninnish Beach

GETTING THERE

Pacific Rim National Park Reserve's Long Beach Unit is off Highway 4, 19 miles (30 km) south of Tofino and 10 miles (16 km) north of Ucluelet.

By car and ferry from Vancouver, the 165-mile (260-km) trip across the Strait of Georgia and then across Vancouver Island takes about six hours. Drive northwest from Vancouver to the Horseshoe Bay Ferry Terminal and take the

Horseshoe Bay-Departure Bay Ferry (www.bcferries.com, 1 hour and 40 minutes, one-way adults $17.20, ages 5-11 $8.60) to Nanaimo. When you leave the Departure Bay ferry terminal, follow the signs to Highway 19/Parksville. After Parksville, exit onto Highway 4 westbound toward Port Alberni. Check your gas gauge; there are no gas stations between Port Alberni and the Pacific coast.

Highway 4 comes to a T at the Tofino-Ucluelet junction. Turn right (north) onto the Pacific Rim Highway toward Tofino. The park's Kwisitis Visitor Centre is 5 miles (8 km) north of the junction.

✪ TOFINO

Like all of the west coast, the Tofino area was First Nations territory where generations of fishers and hunters lived and foraged, both on the mainland and on the islands offshore. Spanish explorers first ventured to the region in the late 1700s, followed quickly by British expeditions, but it wasn't until 1909 that the town of Tofino was officially established, when fishing, logging, and mining were the main occupations along the coast. Tofino's nickname comes from these hard-scrabble jobs and the region's stormy winters: Tough City.

While surfers and other nature-seekers began arriving in the 1960s, the creation of the Pacific Rim National Park Reserve in 1970 and the paving of Highway 4 to the coast in 1972 launched the modern tourist era.

Today, laid-back, surfer-friendly Tofino has a small village around its scenic harbor, where fishing vessels set off to sea, whale-watching and other tour boats dock, and float-planes come and go. The beaches and oceanfront lodges are on the peninsula, south of town.

SIGHTS

The Tofino Botanical Gardens (1084 Pacific Rim Hwy., 250/725-1220, www.tbgf.org, 8am-dusk daily, adults $12, students over age 12 $8), 2 miles (3 km) south of town, offer a refuge from the wilderness of Vancouver Island's wild west coast, with cultivated plants, old-growth rainforest, and works by local artists. Many plants are local, including a tree that's roughly 800 years old, while others include Chilean rainforest vegetation, Himalayan lilies (the world's largest), and other varieties that grow in climates similar to that of British Columbia's coastal regions. Examine the traditional dugout canoe, handmade by First Nations carver Joe Martin, displayed with photos of his family and commentary from his children. Kids may appreciate the chickens and goats that wander the garden's grounds. Named for Charles Darwin and stocked with "books full of dangerous ideas," Darwin's Café (8am-5pm daily Mar.-Oct.) serves coffee, homemade pastries, and light breakfasts and lunches.

TOURS AND EXCURSIONS

To really experience the west coast, get offshore to explore the coastline and nearby islands, and look for the wildlife that populates the region. Most tours operate from March-April through October-November; trips can be postponed or canceled if the seas get too rough. The following

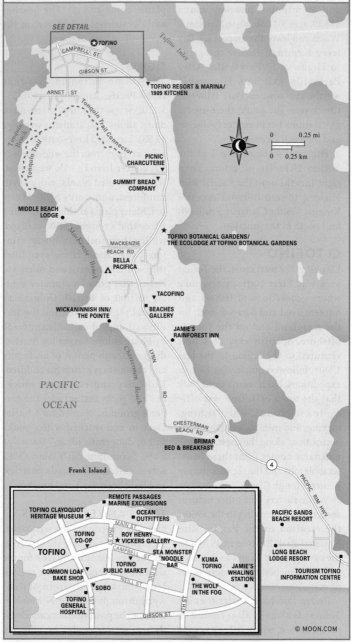

Tofino

SEE DETAIL

Tofino Inlet

★ TOFINO
CAMPBELL ST
GIBSON ST

ARNET ST

Tonquin Trail Connector

Tonquin Beach

Tonquin Trail

▼ TOFINO RESORT & MARINA/
1909 KITCHEN

▼ PICNIC
CHARCUTERIE

▼ SUMMIT BREAD
COMPANY

● MIDDLE BEACH
LODGE

MacKenzie Beach

MACKENZIE
BEACH RD

★ TOFINO BOTANICAL GARDENS/
THE ECOLODGE AT TOFINO BOTANICAL GARDENS

▲ BELLA
PACIFICA

▼ TACOFINO

■ BEACHES
GALLERY

● JAMIE'S
RAINFOREST INN

● WICKANINNISH INN/
THE POINTE

Chesterman Beach

LYNN RD

PACIFIC

OCEAN

CHESTERMAN
BEACH RD

● BRIMAR
BED & BREAKFAST

Frank Island

(4)

PACIFIC RIM HWY

■ PACIFIC SANDS
BEACH RESORT

■ LONG BEACH
LODGE RESORT

■ TOURISM TOFINO
INFORMATION CENTRE

0   0.25 mi
0   0.25 km

REMOTE PASSAGES
MARINE EXCURSIONS

TOFINO CLAYOQUOT
HERITAGE MUSEUM ★

OCEAN
OUTFITTERS

MAIN ST

TOFINO
CO-OP

ROY HENRY
VICKERS GALLERY ★

CAMPBELL ST

TOFINO
TOFINO
PUBLIC MARKET

SEA MONSTER
NOODLE BAR ▼

KUMA
TOFINO ▼

JAMIE'S
WHALING STATION ■

COMMON LOAF
BAKE SHOP ▼

NEILL ST

THE WOLF
IN THE FOG ▼

● SOBO

TOFINO
GENERAL HOSPITAL

1ST ST

4TH ST

GIBSON ST

© MOON.COM

TWO DAYS ON VANCOUVER ISLAND'S WEST COAST

Start your day with a morning stroll along the beach; Chesterman Beach is one of the area's most beautiful. Then wander through the Tofino Botanical Gardens to explore the old-growth rainforest, stopping at the garden's Darwin's Café when it's time for a coffee break.

Have lunch at the orange food truck, Tacofino. Then head for Pacific Rim National Park Reserve to check out the displays in the Kwisitis Visitor Centre and hike near the shore. Later, take a surfing lesson, go swimming, or book a First Nations Dugout Canoe Tour with the excellent guides at T'ashii Paddle School. Have dinner at The Wolf in the Fog, where the don't-miss appetizer is the potato-crusted oyster, and any local seafood is bound to be stellar.

The next morning, pick up coffee and a ginger scone at Common Loaf Bake Shop, or a croissant from Summit Bread Company, before heading for the waterfront for an offshore excursion. Take a full-day trip to Hot Springs Cove, a kayak excursion to Meares Island, or a shorter whale-watching or bear-watching tour.

After your tour, clean up and drive to the Wickaninnish Inn for a cocktail in their window-lined lounge facing the sea. If your budget allows, stay for a special dinner at The Pointe, or if you'd rather have a more casual meal, head into town for a restorative bowl of ramen at Kuma Tofino, or graze on small plates in the window-lined dining room at 1909 Kitchen. Either way, stop to take a few sunset photos over the harbor to remember your west coast adventures.

companies are among those offering tours in the Tofino area:

- **Remote Passages Marine Excursions** (51 Wharf St., 250/725-3330 or 800/666-9833, www.remotepassages.com)

- **Ocean Outfitters** (368 Main St., 250/725-2866 or 877/906-2326, www.oceanoutfitters.bc.ca)

- **T'ashii Paddle School** (250/266-3787 or 855/883-3787, www.tofinopaddle.com)

- **The Adventure Centre at Tofino Resort & Marina** (778/841-0186, www.tofinoresortandmarina.com)

- **The Whale Centre** (411 Campbell St., 250/725-2132 or 888/474-2288, www.tofinowhalecentre.com)

Hot Springs Cove/Maquinna Marine Provincial Park

A full-day trip to these remote hot springs is a highlight for many Tofino visitors. Located 27 nautical miles (50 km) northwest of Tofino, Hot Springs Cove, in Maquinna Marine Provincial Park at the north end of Clayoquot Sound, is accessible only by boat (adults $109-139, under age 13 $89-109) or floatplane (adults $224-229, under age 13 $204-209).

Traveling by boat (1.5-2 hours each way), you may spot whales, sea lions, and even bears or other wildlife, so you might consider this trip an alternative to a separate whale-watching tour. With the floatplane option, you save a little time, traveling one direction by boat, the other on a scenic 20-minute flight.

Once you arrive at the dock, it's a 1-mile (1.6-km) walk on a boardwalk through the rainforest to the natural hot springs. Climb down the rocks and take a natural hot shower in the gushing sulfur springs, then soak in the rock pools. The water temperature averages a soothing 110°F (43°C).

There's a rustic shelter with change rooms and a pit toilet above the springs and a restroom near the docks. Don't forget your bathing suit, towel, and water bottle. Sports sandals or water shoes will protect your feet from the rocks. Bring snacks or a picnic to enjoy before or after you soak.

Meares Island

Declared a park by the Tla-o-qui-aht and Ahousaht First Nations, Meares Island—its traditional name is Wanachis-Hilthhoois—is across the harbor from the village of Tofino.

A popular way to get to the island is on a half-day kayak excursion ($84). Some companies run water shuttles (adults $25-30, under age 12 $15-20) to the island. Tour companies also collect a $5 park fee.

Once you arrive on Meares Island, you can hike through the rainforest on the moderate 1.9-mile (3 km) round-trip Big Tree Trail, which takes you into an old-growth forest, where some trees are more than 1,000 years old.

For experienced hikers, the island's steep, challenging Lone Cone Trail leads up to a 2,395-foot (730-m) peak with panoramic views across the island and the sound. It's only 0.6 mile (1 km) in each direction, but it's essentially a vertical trail.

Whale-Watching

On whale-watching excursions (adults $99-109, under age 13 $75-79) from Tofino, you'll likely spot Pacific gray whales. You might also see humpback whales, bald eagles, sea lions, harbor seals, and occasionally orcas or porpoises.

As on the trips that depart from Victoria, you can choose from a tour

in an inflatable Zodiac, which gives you a choppier but more thrilling ride, or on a larger, more sheltered boat, which would be more comfortable in inclement weather. On either type of craft, whale-watching tours typically last 2.5-3 hours.

Bear-Watching

From Tofino, you can take a boat through Clayoquot Sound to several spots where it's possible to observe the area's resident population of black bears. On these bear-watching excursions (adults $99-109, under age 13 $75-79), the tour boats dock offshore, where, if you're lucky, you'll spot bears foraging along the rocky beaches or in the tidal pools.

You stay on the boat throughout these 2-3-hour tours. Bring a camera with a telephoto lens for the best photos, since the boats must remain a safe distance from the animals.

dugout canoe tour with T'ashii Paddle School

First Nations Dugout Canoe Tours

First Nations-owned T'ashii Paddle School (250/266-3787 or 855/883-3787, www.tofinopaddle.com) offers several excellent paddling tours in hand-carved dugout canoes, where you'll learn about local indigenous communities and their traditional culture.

Departing from **Jamie's Whaling Station** (606 Campbell St.), excursions include a two-hour **Coastal Canoe Tour** (late May-mid-Oct., $65 pp), which is especially lovely at sunset, and a **Meares Island Canoe Tour** (Mar.-Oct., $89 pp), a four-hour paddling and hiking excursion.

RECREATION
Beaches
Sandy beaches line the peninsula that stretches south from Tofino to Ucluelet. Except for Tonquin Beach, all are located off the Pacific Rim Highway, listed here from north to south.

Closest to town, **Tonquin Beach** still feels secluded, as you follow the walking trail—which starts behind Tofino Community Hall (351 Arnet Rd.)—through the rainforest and down the stairs to the beach. Sheltered **MacKenzie Beach** has several resorts and campgrounds.

Beginning surfers hone their skills on the south end of 1.7-mile (2.7-km) **Chesterman Beach,** one of Tofino's most scenic and popular stretches of sand. Toward the beach's north side, you can explore the tide pools at low tide. The Wickaninnish Inn is on North Chesterman Beach.

Home to several resorts, including Pacific Sands and Long Beach Lodge, **Cox Bay Beach** has a popular surf break. At the bay's northern tip, you can explore several tidal caves, accessible only at low tide. Continuing south, you'll reach the beaches in Pacific Rim National Park Reserve, including **Long Beach** and **Wickaninnish Beach.**

surfing in Tofino

Surfing
Tofino is western Canada's **surfing** capital (yes, Canada really has a surfing capital), with plenty of places to take lessons or catch the waves. While you can surf year-round, hard-core surfers come in winter when the waves are biggest; if you're just getting started, summertime is warmest, with the gentlest surf.

With a crew of women as instructors, **Surf Sister Surf School** (250/725-4456, www.surfsister.com) specializes in teaching women to surf, although they offer lessons for both men and women. In addition to standard group lessons ($89 pp), it offers individual ($179), two-person ($119 pp), and three-person ($109 pp) private instruction.

The **Surf Club Adventure Centre** (250/725-2442, www.longbeachlodgeresort.com) at the Long Beach Lodge Resort is another highly regarded surf school, teaching group ($99 pp) and private lessons ($189 pp).

Stand-Up Paddleboarding

T'ashii Paddle School (250/266-3787 or 855/883-3787, www.tofinopaddle.com) offers stand-up paddleboard tours ($65-129), lessons ($80-140), and rentals (2 hours $29, full-day $39). You can also learn SUP surfing—surfing on a stand-up paddleboard ($89-140).

Hiking

The 1.9-mile (3-km) Tonquin Trail (www.tofino.ca/trails) is a moderate path through the rainforest that leads to several lookout points and to the scenic Tonquin, Third, and Middle Beaches, with dramatic rock formations along the shores. The trail starts in town behind the Tofino Community Hall (351 Arnet Rd.), where there's a parking lot.

The Rainforest Education Society (250/725-2560, www.raincoasteducation.org) offers free 1.5-hour interpretive walks in July-August that explore the tide pools and rainforest along Cox Bay. Check the website for the schedule and other details.

Guides from the First Nations-owned T'ashii Paddle School (250/266-3787 or 855/883-3787, www.tofinopaddle.com) lead winter Cultural Walks on the Schooner Cove Trail (10:30am daily mid-Dec.-Mar., $100 for 2 people, $20 each additional person) in Pacific Rim National Park Reserve that combine a gentle hike through the old-growth rainforest with information about local First Nations culture. Book in advance on their website.

FESTIVALS AND EVENTS

In early spring, gray whales begin returning to the waters off Vancouver Island's west coast. During the week-long Pacific Rim Whale Festival (www.pacificrimwhalefestival.com, Mar.), you can learn more about these creatures with presentations, documentary films, guided walks, whale-watching tours, and other events.

Feast Tofino (www.feasttofino.com, Apr.-May) celebrates the region's seafood and its "boat-to-table" food culture, organizing dinners and special events with local and visiting chefs.

FOOD

For a small community, Tofino has a significant food culture, emphasizing innovative uses of local seafood and produce. Outside the summer months, many restaurants keep reduced or varying hours, so call before you set out. Except for The Pointe at the Wickaninnish Inn, Tofino's eating places are casual; patrons often look like they've wandered directly off a boat because, most likely, they have.

Modern Canadian

Tofino's special-occasion restaurant, ❂ The Pointe at the Wickaninnish Inn (500 Osprey Ln., 250/725-3106, www.wickinn.com, 7:30am-2pm and 5pm-10pm daily, dinner $30-46, brunch $16-34) emphasizes local seafood, foraged ingredients, and regional products. The polished staff and walls of curved windows wrapping the ocean panoramas around you don't hurt either. Start with a foie gras tart or a Humboldt squid *sope* (a thick tortilla layered with squid and pickled sea asparagus) as a prelude to teriyaki-glazed steelhead with smoked salmon and squash agnolotti or scallops in a mussel and clam ragout. There are sweets, of course, from a platter of petit fours to unique creations like sea buckthorn mousse with espresso chocolate fudge. Also available is a multicourse tasting menu ($75-105), with optional wine pairings.

Oysters in a potato web? Fried cod cheeks with sea asparagus? Pacific octopus with black lentils and North African spices? Some of the west coast's most imaginative dishes come out of the open kitchen at ✪ **The Wolf in the Fog** (150 4th St., 250/725-9653, www.wolfinthefog.com, 10am-2pm and 5pm-midnight daily, lunch and brunch $13-22, dinner $21-40), where the upstairs dining room sparkles with polished wood and the big windows look out toward the harbor. While there's some serious technique and respect for local ingredients here, the chefs don't take themselves too seriously; the menu suggests buying a six-pack for the kitchen. For your own drinks, try the signature Cedar Sour, with cedar-infused rye. Finish up with the intense dark chocolate blackout or a seasonal fruit creation. The bottom line? Good food, good drinks, good fun.

Overlooking the marina and offshore islands, with picture windows on two sides and portholes framing the views on the third, **1909 Kitchen** (634 Campbell St., 250/726-6122, www.tofinoresortandmarina.com, 7am-11am and 5pm-9:30pm daily, breakfast $6-16, dinner $12-36) at Tofino Resort and Marina shows off the waterfront panoramas. The chef's interest in foraging, fishing, and sourcing regional

"tacos" and more at 1909 Kitchen

ingredients means that the menu of inspired sharing plates might encompass black rice with house-candied salmon, albacore "tacos" (with the fish served raw on radish "paper"), or the day's catch wood-roasted and paired with charred onion-ginger puree. For something simpler, try a pizza—perhaps the side stripe shrimp with chorizo and basil—from the wood-fueled oven. Sweets range from fruit cobblers to s'mores with salted caramel.

Though the name is short for "sophisticated bohemian," airy (and family-friendly) **SoBo** (311 Neil St., 250/725-2341, www.sobo.ca, 11:30am-9:30pm daily, lunch $10-16, dinner $15-30), with sunny yellow walls and floor-to-ceiling windows, is more refined than hippie, serving modern world-beat fare at lunch and dinner. Noon-hour dishes include halloumi cheese and grain salad, huevos rancheros, and pizza, while in the evening, you might try halibut with buttermilk mashed potatoes or whiskey-braised beef brisket. SoBo is justifiably famous for its smoked wild fish chowder.

Asian

When you crave a restorative bowl of ramen, head for Kuma Tofino (101-120 4th St., 250/725-2215, www.kumatofino.com, 4pm-9:30pm daily, $10-14), a modern Japanese eatery. Sake and local craft beer stand up to sharing plates like crispy chicken *karaage*, fresh tuna *tataki*, and salmon croquettes.

For a quick bite in town, the order-at-the-counter Sea Monster Noodle Bar (421 Main St., 250/725-1280, www.seamonsternoodle.com, 11:30am-6:30pm daily, $12-15) offers several varieties of simple, tasty Asian-inspired noodle and rice bowls, from *dan dan* noodles to salmon poke. Try the Thai-style fish curry with fresh cilantro and basil.

Mexican

Before it became a Mexican mini chain with branches in Vancouver and Victoria, Tacofino (1184 Pacific Rim Hwy., 250/726-8288, www.tacofino.com, 11am-8pm daily summer, 11am-6pm daily fall-spring, $4-14) was a taco truck in Tofino. This orange truck parked behind a surf shop south of town channels a surfer vibe with tacos (try the tuna with seaweed and ginger), burritos, and slushie drinks like tangy lime-mint "freshies." Park at one of the long outdoor tables, or take yours to the beach.

Vegetarian

The all-vegetarian, comfort food menu at Bravocados (368 Main St., 250/725-3667, 10am-9pm daily, $12-19), a plant-based bistro in the modern Shore Building, where the garage door-style window opens to the outdoors on sunny days, runs from "appies" to tacos, burgers, and bowls. Try the kimchee poutine (with sweet potato fries, house-made kimchee, and a creamy miso sauce), the vegan "scallops" (made of eggplant), or the Thai curry bowl with locally crafted tempeh.

Bakeries and Cafés

From local hippies to texting teens to travelers, everyone stops into the red house that's home to long-standing Common Loaf Bake Shop (180 1st St., 250/725-3915, 8am-6pm daily) for delectable cinnamon buns, ginger scones, breads, and muffins. They make soup, sandwiches, and pizza too.

It's not only bread at Summit Bread Company (681 Industrial Way, Units C&D, 250/726-6767, www.summitbreadco.com, 7am-4pm daily), where the aromatic baking may lure you to this shop in the south-of-town industrial district. It also turns out croissants, muffins, savory buns, and seasonally changing baked goods to take out. The salted dark chocolate cookie is becoming a local classic.

kimchee poutine at Bravacados

Groceries and Markets

The area's largest grocery store is Tofino Co-op (140 1st St., 250/725-3226, www.tofinocoop.com, 8:30am-9pm daily summer, 8:30am-8pm daily fall-spring). South of town, tiny but well-stocked Beaches Grocery (1184 Pacific Rim Hwy., 250/725-2237, 8:30am-10pm daily) carries fruits and vegetables, baked goods, and other food items such as chips and Asian chili sauce.

Find local produce, prepared foods, and crafts at the Tofino Public Market (Tofino Village Green, 3rd St. and Campbell St., www.tofinomarket.com, 10am-2pm Sat. late May-early Oct.).

ACCOMMODATIONS

Many of Tofino's nicest accommodations are south of town, along the peninsula beaches. Book in advance for summer high season (mid-June-mid-Sept.). In winter, many lodgings offer storm-watching packages, when the big winter surf and rain rolls in. For last-minute lodging, check the "current vacancies" page on the Tourism Tofino website (www.tourismtofino.com).

CAD$150-300

Once a field station for research groups, The Ecolodge at Tofino Botanical Gardens (1084 Pacific Rim Hwy., 250/725-1220, www.tbgf.org, $159-239) is a simple comfortable lodge in the midst of the gardens. Guests gather in the great room for a continental breakfast or to relax; you can browse the lodge's nature library or use the kitchen to prep meals. Eight basic, colorfully decorated rooms share two large baths. Two additional suites, with

private baths, have family-friendly nooks with bunk beds. There are no TVs, but Wi-Fi is included, as is garden admission.

waterfront at Tofino Resort & Marina

To stay close to the departure point for whale-watching trips and other tours as well as the town's cafés and restaurants, consider Tofino Resort & Marina (634 Campbell St., 844/680-4184, www.tofinoresortandmarina.com, $199-339). New owners revamped an old motel above a marina at the south end of Tofino into 62 simple, well-designed rooms in two buildings, all with coffeemakers, kettles, mini fridges, and Wi-Fi. The largest king or queen suites have a small sitting area with a double sofa bed. Request a higher-floor unit for partial ocean views; the least expensive rooms face the parking. You can book whale-watching tours and other activities through the on-site adventure center. Have a beer or casual meal in Hatch Waterfront Pub or inventive contemporary fare at 1909 Kitchen, which both look out to the water.

Overlooking two beaches and the offshore islands, Middle Beach Lodge (400 MacKenzie Beach Rd.,

250/725-2900 or 866/725-2900, www.middlebeach.com, $165-475) offers a variety of accommodations. The original lodge has tiny no-frills rooms with no TVs or closets, but the nicest of these economical units have ocean views. In the main lodge, rooms are slightly larger, with wooden floors and flat-screen TVs; choose an end unit upstairs for the best water vistas. Also on the forested property are roomy cabins with kitchen facilities; some have sleeping lofts, fireplaces, or hot tubs. Take in the panoramic views from the overstuffed chairs in the wood-beamed great room, where a deluxe continental breakfast buffet (included in the rates) is served.

bathtub view at the Wickaninnish Inn

Over CAD$300

The most deluxe lodging on Vancouver Island's west coast is the ✪ **Wickaninnish Inn** (500 Osprey Ln., 250/725-3100 or 800/333-4604, www.wickinn.com, $360-1,020), which nestles into 100 acres (40 ha) of old-growth rainforest on Chesterman Beach. Behind the unassuming gray exteriors, the inn is filled with indigenous art and 75 rustic yet elegant accommodations

with earth-tone furnishings, gas fireplaces, flat-screen TVs hidden in cabinets that open by remote control, soaker tubs, and heated bath floors. The **Ancient Cedars Spa** has seven treatment rooms, including one set dramatically above the rocks; guests can join daily yoga classes. Local musicians perform at the **Driftwood Café** (named for its bar made of driftwood), which serves coffee, pastries, and light meals. **The Pointe,** the inn's premier restaurant, is among the region's finest.

The three gold-and-burgundy guest rooms at the cedar-shingled **BriMar Bed & Breakfast** (1375 Chesterman Beach Rd., 250/725-3410, www.brimarbb.com, $235-375) look right onto Chesterman Beach, close enough to hear the surf. On the 2nd floor, the spacious Moonrise Room has an equally spacious private bath, while the slightly smaller Sunset Room has a private bath across the hall. The secluded Loft Unit, under the eaves, runs the whole length of the top floor. Rates include Wi-Fi and an ample breakfast. Guests can help themselves to coffee and tea at all hours and store snacks in the hallway fridge.

Even if you're not staying at **Long Beach Lodge Resort** (1441 Pacific Rim Hwy., 250/725-2442, www.longbeachlodgeresort.com, $329-509 d, cottages $550-679), have a drink or a meal in the resort's inviting **Great Room,** with walls of windows facing the ocean. The lodge has a well-regarded surf club, where both kids and adults can learn to ride the waves. When it's time to sleep, choose from 41 studio units in the main lodge, with sturdy Douglas fir furnishings, or from 20 two-bedroom cottages in the forest, set back from the beach. Solo travelers: In the off-season, the resort regularly offers discounts for individual guests.

hammock on the beach at Pacific Sands Beach Resort

Opened in 1972 on the beach at Cox Bay, family-friendly **Pacific Sands Beach Resort** (1421 Pacific Rim Hwy., 250/725-3322, www.pacificsands.com, $255-449 d, 2-bedroom units $500-880) has grown to encompass 120 units, all with full kitchens, in several buildings. Most of the modern condo-style beach houses have two bedrooms and views across the lawn to the waterfront. In other buildings, the studio to two-bedroom units are smaller but still feel airy and beachy. The contemporary one-bedroom suites in the newest Oceanside Suites wing have patios or balconies with ocean vistas. The outdoor **Surfside Grill** serves fish-and-chips, seafood chowder, burgers, and tacos, and you can buy drinks, snacks, and quick meals in the lobby. Rent beach cruiser bikes or gather the gang in the gazebo to roast marshmallows.

INFORMATION AND SERVICES

The **Pacific Rim Visitor Centre** (2791 Pacific Rim Hwy., Ucluelet, 250/726-4600, www.pacificrimvisitor.ca, 9am-7pm daily July-Aug., 10am-5pm daily Sept.-June), at the Tofino-Ucluelet junction, where Highway 4 meets the Pacific Rim Highway, provides information about the region.

Tourism Tofino (www.tourismtofino.com) has a detailed website with useful trip-planning tips. They run the **Tofino Information Centre** (1426 Pacific Rim Hwy., Tofino, 250/725-3414 or 888/720-3414, www.tourismtofino.com, 9am-5pm daily June-Sept., 10am-5pm daily Oct.-May), 4.5 miles (7 km) south of downtown Tofino and 15.5 miles (25 km) north of the Tofino-Ucluelet junction.

Small **Tofino General Hospital** (261 Neill St., 250/725-4010, www.islandhealth.ca) offers 24-hour emergency services.

GETTING THERE
Air
Pacific Coastal Airlines (604/273-8666 or 800/663-2872, www.pacificcoastal.com) operates regular flights year-round from the South Terminal at **Vancouver International Airport** (YVR, 4440 Cowley Cres., Richmond, www.yvr.ca, 45 minutes, one-way adults $150-230) to **Tofino-Long Beach Airport** (YAZ, Pacific Rim Hwy., www.tofinoairport.com), which is 7 miles (11 km) southeast of the town and 18 miles (30 km) northeast of Ucluelet.

Harbour Air (604/274-1277 or 800/665-0212, www.harbourair.com, late May-mid-Oct., 1 hour, one-way adults $229-319) flies floatplanes seasonally between the Vancouver Harbour Flight Centre (1055 Canada Pl., behind the Vancouver Convention Centre) and Tofino Harbour (634 Campbell St.), landing near the Tofino Resort & Marina.

Car and Ferry

A road trip from Vancouver to Tofino involves taking a ferry from the mainland to Nanaimo, and then driving west across the island; allow six hours to make the journey.

From Vancouver, drive northwest to the Horseshoe Bay Ferry Terminal and take the Horseshoe Bay-Departure Bay Ferry (www.bcferries.com, 1 hour and 40 minutes, one-way adults $17.20, ages 5-11 $8.60) to Nanaimo.

Although the drive from Nanaimo to Tofino is only 130 miles (210 km), it takes at least three hours, longer if you stop to sightsee en route. When you exit the Departure Bay ferry terminal, follow the signs to Highway 19/Parksville. After Parksville, exit onto Highway 4 westbound toward Port Alberni. Check your gas; there are no gas stations between Port Alberni and the Pacific coast.

Highway 4 winds its way across the island, over and around the mountains that form the island's spine. At several points, the road becomes quite narrow and curvy; don't be in a rush to make this trip. If you find that a line of impatient drivers is forming behind you, use one of the pullouts to move over and allow them to pass.

Highway 4 comes to a T at the Tofino-Ucluelet junction. Turn

right (north) onto the Pacific Rim Highway toward Tofino; it's 20 miles (32 km) from the junction into town.

Bus and Ferry

Tofino Bus (250/725-2871 or 866/986-3466, www.tofinobus.com) can take you to Tofino starting with bus service from Vancouver's Pacific Central Station (1150 Station St., adults $65, seniors and students $59, ages 2-11 $33) to Horseshoe Bay, where you board the Horseshoe Bay-Departure Bay Ferry to Nanaimo. After arriving at the Nanaimo Ferry Terminal, you transfer to the Tofino Bus to the west coast. You must purchase a ferry ticket in addition to the bus fare. The total bus-ferry-bus trip takes 7.5 hours.

Tofino Bus can also take you to Tofino from Nanaimo's Departure Bay Ferry Terminal (4.25 hours, adults $54, seniors and students $49, ages 2-11 $27) and from downtown Victoria (6.5 hours, adults $69, seniors and students $62, ages 2-11 $36).

GETTING AROUND

Easy to explore on foot, the town of Tofino is a few blocks square, with most shops and restaurants along Campbell or Main Streets, between 1st and 4th Streets. To travel between town and the beaches, it's easiest to have your own car, although it's possible to cycle or take a bus, a good idea in the busy summer season when the roads and parking areas can be congested.

Car

From its junction with Highway 4, the Pacific Rim Highway runs 20 miles (32 km) up the peninsula to the town of Tofino, passing Pacific Rim National Park Reserve and beaches along the way. In town, the highway becomes Campbell Street.

If you arrive in Tofino without a car, you can rent one from Budget (188 Airport Rd., 250/725-2060, www.bcbudget.com) at the Tofino airport.

Bus

The free Tofino Shuttle (www.tofinobus.com, 7:30am-10:30pm daily late June-early Sept.) runs during the summer between town and Cox Bay, with stops near several beaches. Buses leave about once an hour in each direction, so check the schedule online before setting out.

Bike

Cycling is a good way to travel between town and the beaches. Ride along the 3.75-mile (6-km) Multi-Use Path, locally known as the MUP, a fairly flat, paved trail that parallels Highway 4 from town to Cox Bay. Plans have been announced to extend the MUP south to the boundary of Pacific Rim National Park Reserve, where it will connect with the ʔapsčiik t'ašii (ups-cheek-TA-shee) trail, a 15-mile (24-km) pathway through the national park, which is planned for a 2020 opening; check with Tourism Tofino (www.tourismtofino.com) for updates.

TOF Cycles (660 Sharp Rd., 250/725-2453, www.tofcycles.com, 9am-6pm daily, 4 hours $30, full-day $35) and Tofino Bikes (1180 Pacific Rim Hwy., 250/725-2722, http://tofinobike.com, 10am-5pm daily, 4 hours $30, full-day $35),

both located between MacKenzie and Chesterman Beaches, rent bikes.

UCLUELET

Once considered the workaday counterpart to more upscale Tofino, 25 miles (40 km) to the north, Ucluelet (population 1,700) is coming into its own as a holiday destination. It's close enough to Pacific Rim National Park Reserve to explore the trails and beaches, and you can also enjoy the sand and hiking routes around town.

SIGHTS AND RECREATION

Ucluelet Aquarium (180 Main St., 250/726-2782, www.uclueletaquarium.org, 10am-5pm daily mid-Mar.-Nov., adults $14, seniors and students $10, ages 4-17 $7) has a rare "catch and release" philosophy. In the spring, staff bring in sealife from the local waters of Clayoquot and Barkley Sounds to populate the kids'-eye-level tanks, releasing them in the autumn back to the wild. The "please touch" displays are fun for youngsters and not-so-youngsters alike.

For hikers, the Wild Pacific Trail (www.wildpacifictrail.com) has several moderate options at the foot of the Ucluelet peninsula, with spectacular views of the Pacific coast. The 1.6-mile (2.6-km) Lighthouse Loop starts and ends on Coast Guard Road south of Terrace Beach, passing the 1915 Amphitrite Lighthouse. The hillier Artist Loop takes you 1.7 miles (2.8 km) along the cliffs starting from either Brown's Beach or Big Beach Park near Black Rock Oceanfront Resort. A short detour off the Artist Loop, the 0.6-mile (1-km) Ancient

along Ucluelet's Wild Pacific Trail

Cedars Loop leads through a forest of old-growth Sitka spruce, western hemlock, and giant red cedar trees. Get a map on the website or from the Pacific Rim Visitor Centre.

FOOD

Stop into **Zoë's Bakery and Café** (250 Main St., 250/726-2253, 7am-4pm daily, $5-10) for pastries, soups, quiche, sandwiches, and other baked goods. Try the Savory Breakfast Egg Bake Thingy, a delicious mash-up of sourdough bread cubes and bacon, topped with an egg. Zoë's is also known for its carrot cake.

Curing its own meats and sourcing ingredients locally may not make this barbecue joint in a little red house nontraditional, but at **Hank's Untraditional BBQ** (1576 Imperial Ln., 250/726-2225, www.hanksbbq.ca, 5pm-9:30pm daily, $24-27), it does make things good. Lead off with spicy hoisin duck wings or panko-crusted cod before muscling into the main event,

whether it's coffee- and cocoa-rubbed beef brisket or barbecued pulled pork.

ACCOMMODATIONS AND CAMPING

The Ucluelet First Nation runs the unique ✪ **Wya Point Resort** (2695 Tofino-Ucluelet Hwy., 250/726-2625 or 844/352-6188, www.wyapoint. com), which has several lodging options on a remote section of coast. Nine wood-frame **lodges** (1-bedroom $349, 2-bedroom $559), decorated with works by First Nations carvers, are upscale cabins, each sleeping 4-6, with solid hand-built bed frames, living rooms with sleep sofas, full kitchens, and spacious decks above Ucluth Beach. Fifteen heated **yurts** ($150-175) made of thick canvas offer more rustic accommodations. You can cook outside on the barbecue and sleep inside on the sofa bed; some yurts also have bunk beds for the kids. Shared washrooms are nearby. The third option is the campground (early-Mar.-mid-Oct., $35-65), where some sites overlook the ocean and others sit in the forest near the beach.

Family-friendly 133-room **Black Rock Oceanfront Resort** (596 Marine Dr., 250/726-4800 or 877/762-5011, www.blackrockresort.com, $199-489) has everything you need for a beach getaway. Modern studios and one-bedroom suites in the main lodge, decorated in earthy greens and blacks, have kitchen facilities, spacious baths with heated floors and soaker tubs, and free Wi-Fi. Choose a fourth-floor room for the best views. Surrounded by trees in separate buildings, the Trail Suites range from studios to two-bedroom units. On the sea-facing deck is a plunge pool and two hot tubs; inside is a small fitness room and spa. When you get hungry, Fetch Restaurant, specializing in seafood, cooks up breakfast, lunch, and dinner; Float Lounge serves drinks and light meals.

INFORMATION AND SERVICES

Get local information at the Pacific Rim Visitor Centre (2791 Pacific Rim Hwy., Ucluelet, 250/726-4600, www.pacificrimvisitor.ca, 9am-7pm daily July-Aug., 10am-5pm daily Sept.-June) at the Tofino-Ucluelet junction.

GETTING THERE

By car and ferry from Vancouver to Ucluelet, the 165-mile (260-km) trip across the Strait of Georgia and then across Vancouver Island takes about six hours. Drive northwest from Vancouver to the Horseshoe Bay Ferry Terminal and take the Horseshoe Bay-Departure Bay Ferry (www.bcferries.com, 1 hour and 40 minutes, one-way adults $17.20, ages 5-11 $8.60) to Nanaimo. When you leave the Departure Bay ferry terminal, follow the signs to Highway 19/Parksville. After Parksville, exit onto Highway 4 westbound toward Port Alberni. Check your gas; there are no gas stations between Port Alberni and the Pacific coast.

Highway 4 comes to a T at the Tofino-Ucluelet junction. Turn left (south) onto the Pacific Rim Highway; Ucluelet is 5 miles (9 km) south of the junction.

WHISTLER AND THE SEA-TO-SKY HIGHWAY

The Sea-to-Sky Highway, one of western Canada's

most stunning roadways, connects Vancouver to the year-round outdoor mecca of Whistler.

Just a two-hour drive, it's perfect for a day trip or as part of a longer exploration. Whistler offers not just North America's largest snow sports resort but also plenty of opportunities for hiking, biking, paddling the glacier-fed lakes, and exploring the region's First Nations heritage.

Between Whistler and Vancouver, the town of Squamish is a hot spot for outdoor activities, including excellent hiking and the region's best white-water rafting. For gentler adventures, Squamish's Sea-to-Sky Gondola delivers stellar mountain views and access to mountaintop hiking trails.

totem pole on the Sea-to-Sky Highway

HIGHLIGHTS

✪ **SEA-TO-SKY GONDOLA:** A 10-minute ride up this Squamish peak gives expansive views of Howe Sound and the surrounding mountains. There's a suspension bridge, lots of hiking trails, and a great patio at the top (page 291).

✪ **BRACKENDALE EAGLES PROVINCIAL PARK:** One of North America's largest populations of bald eagles spends the winter months in this park near Squamish (page 293).

✪ **STAWAMUS CHIEF PROVINCIAL PARK:** For strong hikers, a day hike up the rocky summit known as the Chief is a popular adventure (page 294).

✪ **WHISTLER-BLACKCOMB:** From skiing and snowboarding to hiking, canoeing, rock climbing, and zip-lining, if it's an outdoor adventure, you can do it at this mountain resort (page 299).

✪ **SQUAMISH LIL'WAT CULTURAL CENTRE:** Learn about the Whistler region's First Nations communities at this modern museum and cultural facility (page 304).

✪ **AUDAIN ART MUSEUM:** This beautifully designed museum highlights BC artists from the earliest eras to the present day (page 304).

✪ **SCANDINAVE SPA:** After your Whistler adventures, ease your sore muscles into the hot and cold pools at this Scandinavian-style soaking spa (page 305).

the Cloudraker Skybridge at Whistler-Blackcomb

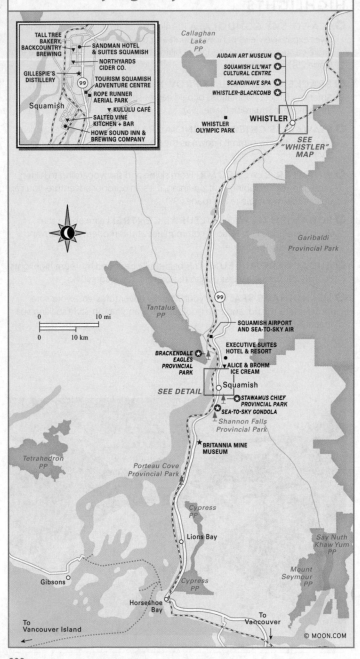

Sea-to-Sky Highway

TALL TREE BAKERY, BACKCOUNTRY BREWING
SANDMAN HOTEL & SUITES SQUAMISH
NORTHYARDS CIDER CO.
GILLESPIE'S DISTILLERY
TOURISM SQUAMISH ADVENTURE CENTRE
ROPE RUNNER AERIAL PARK
Squamish
KULULU CAFÉ
SALTED VINE KITCHEN + BAR
HOWE SOUND INN & BREWING COMPANY

Callaghan Lake PP

AUDAIN ART MUSEUM
SQUAMISH LIL'WAT CULTURAL CENTRE
SCANDINAVE SPA
WHISTLER-BLACKCOMB
WHISTLER

WHISTLER OLYMPIC PARK

SEE "WHISTLER" MAP

Garibaldi Provincial Park

Tantalus PP

SQUAMISH AIRPORT AND SEA-TO-SKY AIR

EXECUTIVE SUITES HOTEL & RESORT

ALICE & BROHM ICE CREAM

BRACKENDALE EAGLES PROVINCIAL PARK

Squamish

SEE DETAIL

STAWAMUS CHIEF PROVINCIAL PARK

SEA-TO-SKY GONDOLA

Shannon Falls Provincial Park

BRITANNIA MINE MUSEUM

0   10 mi
0   10 km

Tetrahedron PP

Porteau Cove Provincial Park

Cypress PP

Lions Bay

Cypress PP

Gibsons

Say Nuth Khaw Yum PP

Mount Seymour PP

Horseshoe Bay

To Vancouver

To Vancouver Island

© MOON.COM

Squamish

Midway between Vancouver and Whistler along the Sea-to-Sky Highway (Hwy. 99), Squamish is perched between the Coast Mountains and Howe Sound. Cafés, local eateries, and a few shops populate the town's laid-back downtown, while along Highway 99, strip malls and fast-food joints give Squamish a mountain-suburban feel. The real action in Squamish is outdoors.

It's a popular destination for all manner of outdoor adventures, including hiking, cycling, rock climbing, sailing, stand-up paddleboarding, and white-water rafting. You can see the area's most famous peak, the Stawamus Chief, from the highway, or tackle the Chief on a day hike.

Squamish takes its name from the Squamish First Nation, the people whose traditional territory encompasses the modern-day town. In more recent times, mining was an important contributor to the local economy; a historic mine is now an attraction. Another Squamish attraction December-February is bald eagles; one of North America's largest populations of eagles spends the winter months near Squamish.

Squamish makes an easy day trip from Vancouver or a stopover between Vancouver and Whistler. It's 40 miles (65 km) from Vancouver to Squamish, a one-hour drive, and 37 miles (60 km) between Squamish and Whistler, which takes 45 minutes.

Britannia Mine Museum

SIGHTS AND ACTIVITIES
BRITANNIA MINE MUSEUM

For much of the 20th century, the Britannia Beach area south of Squamish was copper mining territory. During its heyday, the Britannia Mine produced more copper than any other mine in the British Empire. Workers from more than 50 countries settled here, living in barracks by the water or in a company town high in the surrounding hills.

While the Britannia Mine provided valuable resources and jobs for decades, it also created environmental havoc, particularly on the local water supply. After the mine closed in 1974, its environmental impacts took years to remediate.

The mine site is now the **Britannia Mine Museum** (1 Forbes Way, Britannia Beach, 604/896-2233 or 800/896-4044, www. britanniaminemuseum.ca, 9am-5:30pm daily, adults $35, seniors and students $32, ages 13-17 $29,

SCENIC DRIVE: THE SEA-TO-SKY HIGHWAY

Porteau Cove

Highway 99, the Sea-to-Sky Highway, is one of western Canada's most beautiful drives. In a region full of beautiful drives, that's high praise. At its southern end, the winding road that leads from West Vancouver to Whistler hugs the shores of Howe Sound, where the Gulf Islands rise from the water. You can stop at Horseshoe Bay, where the ferries depart for Vancouver Island and BC's Sunshine Coast, to stroll the harbor and admire the vistas. Another stopping point is Porteau Cove Provincial Park (www.env.gov.bc.ca), which has a small pebbly beach along a scenic stretch of coastline.

In Squamish (www.exploresquamish.com), you have views both of the waterfront and the mountains, particularly the iconic Stawamus Chief that looms above the highway. As you continue toward Whistler (www.whistler.com), the road begins to climb, and both forests and peaks surround you. Keep your camera handy, but pull off at one of the many turnouts to take in the views. At several viewpoints, informational kiosks explore the region's First Nations heritage, a "Cultural Journey" designed in partnership with Whistler's Squamish Lil'wat Cultural Centre (www.slcc.ca).

With rock faces plunging down to the roadway and forested islands offshore, you can easily become distracted by the scenery, so drive carefully. Watch your speed, as the speed limit changes frequently, as do the number of travel lanes. October-March, drivers are required to have winter tires or carry (and know how to use) chains, since sections of Highway 99 can become snow-covered and slippery. Whatever the season, this drive is a striking one, so pack up the car and hit the road from sea to sky.

ages 5-12 $20), where you can explore the mine's complicated history and get a glimpse of what it was like to work in the 130-mile (210-km) network of tunnels underground. Begin the 30-minute tour by donning a hard hat and riding a train into the mine. Guides demonstrate explosives, drilling tools, and how the "muck" (rocks sparkling with copper) was hauled out of the tunnels. Tours are offered throughout the day, but schedules vary seasonally. The temperature in the mine (54°F/12°C) can feel chilly, so bring a sweater.

Above ground, head for the 1923 mill building that rises 20 stories into the hill; inside, where workers had to climb 375 steps to reach the building's highest level, watch "Boom," an entertaining 15-minute multimedia presentation about how workers processed the copper. Nearby, you can also explore a museum building and watch an interesting 15-minute film about the mine's history. The Britannia Mine Museum is 32 miles (52 km) north of Vancouver and 7.5 miles (12 km) south of Squamish, along Highway 99.

SHANNON FALLS PROVINCIAL PARK

Pull off the highway between Britannia Beach and Squamish for a short stroll to BC's third highest waterfall. At Shannon Falls Provincial Park (Hwy. 99, 604/986-9371, www. env.gov.bc.ca, dawn-dusk daily, free), the falls descend 1,100 feet (335 m) in a narrow rushing gush. An easy 0.25-mile (400-m) walking trail leads through the forest to the falls. Beyond the falls, up a short steep trail (there are stairs), you can hike to another viewpoint for a closer look at the cascading waters.

Shannon Falls is 36 miles (58 km) north of Vancouver and 1.25 miles (2 km) south of Squamish. The park has a snack bar and restrooms with flush toilets (mid-May-mid-Oct.).

✪ SEA-TO-SKY GONDOLA

For spectacular views of Howe Sound, the Chief, and the surrounding mountains, take a ride up the Sea-to-Sky Gondola (36800 Hwy. 99, 604/892-2550, www. seatoskygondola.com, 9:30am-6pm

Sun.-Wed., 9:30am-8pm Thurs.-Sat. mid-May-mid-Sept., 10am-5pm daily mid-Sept.-Oct., 10am-4pm daily Nov.-mid-May, adults $48, seniors $44, ages 13-18 $30, ages 6-12 $20). A 10-minute trip in the eight-passenger gondola whisks you up to the 2,790-foot (850-m) summit, where you can enjoy the vistas, have lunch on the deck at the Summit Lodge, and access a network of hiking trails. Purchase your gondola tickets online at least 24 hours before your visit to save a few dollars.

Sky Pilot Suspension Bridge

Once you've taken the gondola to the summit, a highlight is the Sky Pilot Suspension Bridge, a 330-foot (100-m) span that crosses from the Summit Lodge to a viewing platform with expansive views. If you're afraid of heights, don't worry; you don't have to cross the bridge to reach most of the hiking trails.

Another adventure that begins from the gondola summit is the Via Ferrata (604/892-2550, www. seatoskygondola.com, daily May-Oct., tour times vary, over age 7

$109). This "iron way" gives you the experience of rock climbing without needing any special climbing experience. With a guide, you take a short hike down from the Summit Lodge. From there, you clip into a safety cable, cross bridges and a catwalk, and climb a series of steel rungs up the rock face. You'll have beautiful views on this 1.5-hour tour, but skip this activity if you're acrophobic. You have to purchase a gondola ticket in addition to the Via Ferrata tour fee. Kids under eight are not allowed on the Via Ferrata.

The gondola, which closed for extensive refurbishment in 2019, is scheduled to reopen in 2020, when they also plan to launch a new Elevated Tree Walk experience. Check for updates before visiting.

Hiking

A number of hiking trails start at the gondola summit. Two are easy walking paths: the 0.25-mile (400-m) Spirit Trail, a flat loop trail with interpretive panels about the region's First Nations, and the Panorama Trail, a 1-mile (1.6-km) loop that takes you to a lookout with excellent views of the Stawamus Chief.

Also starting from the summit is the moderate Wonderland Trail. This forested 1-mile (1.6-km) loop has a couple of slightly steeper segments before flattening out as it circles small Wonderland Lake.

Experienced hikers can pick from several challenging trails that begin at the gondola summit, including the intermediate Shannon Basin Loop Trail (6 miles/9.7 km) and the more difficult Al's Habrich Ridge Trail (7.5 miles/12 km) and Skyline Ridge Trail (15 miles/24

km). Check with gondola staff for trail conditions before attempting these longer hikes, and be sure you have water, snacks, warm clothing, and a rain-resistant jacket, even if it's sunny and warm when you set out; the mountain weather here can change quickly.

Want a workout? You can hike up to the gondola summit on the Sea-to-Summit Trail and then ride the gondola (one-way $15) back down. Average hikers should allow 3-5 hours for this steady 4.5-mile (7.2-km) climb.

Winter Activities

The Sea-to-Sky Gondola is normally open year-round. December-April, weather permitting, trails are open for winter walking and snowshoeing, and kids can slide down a hill on inner tubes in the tube park. Before planning a winter visit, phone for trail conditions and current operating hours.

Food

The small Basecamp Café (9am-3pm daily) at the gondola base sells coffee, drinks, trail mix, pastries, and a few sandwiches, but it's worth waiting till you get to the Summit Restaurant and Edge Bar (10am-5:30pm daily, $9-14), in the lodge at the top of the gondola, for a meal with a view. The kitchen cooks up burgers, sandwiches, salads, and baked goods and serves beer from Squamish's Howe Sound Brewing Company. In summer, Bodhi's Plaza BBQ sells barbecue, ice cream, and drinks from an outdoor window. If you prefer to picnic, you can bring your own food.

Parking

Although you can park for free in the lot at the gondola base, stays in this lot are limited to three hours. If you're planning to do a longer hike or linger at the top (or if this parking area is full), park in the free lot at Darrell Bay, on Highway 99 opposite Shannon Falls Provincial Park, 0.3 mile (500 m) south of the gondola.

To walk from the Darrell Bay parking area to the gondola base, carefully cross Highway 99 toward Shannon Falls and follow the Shannon Falls Connector Trail, which has signs directing you toward to the Sea-to-Sky Gondola.

Shuttle

To visit the gondola for the day from Vancouver, you can also take the **Squamish Connector shuttle** (hours vary seasonally, round-trip, including lift tickets, adults $89, seniors $79, ages 6-18 $54, under age 6 $35). It picks up passengers in the morning from several points in downtown Vancouver, including the Hyatt Hotel (1098 Melville St.), Library Square (Robson St. and Homer St.), and Waterfront Centre (W. Cordova St.), and will return you to the city in the late afternoon.

FLIGHTSEEING

For up-close views of Squamish's mountains and big-picture vistas over Howe Sound, take a flight-seeing tour with **Sea-to-Sky Air** (Squamish Airport, 46041 Government Rd., 604/898-1975, www.seatoskyair.ca). Among the options are the Sea to Skypilot tour (adults $96), a 25-minute airborne introduction to the region, and the 35-minute Squamish Explorer

(adults $169). Tours depart from the tiny Squamish airport on the town's north side.

❂ BRACKENDALE EAGLES PROVINCIAL PARK

Hundreds of bald eagles come to winter north of Squamish late November-mid-February in the protected 1,865-acre (755-ha) environs of **Brackendale Eagles Provincial Park** (www.env.gov.bc.ca). It's one of the most significant winter eagle populations in North America. In 1994, volunteers counted a record-setting 3,769 eagles in the vicinity.

You can't actually enter the park during the eagle season; it's closed to visitors October-March to provide a protected habitat for the birds. However, you can watch the eagles from across the river. **Eagle Run Park** (Government Rd., dawn-dusk daily), along the municipal dyke, has several viewing points where you can spot the birds. Bring binoculars if you have them. On weekends late November-January, volunteer interpreters staff the Eagle Run viewing area (10am-3pm Sat.-Sun.) and can tell you more about the eagles and their migration patterns.

From Vancouver or points south, follow Highway 99 past downtown Squamish, turn left (west) onto Mamquam Road, and then go right (north) on Government Road toward Brackendale.

BREWERIES AND DISTILLERIES

Squamish has embraced the craft beverage movement, with micro-breweries, cider makers, and distilleries setting up shop around town.

Pizza and beer? What's not to

like, especially with quirkily named brews like "Careful Man, There's a Beverage Here" (an IPA) or "Asking for a Friend" (a raspberry sour)? Pair them with your pies in the pub-style tasting room at Backcountry Brewing (1201 Commercial Way, Suite 405, 604/567-2739, www. backcountrybrewing.com, noon-11pm Mon.-Thurs., noon-midnight Fri., 11am-midnight Sat., 11am-11pm Sun.).

Northyards Cider Co. (38936 Queensway, Suite 9, 604/815-2197, http://northyardscider.com, noon-10pm Mon.-Thurs., noon-11pm Fri.-Sat., noon-8pm Sun.) makes several varieties of cider from BC apples, which is served on tap and in cocktails, alongside charcuterie, cheeses, and other nibbles, in a two-level tasting lounge.

In a space that recalls a basement rec room, Gillespie's Distillery (38918 Progress Way, Unit 8, 604/390-1122, www. gillespiesfinespirits.com, tasting room 1pm-6pm Wed.-Sun., cocktail lounge 5pm-midnight Fri.-Sat.) offers tastings of its products, which include vodka, gin, a raspberry gin, and limoncello. On weekends, the tasting room morphs into a casual cocktail lounge.

RECREATION

HIKING

✪ Stawamus Chief Provincial Park

Looming above Highway 99 north of the Sea-to-Sky Gondola, the rocky cliff known as the Chief has long been a must-do climb for experienced hikers and rock climbers. A challenging but popular day hike takes you from the Chief's base to the top of the cliffs in the Stawamus Chief Provincial Park (Hwy. 99, 604/986-9371, www.env.gov.bc.ca or http://seatoskyparks.com, dawn-dusk daily).

The Chief actually has three summits, and you can choose to hike one or all. First Peak, at 2,000 feet (610 m), draws the most hikers; from the summit, you have great views of Howe Sound. From the parking lot to the First Peak summit is just 2.5 miles (4 km) round-trip. However, because the trail is quite steep, most hikers allow 2-3 hours.

Second Peak, at 2,150 feet (655 m), has lots of viewpoints from its summit, looking across Howe Sound, the town of Squamish, and the mountains in nearby Garibaldi Provincial Park. From the parking lots, it's 3 miles (5 km) round-trip to the Second Peak. Allow 4-5 hours. Third Peak is the tallest of the three summits, rising 2,300 feet (702 m). You can hike to Third Peak directly from the base or continue from the Second Peak trail. Either route is 4.5 miles (7 km) round-trip; allow 5-7 hours.

The hikes up the Chief are considered intermediate-level adventures, but note that on the routes to First and Second Peaks, there are sections where you need to climb ladders or grab onto chains to help you reach the top. For all these hikes, bring water, snacks, a rain jacket, and warm layers. Get an early start, and especially in the summer, hike on a weekday to avoid congestion on these often busy trails.

Garibaldi Provincial Park

The region's largest provincial park, the 750-square-mile

(1,942-square-km) Garibaldi Provincial Park (www.env.gov.bc.ca) extends from Squamish north to Whistler and beyond. Hikers have a lot of territory to explore in this vast park, with more than 55 miles (90 km) of hiking trails.

The park's southernmost section, Diamond Head, is closest to Squamish and includes the park's namesake, the 8,786-foot (2,678-m) Mount Garibaldi. For experienced day hikers, a scenic trail in the Diamond Head area leads up to Elfin Lakes (7 miles/11 km, each way); allow three to five hours one-way. To find the trailhead, turn east off Highway 99 onto Mamquam Road, 2.5 miles (4 km) north of downtown Squamish. Follow the road past the Squamish Golf and Country Club, then turn north (left) onto Highland Way South and follow the road through the Quest University campus. Turn left onto Mamquam Road, which becomes Garibaldi Park Road and which leads to the parking lot. It's 10 miles (16 km) from the highway to the parking area.

Elfin Lakes in Garibaldi Provincial Park

Farther north, you can do several day hikes in the park's Black Tusk/Garibaldi Lake sector. It's a 6-mile (9.7-km) climb to Garibaldi Lake. Allow 3-4 hours each way; the trail has an elevation change of nearly 2,800 feet (850 m). From the same starting point, you can hike to Taylor Meadows. This 4.75-mile (7.6-km) route follows the Garibaldi Lake trail for the first 3.75 miles (6 km) before heading up into the alpine meadows. Allow 3-4 hours each way; the trail also has an elevation change of about 2,800 feet (850 m). The Garibaldi Lake parking lot is 23 miles (37 km) north of Squamish or 12 miles (19 km) south of Whistler, along Highway 99.

At the park's higher elevations, snow is usually on the ground October-June or July. Check the trail conditions report on the website before you set out.

CYCLING

While plenty of serious bicyclists tackle the area's trails and byways, you don't have to be a hard-core mountain biker to explore Squamish on two wheels. Blazing Saddles Adventures (1861 Mamquam Rd., 604/815-7696, www.blazingsaddlesadventures.com) provides a gentler introduction to pedaling along Howe Sound, the Squamish River estuary, and through the woods, offering 2.5-3-hour eco-tours (from $99 pp) on easy-to-ride electric mountain bikes. Tours run spring-fall; call for specific tour times. They also rent e-bikes.

RAFTING

Two rivers in the Squamish area offer white-water rafting adventures. Trips on the Cheakamus River are gentler, with Class I and

II rapids, good for family excursions. The faster **Elaho-Squamish River,** with Class III and IV rapids, will give you more of a thrill. For the Elaho trips, kids generally need to be at least 12 years old and weigh at least 90 pounds (40 kg).

Squamish Rafting Company (40446 Government Rd., 604/898-4677 or 888/498-4677, http:// squamish-rafting.com) offers full-day Elaho River trips (Apr.-Oct., adults $179, ages 12-16 $165) that include a barbecue lunch. They also run half-day Cheakamus River family trips (Apr.-Oct., adults $119, ages 5-16 $79). In winter, when hundreds of eagles nest at Brackendale Eagles Provincial Park, the company operates guided half-day **Wilderness & Eagle Viewing Float Tours** (Nov.-Feb., adults $119, ages 5-16 $79) that enable you to view the eagles from the river, closer than you can see them from the shore.

Canadian Outback Rafting (40900 Tantalus Rd., 866/565-8735, www.canadianoutbackrafting.com) runs Elaho River trips (May-Sept., adults $160, ages 13-16 $140) and Cheakamus River float trips (May-Sept., adults $110, ages 5-16 $75). Whistler-based **Wedge Rafting** (211-4293 Mountain Square, Whistler, 604/932-7171 or 888/932-5899, http://wedgerafting.com) operates Elaho (May-Sept., adults $169, ages 12-16 $149) trips as well.

SAILING
Squamish is located on Howe Sound, North America's southernmost fjord, which you can explore aboard a 40-foot (64-m) sailing yacht with **Canadian Coastal** (www.canadiancoastal.com).

Choose a three-hour afternoon sail ($129 pp) or a four-hour sunset dinner cruise (call for times and rates), departing from Squamish Harbour (37778 Loggers Ln.) near downtown.

PADDLE-BOARDING
Another way to get out on Howe Sound is on a stand-up paddleboard. **Norm Hann Expeditions** (604/848-8792, http://normhann.com) offers guided SUP tours on the fjord's waters. The two-hour **Howe Sound Tour** ($99 pp) includes instruction as well as a guided paddle. On the popular 3.5-hour early-morning **Coffee Tour** ($149 pp), you paddle along Howe Sound en route to a local café for coffee.

ROPE RUNNER AERIAL PARK
While Squamish has plenty of natural adventures, you can challenge your balance and strength on this human-made one. Constructed in a parking lot near the Squamish Adventure Centre, **Rope Runner Aerial Park** (38400 Loggers Ln., 604/892-4623, www.roperunnerpark.com, 10am-3pm Wed.-Sun. mid-Apr.-June, 10am-4pm daily July-Aug., 11am-3pm Sept., 2-hour climbing session adults $47, ages 10-18 $42, ages 7-9 $37) tests you with 50 different elements, from vertical climbs to slack lines. As you venture higher on this ropes course, you'll look over the granite monolith of the Squamish Chief, before you swing back to earth with an optional free fall.

FESTIVALS AND EVENTS
A weekend of outdoor music, from indie to alt-rock to folk and more,

the **Squamish Constellation Festival** (www.constellationfest.ca, July) launched in 2019, highlighting Canadian musicians. Performers have included Serena Ryder, Jessie Reyez, and A Tribe Called Red.

Wondering how lumberjacks get their jollies? At the **Squamish Days Loggers Sports Festival** (www.squamishdays.ca, July-Aug.), a weekend of family fun, you can watch competitions in ax-throwing, tree-climbing, birling (also known as log rolling), and other events, and enjoy pancake breakfasts, bed races, barbecues, and more.

FOOD AND ACCOMMODATIONS

A modern lounge-style dining room in Squamish's oldest building—built in 1910—**Salted Vine Kitchen + Bar** (37991 2nd Ave., 604/390-1910, www.saltedvine.ca, 3pm-9pm Wed.-Sat., 10am-1:30pm and 3pm-9pm Sun., $17-29) serves creative cocktails (including interesting "designated driver" options) and plates to share. During afternoon happy hour, you might snack on a charcuterie platter or gochujang-sauced chicken wings. Later, look for dishes like beet and burrata salad, bucatini with grilled Humboldt squid, or soy-braised short ribs.

You'll have to hunt for tiny **Kululu Café** (38209 Westway Ave., 604/390-3933, 11:30am-3:30pm Mon.-Tues., 11:30am-3:30pm and 5pm-8pm Wed.-Fri., $5-13), a Japanese noodle shop and coffeehouse in a Squamish strip mall. Carefully prepared bowls of tuna poke, spicy *tantan* noodles, organic chicken in a sesame-miso sauce, and other Japanese-style salads, rice, and noodle dishes accompany organic coffees and teas plus a selection of sweets.

Tall Tree Bakery

Stop in early before the goodies sell out at **Tall Tree Bakery** (1201 Commercial Way, Suite 404, 604/849-0951, www.talltreebakery.com, 8am-5pm Wed.-Fri., 9am-4pm Sat.-Sun.), a deliciously aromatic to-go bakeshop, whether you're looking for freshly baked scones, a seasonal fruit Danish, or a sandwich for the trail. The cookies, particularly the cranberry-pecan and double chocolate chip, are excellent, as is the coffee from local roaster Counterpart Coffee.

In the Squamish Town Hub (1861 Mamquam Rd.), a collective of independent boutiques and eateries, **Alice & Brohm Ice Cream** (250/571-9978, www.aliceandbrohm.com, 2pm-8pm Mon.-Fri., noon-8pm Sat.-Sun.) makes creamy soft-serve ice cream from fresh blueberries, blackberries, and other fruit. It offers vegan alternatives. In the same complex, pause for coffee, a muffin, or a sandwich at **Cloudburst Café** (604/567-5646, http://locavorebarandgrill.com, 6am-6pm daily) or have a picnic lunch from the Locavore Food Truck (604/567-5646, http://locavorebarandgrill.com, 11am-4pm Wed.-Sat., 9am-6pm Sun.).

If you want to stay overnight in Squamish, one of the nicest spots is the Executive Suites Hotel and Resort (40900 Tantalus Rd., Garibaldi Highlands, 604/815-0048 or 877/815-0048, www.executivesuitessquamish.com, $125-229 d), where many of the modern studio, one-, and two-bedroom suites with kitchens overlook the mountains. Another mid-range option off Highway 99 is the Sandman Hotel & Suites Squamish (39400 Discovery Way, 604/848-6000 or 800/726-3626, www.sandmanhotels.ca, $149-199).

GETTING THERE AND AROUND
CAR
It's a one-hour, 40-mile (65-km) drive from Vancouver to Squamish via Highway 1 and the Sea-to-Sky Highway. From downtown Vancouver, take West Georgia Street to the Lions Gate Bridge. After crossing the bridge, bear left toward Marine Drive west/Highway 1/Highway 99. Enter Marine Drive and stay in the far right lane to take the first right onto Taylor Way, following signs for "Whistler." Follow Taylor Way up the hill, and exit left onto Highway 1 west. Continue on Highway 1 until it merges with Highway 99, the Sea-to-Sky Highway, which will take you to Squamish.

BUS
While it's easiest to explore Squamish if you have a car, it's possible to get from Vancouver to Squamish on the bus. Designed for commuters, the Squamish Connector (604/802-2119, www.squamishconnector.com, day pass adults $25) can take you between the Squamish Adventure Centre (38551 Loggers Ln.) and downtown Vancouver if your travel times fit with the bus schedule. YVR Whistler SkyLynx buses (604/326-1616, http://yvrskylynx.com) transport passengers from Vancouver International Airport (3 hours, one-way $60) to the Squamish Adventure Centre.

Once you've arrived in Squamish, you can take local buses that BC Transit (604/892-5559, http://bctransit.com/squamish) operates. Use the trip planner on the website to map in-town routes.

INFORMATION AND SERVICES
At the Squamish Adventure Centre, off Highway 99, Tourism Squamish (38551 Loggers Ln., 604/815-4994 or 877/815-5084, www.tourismsquamish.com, 8am-5pm daily mid-May-mid-Sept., 8:30am-4:30pm daily mid-Sept.-mid-May) provides lots of information about the region, including details about hiking trails. The building has a café and restrooms, handy for a Sea-to-Sky pit stop.

Whistler

Nearly three million visitors every year make their way to this mountain town that has a permanent population of only 12,000. Restaurants, pubs, and shops line the walkways of the village's alpine-style pedestrian plaza, where all paths lead, sooner or later, to the ski lifts. Most visitors come to get outdoors—to ski or snowboard in winter, and to hike, cycle, canoe, kayak, rock climb, or zip-line in the warmer months. Others simply want to stroll through the pedestrian village and perhaps ride the gondola to gaze across the mountains.

Just a two-hour drive from Vancouver, Whistler is close enough for a day trip. If you enjoy outdoor adventures, though, you might want to spend two days or more. There's plenty to do!

Whistler has several neighborhoods stretching along Highway 99, with the main Whistler Village about midway through the area. Creekside, where there's a separate base village with its own lifts, and Function Junction, a more industrial area with some of the town's services, are south of Whistler Village. The Upper Village and Blackcomb base areas are north of Whistler Village.

SIGHTS AND ACTIVITIES
✪ WHISTLER-BLACKCOMB
From more than 200 trails for skiing and snowboarding to mountain biking, gondola rides, hiking, zip-lining, and much

more, the two-mountain Whistler-Blackcomb Resort (604/967-8950 or 800/766-0449, www.whistlerblackcomb.com) has scads of outdoor things to do all year long.

Whistler's PEAK 2 PEAK Gondola

PEAK 2 PEAK Gondola
Whistler's PEAK 2 PEAK Gondola (10:15am-5pm daily, adults $70, seniors $63, ages 13-18 $60, ages 7-12 $35) runs 2.7 miles (4.4 km) between Whistler and Blackcomb Mountains. It holds the world's record for the longest unsupported span (that is, the straight-line distance between two towers) at 1.88 miles (3 km) and for the highest lift of its kind, rising 1,427 feet (436 m) above the valley floor. It transports skiers and snowboarders between the two mountains in winter, and spring-fall it's open to sightseers to enjoy the peaks' panoramas.

Allow about two hours for a sightseeing trip on the PEAK 2 PEAK Gondola. The PEAK 2 PEAK ride itself takes about 20 minutes, but to reach the gondola station, you need to take either the Whistler Village

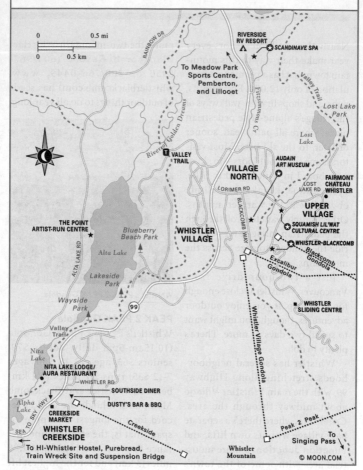

Whistler

0   0.5 mi

0   0.5 km

RAINBOW DR

RIVERSIDE
RV RESORT
★ SCANDINAVE SPA
★

To Meadow Park
Sports Centre,
Pemberton,
and Lillooet

Fitzsimmons Cr.

Valley Trail

Lost Lake
Park

River of Golden Dreams

Lost
Lake

T VALLEY
TRAIL

VILLAGE
NORTH

AUDAIN
ART MUSEUM

LOST Lake Rd

FAIRMONT
CHATEAU
WHISTLER

LORIMER RD

THE POINT
ARTIST-RUN CENTRE ★

Blueberry
Beach Park

WHISTLER
VILLAGE

BLACKCOMB WAY

UPPER
VILLAGE

★ SQUAMISH LIL'WAT
CULTURAL CENTRE

WHISTLER-BLACKCOMB
Blackcomb
Gondola

ALTA LAKE RD

Alta Lake

Excalibur
Gondola

Lakeside
Park

WHISTLER
SLIDING CENTRE

Wayside
Park

99

Whistler Village Gondola

Valley
Trail

Nita
Lake

NITA LAKE LODGE/
AURA RESTAURANT

—WHISTLER RD

SOUTHSIDE DINER

DUSTY'S BAR & BBQ

Alpha
Lake

SEA TO SKY HWY

CREEKSIDE
MARKET

WHISTLER
CREEKSIDE

← To HI-Whistler Hostel, Purebread,
Train Wreck Site and Suspension Bridge

Creekside

Peak 2 Peak

To
Singing Pass

Whistler
Mountain

© MOON.COM

Gondola or the Blackcomb Gondola, which add another 25 minutes each way. If you plan to go hiking, allow additional time.

Gondola tickets are typically cheaper if you buy them online in advance, but check the weather forecast first. The views are obviously best on a sunny clear day.

Cloudraker Skybridge

Crossing the **Cloudraker Skybridge** (www.whistlerblackcomb.com, 10am-4pm Mon.-Thurs., 10am-5:30pm Fri.-Sun. late June-early Sept., 10am-4pm daily early-mid-Sept.), a 425-foot (130-m) suspension bridge high above the Whistler Bowl, feels like walking into the clouds, as you swing gently from Whistler Peak to the West Ridge. A viewing platform on the far side of the bridge, dubbed "The Raven's Eye," gives 360-degree views of the surrounding mountains.

You need to purchase a PEAK 2 PEAK Gondola ticket to access the Skybridge, which is at the Top of the World Summit on Whistler Mountain. Take the Whistler Village Gondola or the PEAK 2 PEAK Gondola to the Roundhouse Lodge, then follow the Peak Express Traverse, a 0.4-mile (0.6-km) gravel walking trail, to the Peak Express chairlift, which takes you to the suspension bridge. Have your camera ready as you ride the chair up; there's a cool view of the bridge hanging above a glacier.

You can return to the Roundhouse on the Peak Express chair. Several hiking trails also start from the Top of the World Summit.

Via Ferrata

Want to try rock climbing but don't have any training or experience? Consider Whistler's Via Ferrata (604/938 9242, www. mountainskillsacademy.com, 4 hours, adults $169, ages 12-18 $149), a guided climbing route that's open to anyone who's reasonably fit, even if you've never done any climbing. The name comes from the Italian for "iron way," and the Via Ferrata route includes a series of iron rungs built into the mountain, which provide handgrips and footholds as you ascend the rock face. You clip on to a series of safety cables during your climb, done in small groups with a guide. Your guide will give you tips as you ascend and talk you through some of the more challenging sections.

The Via Ferrata route starts with a short hike up from the Whistler Roundhouse (at the top of the Whistler Village Gondola) across a boulder field or a snowy slope or both, depending on the season, to the start of the climbing route. After your climb, you hike or take the chairlift back to your starting point. Wear sturdy hiking shoes, and bring a rainproof jacket and a small backpack with water and snacks.

You need to purchase a PEAK 2 PEAK Gondola ticket in addition to the Via Ferrata tour ticket. Via Ferrata tours are seasonal, generally beginning in late June-early July and continuing until early October; tours typically start at 9am or 1pm, but check in advance.

on the Whistler Sky Walk

Whistler Sky Walk

Easier than the Via Ferrata, the Whistler Sky Walk (604/938-9242, www.mountainskillsacademy.com, 2 hours, adults $119, over age 8 $99) is a guided hike along a series of narrow paths and ledges high on the mountain, with several stops to take in the views. As on the Via Ferrata,

ONE DAY IN WHISTLER

If you've come to North America's largest winter sports resort during the ski season, you'll likely spend your day out on the snow. But if you're at Whistler before the snow falls, here's how to organize a great one-day trip.

MORNING

Whistler is on the traditional territory of two First Nations, so start your day with a visit to the modern Squamish Lil'wat Cultural Centre, where you can learn about the history and present-day culture of these communities. The excellent Audain Art Museum has noteworthy collections of Northwest Coast native masks, works by contemporary Vancouver photog-

rest stop on Whistler's Via Ferrata

raphers, and paintings by BC's Emily Carr. If you want to know more about how Whistler became the outdoor resort it is today, wander over to the informative Whistler Museum, which tells the stories of many area entrepreneurs.

AFTERNOON

Then you want to get outdoors, whether you head up the mountain for a ride on the PEAK 2 PEAK Gondola, which wings you between Whistler and Blackcomb Mountains; take in the views as you sway over the Cloudraker Skybridge suspension bridge; challenge yourself with a climb on the Via Ferrata or Whistler Sky Walk; go zip-lining or mountain biking; or simply take a hike. The biggest challenge might be seeing how many activities you can fit into your single day.

When you've had your fill of outdoor adventure, relax at the forested Scandinave Spa, a Scandinavian-style bath experience where you alternate between hot soaks and cold plunges.

EVENING

Choose one of Whistler's top dining rooms, perhaps Araxi or the Bearfoot Bistro, for a leisurely evening meal. At Bearfoot Bistro, you can even have a nightcap in their Ketel One Ice Room, the coldest vodka tasting room in the world—a unique way to cap off your active Whistler day.

---

you clip onto a network of safety cables as you walk the route and over a short suspension bridge. While it could still be difficult for anyone with a fear of heights, the Sky Walk is primarily horizontal, rather than vertical, making it more like a moderately challenging hike than a rockface climb.

You begin the Sky Walk experience with a hike up from the Roundhouse Lodge (at the top of

the Whistler Village Gondola)—the path can be snow-covered early in the season—and after you navigate the Sky Walk, you hike back down to the Roundhouse. Wear hiking shoes, and bring a small daypack with water, snacks, and a rain jacket.

You need to purchase a PEAK 2 PEAK Gondola ticket in addition to the Sky Walk tour ticket. Sky Walk tours run spring-fall.

Lift-Accessed Hiking

Whistler-Blackcomb has lots of hiking trails, from short easy strolls to all-day adventures, that you can access from the lifts or gondolas.

From the top of the Whistler Village Gondola or the Whistler side of the PEAK 2 PEAK Gondola near the Roundhouse Lodge, access the moderate **Harmony Lake Trail and Loop,** a 1.6-mile (2.5-km) round-trip circuit through the forest to pretty Harmony Lake. You can extend this hike on the steeper 0.7-mile (1.1-km) **Harmony Meadows Trail,** which connects to the Harmony Lake route.

For a more challenging hike with panoramic views, take the Peak Express chair (a short walk from the Roundhouse Lodge) to the start of the 5.8-mile (9.4-km) **High Note Trail.** This trail follows the mountain ridges, with great views of the Black Tusk peak in Garibaldi Provincial Park and Cheakamus Lake far below. You can circle back on the trail and ride the lift down, or for an all-day adventure, hike back down to the village; the latter route is about 14 miles (22 km).

Pick up a trail map showing these and other hiking routes at the **Whistler Visitor Centre** (4230 Gateway Dr.) or get one online at the website of **Whistler-Blackcomb** (www.whistlerblackcomb.com).

Lift-Accessed Mountain Biking

Have you seen those cyclists, suited up in knee pads, elbow pads, helmets, and other protective gear, flying down the mountain trails? At Whistler-Blackcomb, you can join them, whether you're learning to mountain bike or whizzing down those trails yourself at North America's largest mountain bike park.

Mid-May-mid-October, more than 70 trails across four different areas are open to mountain bikers, who take their bikes up the lifts. Choose among several different ticket options, from a three-ride sampler to multiday passes to packages that include lift tickets and lessons. Rent bikes through Whistler-Blackcomb or at independent shops around the village.

Winter Sports

In winter, Whistler-Blackcomb has 37 lifts providing access to 200 trails on 8,170 acres (3,300 ha), so you can ski or snowboard for days and still discover new terrain. Whistler Village is at an elevation of 2,214 feet (675 m), while the highest lift takes you up to nearly 7,500 feet (2,284 m), so the weather can be very different at the base than in the alpine regions. Even when there's no snow in the village, the mountains are typically covered in the white stuff late November-April.

Lift tickets (one-day adults $125-150) are most expensive when you walk up to the ticket window and purchase a single-day, same-day ticket. Discounts are available online in advance, for multiday tickets or passes, or sometimes when you buy your tickets as part of a package with lodging. Explore all the pricing options and details at **Whistler-Blackcomb** (604/967-8950 or 800/766-0449, www.whistlerblackcomb.com).

✪ SQUAMISH LIL'WAT CULTURAL CENTRE

For centuries before Whistler was an outdoor holiday destination, indigenous people called the region home. Discover this heritage at the **Squamish Lil'wat Cultural Centre** (4584 Blackcomb Way, 604/964-0999 or 866/441-7522, www.slcc.ca, 9:30am-5pm daily, adults $18, seniors and ages 13-18 $13.50, ages 6-12 $8), a fascinating multimedia exploration of the two First Nations whose traditional territory encompasses the Whistler region.

Squamish Lil'wat Cultural Centre

After rhythmic beats of a drum and a traditional First Nations welcome song greet you, watch a short film about the history and present-day culture of these two communities. Then check out the exhibits, from hand-carved canoes to woven baskets to information about indigenous languages. You can often try out a native craft or chat with "cultural ambassadors," museum staff from the Squamish or Lil'wat communities; in summer, take a guided walk through the adjacent forest, where staff explain the traditional uses of the area's plants. The center's **Thunderbird Café** uses local ingredients in dishes like salmon chowder, venison chili, and bannock (a biscuit-like bread), and the gift shop sells locally made crafts.

✪ AUDAIN ART MUSEUM

Whistler scored an art-world coup when Vancouver businessman and philanthropist Michael Audain decided to build a 56,000-square-foot (5,200-square-m) gallery in this mountain town to house much of his extensive art collection. Focusing on BC artists from the region's earliest eras to the present, the **Audain Art Museum** (4350 Blackcomb Way, www.audainartmuseum.com, 10am-5pm Sat.-Mon. and Wed.-Thurs., 10am-9pm Fri., adults and seniors $18, under age 19 free), in a striking contemporary building in the forest, has one of Canada's largest collections of work by early-20th-century artist Emily Carr; other highlights include 19th-century Northwest Coast masks and Vancouver photography.

Audain Art Museum

WHISTLER MUSEUM

Like many ski "villages" with their alpine facades and purpose-built pedestrian strolls, Whistler can seem like a manufactured community. The Whistler Museum (4333 Main St., 604/932-2019, www.whistlermuseum.org, 11am-5pm Fri.-Wed., 11am-9pm Thurs., $5 donation) tells the history of how the present-day Whistler-Blackcomb resort came to be and the stories of the entrepreneurs and innovators who made it happen.

Another way to learn more about the town and its heritage is to take the museum's one-hour Valley of Dreams Walking Tour (11am daily June-Aug., donation), starting at the Whistler Visitor Centre (4230 Gateway Dr.). You'll hear tales of the community's entrepreneurial women, the year of the naked skiers, and much more.

WHISTLER OLYMPIC PLAZA

Whistler joined Vancouver in hosting the 2010 Winter Olympic Games. One legacy of the games is now a popular photo stop: in front of the colorful Olympic rings that adorn Whistler Olympic Plaza in the village. Also in the plaza is an outdoor amphitheater, where concerts, festivals, and other special events take place.

VALLEA LUMINA

A dreamlike multimedia walk, Vallea Lumina (855/824-9955, www.vallealumina.com, daily late-May-mid-Oct., adults $30-40, ages 6-15 $25-35) incorporates lights, music, and special effects to bring an old-growth forest to life, enabling trees to talk, salmon to glow as they "swim" upstream, and a bear to appear in the smoke of a campfire.

Combining a light show and a self-guided forest walk, Vallea Lumina operates nightly at sundown spring-fall; check the website or phone for seasonal tour times. Tickets include a free shuttle from Whistler Village to the Vallea Lumina location north of town. The walk itself, along a 1-mile (1.6-km) wooded trail, takes about an hour. Although the trail can be dark in places, and there are a lot of stairs, the experience is family-friendly. A shorter winter-season tour is also offered, when the lights reflect across the snow-covered woods.

✪ SCANDINAVE SPA

To unwind after a day on the mountains, head for Scandinave Spa (8010 Mons Rd., 604/935-2424 or 888/935-2423, www.scandinave.com, 10am-9pm daily, adults $70-79, minimum age 19), a Scandinavian-style bath experience set among the trees. You alternate between heat—in a series of hot pools, saunas, and steam baths—and brief cold plunges in a chilled pool or shower, following each sequence with a period of relaxation in the lounges or in a hammock in the forest. To make the experience even more tranquil, the spa has a "silence" policy; you can't talk in the bath area.

Bring your own bathing suit. The spa provides towels and lockers. Several types of massage treatments are available for an additional fee. Scandinave Spa is 2 miles (3.5 km) north of Whistler Village, along Highway 99.

WHISTLER ON A BUDGET

Whistler is one of those destinations where there are more things to do than you could pack into a summer-long stay, but many of those activities can be budget-blowing adventures. If you're watching your loonies but still want to enjoy the best of what Whistler has to offer, follow these tips for organizing your Whistler stay.

- **Come off-season.** If you can schedule your Whistler visit for the spring (May-early June) or fall (Sept.-Oct.), you'll often find lower rates for accommodations and occasional deals for tours and activities.

- **Look for free or low-cost activities.** You can hike or cycle many trails around Whistler without purchasing a lift ticket to go up on the mountain. Go for a swim in area lakes or visit the Whistler Museum (by donation). Window-shopping in the village and walking the Valley Trail are both free too.

- **Maximize your spending.** If you do buy a lift ticket for sightseeing or hiking, get an early start and spend as much time as you'd like up on the mountain. You can stay on the mountain all day on your single ticket.

- **Pack a lunch.** Look for accommodations with kitchen facilities so you can prepare some of your own meals, even if it's just fruit and yogurt for breakfast or a sandwich for the trail. Another option is to have your big meal out at lunch when restaurant prices are a little lower than in the evenings.

- **Go easy on the booze.** Many of Whistler's bars and après-ski hangouts have free live music that you can enjoy for the price of a drink.

TRAIN WRECK SITE AND SUSPENSION BRIDGE

After a freight train derailed near Whistler in 1956, a logging company towed the mangled railcars into the woods nearby, where they were abandoned. Over the years, local graffiti artists began using the train cars as their canvas, and today, Whistler's **train wreck site** (off Jane Lakes Rd., www.whistler.ca, dawn-dusk daily, free), south of town near Cheakamus Crossing, is an unusual outdoor art gallery, with the train cars tagged and retagged with vivid designs.

From Jane Lakes Road, you can follow a section of the Sea-to-Sky Trail that leads to a **suspension bridge** over the Cheakamus River that connects to the train site. It's a 30-minute walk through the woods.

RECREATION
HIKING AND BIKING

Winding 25 miles (40 km) through the Whistler area, the paved **Valley Trail** (www.whistler.ca) is open to both walkers and cyclists. You can follow short stretches of the trail, for example, between the Blackcomb base area and Whistler Village, or head north to Green Lake or south to the Creekside area and beyond.

Close to Whistler Village (follow the Valley Trail), **Lost Lake Park** has several easy hiking and cycling trails. Walkers can circle the lake on the Lost Lake Loop trail, while mountain bikers can follow several single-track routes through the park.

Whistler has several areas of old-growth forest with massive trees. A moderate 5-mile (8-km) loop hike takes you through one of these forests along the **Ancient Cedars Trail,** where the trees are up to 1,000 years old. The trailhead is north of the village; take Highway 99 north past Green Lake and turn left onto 16-Mile Forest Service Road. It's 3 miles (5 km) from the highway to the parking area. Bring mosquito repellent, since this area can be buggy.

Get trail maps showing these and other trails from the Whistler Visitor Centre (4230 Gateway Dr.) or Whistler municipality website (www.whistler.ca).

ZIP-LINING

Fancy a ride on the longest zip line in Canada or the United States? Ziptrek Ecotours (604/935-0001 or 866/935-0001, www.ziptrek.com) offers several different zip-line options, including The Sasquatch (daily May-mid-Oct., 2.5 hours, adults $129, seniors and ages 10-14 $109), which runs more than 7,000 feet (2 km), starting on Blackcomb Mountain and zipping down to the Whistler side.

Ziptrek also offers The Eagle (daily year-round, 2.5-3 hours, adults $149, seniors and ages 6-14 $129), with five zip lines and four treetop bridges. If zip-lining is your passion, combine the Sasquatch and Eagle tours (4.5 hours, adults $219, seniors and ages 10-14 $199). Newcomers to zip-lining or younger kids may prefer The Bear (year-round, 2.5-3 hours, adults $119, seniors and ages 6-14 $99), a slightly gentler combination of zip lines and bridges. Hours vary seasonally.

Superfly Ziplines (211-4293 Mountain Square, 604/932-0647, www.superflyziplines.com, 9am-5pm daily, 3 hours, adults $149, ages 7-12 $109) has a zip-line tour that includes a 0.6-mile (1-km) line that's more than 500 feet (150 m) high.

TREETOP ADVENTURES

If you're looking for an activity that's gentler than zip-lining but still gets you high in the trees, consider a two-hour TreeTrek Canopy Walk (604/935-0001 or 866/935-0001, www.ziptrek.com, daily year-round, adults $49, seniors and ages 6-14 $39), which follows a series of bridges suspended among the old-growth forest on Blackcomb Mountain. The highest of the eight viewing platforms rises 200 feet (60 m) above the forest floor; the oldest trees are 800 years old. On this excursion by Ziptrek Ecotours, your guide will introduce you to the local ecology as you explore the woods.

Want more of a challenge? Superfly's Treetop Adventure Course (211-4293 Mountain Square, 604/932-0647, www.superflyziplines.com, 9am-5pm daily, $69) takes you through the treetops on a ropes course, where you navigate swaying bridges, rope swings, tightropes, and zip lines. Kids not tall enough to reach 71 inches (180 cm) can try the Kids Treetop Adventure Course ($39), designed for youngsters ages 7-14 who can reach to 55 inches (140 cm).

BOBSLED AND SKELETON

During the 2010 Winter Olympic Games, the Whistler Sliding Centre (4910 Glacier Ln., 604/964-0040, www.whistlersportlegacies.com) hosted the bobsled, skeleton, and luge competitions. You can live out your almost-Olympic dreams with rides down the same slippery track that the Olympic athletes used.

Whiz down the track in the Summer Bobsleigh (daily late June-early Sept., adults $109), a bobsled on wheels. A pilot steers your sled, which holds up to four passengers and can reach speeds of 50 mph (80 km/h). Kids must be at least 12 to ride; one youth (ages 12-18) rides free with each paying adult. Participants must be 4-foot-6 to 6-foot-5 (137-196 cm) and weigh 85-285 pounds (39-129 kg).

In winter, the **Bobsleigh Experience** (daily mid-Dec.-Mar., advance reservations required, $189 pp) sends you down the ice at even faster speeds: up to 75 mph (120 km/h). The sled holds a pilot and one or two guests. For this experience, you must be age 14-75; ages 14-16 ride at a 50 percent discount when accompanied by a paying adult. All participants must be 4-foot-6 to 6-foot-8 (137-207 cm) and weigh 90-285 pounds (41-129 kg) with winter clothing on.

If you're really adventurous, ride head-first down the icy track on the **Skeleton** (daily mid-Dec.-Mar., advance reservations required, $189 pp). You get two solo runs, and you may find yourself hurtling down the track at close to 60 mph (100 km/h). Minimum age for the skeleton is 16, and the maximum is 75. All participants must be 4-foot-6 to 6-foot-5 (137-196 cm) and weigh 90-220 pounds (41-100 kg) with winter clothing on.

To reach the Whistler Sliding Centre from Whistler Village, follow Blackcomb Way to Glacier Lane.

WATER SPORTS

One of Whistler's most peaceful outdoor experiences is a kayak or canoe tour along the **River of Golden Dreams. Whistler Eco Tours** (604/935-4900 or 877/988-4900,

www.whistlerecotours.com) offers three-hour guided (adults $140, under age 13 $98) or self-guided (adults $90, under age 13 $63) paddles that start on Alta Lake, travel through a scenic wetlands area, and wrap up at beautiful Green Lake. On the guided tour, your guide will tell you about the area's ecology and give paddling tips. Both the self-guided and guided options are family-friendly and include transportation back to the village.

Whistler Eco Tours also rents single kayaks ($35 per hour) and canoes, double kayaks, stand-up paddleboards, and pedal boats (all $40 per hour) from their base in Wayside Park on Alta Lake, between the village and Creekside.

You can **swim** in several Whistler-area lakes, although the water can be chilly. You'll find beaches at **Alpha Lake** near Creekside, **Alta Lake** between Creekside and the village, **Lost Lake** near the village, and **Green Lake,** a large glacier-fed lake north of the village.

Prefer to do your swimming indoors? Visit **Meadow Park Sports Centre** (8625 Hwy. 99, 604/935-7529, www.whistler.ca, adults $8.75, ages 13-18 $5.25, ages 4-12 $4.50), a public recreational facility with a 25-meter lap pool as well as a kids' pool with a lazy river. Located 2 miles (3 km) north of the village, the center and pool are generally open 6am-10pm daily.

WINTER SPORTS

As an alternative to skiing and snowboarding on Whistler-Blackcomb, go to the **Whistler Olympic Park** (5 Callaghan Valley Rd., 604/964-0060, www.whistlersportlegacies.

com, late Nov.-early Apr., weather permitting) for **cross-country skiing** (adults $29, ages 7-18 $16), **snowshoeing** (adults $17, ages 7-18 $9), and **tobogganing** ($10, $7 each additional person in a vehicle). Gear rentals are available. The park is 15 miles (23 km) from the village; follow Highway 99 south to Callaghan Valley Road.

ENTERTAINMENT

NIGHTLIFE

One of Whistler's most popular pastimes is "après" (aka après-ski, literally "after skiing"). Here are several places where the party starts when the lifts close.

Merlin's Bar and Grill (4553 Blackcomb Way, 604/938-7700, 11am-1am daily), at the Blackcomb Mountain base, often has live music, as does the **Garibaldi Lift Company Bar & Grill** (4165 Springs Ln., 604/905-2220, 11am-1am daily), at the base of the Whistler Village Gondola. In the Creekside area, **Dusty's Bar & BBQ** (2040 London Ln., 604/905-2171, 11am-1am daily) has been pouring pints since the 1960s.

The laid-back **Dubh Linn Gate Irish Pub** (Pan Pacific Whistler Mountainside, 4320 Sundial Cres., 604/905-4047, www.dubhlinngate.com, 7am-1am daily), steps from the Whistler Village lifts, keeps 25 varieties of beer on tap and offers a long list of single-malt scotch. They serve an authentic Irish breakfast and pub fare throughout the day.

For craft beer, head for the Blackcomb base, where **HandleBar** (4557 Blackcomb Way, 604/962-2876, http://handlebar.beer, noon-midnight daily) pours local brews

and offers German-inspired bar food, from pretzels to schnitzel to currywurst.

Bearfoot Bistro (4121 Village Green, 604/932-3433, http://bearfootbistro.com, 6pm-10pm daily) is among Whistler's best restaurants, but it's also a destination for drinkers: Their **Ketel One Ice Room** is the coldest vodka tasting room in the world. Don a heavy parka (which the restaurant provides) and venture into the frosty tasting room, with its carved ice walls and year-round temperature of -25°F (-32°C). Choose a tasting flight ($48) from their selection of 50 different vodkas, made in destinations as diverse as Poland, Ukraine, and Pemberton, BC.

Several Whistler hotels have more sedate drinking scenes—more upscale lounge than rowdy party—including the **Mallard Lounge at the Fairmont Chateau Whistler** (4599 Chateau Blvd., 604/938-8000, www.fairmont.com, 11am-midnight Sun.-Thurs., 11am-1am Fri.-Sat.), known for its martinis and creative seasonal cocktails, and the **Sidecut Bar at the Four Seasons Whistler** (4591 Blackcomb Way, 604/935-3400, www.fourseasons.com, 11am-11pm daily). **Cure Lounge at Nita Lake Lodge** (2131 Lake Placid Rd., 604/966-5700, www.nitalakelodge.com, 11:30am-late daily), in the Creekside area, has a great patio overlooking the lake.

THE ARTS

The **Whistler Arts Council** (604/935-8410, www.artswhistler.com) hosts concerts, films, and other productions at Maury Young Arts Centre (4335 Blackcomb Way), where it also runs a small art gallery (www.thegallerywhistler.com).

See what's happening at The Point Artist-Run Centre (5678 Alta Lake Rd., 604/698-5482, www.thepointartists.com), which presents live music during July-August in the "Sundays at the Point" events, as well as occasional music, film, theater, and dance performances throughout the year. The facility is south of the village on the west side of Alta Lake.

FESTIVALS AND EVENTS
Spring-Summer

Plenty of special events draw visitors to Whistler, particularly late May to Canadian Thanksgiving in mid-October, when there's something on the calendar most weekends.

Bring the kids to the annual Whistler Children's Festival (www.whistlerchildrensfestival.com, July), a weekend of family-friendly arts, crafts, and entertainment ranging from African dancing to First Nations drumming. A "celebration of mindful living," Wanderlust Whistler (www.wanderlust.com, July-Aug.) includes several days of yoga classes, meditation workshops, concerts, lectures, guided hikes, and local food.

Crankworx Freeride Mountain Bike Festival (www.crankworx.com, Aug.) draws wild and crazy mountain bikers to town for a week of downhill and cross-country cycling, stunt riding, and plenty more two-wheeled fun. One of Whistler's top restaurants hosts the Araxi Longtable Series (www.araxi.com, Aug.), lavish alfresco dinners highlighting the region's late-summer bounty.

Fall-Winter

Whistler shows its artistic side during the annual Whistler Writers Festival (www.whistlerwritersfest.com, Oct.), when Canadian and international authors conduct readings, teach seminars, participate on panels, and mingle with guests to discuss their work.

In November, when it's too chilly for hiking and cycling but too early to ski, Whistler hosts the annual Cornucopia Festival (www.whistlercornucopia.com, Nov.), which draws food and wine lovers from far and wide for two weeks of wine-tastings and seminars, guest chef events, special dinners, and extravagant parties.

Whistler Film Festival (www.whistlerfilmfestival.com, Dec.) screens up to 90 movies, including world premieres, features, documentaries, and shorts during this five-day international competition. At least 50 percent of the films are Canadian. You might even spot a celebrity or two.

Whistler hosts one of North America's largest LGBTQ ski weeks, the Whistler Pride and Ski Festival (www.gaywhistler.com, Jan.), eight days of snow sports, après-ski events, parties, concerts, and more.

FOOD

Like many resort towns, Whistler offers several splurge-worthy dining rooms. If you're watching your budget, you'll need to pick your dining spots carefully, but burgers, pizza, and diner-style meals can fuel you up at moderate prices. Another money-saving option, when you're staying in a lodging with kitchen facilities, is to have one or more meals "at home" or pack a lunch for your outdoor adventures.

MODERN CANADIAN

Long considered one of Whistler's top restaurants, ✪ Araxi (4222 Village Square, 604/932-4540, www.araxi.com, 3pm-midnight daily, $30-50) emphasizes regional ingredients like fresh oysters and locally farmed produce. Line-caught tuna is grilled and paired with pearl couscous and minted cucumbers, or try roasted duck breast with polenta and poached pears. Sate your sweet tooth with the warm Valrhona chocolate fondant or the refreshing lemon tart.

Araxi

✪ Aura Restaurant (2131 Lake Placid Rd., 604/966-5715, www.nitalakelodge.com, 6:30am-11am and 5:30pm-9:30pm daily, off-season hours vary, breakfast $12-23, dinner $29-44) at Creekside's Nita Lake Lodge is worth a visit even if you're not staying here, both for its fine contemporary fare and for the lovely lakeside setting. Begin with a seasonal salad or pepper-crusted venison carpaccio; for the main course, try halibut with grilled pineapple salsa, steelhead salmon with fregola salad, or free-range chicken with savoy cabbage. On Meatless Mondays, the restaurant offers a three-course vegan prix fixe option ($39).

With more than 20,000 bottles, ✪ Bearfoot Bistro (4121 Village Green, 604/932-3433, http://bearfootbistro.com, 6pm-10pm daily, prix fixe $76-178 pp) has one of the largest wine cellars in western Canada, the better to pair with its modern Canadian cuisine. Accompanied by live jazz, dinners are multicourse prix fixe affairs that might start with a salad of locally grown root vegetables with popped buckwheat and quince, and continue with pheasant dressed with chestnut brioche and mushroom stuffing or beef striploin with a truffle vinaigrette. Sweets include ice cream whipped up tableside, mixing cream with liquid nitrogen. For a lighter meal—perhaps oysters and champagne, a game burger, or duck confit with a chili-honey glaze—take a seat in the less formal champagne lounge (from 4pm Mon.-Fri., from 3pm Sat.-Sun., $12-22), open from après-ski until late.

At casual, order-at-the-counter Hunter Gather (101-4368 Main St., 604/966-2372, www.huntergatherwhistler.com, noon-10:30pm daily, $15-25), there's local craft beer on tap and lots of local ingredients on the plates. They're known for their smoked meats like brisket, pulled pork, or chicken, but plant lovers may enjoy options like the Pemberton bowl, layered with beets and other veggies, chickpeas, sprouted legumes, and dried fruit in a miso chili vinaigrette.

JAPANESE

A longtime favorite for Japanese fare, upscale **Sushi Village** (11-4340 Sundial Cres., 604/932-3330, http://sushivillage.com, 5:30pm-10pm Mon.-Thurs., noon-2:30pm and 5:30pm-10pm Fri.-Sun., $11-48) has been keeping Whistler in *nigiri, maki,* teriyaki, and tempura since the 1980s.

Part grocery store and part quick-serve Japanese eatery, **Fuji Market** (205-4000 Whistler Way, 604/962-6251, www.fujimarket.ca, 10am-9pm daily, $9-12), in a mini mall near the Whistler Conference Centre, stocks ready-made sushi and cooks up ramen, tempura, and other inexpensive Japanese bites. You can pick up wasabi peas, kimchi, and other Asian ingredients. In the same complex, the market's owners operate a noodle house, **Oyama Ramen** (604/962-6253, www.ohyamaramen.com, 11am-9pm daily, $11-20) and the lively **Harajuku Izakaya** (604/962-7222, www.harajuku.ca, 5pm-10:30pm Sun.-Thurs., 5pm-11pm Fri.-Sat., $5-25), serving sake, beer, and Japanese small plates, including addictive fried brussels sprouts and the "rock and roll" *maki* stuffed with tempura yam, avocado, and other vegetables.

ITALIAN AND PIZZA

In a white-tablecloth dining room with comfortably spaced tables, ✪ **Il Caminetto** (4242 Village Stroll, 604/932-4442, www.ilcaminetto.ca, 5:30pm-11pm daily, $22-59) updates a classic Italian menu with regional products. Kick off your meal with a nectarine and burrata salad or seared scallops paired with a taleggio cheese-stuffed squash blossom, then look for the handmade pasta of the day or the rich wild mushroom risotto. For the secondi, try halibut with sea asparagus or grilled lamb with roasted cauliflower. The lengthy wine list highlights labels from BC and Italy.

A life raft of good value in a sea of expensive eateries, family-friendly **Pasta Lupino** (121-4368 Main St., 604/905-0400, www.pastalupino.com, 11am-9pm daily, lunch $8-14, dinner $14-18) serves a small menu of Italian classics, including spaghetti and meatballs, lasagna, and chicken parmigiana. In the evenings, pasta dinners come with soup or salad, plus homemade focaccia.

The wood-fired oven turns out traditional Neapolitan-style pizzas at **Pizzeria Antico** (101-4369 Main St., 604/962-9226, www.pizzeriaantico.ca, noon-11pm daily, lunch $9-20, dinner $14-20), like the Prosciutto con Ruccola, topped with arugula, prosciutto, tomato, and mozzarella, or the Funghi, sauced with porcini cream and layered with roasted mushrooms and onions. Several fresh salads, grilled paninis (at lunch), and pastas (at dinner) round out the menu.

halibut with sea asparagus at Il Caminetto

SPANISH

Under the same ownership as Araxi, cozy **Bar Oso** (150-4222 Village Square, 604/962-4540, http://baroso.ca, 4:30pm-midnight Mon.-Fri., 11:30am-midnight Sat.-Sun., $9-35) serves up Spanish-style tapas with a BC twist. Nibble wild scallop *crudo* with olives and oranges, a salad of roasted beets with buffalo mozzarella, or a platter of house-made charcuterie. To sip, there are local beers, sangrias, and interesting cocktails.

BURGERS

Splitz Grill (4369 Main St., 604/938-9300, www.splitzgrill.com, 11am-9pm daily, $6-14) has burgers, and not only traditional beef patties: Get lamb, bison, lentil, even salmon. Line up at the counter, order your burger, and choose from a large selection of toppings. Poutine, fries, and beer are the favored accompaniments.

DINERS

For hearty meals served with friendly sass, head for **Southside Diner** (2102 Lake Placid Rd., Creekside, 604/966-0668, www.southsidediner.ca, 7am-9pm Sun.-Thurs., 7am-10pm Fri.-Sat., $9-19) in the Creekside area. Morning menus get you going with breakfast poutine (home fries topped with poached eggs, sausage, cheese curds, and gravy), "big-ass pancakes" (yes, they're big), and the usual egg suspects. Later, you can stuff yourself with burgers, sandwiches, meatloaf, or macaroni and cheese.

VEGETARIAN

You might walk away with a green mustache after slurping down a fresh juice or smoothie at **The Green Moustache** (122-4340 Lorimer Rd., 604/962-3727, http://greenmoustachejuice.com, 8am-6pm daily, $9-15), a tiny juice bar and vegan eatery. In the morning, they serve breakfast bowls, like muesli or chia pudding topped with nuts, berries, and house-made almond or cashew milk. By midday, you might order a big salad or the Buddha Bowl, a blend of rice and quinoa piled high with fresh veggies.

BAKERIES AND CAFÉS

Whistler's best bakery, ✪ **Purebread** (www.purebread.ca) offers an irresistible array of treats, from scones and croissants to lemon crumble bars, salted caramel bars, and oversized brownies. If you're packing for a picnic, try the Dysfunction Ale bread, a hearty loaf made with spent grains from the Whistler Brewing Company. Purebread has two Whistler branches: a convenient **Village location** (Main St., Olympic Plaza, 604/962-1182, 8am-6pm daily) and their original **Function Junction shop** (1-1040 Millar Creek Rd., 604/938-3013, 8:30am-5pm daily) on the south side of town.

It's worth a detour to Creekside for the excellent sourdough cinnamon rolls and fresh baked organic breads at **Bred by Ed** (206-2067 Lake Placid Rd., 604/967-3838, http://edsbred.com, 7:30am-5pm Wed.-Sun.), a take-out bakery in a cozy cottage. Bonus for vegans: Everything on offer is plant-based. You can also find Ed's breads at the coffee and toast bar inside ecologyst (125-4338 Main St., 604/962-7873, http://ecologyst. com, 10am-7pm Sun.-Thurs., 10am-9pm Fri., 9am-9pm Sat.), a Whistler Village boutique selling high-style camp clothing and accessories.

GROCERIES AND MARKETS

The small Whistler Farmers Market (Upper Village Stroll, Blackcomb Village Base, 11am-4pm Sun. May-Oct., 2pm-7pm Wed. July-Aug.) brings locally grown produce and other goodies to the village every weekend late spring-fall, with an additional weekday market in midsummer.

Whistler Marketplace IGA (4330 Northlands Blvd., 604/938-2850, www.marketplaceiga.com, 9am-9pm daily) is the largest and most centrally located grocery store in the village.

Handy to pick up a snack or the toothpaste you forgot, the Whistler Grocery Store (4211 Village Square, 604/932-3628, www.whistlergrocery. com, 8am-11pm daily) keeps long hours and is the closest market to the slopes. If you're staying in the Creekside area, your go-to grocery is Whistler's Creekside Market (305-2071 Lake Placid Rd., 604/938-9301, www.creeksidemarket.com, 7am-10pm daily).

ACCOMMODATIONS AND CAMPING

Whistler accommodations include a range of hotels and condominium buildings. Hotels provide more services, such as on-site restaurants, ski valets, and concierge staff; some, but not all, have kitchenettes or in-room fridges and microwaves. Renting a condo is often less expensive, particularly for a family, and you'll have a kitchen where you can prepare some meals. Many Whistler lodgings charge for overnight parking, so factor that fee into your budget.

Whistler has two peak seasons: in winter for skiing and snowboarding, typically late November-April, and in July-August, when visitors come for hiking, biking, and other summer activities. The most expensive time to stay at Whistler is during the Christmas-New Year holiday, when rates soar. The February-March school holiday weeks are also pricey. During the rest of the year, lodging rates are usually lowest midweek.

Check the Tourism Whistler website (www.whistler.com) for lodging deals, particularly if you're making last-minute plans. The Whistler-Blackcomb website (www.whistlerblackcomb.com) sometimes posts discounts on accommodations as well.

UNDER CAD$150

Built to house athletes during the 2010 Winter Olympics, the HI-Whistler Hostel (1035 Legacy Way, 604/962-0025 or 866/762-4122, www.hihostels.ca, $45-51 dorm, $132-187 d) 5 miles (8 km) south of Whistler Village, offers dorm beds as well as good-value private rooms with flat-screen TVs and en suite baths. Dorms (female, male, or mixed) sleep four, each with bunk beds, reading lights, electrical outlets, lockers, and shared washrooms. Parking and Wi-Fi are included, and common areas include a café, a TV room, a lounge with a pool table, a shared kitchen, and an outdoor terrace. December-February, the hostel has a ski-party atmosphere. Summer is typically quieter, when staff organize hikes, brewery tours, and other activities. BC Transit buses to the village stop out front.

CAD$150-300

Have you ever slept in a "pod"? You can at Canada's first pod hotel. With a central location on the Village Stroll, **Pangea Pod Hotel** (4333 Sunrise Alley, 844/726-4329, www.pangeapod.com, $99-149 s, $170-285 d) has created high-style, high-tech lodgings that are more private than a hostel but less expensive than a typical hotel room. Designed for solo travelers, each of the 88 pods, clustered in eight suites, is outfitted with a double mattress, a lockable cabinet, hangers, charging ports, and a curtain in lieu of a door; in each suite, washrooms are separated into a private shower, a toilet, and vanity rooms. Female-only suites are available. Guests can chill in the living room-like café and lounge or on the rooftop patio. Store your skis, bikes, or other equipment in a gear room dubbed "the toy box."

OVER CAD$300

Catering to skiers and snowboarders in winter, and to cyclists and other active guests in summer, the ✪ **AAVA Whistler Hotel** (4005 Whistler Way, 604/932-2522 or 800/663-5644, www.aavawhistlerhotel.com, $154-450 d, parking $20) will loan you a complimentary GoPro camera to record your day's adventures (neat, right?). While it's not upscale (hotel staff say, "We don't valet your car, but we do valet your bike"), this 192-room lodging feels sociable, with lobby seating areas and a communal work-table with a charging station. There's space to lounge on the outdoor deck around the compact pool and hot tub. Outfitted with one king, two queens, or a queen plus a sofa bed, the guest rooms are crisp and modern, with mini fridges, safes, and one-cup coffeemakers; the prime top-floor units have vaulted ceilings. Wi-Fi and local calls are free. You can walk to the Whistler base in 10 minutes.

the pool at Fairmont Chateau Whistler

Like a grand mountain lodge, the ✪ **Fairmont Chateau Whistler** (4599 Chateau Blvd., off Blackcomb Way, 604/938-8000 or 800/606-8244, www.fairmont.com, $289-699 d, parking $35-39) keeps you comfortable whether you're in your room or exploring the property. The 528 rooms and suites, some with views of the slopes, have down duvets, fluffy bathrobes, flat-screen TVs, and one-cup coffeemakers. A daily resort fee ($15 per room) covers internet access, indoor and outdoor pools, the well-equipped health club, yoga classes, tennis, a shuttle to village destinations, and valet service for your skis, bikes, or golf clubs. The **Mallard Lounge** is popular for après-ski cocktails, and the hotel has several other dining outlets, including **The Grill Room** for steak and seafood and the café-style **Portobello Market & Bakery,** which spans the day from breakfast bowls and pastries to smoked meats and barbecue; it's known for its bacon-maple doughnuts.

Four Seasons Whistler Hotel

With a solicitous staff and all sorts of amenities, ✪ **Four Seasons Whistler Hotel** (4591 Blackcomb Way, 604/935-3400, www.fourseasons.com, $300-634 d, $600-2,200 suites, parking $39-45) is among Whistler's top resort hotels. Decorated in ski-lodge earth tones, the 273 rooms and suites have gas fireplaces, big closets, mini fridges, and flat-screen TVs; ask for an upper-floor unit for slope-side views. Work out in the 24-hour fitness room or swim in the heated outdoor pool. The three hot tubs and eucalyptus steam room are popular après-ski, as is the library-style **Sidecut Bar.** In Whistler's Upper Village, the Four Seasons isn't a ski-in, ski-out property, but the hotel offers a free ski concierge, so

you can leave your gear slope-side. A complimentary car service can take you around town.

On a lake in the Creekside area, ✪ **Nita Lake Lodge** (2131 Lake Placid Rd., 604/966-5700, www.nitalakelodge.com, $249-579 d, 2-bedroom suites $529-869, parking $20-30) is a beautiful setting in any season. The 77 spacious contemporary studio, one-, and two-bedroom suites on four floors have fireplaces, compact kitchenettes hidden in an armoire, and modern baths with rain showers and soaker tubs; the best units have lake views. Activities include lounging in the rooftop hot tubs, kayaking, canoeing, stand-up paddleboarding on the lake, and riding up the Valley Trail on a complimentary bicycle. Restaurants include the more formal **Aura Restaurant,** overlooking the lake, **Cure Lounge & Patio** for burgers, salads, and drinks, and casual **Fix Café,** which serves pastries, coffee, smoothies, and sandwiches. The hotel offers a free shuttle to the village or the Creekside gondola.

Feeling funky? The boutique 41-room **Adara Hotel** (4122 Village Green, 604/905-4009 or 866/502-3272, www.adarahotel.com, $169-409 d, parking $25) goes beyond typical ski-lodge style, starting from its lobby, furnished with curvaceous orange banquettes, a massive stone fireplace, and stylized antler sculptures; grab coffee and a breakfast bar here in the morning. Out on the sundeck is a small hot tub and summer-only pool. Standard rooms have electric fireplaces, French press coffeemakers, mini fridges, microwaves, and modern baths with rain showers, but the coolest units are the lofts, with a bedroom upstairs and a living area below. Wi-Fi is included.

The three-story **Listel Hotel Whistler** (4121 Village Green, 604/932-1133 or 800/663-5472, www.listelhotel.com, $152-459 d, parking $20) is simple but comfortable, with a quiet location off the Village Stroll yet close to the Whistler base lifts. Most of the 98 rooms are standard units with two queens, free Wi-Fi, coffeemakers, and mini fridges. There's a hot tub but no pool on the outdoor patio. Rates include continental breakfast. The excellent **Bearfoot Bistro** is on the property.

At **Summit Lodge Boutique Hotel** (4359 Main St., 604/932-2778 or 888/913-8811, www.summitlodge. com, $172-475 d, parking $20), the 81 studio and one-bedroom suites, with colorful graphic-print walls, all have kitchenettes. Wi-Fi and local calls are included, and you can borrow a complimentary bike to cycle around town. The Asian-style **Taman Sari Royal Heritage Spa** uses traditional Javanese herbs in its treatments. Other hotel amenities include a sauna, a hot tub, and a year-round outdoor pool. You're surrounded by lots of good restaurants, and it's a 10- to 15-minute walk to the lifts.

Location is the draw at the **Crystal Lodge Hotel & Suites** (4154 Village Green, 604/932-2221 or 800/667-3363, www.crystal-lodge. com, $235-589, parking $24), built in the 1980s, with 158 rooms in two sprawling wings directly on the Village Stroll. In the updated south wing, hotel-style rooms and studios are decorated with turquoise headboards, gray accents, and original artwork; the larger north wing units, from studios to three bedrooms, are more traditionally furnished. All rooms have coffeemakers, kettles, fridges, and Wi-Fi. The hotel provides a complimentary bike valet in summer and ski valet in winter. The narrow outdoor pool is open year-round, and the small fitness room is well stocked with cardio equipment.

You can't stay much closer to the lifts than at the 121-unit all-suite **Pan Pacific Whistler Mountainside** (4320 Sundial Cres., 604/905-2999 or 888/905-9995, www.panpacific.com, $279-689 d, parking $28-32), steps from the gondolas. Decorated with cherry-hued Craftsman-style furnishings, the studio, one-bedroom, and two-bedroom units all have full kitchens, gas fireplaces, flat-screen TVs, and DVD players. The studios nominally sleep four, with a queen Murphy bed and a sleep sofa, but the larger suites are more comfortable for families. Other amenities include a heated outdoor saltwater pool, two hot tubs, complimentary Wi-Fi, and free local phone calls. The **Dubh Linn Gate Irish Pub** is popular for drinks and pub fare, with more than 25 beers on tap and live music most nights.

Slightly farther from the gondolas than its sister property, the **Pan Pacific Whistler Village Centre** (4299 Blackcomb Way, 604/966-5500 or 888/966-5575, www. panpacific.com, $169-539 d, parking $28-32) has a more modern boutique feel, but similar amenities: suites ranging from studios to three bedrooms with full kitchens, a saltwater lap pool, two hot tubs, a sauna, and a fitness facility. Rates include breakfast, Wi-Fi, local calls, and a complimentary shuttle to get around the village. You can store your ski or snowboard gear at the Pan Pacific Mountainside.

CAMPING AND CABINS

The Riverside Resort (8018 Mons Rd., 604/905-5533, www.parkbridge. com), 2 miles (3.5 km) north of the village, has several lodging options, including campsites for tents and RVs, yurts, and sturdy log cabins. The 14 family-friendly cabins ($210-250), with solid wood furnishings, have a living room, a small kitchen, a queen bedroom, and a bath on the main level, plus a sleeping loft with two twins. They're equipped with electricity and even a flat-screen TV. Yurts ($105-145) are more rustic but have electricity and heat. Sleeping up to five, most have a bunk bed with a single over a double bed, and either a futon couch or a separate single with a trundle bed. Washrooms with showers are a short walk away. Campsites for RVs ($55-71) include both fully and partially serviced sites. There's a quiet wooded walk-in tent campground ($25-42) with sites along the river. The campground's main building has a small market and café; bicycle rentals are available. Other amenities include guest laundry, free Wi-Fi, a playground, a volleyball court, and a putting course. The Valley Trail crosses the campground property, so you can follow it into town.

CONDO RENTALS

You can book many condo accommodations through the Tourism Whistler (www.whistler.com) and Whistler-Blackcomb (www. whistlerblackcomb.com) websites

and through many of the standard online booking services for hotels. You can also find condos and houses to rent through Airbnb (www. airbnb.com).

Check locally based rental agencies, including alluraDirect (604/707-6700 or 866/425-5872, www.alluradirect.com), which sometimes offer deals that the larger booking services don't have.

INFORMATION AND SERVICES

VISITOR INFORMATION

Tourism Whistler (www.whistler. com) should be your starting point for information about the Whistler region. The website has lots of details about the area, both on and off the mountain, and it runs the year-round Whistler Visitor Centre (4230 Gateway Dr., 604/935-3357 or 877/991-9988) in the village, which supplies maps, answers questions, and books accommodations and activities. Hours vary seasonally, but the visitors center is open at least 8am-5pm daily, and until 9pm-10pm on busy weekends and holidays.

Whistler-Blackcomb (604/967-8950 or 800/766-0449, www. whistlerblackcomb.com) books lift tickets, equipment rentals, ski and snowboard lessons, and accommodations (reservations 604/296-5316 or 888/403-4727) and can provide information about other mountain activities in every season. Check the website for toll-free reservations numbers from many different countries.

Pique Newsmagazine (www. piquenewsmagazine.com) covers the

Whistler area and provides events listings.

MEDICAL SERVICES

The Whistler Health Care Centre (4380 Lorimer Rd., 604/932-4911, www.vch.ca, 8am-10pm daily) provides emergency medical services. Doctors are on-call after hours. Town Plaza Medical Clinic (40-4314 Main St., 604/905-7089, www.medicalclinicwhistler.com) will see visitors for minor issues.

Rexall (103-4360 Lorimer Rd., 604/932-2303, 9am-9pm daily, 4204 Village Square, 604/932-4251, www.rexall.ca, 9am-9pm daily, pharmacy 9am-7pm daily) has two Whistler pharmacies. Shoppers Drug Mart (121-4295 Blackcomb Way, 604/905-5666, www.shoppersdrugmart.ca, 9am-9pm daily) also provides pharmacy services.

GETTING THERE

CAR

Allow about two hours to make the 75-mile (120-km) drive between Vancouver and Whistler along the spectacular Sea-to-Sky Highway.

From downtown Vancouver, take West Georgia Street to the Lions Gate Bridge. Watch the signs carefully as you approach Stanley Park en route to the bridge to stay in the proper lane. The center lane on the three-lane bridge reverses its travel direction at different times of day, typically creating two travel lanes into the city in the morning and two travel lanes toward the North Shore during the afternoon rush hour.

After you cross the Lions Gate Bridge, bear left toward Marine Drive west/Highway 1/Highway 99. Enter Marine Drive and stay in the far right lane to take the first right onto Taylor Way (the sign says "Whistler"). Follow Taylor Way up the hill, and exit left onto Highway 1 west. Continue on Highway 1 until it merges with Highway 99 (the Sea-to-Sky Hwy.). Stay on Highway 99 through Squamish to Whistler.

AIR

A dramatic way to travel between Vancouver and Whistler, if your budget allows, is by floatplane, which takes you above Howe Sound, the Gulf Islands, and the surrounding peaks.

May-September, Harbour Air (604/274-1277 or 800/665-0212, www.harbourair.com, 45 minutes, one-way adults $164-236) flies twice daily in each direction between the Vancouver Harbour Flight Centre (1055 Canada Pl., behind the Vancouver Convention Centre, 604/274-1277) and Green Lake (8069 Nicklaus North Blvd.), 2 miles (3 km) north of Whistler Village. A free shuttle takes passengers between the Green Lake terminal and the village.

BUS

YVR Whistler SkyLynx buses (604/326-1616, http://yvrskylynx.com) take passengers from Vancouver International Airport (3 hours, one-way $65) or downtown Vancouver (2-2.5 hours, one-way $30) to Whistler. The downtown stop is on Melville Street adjacent to the Hyatt Vancouver. Buses also stop at the Squamish Adventure Centre. Check the website for discount offers.

Epic Rides (604/349-1234, www.epicrides.ca, 2 hours, one-way $24) operates several buses daily between Vancouver and Whistler. Late April-mid-November, buses stop downtown outside Burrard Station (Melville St. and Burrard St.). In winter (mid-Nov.-late Apr.), it adds early morning pickups on the UBC campus, at Granville and Broadway, and at Burrard and Comox Streets (at the Sheraton Wall Centre Hotel). Round-trip tickets are a good value at $35 per person.

GETTING AROUND
CAR

Whistler Village is a pedestrian zone, so you have to leave your car outside the village. Whistler has several public parking lots where you can park all day.

Day lots 1 to 5, on Blackcomb Way near Lorimer Road, are closest to Whistler Village. Lots 1, 2, and 3, closest to the lifts, are paid lots ($2.50 per hour, $10 per day) until 5pm; they're free 5pm-8am. Lots 4 and 5 are free in the spring and fall but require payment the rest of the year ($2.50 per hour, $5 per day mid-June-mid-Sept. and mid-Dec.-mid-Apr., free mid-Apr.-mid-June and mid-Sept.-mid-Dec.). Closer to the Blackcomb base, off Glacier Lane, day lots 6, 7, and 8 are open in winter only (free). November-March, you can't park overnight in any of the day lots; April-October, you can park for up to 24 hours.

In the Creekside area, you can park free in the Creekside base underground garage. Follow London Lane off Highway 99.

Public paid parking is available at **Whistler Conference Centre** (4010 Whistler Way, $1 per hour, $15 per day, 24-hour maximum), **Whistler**

Public Library (4329 Main St., $1 per hour, $15 per day, 24-hour maximum), and **Whistler Municipal Hall** (4325 Blackcomb Way, $1 per hour, 2-hour maximum).

BUS

BC Transit (604/932-4020, http://bctransit.com/whistler, $2.50 pp) runs several bus routes through the Whistler area that are useful if you're staying outside the central Whistler Village. The **Whistler Creekside** route travels between the village and Creekside. Other routes, such as the **Cheakamus** route to the HI-Whistler Hostel and Function Junction, or the **Alpine** route to Alpine Meadows and the Meadow Park Sports Centre, link Whistler's residential neighborhoods with the Whistler Gondola Exchange, where you can board the mountain gondola.

Two bus routes are free during the winter season, including the **Upper Village/Benchlands** route that can take you to the village from condos in those neighborhoods, and the **Marketplace Shuttle** between the Whistler Gondola Exchange and the Marketplace shopping center. Bus schedules vary seasonally and by route.

TAXI

Whistler has two local taxi companies: **Whistler Resort Cabs** (604/938-1515, www.resortcabs.com) and **Whistler Taxi** (604/932-3333, www.whistlertaxi.com). Both operate 24 hours daily. Taxi fares average $5 within Whistler Village, $10 between the village and Creekside, and $15 between the village and other Whistler neighborhoods.

BACKGROUND

The Landscape

GEOGRAPHY

Canada is the world's second largest country, covering an immense area of 3,855,230 square miles (nearly 10 million square km). Canadian land stretches from the Atlantic to the Pacific to the Arctic, and shares its long southern boundary, mostly along the 49th parallel, with the United States.

Bordering the Pacific Ocean, British Columbia is the country's westernmost province and its third largest geographically, after Ontario and Quebec; it's about the size of Germany, France, and the Netherlands combined. To the south are the U.S. states of Washington, Idaho, and Montana; to the north are the Yukon and Alaska. More than 60 percent of BC's population is clustered in the province's southwest corner, in and around the city of Vancouver, in the region known as the **Lower Mainland.**

flowers at Vancouver's False Creek

Vancouver is known for its dramatic natural setting, perched between the mountains and the sea. Water surrounds the downtown peninsula, where three bridges cross False Creek, connecting the city center to the rest of the metropolitan area. Two more bridges take you over Burrard Inlet to the city's North Shore, where several mountains dominate the landscape, with three local ski areas and numerous parks. Continuing north, along the strikingly beautiful Sea-to-Sky Highway, you'll reach **Whistler,** North

America's largest winter resort and a year-round outdoor playground; it's a two-hour drive from downtown Vancouver.

Vancouver is a particularly green city, not only for its environmental policies but also for its rainforest setting, with tall trees dominating the region. Douglas fir, western cedar, Sitka spruce, and hemlock all grow in BC's coastal regions, and many of these giants are the tallest in Canada. Even within the city of Vancouver, you can wander through the forests in Stanley Park, on the end of the downtown peninsula, and in Pacific Spirit Regional Park, near the University of British Columbia campus.

Vancouver Island is west of the city of Vancouver, across the Strait of Georgia. It's a big island, measuring 285 miles (460 km) from north to south; from east to west, it's 30-75 miles (50-120 km) across. British Columbia's capital city, Victoria, is on the southeast tip of Vancouver Island, a 90-minute ferry ride or a 35-minute flight from mainland British Columbia.

A spine of mountains, including several approaching 7,000 feet (2,100 m), runs along the center of Vancouver Island. Winding your way between these peaks will take you to the island's western shore, with lovely sandy beaches in the Pacific Rim National Park Reserve and in the nearby communities of Tofino and Ucluelet.

Because coastal British Columbia is near the edge of the large North American tectonic plate and the smaller Juan de Fuca plate, it's in an earthquake zone. Small earthquakes occur with some regularity across the region, although few are felt in the metropolitan areas; the last major earthquake shook the southern BC coast in 1700, with a somewhat smaller one in 1946. However, researchers say that there's a 25 percent chance of a significant quake occurring in the next 50 years.

CLIMATE

Unlike the rest of Canada, coastal British Columbia has a temperate climate, and Victoria has the mildest climate of any Canadian city. The weather in Vancouver and Victoria is similar, although Victoria is normally a degree or two warmer and slightly drier.

In both Vancouver and Victoria, summers are sunny and mild, with daytime temperatures in July-August averaging 68-75°F (20-25°C). In January, the coldest month, expect average temperatures during the day of 41-44°F (5-7°C), dipping close to freezing at night. November-March, it's not terribly cold, but it is rainy, frequently cloudy, and gray. It can snow in the cities, but it's relatively rare, and snow doesn't typically stick around for more than a couple of days. When it's raining in Vancouver, it's often snowing in the North Shore mountains and in Whistler.

Spring comes early to coastal BC, with flowers beginning to bloom in late February-early March. By April, Vancouver's cherry trees blanket the city streets with pink blossoms. It can still rain in spring, but showers are shorter and temperatures milder than during winter. Early autumn (Sept.-Oct.) is another moderate season with comfortable temperatures and less frequent rain.

The region's numerous microclimates can cause surprising variations in weather, even across short distances. The North Shore, where it snows regularly at higher elevations, receives far more rain than downtown Vancouver. In contrast, it rains noticeably less in the suburb of Richmond, where Vancouver International Airport is located, than on the downtown peninsula. Within the city itself are variations: It can be snowing in Vancouver's Point Grey neighborhood or near Queen Elizabeth Park, when at lower elevations, down the hill, in Kitsilano, along False Creek, or downtown, it's raining.

ENVIRONMENTAL ISSUES

Vancouver is a green city, with parks throughout the metropolitan region, citywide recycling initiatives, and programs to encourage everything from environmentally friendly construction to car sharing. Farmers markets are helping provide better access to locally grown food, though most operate only May-October. The city is in the midst of a major initiative to make Vancouver even more bicycle-friendly; a bike-sharing program, launched in 2016, is expanding, and the city continues to build bike lanes on many urban streets.

As residential and commercial towers sprout up throughout metropolitan Vancouver, development has become a major issue. Recent city governments have worked to increase urban density—building up, rather than out—to try to reduce the environmental impact of commuting from the suburbs and, at least in theory, enabling more people to live in the central city. In many districts, historic homes and other structures are being razed to make room for more expensive towers, and neighborhoods are changing in character as they become more densely populated.

History

INDIGENOUS ROOTS

Indigenous people have lived in western Canada for more than 10,000 years. The southwestern corner of British Columbia, where Vancouver is located, is the traditional territory of several indigenous groups, collectively known as the Coast Salish people. Coast Salish territory extends across the Strait of Georgia to Vancouver Island, which is also home to the Nuu-chah-nulth and the Kwakwaka'wakw peoples.

The west coast's natural resources defined the early life of Canada's coastal people. Much of their food came from the sea, where salmon, crab, and other species were abundant. They used the region's large trees, particularly the western red cedar, to construct their homes and longhouses, to carve oceangoing dugout canoes, and to craft massive totem poles, which commemorated the events, histories, and people of these communities. Although totems have come to be a symbol of many indigenous communities, only six west coast First Nations originally carved the poles.

EUROPEAN EXPLORATION

The earliest European explorers to reach North America's west coast were the Spanish, who traveled north from Mexico as early as the 1540s. However, it wasn't until the 1700s that extensive exploration of the region got underway, when Spanish, Russian, French, and British ships all traveled along the coast of what is now British Columbia.

The British left the most lasting legacies, beginning with an expedition in the 1770s that British explorer James Cook captained. Cook became the first non-indigenous person to set foot in what is now British Columbia, when he landed on Vancouver Island's west coast in 1778. Cook's crew included a young sailor named George Vancouver, who had joined the Royal Navy in 1772 when he was just 13 years old.

In 1792, George Vancouver returned to the region as captain of another Pacific Northwest expedition, charged with mapping the coastal areas and negotiating with the Spanish. The mainland beach where Captain Vancouver met with two Spanish captains is known today as Spanish Banks.

In the early 1800s, explorers and fur traders traveled westward across North America. Explorer Simon Fraser, who came from eastern Canada, reached the Pacific after following the river that today bears his name. The Hudson's Bay Company established the first permanent European settlement in the Lower Mainland in 1827 at Fort Langley, east of present-day Vancouver. In 1843, the company set up a trading post on Vancouver Island, naming it Fort Victoria. That post, on the island's southeastern point, would become the city of Victoria.

THE GOLD RUSH

In 1858, nine years after the start of the California gold rush in the United States, miners found gold along British Columbia's Fraser River. Thousands of miners traveled from eastern Canada and from the United States to seek their fortunes. Many Chinese also joined the search for gold, coming from California or directly from China, triggering a major wave of immigration.

Although the gold rush didn't last long, many of these settlers remained in BC and found work in the emerging fishing and lumber industries, businesses that would remain the backbone of the province's economy for years to come.

After two small sawmills began operation in the 1860s along Burrard Inlet, the entrepreneurial Captain John Deighton opened a nearby saloon to quench the millworkers' thirst. Although the district where the saloon was located had officially been named "Granville," Deighton's nickname, "Gassy Jack"—for his habit of telling tall tales—gave the area its more enduring name: Gastown.

WHEN CANADA BECAME A COUNTRY

A milestone year in Canadian history is 1867, when the British Parliament passed the British North America Act, creating the Dominion of Canada as a stand-alone nation, independent of Great Britain. Ontario, Quebec, Nova Scotia, and New Brunswick became the country's first four provinces, joining together at Confederation on July 1, 1867. Canadians celebrate Confederation annually on July 1, now the Canada Day holiday.

British Columbia joined the Canadian Confederation in 1871 (following Manitoba and the Northwest Territories, which came on board in 1870). BC's government signed up with the expectation that the cross-country railroad, under construction to link the east and west, would be completed. It took nearly 15 more years, including a major influx of workers from China, but the Canadian Pacific Railway (CPR) officially finished the 3,100-mile (5,000-km) transcontinental railroad in 1885, when workers drove in the last spike at Craigellachie, BC, in the mountains west of the town of Revelstoke.

IMMIGRATION

The railway opened up the west to rapid settlement and drew large numbers of migrants from eastern Canada, the United States, and Europe, especially from Italy, Ukraine, Poland, Germany, and Hungary. Chinese immigration continued, and small numbers of Japanese began arriving in British Columbia around the same time, many of whom found work along the coast in the fishing industry on boats or in canneries.

At that point, the western terminus of the rail line reached only as far as Port Moody, on Burrard Inlet 12 miles (20 km) east of Vancouver. The CPR's decision to extend the railroad to the fledgling settlement then known as Granville fueled Vancouver's development. Named for the British explorer, the city of Vancouver was officially incorporated in 1886, and the first transcontinental passenger train rolled into town in 1887.

Migrants continued settling in BC throughout the early 1900s. The University of British Columbia was established in 1908, and by the 1920s, Vancouver had become the third largest city in Canada, a position it retains today.

Canada didn't always welcome these immigrants, however. Despite the Chinese role in constructing the railroads, the federal government attempted to restrict further immigration from China. They imposed a "head tax" on every Chinese newcomer. In 1885, the tax was $50; by 1903, it had been raised to $500. In 1923, the Canadian Parliament passed the Chinese Immigration Act, an exclusionary measure that effectively prevented Chinese immigrants from entering Canada. The act was finally repealed in 1947 after World War II.

WORLD WAR II

During the Second World War, more than a million Canadians fought for the Allies, joining Britain, France, Australia, and the United States among the nations who battled the

Axis coalition of Germany, Italy, and Japan.

At home, anti-Asian sentiment began to rise after the 1941 Japanese attack on Pearl Harbor, particularly in British Columbia, which by this time had a well-established Japanese Canadian population, most of whom lived in and around Vancouver. In January 1942, the BC government established a 100-mile (160-km) "security zone" between the Pacific Ocean and the Coast Mountains, extending south to the U.S. border and north to the Yukon. They decreed that all male Japanese Canadians between the ages of 18 and 45 were prohibited from living in the area; they were separated from their families and sent to relocation camps in BC's remote interior regions.

Less than two months later, the government extended the prohibition to all people of Japanese origin and began relocating women, children, and seniors. Overall, more than 22,000 people of Japanese heritage, three-quarters of whom were Canadian citizens, were forcibly relocated, and their land and other property were confiscated. Many spent the war years in these rustic internment camps in British Columbia's Kootenay and eastern mountain regions.

After the war, most of the interned Japanese Canadians were given the choice of moving east of the Rockies or returning to Japan. The majority opted to relocate again, settling in the prairies or farther east in Ontario, although several thousand were sent to Japan. The Japanese were forbidden to return to the BC coast until 1949.

RESIDENTIAL SCHOOLS

Another dark period in Canada's history began in the 1880s, when the Canadian government started establishing residential schools for indigenous children. Children were removed from their families and required to attend these church-run boarding schools, where the objective was to indoctrinate indigenous youth into mainstream Canadian culture by forbidding them from speaking their traditional languages, practicing their customs, or even contacting their parents or relatives. In 1920, Parliament passed the Indian Act, which made it illegal for indigenous children to attend any educational institution other than a residential school.

The vast majority of the 150,000 students sent to these schools suffered through poor education, inadequate food, isolation from their families and culture, and in some cases, physical or sexual abuse. The last residential schools were finally closed in the 1990s. However, the schools' negative legacy continues to affect many indigenous people today, with high rates of alcoholism, drug abuse, domestic violence, and suicide plaguing many communities.

Canada's Assembly of First Nations filed a class action lawsuit against the Canadian government in 2005 for the ongoing trauma that the residential school system had caused. When the suit was settled, and both the federal government and the churches agreed to pay compensation to survivors of the schools, the 2006 Indian Residential Schools Settlement

Agreement became the largest class action settlement in Canadian history. In 2008, Canada's House of Commons publicly apologized for the government's role in creating and maintaining the residential school system. The Truth and Reconciliation Commission, which the federal government subsequently established to investigate the legacy of residential schools, derided the system as "cultural genocide."

CONTEMPORARY TIMES

In recent years, several events triggered significant changes in and around Vancouver. In 1986, Vancouver marked its centennial, hosting Expo '86, a world's fair that focused on developments in transportation and communications. This international exposition took place on a formerly derelict site along False Creek that had been redeveloped to house more than 50 pavilions. Britain's Prince Charles and Princess Diana were among the first visitors, and more than 22 million people visited Expo '86 during its six-month run, with tourists continuing to arrive long after the event officially closed. Vancouver built the city's first SkyTrain line in

anticipation of the Expo, and many other city landmarks, including Canada Place, Science World, BC Place, and the Cambie Bridge, were constructed during this era.

In the late 1980s and early 1990s, thousands of Hong Kong residents immigrated to Canada, and a large percentage settled in British Columbia. Many were afraid of how Hong Kong might change when the United Kingdom handed it over to the Chinese government in 1997. This wave of immigration was the first of several that significantly increased Vancouver's Asian population; many more immigrants arrived from Taiwan and mainland China, beginning in the 1990s and continuing through the present day.

In 2010, Vancouver hosted the Olympic Winter Games, which again turned the world's attention to the region. The Olympics' legacy included a new subway line connecting the airport and downtown as well as the candelabra-like Olympic Cauldron, which has become a waterfront landmark. The residential buildings along False Creek where athletes lived during the Games formed the basis for a new neighborhood, known as the Olympic Village.

Government and Economy

GOVERNMENT

Canada is divided into 10 provinces and three territories. The country has a three-tiered governmental structure, with federal, provincial (or territorial), and municipal governments.

FEDERAL GOVERNMENT

Headquartered in Ottawa, the nation's capital, the federal government is responsible for foreign policy, defense, immigration, and other national issues. Since the country is a constitutional monarchy with roots in the British Commonwealth, Canada's official head of state is the monarch of the United Kingdom. However, the king or queen's role in Canada is largely symbolic; the prime minister is the country's head of government.

Parliament, the national legislature, has two bodies: the elected 338-member House of Commons and the appointed 105-member Senate. The major political parties, to which the House of Commons members belong, include the Liberal Party, Conservative Party, New Democratic Party (NDP), Bloc Québécois, and Green Party. Justin Trudeau, who was elected prime minister in 2015, is the leader of the Liberal Party.

By law, federal elections must now be held at least every four years. In practice, the ruling government has the power to call an election at any time. In addition, if the current government loses a confidence vote in the House of Commons, that vote brings down the government and triggers a new election. Canada's shortest Parliament session lasted just 66 days (in 1979) before the government was brought down. The longest-serving government, from 1911 through 1917, held power for 2,152 days.

PROVINCIAL AND LOCAL GOVERNMENTS

The provincial governments handle health care, education, policing, and highways, among other things. The governmental structure at the provincial level parallels that of the federal government. The head of each provincial government is the premier, a position analogous to a U.S. state governor. Each province and territory has its own legislature.

Although Vancouver is British Columbia's largest city, Victoria is the provincial capital. BC's Legislative Assembly meets in the 1897 provincial Parliament Building, overlooking Victoria's Inner Harbour. The 85 provincial representatives are known as MLAs, members of the legislative assembly. In recent years, two parties have dominated provincial politics in BC: the Liberals and the NDP.

Local issues, such as zoning, city police and firefighting, snow removal, garbage, and recycling, are the municipal governments' purview. The local governments in Vancouver, Victoria, and other BC cities are each led by a mayor, who works with the local city council to determine local policy and regulations.

ECONOMY

Service industries dominate the economies of Vancouver and Victoria. Tourism, including hotels, restaurants, and all sorts of recreation-focused businesses, is a significant pillar of the economy, as are health care, education, financial services, trade (particularly with Pacific Rim countries), and technology. Due to changes in liquor laws, numerous craft breweries have opened in both cities.

A construction boom in both Vancouver and Victoria has kept job growth high in this industry. Outside the urban areas, other industries that contribute significantly to BC's economy include agriculture, forestry (about 60 percent of the province's land is forested), mining, oil and gas extraction, and fishing.

Poverty, drug use, and homelessness are very visible issues on the streets of Vancouver (and to a lesser extent, in Victoria). It's common to see people sleeping in parks, hanging out on the sidewalks, or pushing their possessions in a shopping cart across Vancouver, especially in Gastown, Chinatown, and the east side of downtown. The extent of the problem can surprise visitors, particularly because you'll see people living on the streets, even when those streets are lined with cool restaurants and stylish shops.

While the Vancouver city government has been working on programs to reduce homelessness and increase the availability of affordable housing, those programs have not yet been particularly successful, in part because Vancouver continues to be Canada's most expensive housing market. In mid-2019, although residential real estate prices had declined somewhat, the average purchase price of a single-family detached home was over $1.4 million, and buying even a one-bedroom condo would set you back more than $600,000.

Rental prices are high too. In 2018, the federal government's Canada Mortgage and Housing Corporation reported that the average monthly rent in the city of Vancouver was $1,411 for a one-bedroom apartment and $1,964 for a two-bedroom unit. If you want to live downtown, you'd pay an average of $1,566 for a one-bedroom and $2,330 for a two-bedroom place.

Local Culture

POPULATION

Stretching over a vast landmass, Canada has a population of 37 million (as of 2019). By contrast, the United States, its geographically smaller neighbor to the south, is almost nine times larger in population, with more than 329 million inhabitants. Nearly three-quarters of all Canadians live within 100 miles (160 km) of the U.S. border.

With roughly five million residents, British Columbia is Canada's third most populous province, after Ontario (14 million) and Quebec (8.3 million).

Vancouver is Canada's third largest city, after Toronto and Montreal, and has approximately 2.6 million residents in the metropolitan region. Victoria is BC's capital, but with about 400,000 people, it's significantly smaller than metro Vancouver.

DIVERSITY

Canada's major cities, including Toronto, Montreal, and Vancouver, are among the most multicultural on the planet. Nationwide, more than 20 percent of Canada's population was born outside of the country, but that figure is much higher in urban areas; in Vancouver, 40 percent of residents were born outside Canada. Though the majority of Canadians have their origins in Europe, more than half of the country's recent immigrants have come from Asia, with significant numbers arriving from the Philippines, China, and India. Other major immigrant populations include those coming from the United States, Pakistan, the United Kingdom, Iran, South Korea, Vietnam, Jamaica, and Mexico.

In Vancouver, 70 percent of the region's recent immigrants have arrived from Asia, and overall, more than 40 percent of the population is of Asian descent, including a mix of people born in Canada and those born abroad. It's often called the most Asian major city outside of Asia, and you'll find Asian influences in everything from art and fashion to urban design and food.

While Victoria is becoming increasingly diverse, it's still a far more homogenous community than Vancouver. The majority of the city's citizens trace their roots to the United Kingdom and western Europe; 11 percent of Victoria's population is Asian.

INDIGENOUS CULTURES

Canada has three officially recognized indigenous groups: the First Nations, the Inuit, and the Métis. The Inuit people live primarily in Canada's far north, while the Métis—descendants of French settlers and their First Nations spouses—have historically settled in the prairies and the west. First Nations, the largest indigenous group, is the term for indigenous people who are neither Inuit nor Métis.

In British Columbia today, approximately 6 percent of the population is of indigenous heritage.

Two-thirds are First Nations, representing 200 different communities; most of the rest are Métis.

Of these indigenous people, one in four lives in the Lower Mainland in and around Vancouver, where the largest of the 11 First Nations are the Musqueam, Squamish, and Tsleil-Waututh. Many public events in Vancouver now begin with a statement acknowledging that they're taking place on the traditional territory of these indigenous communities.

Across the Strait of Georgia, Vancouver Island is home to 53 different First Nations, including the Esquimalt and Songhees near Victoria, the Saanich First Nations on the peninsula of the same name north of Victoria, and BC's largest First Nation, the Cowichan, whose territory includes the present-day Cowichan Valley outside Victoria.

FRENCH LANGUAGE AND CULTURE

Ever since European explorers first landed on Canada's shores, both English- and French-speaking colonists settled the country. As a result, Canada has two official languages: English and French. That means that any official federal government communications, from tax forms to airport signs to national park brochures, must be produced in both English and French, and products sold in Canada must contain information on their packaging in both languages.

The province of Quebec is Canada's major francophone region, and there are numerous French-speaking communities in other parts of the country. In British

Columbia, although many people can speak some French and kids study the language in school, only about 70,000 people, or 1.5 percent of the population, have French as their mother tongue. In fact, you're more likely to hear Mandarin, Cantonese, Tagalog, or Punjabi on the streets of Vancouver than you are to hear people speaking French.

RELIGION

Christianity is the major religion in Canada. Nearly 30 percent of Canadians are Catholic, and about 20 percent are Protestant. Conversely, recent census figures indicate that nearly 30 percent of Canadians claim no religious affiliation at all.

Canada's largest non-Christian religious group is Muslim, representing more than 3 percent of the population nationwide. Other major religious groups in Canada include Hindus (1.5 percent of the population), Sikhs (1.4 percent), Buddhists (1.1 percent), and Jews (1 percent).

In British Columbia, these numbers differ somewhat from the nation's population overall. About 40 percent of BC's residents are Christians, and a roughly equal number say that they have no religious affiliation. Nearly 7 percent are Sikhs, 3.4 percent Buddhists, 3.2 percent Muslims, 1.8 percent Hindus, and less than 1 percent Jews.

THE ARTS
LITERATURE

Though she's more often associated with Ontario, where she was born (in 1931) and has lived much of her life, Canadian short-story writer and novelist **Alice Munro** spent the 1950s and 1960s in Vancouver and Victoria. She and her then-husband Jim opened Munro's Books in Victoria in 1963, a classic bookstore that's still operating today. Her many books include *The Lives of Girls and Women* (1971), *Who Do You Think You Are?* (1978), *The View From Castle Rock* (2006), and *Dear Life* (2012). Munro became the first Canadian woman to win the Nobel Prize for Literature, when she received the award in 2013.

Many British Columbia authors have written about the region's Asian communities in both fiction and memoir. In his novel *The Jade Peony* (1995), **Wayson Choy** (1939-2019), who was born in Vancouver, painted a portrait of life in Vancouver's Chinatown in the first half of the 20th century. He continued to explore similar themes in a follow-up work of fiction, *All That Matters,* and in his memoir, *Paper Shadows: A Chinatown Childhood.*

In her novel *Obasan,* Vancouver-born **Joy Kogawa** wrote about the forced relocation and internment of Japanese Canadians in western Canada during World War II, depicted through the eyes of a young Vancouver girl. It's based on her own experiences; Kogawa and her family were required to leave Vancouver and sent to Slocan, BC, during the war. Vancouver author **Jen Sookfong Lee** recounted the family history of three generations in the city's Chinatown in her novel *The End of East* (2007); her more recent works, including *The Better Mother* (2011) and *The Conjoined* (2016), are also set in Vancouver.

Other contemporary BC writers include novelist and artist **Douglas Coupland,** who popularized the term for an entire generation with his 1991 novel, *Generation X: Tales for an Accelerated Culture;* fiction writer **Caroline Adderson,** who has set several of her novels, including *The Sky Is Falling* (2010), in and around Vancouver; and CBC radio and podcast host **Grant Lawrence,** who published the humorous BC-based *Adventures in Solitude: What Not to Wear to a Nude Potluck and Other Stories from Desolation Sound* in 2010. Indigenous author **Eden Robinson** is known for her soon-to-be-a-trilogy of novels, *Son of a Trickster* (2017) and *Trickster Drift* (2019), while UBC professor **Timothy Taylor** earned kudos for his first book of fiction *Stanley Park* (2001).

VISUAL ARTS

The visual artist whose work is perhaps most closely associated with British Columbia is the Victoria-born painter **Emily Carr** (1871-1945), known for her paintings of BC's landscape and its indigenous people. Unusually for a woman of her time, Carr traveled—on her own—to Haida Gwaii and other remote northern communities, where she painted scenes of First Nations' life. You can see Carr's work at the **Vancouver Art Gallery** (www.vanartgallery.bc.ca) and at Whistler's **Audain Art Museum** (www.audainartmuseum.com).

While Carr had no indigenous heritage herself, another well-known BC artist came from mixed European and First Nations ancestry. **Bill Reid** (1920-1998) created more than 1,500 sculptures, carvings, and other works, most of which explore the traditions of the Haida First Nation, to which his mother belonged. Vancouver's **Bill Reid Gallery of Northwest Coast Art** (www.billreidgallery.ca) is dedicated to Reid's work; you can also see his massive sculptures in the Vancouver International Airport and at the **Museum of Anthropology** (http://moa.ubc.ca) on the University of British Columbia campus.

Works by contemporary Musqueam First Nations artist **Susan Point** also greet passengers arriving at Vancouver's airport. Her two towering carvings, *Musqueam Welcome Figures,* stand guard at the entrance to the immigration arrivals area.

Painter and naturalist **Robert Bateman** captured scenes of BC's landscapes and wildlife, which you can view at the **Robert Bateman Centre** (http://batemancentre.org) in Victoria. In the 1950s and 1960s, photographer **Fred Herzog** focused his lens on wildlife of a different sort, taking photos of Vancouver's downtown streets.

The city of Vancouver has a significant **public art program** that places art around the city. Look for works like *A-maze-ing Laughter,* opposite English Bay in the West End, by Beijing-based contemporary artist Yue Minjun, and *The Birds,* two 18-foot-tall (5.5-m) sculptures in the Olympic Village, by Vancouver's Myfanwy MacLeod. Find a directory of local public art on the **City of Vancouver's website** (http://vancouver.ca).

MUSIC

Many musicians and performers with British Columbia connections have gone on to wider acclaim.

Though born in Ontario, rock singer-songwriter **Bryan Adams** launched his early career in Vancouver. Canadian crooner **Michael Bublé** was born and raised in the Vancouver suburb of Burnaby and still maintains homes in the area. **Tegan and Sara,** the powerhouse musical duo (and identical twins), reside at least part-time in Vancouver.

Singer-songwriter **Sarah McLachlan,** who founded the Lilith Fair tours highlighting women musicians, established the Sarah McLachlan School of Music in Vancouver, which provides free music instruction to local at-risk youth.

Singer **Nelly Furtado** was born in Victoria, and jazz artist **Diana Krall,** who's married to fellow musician Elvis Costello, also has island roots; she hails from the city of Nanaimo.

FILM AND TV

Vancouver and Toronto vie for the title of **Hollywood North,** since both cities are popular filming locations for movies and TV series.

Recent movies shot in or around Vancouver include *Deadpool* (2015) and *Deadpool 2* (2018), starring Vancouver native Ryan Reynolds; *Tomorrowland* (2015), with George Clooney; *50 Shades of Grey* (2014), based on the popular book of the same name; *Meditation Park* (2017), from Vancouver director Mina Shum, featuring Sandra Oh; *Big Eyes* (2014), directed by Tim Burton and starring Amy Adams; and Casey

Affleck's 2019 drama, *Light of My Life*.

Although the number of movies being made in Canada rises and falls with the relative strength of the U.S. and Canadian dollars (when the Canadian dollar is weaker compared to the U.S. currency, it's cheaper to make films north of the border), it's not unusual to stumble upon a film set as you wander around Vancouver. To increase your chances of spotting a celebrity when you're in town, check the Creative BC website (www.creativebc.com), which lists movies and TV shows currently filming in British Columbia.

FOOD AND DRINK

British Columbia is well-regarded for its seafood, particularly salmon, halibut, oysters, and spot prawns, caught in Pacific waters. A sweetened cured fish, salmon candy, is a surprisingly delicious local snack. Much of Vancouver's produce, from greens to blueberries, comes from the Fraser Valley, east of the city, with more fruits and vegetables from farms in the Okanagan Valley or on Vancouver Island. With its large Asian population, Vancouver has some of North America's best Chinese food, as well as good Japanese, Korean, and Vietnamese fare, and many non-Asian restaurants incorporate Pacific Rim influences in their dishes.

Look for British Columbia wines from the Okanagan Valley or Vancouver Island, as well as craft beers from Vancouver, Victoria, Whistler, and elsewhere around the province. BC is home to a growing number of craft spirits makers, who produce much of the gin, vodka, and whiskey that you find in the region's cocktail bars.

ESSENTIALS

Getting There

AIR

Vancouver International Airport (YVR, 3211 Grant McConachie Way, Richmond, 604/207-7077, www.yvr.ca) is a major international gateway with flights from across Canada, the United States, Mexico, Europe, Asia, and the Pacific. The airport is south of the city center in the suburb of Richmond. It's 25 minutes from the airport to downtown by public transit, taxi, or by car. All the major car rental companies have offices at the airport.

To get to most Vancouver destinations from the airport by taxi, you'll pay a flat rate by zone ($31-37). The Canada Line branch of the SkyTrain subway network stops at the airport. One-way adult fares ($8-9.25) from the airport to downtown vary by time of day. Returning to the airport from downtown costs $3-4.25.

Vancouver International Airport

TRAIN

Pacific Central Station (1150 Station St.), near the intersection of Main and Terminal Streets on the edge of Chinatown, is Vancouver's passenger rail depot. It's also the city's long-distance bus station.

AN AIRPORT ART TOUR

Airports aren't normally designed for lingering (at least voluntarily), but the Vancouver International Airport (YVR) has made visitors' time in the terminals more enjoyable by assembling a striking set of artworks. In fact, the airport now houses one of the world's largest collections of Northwest Coast indigenous art. Here's a guide to the notable pieces to look for as you begin or end your Vancouver air travels.

If you're arriving from outside Canada, several pieces of art welcome you into the customs hall. At the top of the escalators above the customs area, *Flight (Spindle Whorl)*, by Susan Point, a Coast Salish artist from the Musqueam First Nation, is the world's largest Coast Salish spindle whorl, measuring 15.7 feet (4.8 m) in diameter. This circular red cedar carving uses traditional images to illustrate flight. Point also carved the two 17-foot-tall (5.2-m) *Musqueam Welcome Figures* that flank the escalators into the immigration arrivals area.

Travelers arriving on flights from the United States typically walk through the airport's Pacific Passage, where *Hetux*, a mythological Thunderbird, appears to fly above the walkway. Artist Connie Watts, who is of Nuu-chah-nulth, Gitxsan, and Kwakwaka'wakw ancestry, crafted the piece from powder-coated aluminum and stained birch panels.

One of the airport's most famous sculptures is between the U.S. and international departure counters. Haida First Nations artist Bill Reid created *The Spirit of Haida Gwaii: The Jade Canoe*, a jade-green bronze-cast work, in 1994. Behind Reid's work is *The Great Wave*, Lutz Haufschild's glass wall that depicts BC's ocean and coastline.

In the domestic terminal, a contemporary carved and painted 35-foot (11-m) cedar pole, *Celebrating Flight*, by Haida artist Don Yeomans, incorporates LED lights, Chinese characters, and Celtic knots along with its indigenous imagery. On Level 2, also in the domestic terminal, look for *Hugging the World*, a red cedar carving suspended from the ceiling and depicting Eagle and Raven figures, by notable artist Robert Davidson. In the same area is Richard Hunt's *Thunderbird and Killer Whale* and Dempsey Bob's red cedar *Human/Bear Mask*.

So stay alert to your surroundings as you arrive at or depart from YVR. Beyond the typical coffee shops, baggage carousels, and departure gates, there's a world of indigenous art to explore.

AMTRAK

Amtrak (800/872-7245, www.amtrak.com), the U.S. passenger rail carrier, runs trains to Vancouver from Seattle, Washington (one-way adults from US$44), and Portland, Oregon (one-way adults from US$51). Make connections in Seattle or Portland to U.S. points farther south or east. Trains from Seattle (5.5 hours) operate twice a day; the direct Portland-Vancouver train (8 hours) runs once a day in each direction. These trains have electrical outlets and free Wi-Fi in both standard economy and business classes; the latter seats give you additional legroom.

Tip for cyclists: You can walk your bike onto the Seattle or Portland trains for a fee of US$5.

VIA RAIL

Canada's national passenger rail carrier, VIA Rail (514/989-2626 or 888/842-7245, www.viarail.ca), runs cross-country trains to Vancouver from Toronto. The major stops along the Toronto-Vancouver route of *The Canadian*, VIA Rail's flagship train, are Winnipeg (Manitoba), Saskatoon (Saskatchewan),

Edmonton and Jasper (Alberta), and Kamloops (British Columbia).

If you do the 2,775-mile (4,466-km) Toronto-to-Vancouver rail trip nonstop, it's a four-night, three-day journey. *The Canadian* operates three times a week in each direction May-mid-October, and twice a week mid-October-April. It's possible to get off en route and continue your journey on a subsequent train. For example, you could take the train from Toronto to Jasper in the Canadian Rockies, get off the train for 2-3 days, and catch the next train onward to Vancouver.

VIA Rail offers several classes of service on *The Canadian.* In **Economy class,** the cheapest option, you have a reclining seat and access to a restroom (but no shower). Meals aren't included, although you can buy meals and snacks on the train or outside the train during a few brief stopovers.

A more comfortable alternative is **Sleeper Plus class,** which offers several choices of accommodations. The least expensive is either an upper or lower **berth,** which is a seat by day that converts into a bunk, shielded by a heavy curtain, at night. Berth passengers have access to men's and women's restrooms and private shower rooms in the corridor.

Another Sleeper Plus option is a **cabin,** which can sleep 1-4 people. Cabins have their own toilets and sinks, and passengers can use the shower rooms in the corridor. Note that in the one-person cabin, the bed folds down over the toilet, so if you need to use the facilities during the night, you have to fold up your bed or use the restroom in the hallway.

The top-end sleeper accommodations are in **Prestige Sleeper class,** which offers a more modern cabin with a private bathroom and shower. These units have an L-shaped leather couch by day with a Murphy bed for two that folds down at night.

All the Sleeper class fares include three meals daily in the dining car, nonalcoholic drinks, and access to both a window-lined viewing car and the bar-snack car, with complimentary coffee, tea, fruit, and cookies.

Outside the busy summer travel season, VIA Rail frequently offers discounts of up to 50 percent off their standard fares. Check their website or sign up for their newsletter to find out about seat sales. They also offer occasional last-minute travel deals, which are posted on the **VIA Rail website** (www.viarail.ca).

THE ROCKY MOUNTAINEER

The **Rocky Mountaineer** (1755 Cottrell St., at Terminal Ave., 604/606-7245 or 877/460-3200, www.rockymountaineer.com, mid-Apr.-mid-Oct.) is a privately run luxury train that offers rail trips between Vancouver, Banff, Lake Louise, Jasper, and Calgary. You can travel round-trip from Vancouver to the Canadian Rockies and back, or you can book a one-way journey through the Rockies from Vancouver to Calgary (or vice versa). Another route starts in Seattle and stops in Vancouver before continuing to the Rockies. Rocky Mountaineer trains travel during the day and stop overnight in Kamloops, where you stay in a hotel, en route to or from the Rockies.

Unlike a standard train trip,

many Rocky Mountaineer packages include activities that range from gondola rides to helicopter tours, as well as accommodations along the way. It's also possible to book a Rocky Mountaineer holiday that covers rail fare and accommodations only; for example, they offer two-day train trips between Vancouver and Lake Louise, Banff, or Jasper. Rail packages start at $1,741 per person and vary by destinations, number of travel days, and the level of service and accommodations.

Rocky Mountaineer trains do not use Vancouver's Pacific Central Station, where VIA Rail and Amtrak trains depart; they have a separate depot nearby.

BUS

Bolt Bus (877/265-8287, www. boltbus.com, one-way adults from US$25) provides bus service between Seattle and Vancouver, arriving at and departing from Pacific Central Station (1150 Station St., Vancouver). Quick Shuttle (604/940-4428 or 800/665-2122, www.quickcoach.com, one-way adults from US$43) runs buses between Seattle and Vancouver as well, stopping at Canada Place; it will pick up or drop off passengers at a number of downtown hotels, with advance reservations.

CAR

Coming from the United States, Interstate 5 takes you north from Seattle to the U.S.-Canada border. When you pass through border control, you'll be on Highway 99 in British Columbia, which leads to metropolitan Vancouver.

The main east-west route across Canada is Highway 1, the Trans-Canada Highway. It's possible to follow Highway 1 from eastern Canada, Calgary, and the Canadian Rockies all the way to Vancouver; however, it's not the fastest route.

If you're coming from Calgary or Banff to Vancouver, follow Highway 1 west into British Columbia and continue west to the city of Kamloops. From Kamloops, take Highway 5, the Coquihalla Highway, southbound, toward Merritt and Hope. Highway 5 meets Highway 3, which you take westbound to rejoin Highway 1 at the town of Hope and continue west to Vancouver.

From Jasper to Vancouver, the shortest route is to follow Highway 16 west to Highway 5, where you turn south toward Kamloops. At Kamloops, continue south on Highway 5, to Highway 3 west, to Highway 1 west.

Getting Around

You don't need a car to get around downtown Vancouver. The downtown peninsula is easy to navigate on foot, cabs are readily available, and the city has a good public transportation system with its SkyTrain subway and comprehensive bus network. It can be faster to go by car to some places outside downtown, like the University of British Columbia or the North Shore, but these destinations are not difficult to reach by transit.

PUBLIC TRANSPORTATION

TransLink (604/953-3333, www.translink.ca) runs the city's public transportation system. Use the Trip Planner feature on the TransLink website to plot your route.

TRANSIT FARES AND PASSES

Vancouver transit fares (adults 1-zone $3, 2-zone $4.25, 3-zone $5.75, ages 5-13, students, and seniors 1-zone $1.95, 2-zone $2.95, 3-zone $3.95) are divided into three zones, based on the distance you travel. Pay a basic one-zone fare if:

- your trip is entirely within the Vancouver city limits.
- you're traveling only by bus. All bus trips are one zone, regardless of distance.
- you're traveling anywhere after 6:30pm weekdays or all day Saturday-Sunday and holidays.

If you're taking the SkyTrain between downtown Vancouver and the airport before 6:30pm Monday-Friday, you need to pay a two-zone fare. During those hours, the SeaBus between Vancouver and North Vancouver is also a two-zone trip.

When you board the SkyTrain at the YVR Airport Station, you pay a $5 surcharge in addition to the regular transit fare.

If you're going to be riding transit extensively, buy a day pass (adults $10.50, seniors, students, and ages 5-13 $8.25), which covers one day of unlimited travel on the SkyTrain, buses, and SeaBus across all zones.

How to Buy Tickets and Passes

At SkyTrain or SeaBus stations, buy a ticket or day pass from the vending machine, which accepts cash, credit cards, and debit cards. Alternatively, without buying a ticket, you can "tap to pay," scanning your credit card or mobile device equipped with Apple Pay, Google Pay, or Samsung Pay directly at the fare gates. Each person tapping must have his or her own card, and you can tap to pay regular adult fares only (there are no youth or senior discounts). Tap your card when you enter the station and tap out when you exit; your fare, based on the zones you've traveled, will be charged to your credit card.

On the bus, you can pay your fare in cash with exact change or tap in with a credit card or mobile device; you don't have to tap out when you get off the bus, because all bus trips are a one-zone fare. If you've bought a ticket on the SkyTrain or SeaBus within the previous 90 minutes, you can use that same ticket on the bus.

For any mode of travel, you

can also buy a **Compass Card,** an electronic stored-value card, which gives you a **discounted fare** (adults 1-zone $2.40, 2-zone $3.45, 3-zone $4.50). Buy Compass Cards at station vending machines, online (www.compasscard.ca), or at London Drugs stores around the city.

When you purchase a Compass Card, you're charged a $6 card deposit. You can get your deposit back when you no longer need the card, either by returning your card in person to the **Compass Customer Service Centre** (Stadium-Chinatown Station) or to the **West Coast Express Office** (Waterfront Station), or by mailing or emailing in a refund request. See the TransLink website for mail-in refund instructions.

How to Use a Compass Card

Before boarding the SkyTrain or SeaBus, tap your Compass Card at the fare gates. After your trip, tap your card as you exit the station, so the system can calculate the correct fare and debit it from your card balance. **Remember to tap out,** or you'll be charged the maximum fare.

When you board a bus, tap your card on the card reader. You don't have to tap out when you get off the bus, since all bus trips are a one-zone fare.

SKYTRAIN

Vancouver's **SkyTrain subway** has two lines that converge downtown at Waterfront Station and a third line that travels to some of the city's eastern suburbs.

Traveling to or from Waterfront Station, the **Canada Line** (4:45am-1:15am daily) makes several downtown stops. Its two branches can take you between downtown and the airport (take the YVR branch) or other destinations in Richmond (the Richmond-Brighouse branch). If you're heading anywhere downtown or along the Cambie Corridor, you can take any Canada Line train; going south, the two branches diverge at Bridgeport Station.

The **Expo Line** (5am-1:30am Mon.-Fri., 6am-1:30am Sat., 7am-12:30pm Sun.) travels between downtown and the Vancouver suburbs of Burnaby, New Westminster, and Surrey, east of the city. Going east, the Expo Line splits into two branches, one terminating at King George Station in Surrey, and the other going to Production Way-University Station in Burnaby. Take either branch from downtown to Chinatown, Main Street (near Science World), or Commercial Drive.

The **Millennium Line** (5am-1:30am Mon.-Fri., 6am-1:30am Sat., 7am-12:30pm Sun.) serves Vancouver's northeastern suburbs, operating between VCC-Clark Station and Lafarge Lake-Douglas Station in Coquitlam. Transfer between the Millennium and Expo Lines at Commercial-Broadway, Production Way-University, and Lougheed Town Centre Stations.

BUS

The main bus routes in downtown Vancouver run along Granville, Burrard, Robson, Georgia, Pender, Hastings, and Davie Streets. Useful routes outside downtown travel along West 4th Avenue, Broadway,

Oak, Cambie, and Main Streets, and along Commercial Drive.

At any bus stop, text the posted stop number to 33333 and you'll receive a reply listing the next buses scheduled to arrive at that stop. For real-time bus arrival data, enter your stop number into the **Next Bus** page (http://nb.translink.ca) on the TransLink website. Signs at every bus stop show the stop number.

Bus schedules vary by route, but regular service begins 5am-6am and runs until 1am-2am. Vancouver also has 10 **Night Bus** routes that provide limited service into the wee hours; get schedules on the **TransLink website** (www.translink.ca).

FERRY
AQUABUS AND FALSE CREEK FERRIES

Two privately run ferry services shuttle passengers across False Creek between downtown, Granville Island, Science World, and several other points. Schedules vary seasonally, but in summer, service starts around 6:45am-7am and continues until after 10pm. These ferries aren't part of the TransLink system and require separate tickets.

The colorful **Aquabus ferries** (604/689-5858, www.theaquabus. com, adults $3-7, day pass $16, seniors and ages 4-12 $1.75-5, day pass $14, bikes $0.50) stop at the foot of Hornby Street, Granville Island, Yaletown's David Lam Park, Stamps Landing, Spyglass Place near the Cambie Bridge, the foot of Davie Street in Yaletown, Plaza of Nations,

ferries crossing False Creek in Yaletown

and Olympic Village. They operate 12-passenger mini ferries as well as 30-passenger boats that accommodate bicycles.

False Creek Ferries (604/684-7781, www.granvilleislandferries. bc.ca, adults $3.50-8, day pass $16, seniors and ages 4-12 $2.25-4.50, day pass $14) follow a similar route, stopping at the Vancouver Aquatic Centre in the West End, Granville Island, Vanier Park (near the Maritime Museum and Museum of Vancouver), David Lam Park, Stamps Landing, Spyglass Place, the foot of Davie Street, Plaza of Nations, and Olympic Village.

SEABUS

The SeaBus (604/953-3333, www. translink.ca) ferry is the fastest route between downtown's Waterfront Station and North Vancouver's Lonsdale Quay, taking just 12 minutes to cross Burrard Inlet. TransLink bus and SkyTrain tickets are valid on the SeaBus.

TAXI

In downtown Vancouver, you can usually hail taxis on the street or find cabs waiting at hotels, restaurants, bars, and transit stations.

You can also phone for a cab or book one online. Local taxi companies include Blacktop & Checker Cabs (604/731-1111, www.btccabs. ca), MacLure's Cabs (604/831-1111, www.maclurescabs.ca), Vancouver Taxi (604/871-1111, www.avancouvertaxi.com), and Yellow Cab (604/681-1111, www. yellowcabonline.com).

Vancouver taxis are metered, with a base fare of $3.30 plus $1.89 per kilometer, except for trips

starting at Vancouver International Airport. From the airport, you'll pay a flat rate by zone ($31-37) to most Vancouver destinations. Cabs accept cash and credit cards.

After extended deliberations, the city of Vancouver has announced that it would allow ride-sharing companies, including Uber and Lyft, to begin offering services in Vancouver. Ride-sharing services are expected to launch in 2020.

DRIVING

By law, you must wear a seat belt when you're driving in BC.

PARKING

Vancouver's on-street parking meters ($1-6 per hour) operate 9am-10pm daily, including holidays. Rates vary by location. You can park at most metered spaces for up to two hours. Pay for parking using coins, credit cards, or the Pay by Phone app (604/909-7275, www. paybyphone.com).

Find locations and rates for the EasyPark city-run parking garages and lots online (www.easypark.ca), or look for their bright orange signs. EasyPark garages are usually less expensive than privately owned parking facilities.

Many residential neighborhoods, including the West End, Kitsilano, and Main Street, reserve some street parking for residents. Don't park in spaces marked "Parking by permit only," or you can be ticketed.

CAR RENTAL

The major car rental companies have offices at Vancouver International Airport, including Alamo (604/231-1400 or

888/826-6893, www.alamo.ca), Avis (604/606-2847 or 800/230-4898, www.avis.ca), Budget (604/668-7000 or 800/268-8900, www.budget.ca), Discount (604/207-8140 or 800/263-2355, www.discountcar.com), Dollar (604/606-1656 or 800/800-6000, www.dollar.com), Enterprise (604/303-1117 or 800/261-7331, www.enterprise.com), Hertz (604/606-3700 or 800/654-3001, www.hertz.ca), National (604/273-6572 or 888/826-6890, www.nationalcar.ca), and Thrifty (604/207-7077 or 800/847-4389, www.thrifty.com). Most also have downtown locations.

Visas and Officialdom

For the most up-to-date requirements for visitors coming to Canada, visit Citizenship and Immigration Canada (www.cic.gc.ca).

Important note: If you have a criminal record, including misdemeanors or driving while impaired (DWI), no matter how long ago, you can be prohibited from entering Canada, unless you obtain a special waiver well in advance of your trip. Refer to the Citizenship and Immigration Canada website for additional information.

PASSPORTS AND VISAS

U.S. CITIZENS

The simple answer to the question of what documents U.S. citizens need to visit Canada is "a valid passport." If you are driving over the border, you can use a NEXUS card, issued as part of the U.S. government's Trusted Travel Program, as your entry document. See the U.S. Customs and Border Protection website (www.cbp.gov) for NEXUS details.

If you're driving, a valid U.S. Passport Card can also be used instead of a passport. Get more information about U.S. Passport Cards, which cannot be used for air travel, from the U.S. State Department (www.travel.state.gov).

Several U.S. states and Canadian provinces issue Enhanced Drivers Licenses that can be used as an alternative to a passport or passport card when you're crossing a land border; they're not valid for air travel. The U.S. Customs and Border Protection website (www.cbp.gov) has details about Enhanced Drivers Licenses.

Citizens of the United States do not need a visa to visit Canada for stays of less than six months.

CITIZENS OF OTHER COUNTRIES

All other foreign visitors to Canada must have a valid passport, and depending on your nationality, you may also need either a visitor visa or an Electronic Travel Authorization (eTA). Check with Citizenship and Immigration Canada (www.cic.gc.ca) to confirm what documents you require.

British, Australian, and New Zealand citizens don't require a visa, nor do citizens of many European nations. However, in 2016, Canada introduced the Electronic Travel Authorization (eTA), which is required for visa-exempt visitors who are traveling to Canada by air. For example, a British citizen who is driving into Canada from the U.S. would not require a visa or an eTA but would need the eTA to fly into Canada. If you need an eTA, apply for this document online on the Citizenship and Immigration Canada website (www.cic.gc.ca).

EMBASSIES AND CONSULATES

U.S. citizens in Vancouver, Victoria, or other parts of western Canada can get assistance from the U.S. Consulate General-Vancouver (1075 W. Pender St., Vancouver, 604/685-4311, www.vancouver. usconsulate.gov).

British nationals needing consular assistance can contact the British Consulate General-Vancouver (1111 Melville St., Suite 800, Vancouver, 604/683-4421, www.gov.uk).

The Australian Consulate and Trade Commission, Vancouver (1075 W. Georgia St., Suite 2050, Vancouver, 604/694-6160, www. canada.embassy.gov.au) provides consular assistance to Australian citizens in western Canada, while the New Zealand Consulate General, Vancouver (1050 W. Pender St., Suite 2250, Vancouver, 604/684-7388, www.nzembassy. com/canada) can assist citizens of New Zealand.

CUSTOMS

Visitors to Canada can bring a reasonable amount of personal baggage, including clothing, camping and sports equipment, cameras, and computers for personal use.

Travelers must declare all food, plants, or animals they bring into Canada. In general, you're allowed to bring food for personal use, although there are restrictions on fresh fruits, vegetables, meats, and dairy products. Get the latest information from the Canadian Food Inspection Agency (www. inspection.gc.ca).

As long as you're of legal drinking age (19 in BC), you can bring a small amount of alcohol into Canada duty- and tax-free. You're allowed to bring *one* of the following: two bottles of wine (up to 53 fluid ounces or 1.5 liters), one standard bottle of other alcohol (40 ounces or 1.14 liters), or 24 cans or bottles of beer or ale (up to a total of 287 ounces or 8.5 liters). Visitors are also allowed to bring in up to 200 cigarettes or 50 cigars.

Although Canada legalized recreational cannabis use in 2018, it's illegal to transport the drug across international borders, so don't take it into or out of Canada. In general, visitors cannot bring weapons into Canada. Check the detailed requirements with the Canada Border Services Agency (www.cbsa.gc.ca).

Note that when you're flying to Canada from the United States or other international destinations, you clear immigration and customs at the Canadian airport after you land in Canada. However, if you're flying to the United States from Vancouver, Calgary, or other major Canadian cities, you clear U.S. immigration and customs at the Canadian airport *before* you board your flight. For example, if you were traveling from Vancouver to Los Angeles, you would clear U.S. immigration and customs at the Vancouver airport. Allow extra time for these immigration and customs procedures, in addition to the time it takes for standard airport passenger screening.

WORKING IN VANCOUVER

To work in Vancouver, Victoria, Whistler, or elsewhere in Canada, you must apply for and receive a work permit *before* you enter the country. The government agency responsible for work permits is Citizenship and Immigration Canada (www.cic.gc.ca). In general, you must have a job offer from a Canadian company in order to apply for a work permit.

However, if you're between the ages of 18 and 30-35, you might qualify for the International Experience Canada program, which enables young people to come to Canada on a working holiday (combining short-term work and travel), for an internship, or to work temporarily to gain international experience in your chosen profession. The International Experience Canada program is available to citizens of 32 countries, with varying options available depending on what country you're from. Use the planning tool on the Citizenship and Immigration Canada website to determine if you're eligible for the program and what options you might have.

The International Experience Canada program is not available to U.S. citizens. However, you may be able to work with an organization that helps arrange short-term work programs in Canada. Read more about applying through one of these "Recognized Organizations" on the Citizenship and Immigration Canada website.

STUDYING IN VANCOUVER

To go to school in Canada, you must apply for and receive a study permit *before* you enter the country. Citizenship and Immigration Canada (www.cic.gc.ca) is the government agency responsible for study permits.

Vancouver is a popular destination for people who want to study English. The city has numerous language schools catering to foreign students. Languages Canada (www.languagescanada.ca) has more information about language study in Vancouver and elsewhere in Canada.

Health and Safety

Vancouver and Victoria are generally safe destinations, with no significant health issues for visitors. Travelers should use caution and be aware of their surroundings, especially at night. In Vancouver, avoid walking or running alone through the interior of Stanley Park or Pacific Spirit Regional Park, as many trails are quite remote; however, the Seawall path around Stanley Park is well traveled dawn-dusk.

EMERGENCY AND MEDICAL SERVICES

Call 911 for assistance in an emergency. In British Columbia, to speak with a nurse for medical information 24 hours a day, call 811 to reach the HealthLink BC service (www.healthlinkbc.ca). You can also phone HealthLink BC (604/215-8110).

HOSPITALS

Vancouver General Hospital (920 W. 10th Ave., 604/875-4111, www.vch.ca) has a 24-hour emergency room that will assist patients ages 17 and older. If children under 17 need emergency medical attention, take them to BC Children's Hospital (4480 Oak St., 604/875-2345 or 888/300-3088, www.bcchildrens.ca).

Downtown, you can get 24-hour emergency care at St. Paul's Hospital (1081 Burrard St., 604/682-2344, www.providencehealthcare.org). On the University of British Columbia campus, the UBC Urgent Care Clinic (UBC Hospital, Koerner Pavilion, 2211 Wesbrook Mall, 604/822-7121, www.vch.ca, 8am-10pm daily) is a good choice for X-rays and nonemergency medical issues.

Check the website Emergency Wait Times (www.edwaittimes.ca) for the estimated waiting time at local emergency rooms.

PHARMACIES

Several locations of Shoppers Drug Mart (www.shoppersdrugmart.ca) have 24-hour pharmacies, including branches in the West End (1125 Davie St., 604/669-2424), near Vancouver General Hospital on Broadway (885 W. Broadway, 604/708-1135), and in Kitsilano (2302 W. 4th Ave., 604/738-3138). Other centrally located branches have extended hours, including downtown at Robson and Burrard (748 Burrard St., 778/330-4711, 8am-midnight daily) and Yaletown (1006 Homer St., 604/669-0330, 8am-midnight Mon.-Sat., 9am-midnight Sun.).

London Drugs (www.londondrugs.com), another Canadian pharmacy chain, has several downtown locations that are open late, including 710 Granville Street (604/448-4802, 8am-10pm Mon.-Fri., 9am-10pm Sat., 10am-8pm Sun.) and 1187 Robson Street (604/448-4819, 9am-10pm Mon.-Sat., 10am-10pm Sun.).

HEALTH INSURANCE

If you become ill or injured while traveling in British Columbia, go to the nearest hospital emergency room or walk-in health clinic.

If you're a resident of another Canadian province, your provincial health plan may not provide health coverage while you're out of your home province. If the plan does provide coverage, it may pay only the amount it would pay for the service in your home province, not what you might be billed in British Columbia. Either way, before your trip, it's a good idea to purchase supplemental travel health insurance to cover any unexpected medical costs while you're on the road.

If you live outside Canada, make sure that you have health insurance that will cover you and your family in Canada. You normally have to pay for medical services provided in Canada and then file a claim with your health insurance provider after you return home.

CRIME

Compared to many cities around the world, Vancouver is relatively safe. The most prevalent crimes are property crimes. Bicycle thefts are a particular problem, and car break-ins happen more frequently than anyone would like. Don't leave valuables in your car, and always lock your bike.

Vancouver has a significant homeless population, many of whom congregate on the streets of Gastown and Chinatown, particularly along sections of Hastings Street, near Main Street. While that isn't a reason to avoid the area, use caution as you would in any urban neighborhood. Hop on the bus or take a cab if you're in this part of the city late at night.

Travel Tips

WHAT TO PACK

In casual Vancouver, decent slacks and a blouse or collared shirt would be appropriate attire almost anywhere. You can dress up a bit when you're eating out, and many people bring out their finery if they're attending the opera, the symphony, or a dance club.

Bring comfortable walking or hiking shoes, and clothes for the outdoors. In summer, bring a jacket or sweater for the cool evenings; even during the day, temperatures rarely rise much above 75°F (24°C).

If you're visiting October-May, pack rain gear; a good rain jacket and an umbrella will protect you from the inevitable drizzle and frequent downpours. Temperatures typically don't drop below freezing in the city, but it can be cool enough that you'll want a hat and gloves November-March.

DRINKING AND SMOKING

In Canada, each province sets its own laws regulating activities such as drinking, smoking, and drug use. The drinking age in British Columbia is 19.

Each province has its own laws about when and where you can smoke tobacco, and some cities have laws that are more restrictive than those at the provincial level. You must be 19 to smoke in BC, and you can't smoke in any indoor public place, including restaurants, bars, shopping centers, and public transit, or in a car where anyone under age 16 is a passenger. Vancouver also prohibits smoking at any city parks or beaches and on restaurant patios.

CANNABIS IN CANADA

In 2018, recreational cannabis use became legal across Canada. In general, that means that, throughout the country, adults can possess up to 30 grams of legal cannabis and use or share up to 30 grams with other adults. You must be at least 19 in BC to legally use marijuana, and you have to obey the same laws in each province and city about where you can smoke that apply to tobacco.

Note that it is illegal to transport cannabis across international borders, so any that you buy in Canada must stay in Canada. Each province has its own rules about where you can legally buy cannabis products. In British Columbia, cannabis is being sold at government-run stores, a limited number of licensed private retailers, and the BC government's online shop.

For more details, refer to the Government of Canada website (www.canada.ca) and to British Columbia's cannabis information site (www.cannabis.gov.bc.ca).

ACCESS FOR TRAVELERS WITH DISABILITIES

Many of western Canada's attractions, hotels, restaurants, entertainment venues, and transportation options are accessible to travelers with disabilities. A useful general resource about accessible travel to and around Canada is the government's Access to Travel website (www.accesstotravel.gc.ca). It includes details about transportation between and around BC cities and towns, as well as general tips and travel advice.

Most national and provincial parks offer accessible facilities. Many picnic areas, campsites, and park washrooms, as well as some trails, can accommodate wheelchairs and other mobility aids. Get details on facilities in specific parks from Parks Canada (www.pc.gc.ca) or BC Parks (www.env.gov.bc.ca).

TRAVELING WITH CHILDREN

Western Canada is an extremely family-friendly destination. Not only are there tons of fun things for families to do, but plenty of resources also help support traveling families or make travel more affordable.

Many museums, attractions, and recreational facilities offer free admission for kids under a certain age (often 5-6, but sometimes 11-12). Many offer discounted family admission rates, which generally include two adults and at least two children. Ask about family discounts when you're buying tickets.

Kids stay free at many major hotels. Other good lodging options for traveling families, besides the typical chain motels, include suite hotels (in cities) and cabins or cottages (in more rural areas), which often provide more space for the money, as well as kitchen facilities where you can prepare your own food. Some bed-and-breakfasts don't accept kids, so always ask.

Many restaurants in Canada offer children's menus with a few kid-approved food selections. Encourage your kids to try new things, though, since they may surprise you with their newfound love for bison burgers, handmade noodles, or sushi.

When you're visiting a national park or national historic site with kids, ask for a free **Parks Canada Xplorer** booklet, which has child-friendly activities to help them explore that destination. At most parks, Parks Canada staff offer interpretive programs, from wildlife talks to guided hikes, that are designed for kids or suitable for families; ask at the park visitors center or check the **Parks Canada website** (www.pc.gc.ca) for details and schedules.

Note that if only one parent is traveling with his or her children, the Canadian government recommends that the parent carry a written letter of permission from the other parent. Divorced parents who share custody should also travel with a copy of their legal custody documents. If you are traveling with a child who isn't your own (or for whom you're not the legal guardian), you should carry written permission from the parents or guardians indicating that you're allowed to travel with the child. You may be asked to present these letters at the border when you enter Canada. For a sample letter of consent, see the **Travel and Tourism** section of the Government of Canada's website (www.travel.gc.ca).

SENIOR TRAVELERS

The good thing about getting older is that you can often get discounts. Many BC attractions, lodgings, and transportation providers offer discounts for seniors. Normally, you need to be 65 to qualify for a senior discount, although occasionally these discounts are extended to travelers at age 60-62.

Parks Canada offers discounts at the country's national parks and national historic sites, with reduced rates for single-day admissions and annual passes.

LGBTQ TRAVELERS

Canada is far more welcoming to LGBTQ travelers than many other destinations. Marriage equality is the law in Canada.

Vancouver has a large LGBTQ community. The hub of the community is along Davie Street in the city's West End, with another popular area along Commercial Drive in East Vancouver, although accommodations, restaurants, and other facilities across the city (and indeed across BC) welcome gay, lesbian, bisexual, transgender, and queer travelers. **Tourism Vancouver** (www.tourismvancouver.com) publishes a quarterly LGBTQ newsletter, *Out in Vancouver.* **Gayvan Travel Marketing** (www.gayvan.com) can tell you more about the local community, events, and resources.

Other resources for gay and lesbian travel to Canada include **Travel Gay Canada** (www.travelgaycanada. com), the country's gay and lesbian tourism association, and **TAG Approved** (www.tagapproved.com), which highlights gay-friendly hotels and attractions.

MONEY

Canada's currency is the dollar, and like its U.S. counterpart, it's divided into 100 cents. Canadian bills include $5, $10, $20, $50, and $100 denominations. Coins include 5, 10, and 25 cents, and 1 and 2 dollars; Canada has discontinued use of the penny (1-cent coin), so prices for cash purchases are rounded to the nearest five cents. The gold-colored one-dollar coin is called the "loonie," for the picture of the loon on its back. The two-dollar coin is nicknamed the "toonie" (since it's equal to two loonies). Throughout this book, prices are listed in Canadian dollars unless otherwise specified.

Major credit cards, including Visa, MasterCard, and American Express, are accepted throughout British Columbia, although some smaller establishments may take payment in cash only. You'll find automated teller machines (ATMs)—which Canadian banks call automated banking machines, or ABMs—in almost every town. Debit cards are also widely accepted through the region.

Bank of Canada (www. bankofcanada.ca), the Canadian central bank, publishes the official exchange rate between Canadian dollars and other currencies. You can exchange U.S. dollars, euros, British pounds, Australian dollars, and other major currencies for Canadian dollars at banks across BC or at currency exchange dealers in Vancouver, Victoria, and Whistler. Some BC businesses will accept U.S. dollars, although the exchange rate is usually worse than the official rate, and you'll get change back in Canadian funds. You're nearly always better off paying in Canadian currency or using a credit card.

TAXES

Purchases in Canada are subject both to a federal Goods and Services Tax (GST) and, in most provinces, to an additional provincial sales tax (PST). The GST is currently 5 percent, and in British Columbia, the PST adds 7 percent. Not every item you buy is subject to both types of sales tax; basic groceries and prepared food, books, newspapers, magazines, and children's clothing are all exempt from BC's sales tax.

However, on accommodations, you'll pay an 8 percent PST, plus an additional municipal and regional district tax of up to 3 percent. British Columbia charges a 10 percent tax on liquor.

WEIGHTS AND MEASURES

Canada officially uses the metric system. Distances and speed limits are marked in kilometers, gasoline and bottled beverages are sold by the liter, and weights are given in grams or kilograms. Electricity service in Canada is 120 volts at 60 hertz, the same as in the United States, with the same types of plugs.

British Columbia has two time zones. Vancouver, Victoria, and Whistler, along with most of the province, are in the Pacific time zone. British Columbia observes daylight saving time: Clocks move forward one hour on the second Sunday in March and turn back one hour on the first Sunday of November.

TOURIST INFORMATION

Near Canada Place, the Tourism Vancouver Visitor Centre (200 Burrard St., plaza level, 604/683-2000, www.tourismvancouver.com, 9am-5pm daily) provides helpful information about the city.

Tourism Vancouver's **Inside Vancouver blog** (www.insidevancouver.ca) details goings-on around town and provides event listings. **Destination BC** (www.hellobc.com), the provincial tourism agency, has a useful website with information about Vancouver and destinations across the province. The **City of Vancouver** website (http://vancouver.ca) provides details about city-run parks, theaters, and transportation. **TransLink** (www.translink.ca), the city's public transit system, has an online trip-planning function that can help you get around town.

COMMUNICATIONS AND MEDIA

The city's local daily newspapers include the *Vancouver Sun* (www.vancouversun.com) and *Vancouver Province* (www.theprovince.com). The daily Toronto-based *Globe and Mall* (www.theglobeandmail.com) covers news across Canada, including Vancouver, as does the CBC (www.cbc.ca), Canada's public television and radio outlet.

The *Georgia Straight* (www.straight.com) provides arts and entertainment listings, restaurant reviews, and area news. The *Vancouver Courier* (www.vancourier.com), **Vancouver Is Awesome** (http://vancouverisawesome.com), and the **Daily Hive** (http://dailyhive.com/vancouver) are other local news outlets. *Vancouver Magazine* (www.vanmag.com), a glossy monthly also available online, covers city news, restaurants, and events.

The online **Scout Magazine** (http://scoutmagazine.ca) features Vancouver restaurant, food, and culture stories. **Miss 604** (www.miss604.com) is a well-established local blog, with lots of information about things to do in the region.

Recreation

NATIONAL, PROVINCIAL, AND REGIONAL PARKS

NATIONAL PARKS

Parks Canada (888/773-8888, www.pc.gc.ca) is the agency responsible for the country's national parks. You can purchase an annual **Parks Canada Discovery Pass** (adults $68, seniors $58, family or group $137), valid at more than 80 national parks, national marine conservation areas, and national historic sites across the country. Visiting these sites is currently free for kids up to age 17. The family or group pass is good for up to seven people arriving together at a particular site. If you're going to visit several parks and historic sites during your travels, a Discovery Pass can be a good value.

If you purchase your Discovery Pass at the beginning of a month, your pass will be valid for 13 months rather than 12, since the pass expires on the last day of the month in which you bought it.

You can buy a Discovery Pass online or by phone from Parks Canada or in person at any national park or historic site. If you've already bought a day pass to a park or historic site within the past 30 days, you can credit the price of that ticket toward a Discovery Pass.

PROVINCIAL PARKS

British Columbia has more than 1,000 provincially managed parks and protected areas, run by **BC Parks** (www.env.gov.bc.ca). The BC Parks system is the second largest group of parks in Canada; only the country's national park system protects a larger area. The first provincial park in British Columbia, Strathcona Park on Vancouver Island, opened in 1911.

Among the most visited parks near Vancouver are **Cypress Provincial Park** (www.cypressmountain.com) on the North Shore, **Shannon Falls Provincial Park** (www.env.gov.bc.ca) and **Stawamus Chief Provincial Park** (http://seatoskyparks.com) in Squamish, and **Garibaldi Provincial Park** (www.env.gov.bc.ca), which extends from Squamish north to Whistler and beyond.

While there are fees to camp in BC's provincial parks, day use at most BC parks is free.

REGIONAL AND URBAN PARKS

At the end of Vancouver's downtown peninsula, **Stanley Park** is the city's marquee park, with 1,000 acres (400 ha) of rainforest, beaches, and walking trails. Near the University of British Columbia campus on Vancouver's West Side, **Pacific Spirit Regional Park** is even larger. This rainforest park measures more than 1,800 acres (760 ha), with 40 miles (70 km) of hiking paths. On the North Shore, West Vancouver's **Lighthouse Park** (www.lighthousepark.ca) rewards visitors with beautiful waterfront views.

HIKING

British Columbia has plenty of opportunities to hit the trail, whether you're looking to tromp around in the woods for an afternoon or set off on a multiday hiking adventure. In Vancouver, you can hike in **Stanley Park** or **Pacific Spirit Regional Park.**

Just outside the city, there are numerous hiking routes on the North Shore, from the iconic **Grouse Grind** (www.grousemountain.com) to the trails in **Cypress Provincial Park** (www.cypressmountain.com). North Vancouver's **Lynn Canyon Park** (www.lynncanyon.ca) has a **suspension bridge** that's free to cross, as well as several easy-to-moderate hiking paths.

Within an hour's drive of Vancouver, the Squamish area is a popular hiking destination. Among the area's best hikes is the climb up "The Chief," the imposing rock cliff in **Stawamus Chief Provincial Park** (http://seatoskyparks.com). Hikers also gravitate to the 750-square-mile (1,942-square-km) **Garibaldi Provincial Park** (www.env.gov bc.ca) for its more than 55 miles (90 km) of hiking trails.

Whistler has several hiking trails in or near the village, including the 25-mile (40-km) **Valley Trail** (www.whistler.ca) that's open to both walkers and cyclists. Up on the mountain, **Whistler-Blackcomb** (www.whistlerblackcomb.com) has numerous hiking trails of all levels that you can access from the lifts or gondolas.

BIKING

Mountain bikers head for the North Shore, particularly the trails near the three local ski hills, **Grouse** (www.grousemountain.com), **Cypress** (www.cypressmountain.com), and **Mount Seymour** (www.mountseymour.com). **Whistler-Blackcomb** (www.whistlerblackcomb.com) is a mecca for mountain bikers, with more than 70 trails open mid-May-mid-October.

In bike-friendly Victoria, you can cycle around the city or pedal a longer rail trail. The 35-mile (55-km) **Galloping Goose Trail** runs along a former rail line from Victoria west to the town of Sooke, and the 18-mile (29-km) **Lochside Regional Trail** connects Victoria and Swartz Bay, where most ferries from Vancouver dock.

WATER SPORTS

You can go **swimming** at Vancouver's many oceanfront beaches, including **English Bay** and **Sunset Beaches** in the West End, **Second** and **Third Beaches**

in Stanley Park, and **Kitsilano, Jericho, Locarno,** and **Spanish Banks Beaches** on the West Side. Even in summer, though, the water temperature is rarely above 21°C (70°F).

Vancouver's several large public pools, particularly **Kitsilano Pool** and Stanley Park's **Second Beach Pool,** are warmer alternatives. You can swim indoors at the **Vancouver Aquatic Centre** (1050 Beach Ave.) in the West End.

You don't have to leave central Vancouver to go **kayaking or stand-up paddleboarding** either. **Ecomarine Paddlesports Centre** (www.ecomarine.com) rents kayaks and stand-up paddleboards at Granville Island, and they have kayaks for rent at Jericho Beach as well. You can also rent kayaks and stand-up paddleboards from **Creekside Kayaks** (www.creeksidekayaks.ca) on False Creek and from **Vancouver Water Adventures** (www.vancouverwateradventures.com), which has outlets at English Bay Beach, Granville Island, and Kitsilano Beach. Another destination for **kayaking** is **Deep Cove** (www.deepcovekayak.com) on Vancouver's North Shore, where you can paddle through the scenic waters of the Indian Arm fjord.

For **white-water rafting,** head for Squamish, north of Vancouver, where several outfitters offer trips on the gentle **Cheakamus River** and the faster **Elaho-Squamish River.**

Western Canada's top **surfing** spot is **Tofino,** on Vancouver Island's west coast. Hard-core surfers suit up and hit the waves in the winter, when the surf is largest.

Summer brings gentler waves and somewhat warmer temperatures.

WINTER SPORTS

In winter, you can **ice-skate** at a public rink in **Robson Square downtown** (www.robsonsquare. com) or at the **Richmond Olympic Oval** (http://richmondoval. ca). **Grouse Mountain** (www. grousemountain.com) also has a mountaintop skating rink.

On Vancouver's North Shore, less than 45 minutes from downtown, three local mountains, **Grouse** (www.grousemountain.com), **Cypress** (www.cypressmountain. com), and **Mount Seymour** (www. mountseymour.com), offer **downhill skiing** and **snowboarding.** The ski season on the North Shore typically runs from December-March. You can go **snowshoeing** at all three mountains, and Cypress offers **cross-country skiing** too.

North America's largest snow sports resort is just a two-hour drive from downtown Vancouver.

Whistler-Blackcomb (www. whistlerblackcomb.com) has more than 200 trails for skiing and snowboarding. The mountain is usually open November-April. Weather permitting, you can even go glacier skiing on Blackcomb Mountain in the summer.

WHALE-WATCHING

Whale-watching trips depart regularly from Vancouver's Granville Island, from the village of Steveston in Richmond south of Vancouver, and from the Inner Harbour in Victoria. These trips typically take you either among the Gulf Islands or south to Washington's San Juan Islands, depending on where whales have been spotted. Whale-watching season runs April-October.

On Vancouver Island's west coast, the Tofino area is another prime spot for whale-watching trips. A number of operators run whale-watching cruises from Tofino harbor from March-April through October-November.

RESOURCES

Suggested Reading

GENERAL INFORMATION

Citizenship and Immigration Canada. *Welcome to Canada: What You Should Know.* Ottawa: Government Services Canada, 2013. A government publication that provides a useful overview of the Canadian immigration process and of life in Canada.

Ferguson, Will. *Canadian History for Dummies.* Toronto: Wiley, 2005. The essentials of Canadian history distilled into a humorous, easy-to-read guide.

HISTORY AND CULTURE

Adderson, Caroline. *Vancouver Vanishes: Narratives of Demolition and Revival.* Vancouver: Anvil Press, 2015. A collection of essays and photographs chronicling how Vancouver is changing, as an increasing number of homes built in the 1920s-1940s are torn down to make way for newer structures.

Coupland, Douglas. *Souvenir of Canada.* Vancouver: Douglas & McIntyre, 2002. A Vancouver-based artist and author dissects Canadian culture in a series of quirky essays and photos.

Davis, Chuck. *The Chuck Davis History of Metropolitan Vancouver.* Vancouver: Harbour Publishing, 2011. Running nearly 600 pages, this timeline of the city's history from the 1750s to modern times is packed with facts and local trivia.

Herzog, Fred. *Fred Herzog: Photographs.* Vancouver: Douglas & McIntyre, 2011. Vivid color photos of life on Vancouver's streets, primarily in the 1950s-1960s, by a noted local photographer.

Johnson, Pauline. *Legends of Vancouver.* Vancouver: Douglas & McIntyre, 1971. In this book, originally published in 1911, Johnson, who was born to a Mohawk father and English mother, shares Coast Salish narratives about the Vancouver region that she learned from conversations with a Squamish First Nations chief, Joseph Capilano. Johnson's ashes are buried in Vancouver's Stanley Park.

FOOD

Dhalwala, Meeru and Vikram Vij. *Vij's: Elegant and Inspired Indian Cuisine.* Vancouver: Douglas & McIntyre, 2006. Recipes from Vancouver's most famous Indian restaurant.

Mundy, Jane. *The Ocean Wise Cookbook 2: More Seafood Recipes That Are Good for the Planet.* Vancouver: Whitecap Books, 2015. In partnership with the Vancouver Aquarium, a Vancouver-based food and travel writer has compiled more than 100 recipes for sustainable seafood from leading Canadian chefs.

Sasvari, Joanne. *Vancouver Eats: Signature Recipes from the City's Best Restaurants*. Vancouver: Figure 1 Publishing, 2018. An extensive collection of recipes from chefs working in Vancouver and Whistler.

Yuen, Stephanie. *East Meets West: Traditional and Contemporary Asian Dishes from Acclaimed Vancouver Restaurants*. Vancouver: Douglas & McIntyre, 2012. A look at Vancouver's Asian cuisine through recipes adapted from local chefs.

FICTION

Adderson, Caroline. *The Sky Is Falling*. Toronto: Thomas Allen, 2010. Following a group of student idealists who share a Vancouver house, this novel is set in both 1984 and 2004, when the end of the world seemed close at hand.

Choy, Wayson. *The Jade Peony*. Vancouver: Douglas & McIntyre, 1995. A portrait of life in Vancouver's Chinatown in the early 20th century.

Kogawa, Joy. *Obasan*. Toronto: Penguin, 2003 (first published 1981). The internment and forced relocation of Japanese-Canadians in western Canada during World War II, depicted through the eyes of a young girl living in Vancouver.

Lee, Jen Sookfong. *The Better Mother*. Toronto: Alfred A. Knopf, 2011. A local author weaves a tale of a young Chinese boy and a burlesque dancer who cross paths in Vancouver's Chinatown.

Robinson, Eden. *Son of a Trickster*. Toronto: Knopf Canada, 2016. This coming-of-age story is the first in a trilogy by a Vancouver-based author of indigenous heritage.

Taylor, Timothy. *Stanley Park*. Toronto: Vintage Canada, 2001. Locavore chefs, coffee magnates, and the homeless cross paths in this thriller set in and around Vancouver's largest green space.

Internet Resources

CANADA

Destination Canada
www.canada.travel
The government of Canada's official guide to travel across the country.

Parks Canada
www.pc.gc.ca
The federal government agency that manages national parks and national historic sites across Canada. The Parks Canada website has details about things to do, camping, hiking, and other activities in parks throughout the country.

Parks Canada Reservation Service
www.reservation.pc.gc.ca
Reservations booking service for Canada's national park campgrounds.

Citizenship and Immigration Canada
www.cic.gc.ca
The federal government agency responsible for overseeing visitors and immigrants to Canada, including information about visitor visas, work permits, study permits, and applications for permanent residence.

Canada Border Services Agency
www.cbsa-asfc.gc.ca
The federal government agency that manages Canada's borders, including what items visitors can bring into Canada. Their website also shows wait times at highway border crossings.

Environment Canada
www.weather.gc.ca
Provides weather forecasts and historical weather data for locations across Canada.

BRITISH COLUMBIA

Destination British Columbia
www.hellobc.com
British Columbia's provincial tourism agency, which provides travel tips and information for the region and operates a network of visitors centers.

BC Parks
www.env.gov.bc.ca
The agency responsible for managing British Columbia's provincial parks. The website includes listings for each park, with maps, fees, and other details.

British Columbia Wine Institute
www.winebc.com
Has a detailed website with information about wineries and wine-touring tips in the Okanagan, Vancouver Island, and elsewhere in British Columbia.

Tourism Vancouver
www.tourismvancouver.com
Vancouver's tourism agency provides event schedules, tips for getting around, neighborhood profiles, and other information about the city's sights, hotels, restaurants, shops, and experiences.

Tourism Vancouver Island
www.vancouverisland.travel
Their free guide to things to do across Vancouver Island is available online and in print from area visitors centers.

Destination Greater Victoria
www.tourismvictoria.com
Promoting tourism in the city of Victoria, this organization runs a year-round information center on Victoria's Inner Harbour and provides information about attractions and activities, events, accommodations, and restaurants.

Tourism Whistler
www.whistler.com
Representing the Whistler region, this tourism agency has information to help you plan a mountain trip in any season.

Index

Restaurants Index

Nightlife Index

Shops Index

Hotels Index

Photo Credits

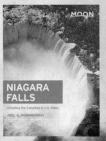

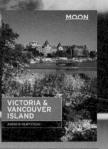

More Guides for Urban Adventure

AMSTERDAM WALKS
See the City Like a Local

LONDON WALKS
See the City Like a Local

NEW YORK CITY WALKS
See the City Like a Local

TOKYO WALKS
See the City Like a Local

ASHEVILLE & THE GREAT SMOKY MOUNTAINS

BOSTON
CAMERON SPERANCE

CLEVELAND
DOUGLAS TRATTNER

LOS ANGELES

MEXICO CITY

MONTRÉAL
ANDREA BENNETT

NASHVILLE
MARGARET LITTMAN

New Orleans
LOCAL SPOTS BEYOND THE FRENCH QUARTER

NEW YORK CITY
CHRISTOPHER KOMPANEK

OSLO
DAVID NIKEL

PORTLAND

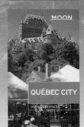
QUÉBEC CITY
ANICK GREENENNET

REYKJAVÍK
JENNA GOTTLIEB

SEATTLE

VANCOUVER
NEIGHBORHOOD WALKS • OUTDOOR ADVENTURES • BELOVED LOCAL SPOTS

WASHINGTON DC

MAP SYMBOLS

═══ Major Hwy	Pedestrian Friendly	-------- Trail	·········· Ferry
─── Road/Hwy	Tunnel	▪▪▪▪▪ Stairs	⊣─⊢ Railroad

- ■ **Sights**
- ■ **Restaurants**
- ■ **Nightlife**
- ■ **Arts and Culture**
- ■ **Recreation**
- ■ **Shops**
- ■ **Hotels**

- ⊛ City/Town
- ◉ State Capital
- ○ National Capital
- ✪ Highlight
- ★ Point of Interest
- • Accommodation
- ▼ Restaurant/Bar
- ■ Other Location

- ▲ Mountain
- ✦ Unique Feature
- 🖋 Waterfall
- ▲ Park
- ⏶ Archaeological Site
- **TH** Trailhead
- **P** Parking Area

CONVERSION TABLES

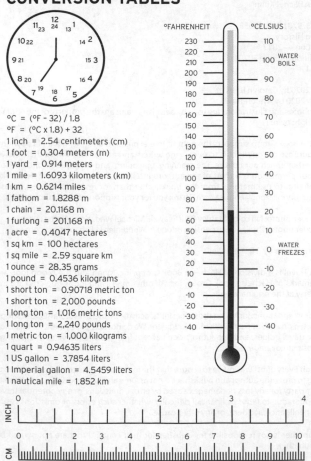

°C = (°F - 32) / 1.8
°F = (°C x 1.8) + 32
1 inch = 2.54 centimeters (cm)
1 foot = 0.304 meters (m)
1 yard = 0.914 meters
1 mile = 1.6093 kilometers (km)
1 km = 0.6214 miles
1 fathom = 1.8288 m
1 chain = 20.1168 m
1 furlong = 201.168 m
1 acre = 0.4047 hectares
1 sq km = 100 hectares
1 sq mile = 2.59 square km
1 ounce = 28.35 grams
1 pound = 0.4536 kilograms
1 short ton = 0.90718 metric ton
1 short ton = 2,000 pounds
1 long ton = 1.016 metric tons
1 long ton = 2,240 pounds
1 metric ton = 1,000 kilograms
1 quart = 0.94635 liters
1 US gallon = 3.7854 liters
1 Imperial gallon = 4.5459 liters
1 nautical mile = 1.852 km

MOON VANCOUVER
Avalon Travel
Hachette Book Group
1700 Fourth Street
Berkeley, CA 94710, USA
www.moon.com

Editor: Kristi Mitsuda
Series Manager: Leah Gordon
Copy Editor: Christopher Church
Graphics and Production Coordinator: Ravina Schneider
Cover Design: Charles Brock
Interior Design: Megan Jones Design
Moon Logo: Tim McGrath
Map Editor: Kat Bennett
Cartographers: Brian Shotwell, John Culp, Vivienne von Welczeck
Proofreaders: Rosemarie Leenerts, Diana Smith
Indexer: Rachel Kuhn

ISBN-13: 9781640499058
Printing History
1st Edition — 2017
2nd Edition — June 2020
5 4 3 2 1